The Editor

ROBERT S. MIOLA, the Gerard Manley Hopkins Professor of English and Lecturer in Classics at Loyola University in Maryland, has written and lectured widely on Shakespeare, classical literature, and early modern Catholicism. His publications include *Shakespeare's Rome*, *Shakespeare and Classical Tragedy*, *Shakespeare and Classical Comedy*, the Norton Critical Edition of *Hamlet*, editions of Ben Jonson's *Every Man in His Humor* and *The Case Is Altered*, and *Early Modern Catholicism: An Anthology of Primary Sources*.

W. W. NORTON & COMPANY, INC.
Also Publishes

ENGLISH RENAISSANCE DRAMA: A NORTON ANTHOLOGY
edited by David Bevington et al.

THE NORTON ANTHOLOGY OF AFRICAN AMERICAN LITERATURE
edited by Henry Louis Gates Jr. and Nellie Y. McKay et al.

THE NORTON ANTHOLOGY OF AMERICAN LITERATURE
edited by Nina Baym and Robert Levine et al.

THE NORTON ANTHOLOGY OF CHILDREN'S LITERATURE
edited by Jack Zipes et al.

THE NORTON ANTHOLOGY OF DRAMA
edited by J. Ellen Gainor, Stanton B. Garner Jr., and Martin Puchner

THE NORTON ANTHOLOGY OF ENGLISH LITERATURE
edited by Stephen Greenblatt et al.

THE NORTON ANTHOLOGY OF LATINO LITERATURE
edited by Ilan Stavans et al.

THE NORTON ANTHOLOGY OF LITERATURE BY WOMEN
edited by Sandra M. Gilbert and Susan Gubar

THE NORTON ANTHOLOGY OF MODERN AND CONTEMPORARY POETRY
edited by Jahan Ramazani, Richard Ellmann, and Robert O'Clair

THE NORTON ANTHOLOGY OF POETRY
edited by Margaret Ferguson, Mary Jo Salter, and Jon Stallworthy

THE NORTON ANTHOLOGY OF SHORT FICTION
edited by R. V. Cassill and Richard Bausch

THE NORTON ANTHOLOGY OF THEORY AND CRITICISM
edited by Vincent B. Leitch et al.

THE NORTON ANTHOLOGY OF WORLD LITERATURE
edited by Martin Puchner et al.

THE NORTON FACSIMILE OF THE FIRST FOLIO OF SHAKESPEARE
prepared by Charlton Hinman

THE NORTON INTRODUCTION TO LITERATURE
edited by Kelly J. Mays

THE NORTON READER
edited by Linda H. Peterson and John C. Brereton et al.

THE NORTON SAMPLER
edited by Thomas Cooley

THE NORTON SHAKESPEARE, BASED ON THE OXFORD EDITION
edited by Stephen Greenblatt et al.

For a complete list of Norton Critical Editions, visit
wwnorton.com/college/English/nce

A NORTON CRITICAL EDITION

William Shakespeare
MACBETH

THE TEXT OF *MACBETH*

THE ACTORS' GALLERY

SOURCES AND CONTEXTS

CRITICISM

AFTERLIVES

RESOURCES

SECOND EDITION

Edited by

ROBERT S. MIOLA

LOYOLA UNIVERSITY IN MARYLAND

W · W · NORTON & COMPANY · *New York* · *London*

W. W. Norton & Company has been independent since its founding in 1923, when William Warder and Mary D. Herter Norton first published lectures delivered at the People's Institute, the adult education division of New York City's Cooper Union. The Nortons soon expanded their program beyond the Institute, publishing books by celebrated academics from America and abroad. By mid-century, the two major pillars of Norton's publishing program—trade books and college texts—were firmly established. In the 1950s, the Norton family transferred control of the company to its employees, and today—with a staff of four hundred and a comparable number of trade, college, and professional titles published each year—W. W. Norton & Company stands as the largest and oldest publishing house owned wholly by its employees.

Production manager: Sean Mintus

Library of Congress Cataloging-in-Publication Data

Shakespeare, William, 1564–1616.
  Macbeth : the text of Macbeth, the actors' gallery, sources and contexts, criticism, afterlives, resources / William Shakespeare ; edited by Robert S. Miola, Loyola University in Maryland.—Second edition.
        pages cm—(A Norton critical edition)
  Includes bibliographical references.

  ISBN 978-0-393-92326-1 (pbk.)

  1. Macbeth, King of Scotland, active 11th century—Drama.
  2. Shakespeare, William, 1564–1616. Macbeth—Sources.
  3. Macbeth, King of Scotland, active 11th century—In literature.
  4. Shakespeare, William, 1564–1616. Macbeth.   5. Kings and rulers—Succession—Drama.   6. Regicides—Drama.   7. Scotland—Drama.   I. Miola, Robert S., editor of compilation.   II. Title.
  PR2823.A2M56 2014
  822.3'3—dc23

                                                                    2013021933

W. W. Norton & Company, Inc., 500 Fifth Avenue,
New York, NY 10110
wwnorton.com

W. W. Norton & Company Ltd., Castle House,
75/76 Wells Street, London W1T 3QT

1 2 3 4 5 6 7 8 9 0

Contents

Illustrations

Macbeth
Fall → pity & terror
Ancient playwrights
→ human struggles w/gods,
fate + free will, crime + punishment
guilt & suffering

Introduction

Like the ancient tragedies, Shakespeare's *Macbeth* depicts a fall
that evokes, according to Aristotle's prescription in the *Poetics*, both
pity and terror. Though ancient playwrights believed in different
deities and ethical systems, they too depicted humans struggling
with the gods, with fate and free will, crime and punishment, guilt
and suffering. Sophocles (fifth century B.C.E.), for example, portrays
Oedipus, solver of the Sphinx's riddle and King of Thebes, who
discovers that all along he has been fulfilling, not fleeing, the curse
of Apollo and its dread predictions. "Lead me away, O friends, the
utterly lost (τὸν μέγ' ὀλέθριον), most accursed (τὸν καταρατότατον),
and the one among mortals most hated (ἐχθρότατον) by the gods!"
(1341–43). In several plays that provided models for *Macbeth*, Seneca
(d. 65 C.E.) presents men and women saying the unsayable, doing
the unthinkable, and suffering the unimaginable. The witch Medea
slays her own children in a horrifying act of revenge. In contrast to
Euripides' *Medea*, which ends in a choral affirmation of Zeus's justice and order, Seneca's play concludes with Medea's transformation
into something inhuman: she leaves the scene of desolation in a
chariot drawn by dragons, bearing witness, wherever she goes, that
there are no gods, *testare nullos esse, qua veheris, deos* (1027). Driven
mad by the goddess Juno, Seneca's Hercules in *Hercules Furens* kills
his children, then awakens to full recognition of his deed in suicidal grief and remorse (below, 152–55). These tragic heroes struggle
against the gods and themselves.

Such classical archetypes inform tragedy in the West, Seneca
especially shaping Elizabethan tragedy. *Medea* and *Hercules Furens*
partly account for the child-killing so prominent in *Macbeth*. (Seneca
here joins with native traditions of medieval drama, represented
below by Herod's massacre of holy innocents, see 154–55.) Child-
killing, as many have noted, appears both in the stage action of
Shakespeare's play—the murder of Macduff's children, the bloody
child apparition—and in its language, for example, in Lady Macbeth's terrible hyperbole:

> I have given suck, and know
> How tender 'tis to love the babe that milks me;

John Turturro and Katherine Borowitz in *Men of Respect* (1990).
© Columbia Pictures. Courtesy of the Everett Collection.

> I would, while it was smiling in my face,
> Have plucked my nipple from his boneless gums
> And dashed the brains out, had I so sworn as you
> Have done to this. (1.7.54–59)

These lines, transformed, take on a contemporary urgency in William Reilly's film adaptation *Men of Respect* (1991); there, Ruthie (Lady Macbeth) reminds her husband of her abortion: "I know what it is to have a life inside me, and squashing it out because it's not the right time, it's too difficult. I know what it is to kill for you." Like Lady Macbeth, the murdering mother here forces her husband into a guilty and awed submission.

Seneca may have directly inspired Lady Macbeth herself. When Medea invokes the gods, she asks them to "exile all foolish fear and pity" from her mind; alone, she rouses herself to a terrible deed of self-creation (below, 152–54). In her famous soliloquy Lady Macbeth asks the spirits to "unsex" her, to "stop up th'access and passage to remorse," to take her "milk for gall" (1.5.36ff.). Of course, the differences between the two women loom large and important. Medea achieves a unique selfhood in *scelus* ("crime"); altering the universe by transgressing the bounds of the natural, she becomes a supernatural creation who flies away like a god. Instead of such apotheosis, however, Lady Macbeth comes crashing down. Tormented by guilt and sleeplessness, she last appears in the sleepwalking scene

LMB → rise + fall
MB

(5.1) a ghost of her former self, haunted, frightened, broken, "like the bony carcass left bare by a vulture," observed the Italian actress Adelaide Ristori, "eaten up by the remorse preying on her mind" (below, 109). Perhaps the most celebrated actress in this role, Sarah Siddons (1755–1831) portrayed Lady Macbeth washing her hands vehemently; she imagined her character "with wan and haggard countenance, her starry eyes glazed with the ever-burning fever of remorse, and on their lids the shadows of death" (below, 96). Medea transforms herself; Lady Macbeth dies offstage.

Macbeth also experiences a breathtaking rise and crashing fall. He appears first as a classical warrior hero, "valor's minion," the bridegroom of Bellona, Roman goddess of war (1.2.19, 56). At a crucial point in the action he justifies the decision to kill Banquo in Senecan fashion: "Things bad begun make strong themselves by ill" (3.2.54) echoes Seneca's proverbial saying, *per scelera semper sceleribus tutum est iter* (*Agamemnon*, 115), "The safe way for crime is through more crimes." But there is no safe way for crimes in Macbeth's world; not even Bellona's bridegroom can carve out his passage with brandished steel and bloody execution. Dagger in blood-stained hand, Macbeth suffers like no classical hero; at the very moment of his triumphant murder, he hears the sleeping guards wake:

> MACBETH   One cried "God bless us!" and "Amen!" the other,
> As they had seen me with these hangman's hands.
> List'ning their fear, I could not say "Amen"
> When they did say "God bless us!"
> LADY MACBETH   Consider it not so deeply.
> MACBETH   But wherefore could not I pronounce "Amen"?
> I had most need of blessing, and "Amen"
> Stuck in my throat. (2.2.29–36)

Macbeth expresse[s]
What he's done wrong → other plays do, x

In David Garrick's celebrated eighteenth-century performance of this scene the self-reproach ("these hangman's hands") widened into a "wonderful expression of heartfelt horror" (below, 89). Here that reproach accompanies an urgent need for God's blessing and the solace of prayer. Unable to say "Amen," Macbeth expresses a childlike incomprehension and astonishment at what he has done and become. This extraordinary moment marks the differences between him and his classical predecessors, and from the cruel, remorseless tyrant Shakespeare found in Holinshed's *Chronicles* (1587), the main source of the play.

This moment takes us into the heart of Macbeth's tragedy: he has most need of God's blessing and cannot say "Amen." An imperfect man in a brutal, fallen world, Macbeth needs to be saved but, instead, chooses to save himself, and suffers miserably for his choice. Macbeth's abortive prayer thus illuminates the moral world of the play, the ethical universe in which he must live and die. And we must surely share, at first, in his momentary astonishment: why, after all, can't the man who has just butchered his guest, kinsman, and king manage to mouth an "Amen," even if insincere? What stops him, what sticks the word in his throat? Is it the involuntary reflex of a defeated conscience, as Menteith later suggests: "all that is within him does condemn / Itself for being there" (5.2.24–25). Or is it some divine refusal to tolerate yet another transgression? The play affords no window through which to look this deeply into Macbeth's soul, but one thing is clear: Macbeth's inability to say "Amen" signals the futility of his crime. Human action and the will to power may prevail in Medea's world but not here, where the immutable order of moral law appears in the interior workings of conscience and the exterior natural world.

Ninagawa's stylized kabuki *Macbeth* (1980, and after) expressed this ordered natural world by featuring a beautiful cherry tree and its blossoms on stage, a stunning visual contrast to the unnatural human barbarity on display. Macbeth himself fears that the very stones will reveal his crime, will prate of his whereabout (2.1.58). The night of the King's murder is "unruly": chimneys fall, laments and strange screams of death fill the air, the owl clamors, the earth shakes (2.3.49–56). After, an unnatural darkness strangles the sun, a mousing owl kills a falcon, and Duncan's horses eat each other (2.4.5–18). In the Globe performance of 1611, Simon Forman reports, the blood on Macbeth's hands "could not be washed off by any means, nor from his wife's hands" (below, 225). After Banquo's ghost returns, Macbeth says that stones move, trees speak, and birds ("maggot-pies and choughs and rooks") reveal "the secret'st man of blood" (3.4.125–28). The mix of legend, superstition, and mirabilia here points to providential order in nature; the capricious pagan gods Apollo, Juno, and Zeus do not rule in this world, but the just Judaeo-Christian God, the God who will return at the Last Judgment, the day of the great doom, when the dead rise from their graves and walk like sprites (2.3.74–76).

This God, creator of nature and moral order, figures centrally in Holinshed's *Chronicles*: "almighty God showed himself thereby to be offended most highly for that wicked murder of King Duff, and, surely, unless the offenders were tried forth and punished for that deed, the realm should feel the just indignation of the divine judgment for omitting such punishment as was due for so a grievous an offense" (below, 160). And this God makes a surprising number of appearances (fifteen total) in the language of Shakespeare's dark, bloody play, rife with scenes of evil supernaturalism and murderous ambition. Coleridge noted long ago that the witches "strike the keynote" (below, 234) of the play, but there is an insistent, if quieter, divine counterpoint. Orson Welles heard and amplified this music in his 1948 film version, often employing the symbol of the cross amidst the gnarled trees and stone of his primitive Scotland, adding a Holy Father to conduct a service against Satan and oppose the rising evil. So did Trevor Nunn in his 1976 production, beginning with the witches' black mass ritual and ending when "the glimmer of Christianity arrived like a fragile dawn" (ed. Bate and Rasmussen, 2009, 149). In Shakespeare's text Ross greets Duncan with unintentional irony, "God save the King!" (1.2.48). Immediately after the murder Banquo declares himself to stand "in the great hand of God" (2.3.129) against treasonous malice. Malcolm asks "God above" (4.3.120) to regulate the alliance with Macduff, echoing the lord who hoped that "Him above" (3.6.32) would ratify the rebellion against Macbeth. Witnessing Lady Macbeth sleepwalking, the Doctor does what Macbeth could not: he says a spontaneous prayer: "God, God, forgive us all" (5.1.68). The Captain compares the opening battle to Golgotha (1.2.40), place of the Crucifixion; Malcolm later praises Siward as the oldest and best soldier in "Christendom" (4.3.192). Commissioning the murderers, Macbeth pointedly asks, "Are you so gospeled / To pray for this good man and for his issue, / Whose heavy hand hath bowed you to the grave / And beggared yours for ever?" (3.1.88–91). Whether or not he alludes specifically to Matthew 5:44 ("Love your enemies and pray for those who persecute you"), Macbeth here invokes the God whom he has disobeyed and the moral order he has violated. And once again, he adverts to prayer, this time thinking it the cowardly alternative to the manly action of murder. murder ──➤ prayer

King Macbeth's newfound contempt for the gospel and prayer marks his moral deterioration. "Had I but died an hour before this chance, / I had lived a blessèd time" (2.3.89–90), he himself said earlier. But such blessing as he required and yearned for now lies out of reach and out of mind. Lennox, ironically, hopes that a "swift blessing" (3.6.48) in the form of divine aid and the English army will come to remove Macbeth and relieve sick, suffering Scotland. The imagery of disease runs importantly throughout the play: Macbeth thinks of life as a "fitful fever" (3.2.23); "he cannot buckle his distempered cause / Within the belt of rule" (5.2.15–16). Scotland "bleeds, and each new day a gash / Is added to her wounds" (4.3.40–41); the invading Malcolm is the "med'cine of the sickly weal" (5.2.27). And the English King Edward, in purposeful contrast to King Macbeth, is a religious curer who gives "holy prayers" and the "healing benediction" to the afflicted, who has "a heavenly gift of prophecy" (4.3.154–57). "Sundry blessings hang about his throne" (4.3.158), while Macbeth becomes "a hand accursed" (3.6.50), receiving not love or honor but "curses, not loud but deep" (5.3.27).

In the Shakespeare play that most embodies the "principle of contrast" and moves "upon the verge of an abyss," in William Hazlitt's fine phrasing (*Characters*, 1817, 23–24), other religious antitheses mark Macbeth's decline. Early on he imagines Duncan's virtues as angels pleading trumpet-tongued against the murder, and pity as heaven's cherubim blowing the horrid deed in every eye (1.7.18–24). He declares himself the kind of man who could appall the devil (3.4.61), but chooses to side with him and his minions. Too late he realizes that the witches are "juggling fiends" (5.7.49) and that he has been deceived by the "equivocation of the fiend / That lies like truth" (5.5.43–44). The association of witches, equivocation, and the devil, many have noted, draws resonance from the anti-Catholic fervor following the discovery of the Gunpowder plot; the Porter alludes to one of the convicted conspirators, the Jesuit Henry Garnet, who wrote a treatise on equivocation and was executed in 1606: "Faith, here's an equivocator that could swear in both the scales against either scale, who committed treason enough for God's sake, yet could not equivocate to heaven" (2.3.7–10) (below, 218–19, and Bill Cain's *Equivocation*, also below, 365–76). Submitting to the paltering, equivocal witches, Macbeth becomes increasingly identified with the devil: Macduff wants to confront "this fiend of Scotland" (4.3.233); Malcolm calls him "devilish Macbeth" (4.3.117). Hearing Macbeth name himself, Young Siward proclaims, "The devil himself could not pronounce a title / More hateful to mine ear"; "No, no more fearful" (5.7.8–9), Macbeth responds. Macbeth himself invokes the Prince of Darkness: "The devil damn thee black, thou cream-faced loon!" (5.3.11). He who had most need of blessing now turns the other way for curses, even threatening the witches themselves: "Deny me this [the truth about Banquo's issue] / And an eternal curse fall upon you!" (4.1.103–104).

Given the company he keeps, we should not be surprised that Macbeth's enemy, Hecate, probably a later addition by Thomas Middleton, delivers the most telling commentary on his spiritual state: "He shall spurn fate, scorn death, and bear / His hopes 'bove wisdom, grace, and fear. / And you all know security / Is mortals' chiefest enemy" (3.5.30–33). Hecate, leader of the witches, here plays orthodox preacher, echoing numerous homilies and popular theology pamphlets ("you all know") on the dangers of "security," i.e., spiritual overconfidence and complacency, repose in the pleasures of this world. In 1584 John Stockwood published *A Very Fruitful and Necessary Sermon* "to the wakening and stirring up of all such as be lulled asleep in the cradle of security or carelessness" (title page). Similarly, the title page of Thomas Rogers's *The Enemy of Security* (1591) exhorts the reader to watch and pray, "pray continually." About the time of *Macbeth* William Est preached in *The*

Scourge of Security (1609) that neglect of prayer led to the return of the unclean spirit. In the same year Thomas Draxe explained that the substance of security is contained in the words "I sleep" and the antidote in the phrase "but mine heart waketh" (*The Church's Security,* sigs. B1v–B2). This homiletic fervor motivated John Downame's A *Treatise of Security* (1622), written "to rouse up" sinners "out of this sleep or rather lethargy of security" (Epistle Dedicatory).

Hecate's precise spiritual diagnosis, then, evokes a discrete, clearly outlined, and abundantly available complex of image and exhortation. Shakespeare fully engages this familiar complex but reverses its basic logic: the sleepless Macbeth ever waketh in his cradle of security, not lulled, but racked "in the affliction of these terrible dreams / That shake us nightly' (3.2.18–19). The pervasive images of sleeplessness in the play have been well remarked, of course—the bewitched insomniac sailor who dwindles, peaks, and pines (1.3.19–26), the mysterious cry, "'Sleep no more! / Macbeth does murder sleep'" (2.2.38–39), Macbeth's subsequent yearning for "sleep that knits up the raveled sleeve of care, / The death of each day's life, sore labor's bath, / Balm of hurt minds, great nature's second course, / Chief nourisher in life's feast" (40–43), the sleepwalking Lady Macbeth. But to contemporary audiences they must have derived their force from Shakespeare's daring inversion of conventional rhetoric and moral formula. His Macbeth is agonizingly and unremittingly awake, stung by his conscience, the agenbyte of inwit, that full, tormenting, relentless awareness of his sin.

Another terror of the play is that Macbeth's gains are negligible and indistinct, his losses large and clearly articulated: "honor, love, obedience, troops of friends, / I must not look to have" (5.3.25–26). Macbeth cannot eat or sleep in peace; he loses his wife, as Ian McKellen noted of his performance with Judi Dench: "the story of their progression is of them getting separated from the bliss of that union" (below, 120). Accordingly, the earthly highlands of Scotland are never so precisely mapped as the spiritual landscapes Macbeth traverses. Some of the Scottish references, Saint Colme's Inch (or Inchcolm isle) (1.2.63) and Colmekill (2.4.33), even point to the other world, where the real drama transpires: both localities pay nominal tribute to St. Columba (521–97), the abstemious missionary to northern Scotland who preached, worked miracles, and converted the pagan Picts and Druids to Christianity. Appropriately, Duncan's body is carried to the "sacred storehouse of his predecessors" (2.4.34) at Colmekill, the monastic "cell of Columba" in Iona, off the west of Scotland. The forces of Christianity thus align themselves in death as in life against the pagan barbarism of Scotland. Macbeth moves between these two opposed realms, as between blessings and curses, angels and devils, and, like one of Hamlet's crawling fellows, between heaven and hell. Lady Macbeth wants the "dunnest smoke of hell" to beshroud the world so that heaven cannot "peep through the blanket of the dark / To cry 'Hold, hold'" (1.5.48–51). "The heavens, as troubled with man's act," the murder, threaten "his bloody stage" (2.4.5–6) with natural disruptions and cosmic events. Macduff says that "new sorrows / Strike heaven on the face" (4.3.5–6). Heaven often appears as a metonym for divine providence. Lennox hopes, if it "please heaven" (3.6.19), that Macbeth will not get his hands on Duncan's heirs. The messenger says to Macduff's doomed wife, "heaven preserve you" (4.2.69); Macduff asks if heaven looked on at the slaughter of his wife and children (4.3.223–24). Heaven grants the gifts of healing and prophecy to King Edward (4.3.149ff.). Most significantly, heaven appears in contrast to hell as the after-life abode of the blessed and just, the place of peace and happiness. Again, Macbeth himself points the moral before the murders of Duncan and Banquo: the ringing bell summons the king "to heaven or to hell" (2.1.64); and Banquo's soul "If it find heaven, must find it out tonight" (3.1.142).

On the opposing side, the Porter imagines himself keeping the gate in hell and comments on the condemned residents. Though reviled by many, including Samuel Taylor Coleridge ("disgusting," below, 233), this great serio-comic scene (2.3) appropriately gives, as Harry Levin observes, the other place a local habitation and a name. The Macbeths walk the broad and royal road to hell, in fact, sometimes seem already to live there. Reliving her crimes over and over again, Lady Macbeth, one of the living dead, murmurs "Hell is murky" (5.1.31). In Trevor Nunn's celebrated production, Judi Dench turned this into a discovery—[*gasp*] "Hell is murky"—as she recoiled from the abyss opening for her. Then she let out a chilling, suspended scream, part animal cry, part hell-fire howl. Hearing a night shriek, Macbeth observes: "I have supped full with horrors. / Direness, familiar to my slaughterous thoughts, / Cannot once start me" (5.5.13–15). Macduff calls Macbeth a "hell-kite" and a "hell-hound" (4.3.217; 5.7.33), thus echoing his pronouncement, "Not in the legions / Of horrid hell can come a devil more damned / In evils to top Macbeth" (4.3.55–57).

Damned in evils. *Macbeth* takes us on a thrilling, terrifying journey into the heart and soul of the damned. Staging the morality-play sequence of temptation, sin, and death, Shakespeare degrades repentance in this Everyman to a melancholy remorse, leaving both Macbeths to the consequences of their actions, to the "deep damnation of his [the King's] taking-off" (1.7.20). The resulting portraits of sin, punishment, and damnation stand worthily next to those of Dante's *Inferno*, to Ezzelino the tyrant in Phlegethon, the boiling river of blood (Canto 12); to Vanni Fucci, defiant and making an obscene gesture to God (Canto 25); to Ugolino, who eats the bodies of his dead children (Canto 33); to Fra Alberigò and Branca Doria, whose souls are already in hell though their bodies live on earth (Canto 33), to the traitors Judas, Brutus, and Cassius, writhing from the mouths of Satan in the ice of Judecca (Canto 34). Such compelling, full-bodied figures all contrast with the sterilized wraiths of the native *de casibus* tradition, tediously moralizing their histories, reciting their faults, and preaching repentance. Dante and Shakespeare portray the sinners themselves, living human beings, groaning sweating suffering, cursing, excusing, regretting, all their faults and imperfections on their heads, their sins in full and flagrant blossom. And, like Macbeth, the damned souls throughout the nine circles of Dante's *Inferno* are capable of every kind of speech noise, eloquence, and remorse, save one: they cannot pray.

The play's focus on damnation inspired one twentieth-century actor, Derek Jacobi, to summarize his conception of the lead role thus: "I tried to plot his journey from the golden boy of the opening to the burnt-out loser accepting his own damnation of the conclusion" (*Players of Shakespeare 4*, 1998, 210). This journey, we should remember, Shakespeare consciously constructs from numerous possibilities in Holinshed's account. In his notes for plays and poems John Milton apparently envisioned a different kind of *Macbeth*; starting with the conference of Malcolm and Macduff (4.3) and including the ghost of Duncan, he imagined perhaps a political play in the form of a classical revenge tragedy. Shakespeare's drama of damnation, by contrast, purposefully evokes and engages contemporary theology, particularly the disputes about divine foreknowledge, human responsibility, the nature of grace, and the freedom of the human will. These disputes occupied preachers on the pulpit as well as the best theological minds of the early modern period. Asserting the total efficacy of God's foreknowledge and divine grace in his *Thirty-Sixth Article*, the Protestant reformer Martin Luther emphatically denied the existence of free will:

> I misspoke when I said that free will before grace exists in name only; rather I should have simply said "free will is a fiction among real things, a name with no reality." For no one has it within his control to intend anything, good or evil, but rather, as was rightly taught by the article of Wyclif which was condemned at Constance, all things occur by absolute necessity. (below, 177)

Arguing that free will cooperates with grace, Erasmus responded to Luther, at one point in the voice of a Bible reader, speaking to God:

"Why complain of my behaviour, when all my actions, good or bad, are performed by you in me regardless of my will? Why reproach me, when I have no power to preserve the good you have given me, or keep out the evil you put into me? Why entreat me, when everything depends on you, and happens as it pleases you? Why bless me, as though I had done my duty, when whatever happens is your work? Why curse me, when I sinned through necessity?" What is the purpose of such a vast number of commandments if not a single person has it at all in his power to do what is commanded? (below, 182)

Erasmus contends that the doctrine of predestination invalidates God's commandments and renders absurd the concept of divine justice.

The controversy provides an illuminating context for the depiction of witches, sin, and punishment in *Macbeth*. First, it disposes summarily the notion that the weïrd sisters can in any sense possess or control Macbeth. Those early Protestants and Catholics who believe in witches never grant to them such power. Instead, they debate the nature of God's foreknowledge and the predestination of the elect and reprobate, the saved and the damned. Whatever his personal convictions, Shakespeare clearly adopts a Catholic view of the action and theology of free will in this play. Macbeth repeatedly adverts to the terror implicit in free will, in his awesome power to choose good or evil: "I dare do all that may become a man; / Who dares do more is none" (1.7.46–47). He never contemplates the predispositions of fate or the deity, but thinks instead on the consequences of his choices and actions, consequences he would desperately evade and deny. Recalling the prophecy about Banquo, he emphasizes his own responsibility and autonomous agency:

> If't be so,
> For Banquo's issue have I filed my mind,
> For them the gracious Duncan have I murdered,
> Put rancors in the vessel of my peace
> Only for them, and mine eternal jewel
> Given to the common enemy of man
> To make them kings, the seeds of Banquo kings! (3.1.64–70)

Macbeth has chosen evil, in his words, "given" his soul to the devil. To emphasize the point, Shakespeare departs from Holinshed in his depiction of Banquo, who originally encourages him in jest to "purchase" (below, 163) the crown, and who knows in advance of the assassination. Shakespeare's Banquo, a clear foil to Macbeth, freely and steadfastly resists temptation: first he prays, "Merciful powers, / Restrain in me the cursèd thoughts that nature / Gives way to in repose" (2.1.7–9); then he confronts Macbeth directly, asserting that he must lose no honor, must keep his "bosom franchised and allegiance clear" (2.1.28). Rejecting the Protestant dichotomy between the elect and reprobate, Shakespeare deploys the Catholic view of free will perhaps from theological conviction, but more certainly from theatrical necessity. For the doctrine of predestination renders human action essentially undramatic: when the end is known, preordained, and absolutely just, there can be no real choice, suspense, conflict, or resolution. This conception of divine justice and human action renders pity an impertinence, terror a transgression, and tragedy an impossibility.

Consider, for example, the death of the reprobate, as described by the popular Calvinist William Perkins, *A Golden Chain, a Description of Theology containing the Order of the Causes of Salvation and Damnation* (1591): "The reprobates when they die do become without sense and astonied like unto a stone; or else they are overwhelmed with a terrible horror of conscience, and despairing of their salvation, as it were, with the gulf of the sea overturning them" (sig. V5). Perkins illustrates the first option with the story of Nabal who hears of God's judgment against him: "his heart died within him; he became like a stone. About ten days later the Lord struck Nabal, and he died" (1 Kings 23:37–38). He illustrates the second with the story of Judas, who hanged himself in despair (Matthew 27:5). However these ends may compare to the death of Lady Macbeth off-stage, they contrast jarringly with Macbeth's final moments—with his somber reflections and military resurgence. Here as throughout the play, the vitality and eloquence of Macbeth distinguish him from the reprobate of the popular imagination, the heart-dead stone, Nabal, or the despairing, suicidal Judas. Shakespeare presents instead a tragedy of free will and damnation.

Another contemporary controversy, the debate over regicide, also informs *Macbeth*, just as it does, *mutatis mutandis*, Shakespeare's history plays and other tragedies. *Macbeth*, however, features not one regicide but two. The play asks that we condemn the murder of King Duncan, and, with equal conviction, applaud the murder of King Macbeth. To ensure the condemnation Shakespeare denies Macbeth a coronation scene and suppresses Holinshed's notice of Duncan's inadequacies, Macbeth's possible claim to the crown, and his years of just rule. Thus Shakespeare portrays the first regicide as a monstrous rebellion, in accord with the Elizabethan *Homily against Disobedience* (below, 207–13) and the beliefs of Banquo's descendant, King James I, proponent of the divine right of kings. To portray the second regicide as virtuous restoration, Shakespeare amplifies the witches, the sinister influence of Lady Macbeth, and Macbeth's crimes. But according to the *Homily* and divine right

theory, even bad kings had to be obeyed and tolerated: "let us either
deserve to have a good prince, or let us patiently suffer and obey such
as we deserve" (below, 209). To justify the second regicide, Shakespeare draws upon the opposing resistance theory, which holds that
citizens owe obedience to kings but not to tyrants, i.e., rulers who by
unlawful entrance or vicious practice forfeit their rights of sovereignty. The Jesuit Juan de Mariana, for example, argued that, under
certain circumstances, anyone may depose a tyrant for the good of
the commonwealth and in so doing earn gratitude and praise (below
214–18).

Accordingly, Shakespeare repeatedly portrays King Macbeth as a
tyrant both in the language and the action of the play. Macduff
calls him "an untitled tyrant, bloody sceptred" (4.3.104), neatly
alluding to both his unlawful entrance (by assassination) and vicious
practice (the subsequent murders). "This tyrant holds the due of
birth" (3.6.25) from Duncan's son; the "sole name" of this tyrant
"blisters our tongues" (4.3.12). Like the archetypal Herod, the tyran-
nical Macbeth massacres the innocents. Macduff threatens to display Macbeth's picture on a pole with the legend "Here may you see
the tyrant" (5.7.57). And, accordingly, Shakespeare depicts the
deposer Macduff as "anyone," as an ordinary, flawed man. Macduff
makes the fatal error of leaving his wife and children unprotected;
he has no claim to fame except his birth by Caesarean section; and,
as one Royal Shakespeare Company actor who had played the role
five times observed to me, he is typically ineloquent or silent: relat-
ing Duncan's murder to others, Macduff says, "Do not bid me
speak" (2.3.68); Malcolm urges him, "give sorrow words" (4.3.209);
"I have no words / My voice is in my sword" (5.7.36–37), Macduff
says later to Macbeth. In his operatic *Macbeth* (1847, 1865) Giuseppe
Verdi amplified this voice into an entire chorus of Scottish refugees,
lamenting their country's oppression, *Or che tutta a' figli tuoi / Sei
conversa in un avel*, "Now that for all your children, / You have
become a tomb."

In this, as in other regards, the eloquent Macbeth, speaking fully
thirty percent of the play's lines, stands in colossal contrast with
the avenger and putative hero, Macduff. Shakespeare thus recapit-
ulates the strategy of his previous tyrant play, *Richard III*, wherein
Richmond's forgettable piety opposes Gloucester's grand and
thrilling blasphemy. But both blasphemy and piety in many forms
resound throughout Macbeth's speech—alternating, simultaneous,
interdependent—creating memorable and musical discord. Blasphemy appears in the eerie invocation to night and "its bloody and
invisible hand," which Macbeth hopes will "cancel and tear to
pieces that great bond" that keeps him pale (3.2.45–49). It continues throughout the consultation with the witches (4.1). And, at the

last, Macbeth, perversely mimicking his former valor instead of repenting, redefines the very terms of salvation and damnation: "Before my body / I throw my warlike shield. Lay on, Macduff, / And damned be him that first cries, 'Hold, enough'!" (5.7.62–64). Identifying "him" as God by pointing toward the heavens, Derek Jacobi's Macbeth pointed the blasphemy with a curse against the deity. Less explicitly, an equally potent denial appears in the world-weary nihilism of Macbeth's famous meditation:

> Tomorrow, and tomorrow, and tomorrow
> Creeps in this petty pace from day to day
> To the last syllable of recorded time,
> And all our yesterdays have lighted fools
> The way to dusty death. Out, out, brief candle,
> Life's but a walking shadow, a poor player
> That struts and frets his hour upon the stage
> And then is heard no more. It is a tale
> Told by an idiot, full of sound and fury,
> Signifying nothing. (5.5.19–28)

Only those who have experienced some elevation can fall to this nadir; and the Macbeth who piously believed in evenhanded justice and heaven's cherubim (1.7.10, 22), we recall, once saw life as a feast nourished by that very same progression of days, each capped by restorative sleep (2.2.40–43). Then the diurnal rhythms of waking and sleeping expressed not meaninglessness but moral order. This deep belief in moral order motivates Macbeth's distinctive verse music, his piety, like his blasphemy, taking various shapes and forms. Seconds after the murder Macbeth feels an incredulous repulsion and self-alienation: "What hands are here? Ha, they pluck out mine eyes!" "To know my deed 'twere best not know myself" (2.2.62, 76). Soon after, pretending to mourn the King, he speaks truer than he intends: "from this instant / There's nothing serious in mortality. / All is but toys. Renown and grace is dead. (2.3.90–92). Racked by his guilty conscience, the man who yearned for renown and grace soon envies his victim:

> Better be with the dead,
> Whom we, to gain our peace, have sent to peace,
> Than on the torture of the mind to lie
> In restless ecstasy. (3.2.19–22)

There is even a clear moment of moral vision and remorse in the final meeting with Macduff:

> Of all men else I have avoided thee.
> But get thee back. My soul is too much charged
> With blood of thine already. (5.7.34–36)

[handwritten margin notes: "collapses present, future past" with arrow, "'to do'" ; "evil driving force" ; "thrill, misery, evil"]

The eloquent and elegiac register of such piety rarely survives translation or adaptation. Plangent and moving, it arrests the hero's descent into darkness while marking the speed and distance of his fall. Coleridge thought *Macbeth* "the most rapid" of Shakespeare's plays, "being wholly and purely tragic" (below, 233). Consequences follow so quickly and inevitably that they seem embedded in actions themselves, even in the thoughts preceding action. The confusion of tenses attending the verb "to do" sometimes collapses past, present, and future so that planning, acting, and suffering become coexistent aspects of the same crime. Lady Macbeth urges:

> Thou'dst have, great Glamis,
> That which cries "Thus thou must do," if thou have it,
> And that which rather thou dost fear to do
> Than wishest should be undone. (1.5.20–23)

And Macbeth contemplates, "If it were done when 'tis done, then 'twere well / It were done quickly" (1.7.1–2); he resolves, "I go, and it is done" (2.1.62). The interconnectedness of conception, execution, and consequence heightens the sense of Macbeth's dizzying plunge and, once begun, its inevitability. "I have done the deed" (2.2.14), he says simply after the murder. "What's done is done" (3.2.12), Lady Macbeth counsels; and then later in a rueful echo while sleepwalking, she says, "what's done cannot be undone" (5.1.60–61). Writing a travesty of *Macbeth* in the nineteenth century, Francis Talfourd shrewdly seized upon this inevitability to turn the play into topsyturvy burlesque. In his version Duncan returns from the dead, nodding and winking at Macduff, and reclaims his crown. Before Banquo and Lady Macbeth return arm-in-arm from the nether world, Macbeth rises and addresses the King:

> I tender, sir, of course, my resignation,
> Since all's in train for me to leave my station.
> So at your feet I lay my regal diadem
> Without regret, nor wish again that I had 'em. (below, 332)

The comic fantasy strikes at the heart of Shakespeare's play, where evil freely chosen becomes a driving force, propulsive, uncontrollable, irreversible, irrevocable. As director Gregory Doran observed, "in *Macbeth*, if anyone had time to think the events wouldn't happen. The furious pace of the text is crucial: things happen in this terrible whirlwind" (ed. Bate and Rasmussen, 2009, 159).

Thus the play enables us to experience the thrill and misery of evil as few others. Before playing Macbeth, Antony Sher interviewed two murderers to learn how it actually felt to kill someone, before, during, and after (below 127). Recoiling from this heart of darkness, William Davenant emphasized the positives and affirmed the existence of moral order: he greatly expanded the role of Macduff's wife to provide a clear contrast to Lady Macbeth, the good wife matched against the evil one. His successful seventeenth-century adaptation also presented a Macbeth who died not with a defiant snarl but with a belated confession of folly, "Farewell vain world, and what's most vain in it, ambition" (below, 320). Such changes diminish the evil in Shakespeare's play, reducing it to comfortable and conventional moral schema. Expanding the witches' roles, Davenant likewise relocated the evil safely in the other, in the non-human. Such revision can constitute a strategy of evasion, modern critics remind us, for the witches release and reveal the evil in human beings and their social orderings. Stephen Orgel comments that witches "live outside the social order but embody its contradictions": their gender indeterminacy, women with beards, females played originally by male actors, suggest that nature is "anarchic, full of competing claims, not ordered and hierarchical" (below, 260). Director Rupert Goold brilliantly cast the witches as hospital nursing sisters, "people we trust and look to in times of need and custodians of life and death in most people's lives, so more problematic if evil" (ed. Bate and Rasmussen, 2009, 151). Evil cannot be summarily demonized, dislocated, and dismissed.

Early modern controversy supports modern critical insight about the ambivalent nature of the witches as both demonic and human, as both other and ourselves. James I depicted them as "ungodly creatures, no better than devils" (below, 197) in a pamphlet, *News from Scotland* (1591), and later in his *Daemonology* (1597). He spoke about their supernatural powers to create storms and topple kings. James was writing against such sceptics as Reginald Scot (*The Discovery of Witchcraft*, 1584), who thought witches ordinary people, either deluders or deluded themselves, "women which be commonly old, lame, blear-eyed, pale, foul, and full of wrinkles, poor, sullen, superstitious, and papists, or such as know no religion in whose drowsy minds the devil hath gotten a fine seat; so as what mischief, mischance, calamity, or slaughter is brought to pass, they are easily persuaded the same is done by themselves" (below, 191). Shakespeare's play takes full advantage of the controversy without deciding it: *Macbeth* provides chilling testimony to the existence of supernatural evil and the forbidden black arts, well according with popular superstition and James's views. But, the play insists equally, Macbeth desires the crown before his first encounter with the witches. And when he later seeks them out on his own, they anticipate his arrival by saying, "Something wicked this way comes" (4.1.45). Clearly, the evil lives within Macbeth, within his human ambition; and his faith in the witches both evokes and sustains them. Their existence and power depend, as Scot insists, on human credulity and weakness. They reside in our lusts, hatreds, and sins.

Though created in a language arising from specific theological and political contexts, Shakespeare's *Macbeth* has come to new life in strange and marvelous adaptations (see Holland's survey of films below, 270–94). Eugène Ionesco makes *Macbeth* into an absurdist fantasy that depicts a world of political incoherence and moral vacuity (below, 340–48); Tom Stoppard restages the play to protest communist suppression of art and to explore the meaning of language (*Cahoots Macbeth*, 1980). Bill Cain's brilliantly revisionist *Equivocation* (2009) imagines *Macbeth* as Shakespeare's indictment of Robert Cecil, the true author of the Gunpowder Plot (below, 365–76).

Akira Kurosawa's admired 1957 film, *Throne of Blood*, or *The Castle of the Spider's Web*, transposes the tale to medieval Japan. There the white-haired Forest Spirit sits at a spinning wheel in a hut of sticks, tempting and mocking humans. The gruff, passionate Samurai warlord, Washizu, goaded by his wife, the still, formal, precise, and menacing automaton, Asaji, slays Lord Kuniharu. Washizu then kills his friend Miki, whose spirit returns to the banquet. The labyrinthine forest finally takes spectacular revenge as volleys of hissing arrows strike and stick in Washizu, staggering desperately and defiantly on the wall of his castle (see below, 284). A final arrow pierces him in the neck as mist shrouds both the castle and the forest. In the early 1970s the South African playwright Welcome Msomi staged another brilliant retelling, *uMabatha*, based partly on the life of Shaka Zulu, an early nineteenth-century chief famous for his military skill and brutality. The Sangoma, or witchdoctors, spit, beat drums, throw bones, and prophesize greatness for the warrior Mabatha. His wife, Kamdonsela, invokes her ancestors to make her heart like the devil's thorn, her blood like mamba's poison. Mabatha kills Chief Dangane and his friend Bhangane, and resolves to kill the wife and children of Mafudu: "My thoughts were children, tortoise-slow / But now I will strike / Swifter than the crouching lion / Who smells the terror of his prey" (below, 360–61). Mafudu returns to slay Mabatha, deceived by the Sangomas' prophecies.

Such radical and daring adaptations treat the play as a myth about the mystery of evil, infinitely translatable into new series of haunting images and actions. Whether reflecting or departing from its origins, whether set in medieval Scotland or in some other land and culture, Shakespeare's *Macbeth* still stirs our deepest desires and fears.

ROBERT S. MIOLA
LOYOLA UNIVERSITY IN MARYLAND

The Text of
MACBETH

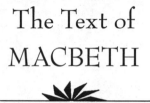

Character List

KING Duncan of Scotland
MALCOLM, his son, later Prince of Cumberland
DONALDBAIN, another son
CAPTAIN in King Duncan's army

MACBETH, Thane of Glamis, later Thane of Cawdor, later King of
    Scotland
Three MURDERERS, attending Macbeth
A PORTER at Macbeth's Castle
SEYTON, a servant of Macbeth
LADY MACBETH, Macbeth's wife, later Queen of Scotland
GENTLEWOMAN, servant of Lady Macbeth
Scottish DOCTOR, attending Lady Macbeth

Six WITCHES, including the three weïrd sisters
HECATE, leader of the witches
Three APPARITIONS: an armed head, a bloody child, a child
    crowned
A show of eight KINGS

BANQUO, a thane of Scotland, later appearing as a GHOST
FLEANCE, his son

MACDUFF, Thane of Fife
WIFE of Macduff
SON, child of Macduff and Wife

LENNOX
ROSS
MENTEITH   } Scottish thanes
ANGUS
CAITHNESS

English DOCTOR
OLD MAN
SIWARD, English Earl of Northumberland
YOUNG SIWARD, his son
MESSENGER
LORD

3

SERVANT
SOLDIER

Lords, Soldiers, Servants, Drummers, a Sewer

The Tragedy of Macbeth

I.I

Thunder and lightning. Enter three WITCHES.
FIRST WITCH   When shall we three meet again?
  In thunder, lightning, or in rain?
SECOND WITCH   When the hurly-burly's done,
  When the battle's lost and won.
THIRD WITCH   That will be ere the set of sun.   5
FIRST WITCH   Where the place?
SECOND WITCH   Upon the heath.
THIRD WITCH   There to meet with Macbeth.
FIRST WITCH   I come, Grimalkin!
ALL   Paddock calls anon!   10
  Fair is foul, and foul is fair,
  Hover through the fog and filthy air.

                                                    Exeunt.

I.2

Alarum within. Enter KING [*Duncan*], MALCOLM, DONALD-
  BAIN. LENNOX, *with Attendants, meeting a bleeding* CAPTAIN.
KING   What bloody man is that? He can report,
  As seemeth by his plight, of the revolt
  The newest state.
MALCOLM   This is the sergeant
  Who like a good and hardy soldier fought
  'Gainst my captivity. —Hail, brave friend!   5

1.1. **Location: outdoors.**
3. **hurly-burly**: commotion.
7. **heath**: open, uncultivated ground with low shrubs.
9. **Grimalkin**: gray cat, the name of the witch's familiar (attendant spirit).
10. **SP ALL**: Editors have unnecessarily made this line start a dialogue between the Second Witch and Third Witch; **Paddock**: toad, another familiar; **anon**: at once.
1.2. **Location: a military camp.**
0.1. SD *Alarum*: a call to arms by a trumpet or other instrument; *within*: behind the back
  wall of the stage.
3. **sergeant**: a military officer; the rank is probably "captain," as indicated by the stage
  direction and speech prefixes.

Say to the King the knowledge of the broil
As thou didst leave it.
CAPTAIN   Doubtful it stood, → battle
As two spent swimmers that do cling together
And choke their art. The merciless Macdonald—
Worthy to be a rebel, for to that   10
The multiplying villainies of nature
Do swarm upon him—from the Western Isles
Of kerns and galloglasses is supplied;
And Fortune, on his damnèd quarry smiling, →
Showed like a rebel's whore. But all's too weak,   15
For brave Macbeth—well he deserves that name—
Disdaining Fortune with his brandished steel, →
Which smoked with bloody execution,
Like valor's minion carved out his passage
Till he faced the slave,   20
Which ne'er shook hands nor bade farewell to him,
[Till he unseamed him from the nave to th' chops,] → split him
And fixed his head upon our battlements.   open
KING   O valiant cousin, worthy gentleman!
CAPTAIN   As whence the sun 'gins his reflection,   25
Shipwrecking storms and direful thunders,
So from that spring whence comfort seemed to come,
Discomfort swells. Mark, King of Scotland, mark:
No sooner justice had, with valor armed,
Compelled these skipping kerns to trust their heels,   30
But the Norwegian lord, surveying vantage,

6. **broil**: battle.
8. **spent**: exhausted.
9. **choke their art**: make impossible the art of swimming.
10. **that**: that end.
11. **villainies of nature**: (1) evil aspects of his nature; (2) villainous rebels.
12. **Western Isles**: the Hebrides and, perhaps, Ireland.
13. **kerns**: light-armed Irish foot soldiers; **galloglasses**: soldiers on horse with axes.
14–15. **Fortune . . . whore**: Fortune, seeming to favor its intended victim Macdonald (**quarry**), appeared to be his consort. (Fortune was proverbially a strumpet and unfaithful, so the metaphor is ominous for Macdonald.)
19. **minion**: darling.
20. **slave**: Macdonald.
21. **Which**: who.
22. Till he split him open from the navel to the jaws.
24. **cousin**: a general term of affection, here indicating a specific familial relation; see 1.7.13.
25. **whence**: from the place where; **'gins his reflection**: begins its turning back across the sky.
26. If the verb **come** (27) is understood at the end of the line, there is no need to add "break" or some such word, as editors often do. The movement of the sun after the spring equinox was thought to cause storms.
27. **spring**: (1) season of spring; (2) source.
30. **skipping . . . heels**: flighty foot-soldiers to retreat.
31. **surveying vantage**: seeing an advantage.

With furbished arms and new supplies of men
Began a fresh assault.

KING   Dismayed not this our captains, Macbeth and Banquo?

CAPTAIN   Yes, as sparrows eagles or the hare the lion.   35
If I say sooth, I must report they were
As cannons overcharged with double cracks;
So they doubly redoubled strokes upon the foe.
Except they meant to bathe in reeking wounds,
Or memorize another Golgotha,   —→ *biblical allusion*   40
I cannot tell—
But I am faint. My gashes cry for help.

KING   So well thy words become thee as thy wounds;
They smack of honor both. —Go get him surgeons.
                              [*Exit* CAPTAIN, *attended.*]

          Enter ROSS *and* ANGUS.
Who comes here?

MALCOLM   The worthy Thane of Ross.   45

LENNOX   What a haste looks through his eyes!
So should he look that seems to speak things strange.

ROSS   God save the King!

KING   Whence cam'st thou, worthy thane?

ROSS   From Fife, great King,   50
Where the Norwegian banners flout the sky
And fan our people cold.
Norway himself, with terrible numbers,
Assisted by that most disloyal traitor,
The Thane of Cawdor, began a dismal conflict.   55
allusion Till that Bellona's bridegroom, lapped in proof,
Confronted him with self-comparisons,
Point against point, rebellious arm 'gainst arm,
Curbing his lavish spirit. And to conclude,

32. **furbished**: scoured.
36. **sooth**: truth.
37. **cracks**: charges of gunpowder.
38. **So they**: they so.
39. **Except**: unless.
40. **memorize another Golgotha**: make the battle as memorable as the Biblical Gol-
    gotha ("the place of the skull"), where Christ was crucified (Mark 15:22).
45. **Thane**: a landowner and chief of a clan, equivalent to an English earl.
46. **looks through**: appears in.
47. **seems to**: seems about to.
50. **Fife**: county on the east coast of Scotland.
51. **flout**: mock.
52. **fan . . . cold**: make . . . afraid.
53. **Norway**: the King of Norway (Sweno).
55. **dismal**: ominous.
56. **Bellona**: Roman goddess of war (imagined as wife to Macbeth, the **bridegroom**);
    lapped in proof: (1) wearing proven armor; (2) wrapped in experience.
57. **self-comparisons**: powers comparable to his own.
59. **lavish**: wild.

The victory fell on us—
KING   Great happiness!—
ROSS   That now Sweno,   60
  The Norways' king, craves composition.
  Nor would we deign him burial of his men
  Till he disbursèd at Saint Colme's Inch
  Ten thousand dollars to our general use.
KING   No more that Thane of Cawdor shall deceive   65
   Our bosom interest. Go pronounce his present death,
   And with his former title greet Macbeth.
ROSS   I'll see it done.
KING   What he hath lost noble Macbeth hath won.

                                        Exeunt.

                          1.3
    Thunder. Enter the three WITCHES.
FIRST WITCH   Where hast thou been, sister?
SECOND WITCH   Killing swine.
THIRD WITCH   Sister, where thou?
FIRST WITCH   A sailor's wife had chestnuts in her lap,
   And munched, and munched, and munched.   5
   "Give me," quoth I.
   "Aroint thee, witch!" the rump-fed runnion cries.
   Her husband's to Aleppo gone, master o' the *Tiger*,
   But in a sieve I'll thither sail,
   And like a rat without a tail,   10
   I'll do, I'll do, and I'll do.
SECOND WITCH   I'll give thee a wind.
FIRST WITCH   Thou'rt kind.
THIRD WITCH   And I another.
FIRST WITCH   I myself have all the other,   15

---

61. **Norways'**: Norwegians'; **composition**: agreement, peace treaty.
62. **deign**: grant.
63. **Saint Colme's Inch**: Inchcolm, an isle near Edinburgh. **Colme's** is disyllabic, derived from St. Columba (521–97), who preached, worked miracles, and converted the Northern Picts to Christianity (see 2.4.33n.).
64. **dollars**: silver coins, probably German *thalers*, used throughout Europe.
66. **bosom interest**: heart's trust; **present**: immediate.
1.3. **Location**: a heath.
6. **quoth**: said.
7. **Aroint**: begone; **rump-fed**: (1) fed on rump meat; (2) fat-rumped; **runnion**: woman (an abusive term).
8. **Aleppo**: trading city in Northern Syria; *Tiger*: name of a ship.
9. **sieve**: Witches were commonly thought to sail in sieves.
10. **rat . . . tail**: Transformed witches sometimes had bodily defects.
11. **do**: (1) act; (2) have sexual intercourse.
16. And I control the ports where the winds blow.

And the very ports they blow,
All the quarters that they know
I'th' shipman's card.
I'll drain him dry as hay.
Sleep shall neither night nor day   20
Hang upon his penthouse lid;
He shall live a man forbid.
Weary sennights nine times nine
Shall he dwindle, peak, and pine.
Though his bark cannot be lost,   25
Yet it shall be tempest-tossed.
Look what I have.

SECOND WITCH   Show me, show me.

FIRST WITCH   Here I have a pilot's thumb,
Wrecked as homeward he did come.   30
　　　　　Drum within.

THIRD WITCH   A drum, a drum!
Macbeth doth come!

ALL [*dancing in a circle*]   The weïrd sisters, hand in hand,
Posters of the sea and land,
Thus do go, about, about,   35
Thrice to thine, and thrice to mine,
And thrice again to make up nine.
Peace, the charm's wound up.
　　　　　Enter MACBETH *and* BANQUO.

MACBETH   So foul and fair a day I have not seen.

BANQUO   How far is't called to Forres? What are these,   40
So withered and so wild in their attire,
That look not like th'inhabitants o'th' earth,
And yet are on't? —Live you? Or are you aught
That man may question? You seem to understand me
By each at once her choppy finger laying   45
Upon her skinny lips. You should be women.

---

17. **quarters**: directions.
18. **shipman's card**: nautical map.
19. By sexual intercourse, presumably, as a succubus (demon in female form).
21. **penthouse lid**: eyelid (projecting over the eye like a **penthouse**).
22. **forbid**: cursed.
23. **sennights**: weeks (seven nights).
24. **peak**: waste away.
25. **bark**: ship.
30. **SD *Drum***: a signal for the entrance of military characters.
33. **weïrd**: fateful (from **wyrd**, "fate"), pronounced disyllabically, with a suggestion of the uncanny. Audiences might have heard "wayward" too, which appears elsewhere in the play (3.5.11).
34. **Posters of**: travelers over.
40. **called**: said to be; **Forres**: Scottish town.
43. **aught**: anything.
45. **choppy**: chapped.

And yet your beards forbid me to interpret
That you are so.
MACBETH   Speak, if you can. What are you?
FIRST WITCH   All hail, Macbeth! Hail to thee, Thane of Glamis!
SECOND WITCH   All hail, Macbeth! Hail to thee, Thane of
    Cawdor!   50
THIRD WITCH   All hail, Macbeth, that shalt be king hereafter!
BANQUO   Good sir, why do you start and seem to fear
    Things that do sound so fair? —I'th' name of truth,
    Are ye fantastical or that indeed
    Which outwardly ye show? My noble partner   55
    You greet with present grace and great prediction
    Of noble having and of royal hope
    That he seems rapt withal. To me you speak not.
    If you can look into the seeds of time
    And say which grain will grow and which will not,   60
    Speak then to me, who neither beg nor fear
    Your favors nor your hate.
FIRST WITCH   Hail!
SECOND WITCH   Hail!
THIRD WITCH   Hail!   65
FIRST WITCH   Lesser than Macbeth, and greater.
SECOND WITCH   Not so happy, yet much happier.
THIRD WITCH   Thou shalt get kings, though thou be none.
    So all hail, Macbeth and Banquo!
FIRST WITCH   Banquo and Macbeth, all hail!   70
MACBETH   Stay, you imperfect speakers, tell me more.
    By Finel's death I know I am Thane of Glamis,
    But how of Cawdor? The Thane of Cawdor lives,
    A prosperous gentleman, and to be king
    Stands not within the prospect of belief,   75
    No more than to be Cawdor. Say from whence
    You owe this strange intelligence, or why

---

49. **All hail**: Shakespeare associated this phrase with Judas's betrayal of Jesus (Matthew
    26.49) in 3 *Henry VI* (5.7.33–34) and *Richard II* (4.1.169–71).
52. **start**: flinch, recoil.
54. **fantastical**: creatures of fantasy.
56. **grace**: honor.
58. **rapt**: entranced; **withal**: with it.
68. **get**: beget.
71. **imperfect**: unfinished.
72. **Finel**: Macbeth's father.
73–74. An apparent contradiction (explicable as an oversight or an incomplete revision)
    to 1.2.54–58, which describes Macbeth's victory over Cawdor.
75. **prospect**: possibility.
77. **owe**: own; **intelligence**: news.

Upon this blasted heath you stop our way
With such prophetic greeting. Speak, I charge you.

                                    WITCHES *vanish.*

BANQUO   The earth hath bubbles as the water has,   80
And these are of them. Whither are they vanished?

MACBETH   Into the air. And what seemed corporal
Melted as breath into the wind. Would they had stayed.

BANQUO   Were such things here as we do speak about?
Or have we eaten on the insane root   85
That takes the reason prisoner?

MACBETH   Your children shall be kings.

BANQUO   You shall be king.

MACBETH   And Thane of Cawdor too. Went it not so?

BANQUO   To th'selfsame tune and words. —Who's here?
        Enter ROSS *and* ANGUS.

ROSS   The King hath happily received, Macbeth,   90
The news of thy success; and when he reads
Thy personal venture in the rebels' fight,
His wonders and his praises do contend
Which should be thine or his. Silenced with that,
In viewing o'er the rest o'th' selfsame day,   95
He finds thee in the stout Norwegian ranks,
Nothing afeard of what thyself didst make,
Strange images of death. As thick as hail
Came post with post, and every one did bear
Thy praises in his kingdom's great defense   100
And poured them down before him.

ANGUS   We are sent
To give thee from our royal master thanks,
Only to herald thee into his sight,
Not pay thee.

ROSS   And for an earnest of a greater honor,   105
He bade me, from him, call thee Thane of Cawdor;

---

78. **blasted**: blighted, often by a supernatural agent.
79. **SD** *vanish*: Probably by use of the trap door or smoke from burning resin.
82. **corporal**: bodily.
85. **insane root**: plant causing insanity (probably henbane).
91. **reads**: considers.
93–94. **His . . . his**: His astonishment strikes him into awed silence but also stimulates
    the conflicting impulse to praise and reward.
97. Not at all afraid of what you yourself created.
98. **hail**: Some defend Folio's "Tale," but "thick as hail" is proverbial (Dent HI 1, see
    Resources).
99. **post with post**: messenger after messenger.
103. **herald**: usher.
105. **earnest**: token payment.

In which addition, hail, most worthy thane,
For it is thine.
BANQUO   What, can the devil speak true?
MACBETH   The Thane of Cawdor lives. Why do you dress me
In borrowed robes?
ANGUS   Who was the thane lives yet,   110
But under heavy judgment bears that life
Which he deserves to lose.
Whether he was combined with those of Norway,
Or did line the rebel with hidden help
And vantage, or that with both he labored   115
In his country's wrack, I know not.
But treasons capital, confessed and proved,
Have overthrown him.
MACBETH [*aside*]   Glamis, and Thane of Cawdor!
The greatest is behind. —Thanks for your pains.
[*aside to* BANQUO] Do you not hope your children shall be kings,   120
When those that gave the Thane of Cawdor to me
Promised no less to them?
BANQUO [*aside to* MACBETH] That trusted home
Might yet enkindle you unto the crown.
Besides the Thane of Cawdor. But 'tis strange,
And oftentimes to win us to our harm,   125
The instruments of darkness tell us truths,
Win us with honest trifles, to betray's
In deepest consequence.
—Cousins, a word, I pray you.
                    [*He converses apart with* ROSS *and* ANGUS.]
MACBETH [*aside*]   Two truths are told,
As happy prologues to the swelling act   130
Of th'imperial theme. —I thank you, gentlemen.
[*aside*] This supernatural soliciting
Cannot be ill, cannot be good. If ill,
Why hath it given me earnest of success

107. **addition**: title.
114. **line the rebel**: fortify Macdonald.
116. **wrack**: ruin.
117. **capital**: punishable by death.
119. **behind**: still to come.
122. **home**: all the way.
126. **darkness**: evil, especially demonic.
128. **deepest consequence**: gravest outcome.
129. **Cousins**: fellow lords.
130. **swelling act**: developing drama.
131. **imperial theme**: the subject of kingship.
132. **soliciting**: urging.

Commencing in a truth? I am Thane of Cawdor.   135
If good, why do I yield to that suggestion
Whose horrid image doth unfix my hair
And make my seated heart knock at my ribs
Against the use of nature? Present fears
Are less than horrible imaginings.   140
My thought, whose murder yet is but fantastical,
Shakes so my single state of man
That function is smothered in surmise,
And nothing is but what is not.

BANQUO   Look how our partner's rapt.   145

MACBETH [*aside*]   If chance will have me king, why, chance may
    crown me
Without my stir.

BANQUO   New honors come upon him,
    Like our strange garments, cleave not to their mold
    But with the aid of use.

MACBETH [*aside*]   Come what come may,
    Time and the hour runs through the roughest day.   150

BANQUO   Worthy Macbeth, we stay upon your leisure.

MACBETH   Give me your favor. My dull brain was wrought
    With things forgotten. Kind gentlemen, your pains
    Are registered where every day I turn
    The leaf to read them. Let us toward the King.   155
    [*aside to* BANQUO] Think upon what hath chanced, and at more
        time,
    The interim having weighed it, let us speak
    Our free hearts each to other.

BANQUO [*aside to* MACBETH]   Very gladly.

MACBETH [*aside to* BANQUO]   Till then, enough. —Come,
    friends.

                                                  Exeunt.

137. **horrid**: bristling; **unfix**: make stand.
139. **use**: custom.
141. **whose**: in which; **fantastical**: imaginary.
142. **single . . . man**: weak human condition.
143. **function**: ability to act; **surmise**: speculation.
144. Nothing exists in the present but thoughts about the future.
147. **stir**: acting; **come**: having come.
148. **cleave . . . mold**: do not fit the body's form.
149. **Come . . . may**: Let whatever will happen happen, a proverbial expression (Dent C529, see Resources).
150. Even the roughest days come to an end.
152. **favor**: goodwill.
154. **registered**: recorded (in my mind).
155. **leaf**: page.
157. **The . . . it**: having considered the matter in the meantime.

I.4

Flourish. Enter KING, LENNOX, MALCOLM, DONALDBAIN,
and Attendants.

KING   Is execution done on Cawdor? Or not
Those in commission yet returned?

MALCOLM   My liege,
They are not yet come back. But I have spoke
With one that saw him die, who did report
That very frankly he confessed his treasons,   5
Implored your highness' pardon, and set forth
A deep repentance. Nothing in his life
Became him like the leaving it. He died
As one that had been studied in his death
To throw away the dearest thing he owed   10
As 'twere a careless trifle.

KING   There's no art
To find the mind's construction in the face.
He was a gentleman on whom I built
An absolute trust.

    Enter MACBETH, BANQUO, ROSS, *and* ANGUS.
                —O worthiest cousin!
The sin of my ingratitude even now   15
Was heavy on me. Thou art so far before
That swiftest wing of recompense is slow
To overtake thee. Would thou hadst less deserved,
That the proportion both of thanks and payment
Might have been mine. Only I have left to say,   20
More is thy due than more than all can pay.

MACBETH   The service and the loyalty I owe
In doing it pays itself. Your highness' part
Is to receive our duties, and our duties
Are to your throne and state, children and servants,   25

1.4. Location: the King's camp or palace.
0.1. SD *Flourish*: a trumpet signal indicating the entrance or exit of royal authority.
Flourishes honor King Duncan and later King Malcolm (5.7.64.4 SD, 89 SD) but never
the usurper Macbeth.
1. Or not: or are not; in commission: commissioned (to execute Cawdor); liege: superior
to whom one owes service.
8. Became: graced, befitted.
9. studied: prepared by study.
10. owed: owned.
11. careless: uncared for.
16. before: ahead (in time and in deserving).
19. proportion: just and satisfactory reckoning.
23. it: my duty.
24–25. and . . . servants: We owe duty to your throne and high rank just as children owe
duty to their parents, and servants to their masters.

Which do but what they should by doing everything
Safe toward your love and honor.
KING   Welcome hither.
I have begun to plant thee and will labor
To make thee full of growing.—Noble Banquo,
That hast no less deserved nor must be known   30
No less to have done so, let me enfold thee
And hold thee to my heart.
BANQUO   There if I grow,
The harvest is your own.
KING   My plenteous joys,
Wanton in fullness, seek to hide themselves
In drops of sorrow.—Sons, kinsmen, thanes,   35
And you whose places are the nearest, know
We will establish our estate upon
Our eldest, Malcolm, whom we name hereafter
The Prince of Cumberland; which honor must
Not unaccompanied invest him only,   40
But signs of nobleness, like stars, shall shine
On all deservers. [*to* MACBETH] From hence to Inverness,
And bind us further to you.
MACBETH   The rest is labor which is not used for you.
I'll be myself the harbinger and make joyful   45
The hearing of my wife with your approach.
So humbly take my leave.
KING   My worthy Cawdor!
MACBETH [*aside*]   The Prince of Cumberland! That is a step
On which I must fall down or else o'erleap,
For in my way it lies. Stars, hide your fires,   50
Let not light see my black and deep desires;
The eye wink at the hand; yet let that be
Which the eye fears, when it is done, to see.   *Exit.*
KING   True, worthy Banquo, he is full so valiant,
And in his commendations I am fed;   55
It is a banquet to me. Let's after him,

27. **Safe toward**: to make safe.
28. **plant**: nurture.
31. **enfold**: embrace.
34. **Wanton**: profuse.
37. **establish . . . upon**: name as heir to the throne. (The monarchy was not hereditary.)
39. **Prince of Cumberland**: an honorific title designating the next king.
40. **Not unaccompanied invest**: not alone adorn.
42. **Inverness**: "Mouth of the River Ness," the city where Macbeth's castle is located.
44. **rest**: repose.
45. **harbinger**: forerunner.
52. **The . . . hand**: Let the eye see not what the hand does.
54. **full so valiant**: fully as valiant (as you say).
55. **his commendations**: praises of him.

Whose care is gone before to bid us welcome.
It is a peerless kinsman.

Flourish. Exeunt.

I.5

Enter Macbeth's Wife [LADY MACBETH] *alone with a letter.*
LADY MACBETH [*reads*]   "They met me in the day of success, and
I have learned by the perfect'st report they have more in them
than mortal knowledge. When I burned in desire to question
them further, they made themselves air, into which they vanished. Whiles I stood rapt in the wonder of it came missives   5
from the King, who all-hailed me 'Thane of Cawdor,' by which
title before these weïrd sisters saluted me and referred me to
the coming on of time with 'Hail, king that shalt be!' This
have I thought good to deliver thee, my dearest partner of
greatness, that thou mightst not lose the dues of rejoicing by   10
being ignorant of what greatness is promised thee. Lay it to
thy heart, and farewell."
Glamis thou art, and Cawdor, and shalt be
What thou art promised. Yet do I fear thy nature;
It is too full o'th' milk of human kindness   15
To catch the nearest way. Thou wouldst be great,
Art not without ambition, but without
The illness should attend it. What thou wouldst highly,
That wouldst thou holily; wouldst not play false,
And yet wouldst wrongly win. Thou'dst have, great Glamis,   20
That which cries "Thus thou must do" if thou have it,
And that which rather thou dost fear to do
Than wishest should be undone. Hie thee hither,
That I may pour my spirits in thine ear
And chastise with the valor of my tongue   25
All that impedes thee from the golden round,

1.5. **Location: Inverness. Macbeth's castle.**
2. **perfect'st report**: most reliable evidence.
5. **missives**: messengers;
6. **all-hailed**: greeted.
10. **dues**: due measure.
15. **milk . . . kindness**: compassion natural to humankind.
18. **illness**: evil that; **wouldst highly**: would have or do greatly.
20–21. **Thou'dst . . . it**: You must have, great Glamis, a voice that cries "Thus you must do" (i.e., kill the king), if you would attain the crown.
22–23. **And . . . undone**: And you would rather have Duncan dead (even though you fear killing him) than wish him alive again after he is gone.
23. **Hie**: hurry.
24. **spirits**: supernatural assistants to evil (see 36ff.).
25. **valor**: power.
26. **round**: crown.

Which fate and metaphysical aid doth seem
To have thee crowned withal.
  Enter MESSENGER.
       What is your tidings?
MESSENGER The King comes here tonight.
LADY MACBETH   Thou'rt mad to say it!
 Is not thy master with him, who, were't so,   30
 Would have informed for preparation?
MESSENGER So please you, it is true. Our thane is coming.
 One of my fellows had the speed of him,
 Who, almost dead for breath, had scarcely more
 Than would make up his message.
LADY MACBETH   Give him tending; 35
 He brings great news.   *Exit* MESSENGER.
      The raven himself is hoarse
 That croaks the fatal entrance of Duncan
 Under my battlements. Come, you spirits
 That tend on mortal thoughts, unsex me here,
 And fill me from the crown to the toe top-full   40
 Of direst cruelty! Make thick my blood,
 Stop up th'access and passage to remorse,
 That no compunctious visitings of nature
 Shake my fell purpose nor keep peace between
 Th'effect and it. Come to my woman's breasts   45
 And take my milk for gall, you murd'ring ministers,
 Wherever in your sightless substances
 You wait on nature's mischief. Come, thick night,
 And pall thee in the dunnest smoke of hell,
 That my keen knife see not the wound it makes,   50

---

27. metaphysical: supernatural.
28. withal: with.
31. informed for preparation: sent us word so that we could prepare for the visit.
33. had . . . him: traveled more quickly than he.
34. more: more breath.
36. raven: a bird of evil portent.
37. fatal: (1) directed by fate; (2) deadly to Duncan.
39. mortal: (1) human; (2) murderous; **here**: At this word actresses have sometimes gestured to breast or groin.
41. Make . . . blood: Thickened blood supposedly blocked the operation of emotions like pity and fear.
43. compunctious visitings: feelings of compassion or guilt.
44. fell purpose: cruel intention; **keep peace**: intervene.
45. Th'effect and it: the consequence (i.e., the King's murder) and my **fell purpose**.
46. take . . . gall: (1) replace my milk with gall, i.e., bile, associated with envy and hatred; (2) take evil from my breasts by nursing at them.
47. sightless substances: invisible presences.
48. wait on: attend, aid.
49. pall: cover (as with a funeral cloth); **dunnest**: darkest.

Nor heaven peep through the blanket of the dark
To cry "Hold, hold!"

    Enter MACBETH.

                     Great Glamis, worthy Cawdor,
Greater than both by the all-hail hereafter!
Thy letters have transported me beyond
This ignorant present, and I feel now   55
The future in the instant.

MACBETH   My dearest love,
Duncan comes here tonight.

LADY MACBETH   And when goes hence?

MACBETH   Tomorrow, as he purposes.

LADY MACBETH   Oh, never
Shall sun that morrow see!
Your face, my thane, is as a book where men   60
May read strange matters. To beguile the time,
Look like the time; bear welcome in your eye,
Your hand, your tongue. Look like th'innocent flower,
But be the serpent under't. He that's coming
Must be provided for. And you shall put   65
This night's great business into my dispatch,
Which shall to all our nights and days to come
Give solely sovereign sway and masterdom.

MACBETH   We will speak further.

LADY MACBETH   Only look up clear.
To alter favor ever is to fear.   70
Leave all the rest to me.

                             Exeunt.

1.6

Hautboys and torches. Enter KING, MALCOLM, DONALDBAIN,
BANQUO, LENNOX, MACDUFF, ROSS, ANGUS, *and Attendants.*

KING   This castle hath a pleasant seat.
The air nimbly and sweetly recommends itself
Unto our gentle senses.

---

53. **all-hail hereafter**: the future in which everyone will salute you as king.
61. **beguile the time**: deceive present observers.
62. **Look . . . time**: Act the way people now expect you to act.
65. **provided for**: prepared for (as guest and as murder victim).
66. **dispatch**: management.
69. **look up clear**: look calm.
70. To change expression (**favor**) is always to show fear.
1.6. Location: before Macbeth's castle.
0.1. SD *Hautboys*: woodwind instruments, ancestors of the softer-toned oboe.
1. **seat**: site.

BANQUO   This guest of summer,
The temple-haunting martlet, does approve
By his loved mansionry that the heavens' breath   5
Smells wooingly here. No jutty, frieze,
Buttress, nor coign of vantage, but this bird
Hath made his pendent bed and procreant cradle.
Where they must breed and haunt, I have observed,
The air is delicate.
             Enter LADY MACBETH.

KING   See, see, our honored hostess!   10
—The love that follows us sometime is our trouble,
Which still we thank as love. Herein I teach you
How you shall bid God 'ield us for your pains,
And thank us for your trouble.

LADY MACBETH   All our service
In every point twice done and then done double   15
Were poor and single business to contend
Against those honors deep and broad wherewith
Your majesty loads our house. For those of old,
And the late dignities heaped up to them,
We rest your hermits.

KING   Where's the Thane of Cawdor?   20
We coursed him at the heels and had a purpose
To be his purveyor; but he rides well,
And his great love, sharp as his spur, hath holp him
To his home before us. Fair and noble hostess,
We are your guest tonight.

---

4. martlet: name used for a number of birds, especially the swallow and house-martin;
approve: confirm.
5. loved mansionry: beloved nest-building.
6. wooingly: enticingly; **jutty**: projection (from a building); **frieze**: painted or carved
band above or at the top of a wall.
7. coign of vantage: a projecting corner, affording a good observation point.
8. pendent: hanging; **procreant**: for breeding.
10. delicate: pleasant.
11–12. The love . . . love: The attentions of others can sometimes be a nuisance, but we
still appreciate the love that motivates them. (The King graciously acknowledges the
trouble of hosting him but hopes that he is still welcome.)
13. bid . . . pains: ask God to reward me (**God 'ield us**) for putting you to trouble
(because my visit is motivated by love).
16. single business: slight exertion ("busy-ness").
16–17. contend Against: match, vie with.
18. those of old: the former honors you bestowed.
19. late: recent.
20. rest your hermits: remain faithful petitioners to God on your behalf (like **hermits**,
i.e., beadsmen who offered prayers for benefactors).
21. coursed: pursued.
22. purveyor: domestic officer who preceded the King or other great personages and
arranged for lodging and supplies.
23. holp: helped.

LADY MACBETH   Your servants ever   25
  Have theirs, themselves, and what is theirs in count
  To make their audit at your highness' pleasure,
  Still to return your own.
KING   Give me your hand;
  Conduct me to mine host. We love him highly
  And shall continue our graces towards him.   30
  By your leave, hostess.

                                      Exeunt.

1.7

Hautboys. Torches. Enter a Sewer, and divers Servants
with dishes and service over the stage.
  Then enter MACBETH.
MACBETH If it were done when 'tis done, then 'twere well
  It were done quickly. If th'assassination
  Could trammel up the consequence and catch
  With his surcease success—that but this blow
  Might be the be-all and the end-all!—here,   5
  But here, upon this bank and shoal of time,
  We'd jump the life to come. But in these cases
  We still have judgment here, that we but teach
  Bloody instructions which, being taught, return
  To plague th'inventor. This even-handed justice   10
  Commends th'ingredients of our poisoned chalice
  To our own lips. He's here in double trust:
  First, as I am his kinsman and his subject,
  Strong both against the deed; then, as his host,
  Who should against his murderer shut the door,   15
  Not bear the knife myself. Besides, this Duncan

---

26. **Have theirs**: have their servants; **what is theirs**: whatever they own; **count**: trust (from the King).
27. **make their audit**: render an account.
28. **Still . . . own**: always to render back to you as truly yours (since whatever they own they only have in trust from you).
1.7. **Location: Inverness. Macbeth's castle.**
0.1. SD *Sewer*: chief waiter.
0.2. SD *service*: a meal and the accompanying equipment.
1–2. **If . . . quickly**: If the whole business of murder could end with the killing itself, then it would be good to kill the King quickly.
3. **trammel . . . consequence**: catch (as in a net) the effects and results.
4. **his surcease**: (1) Duncan's death; (2) the cessation of consequence; **success**: (1) whatever follows; (2) a favorable outcome; (3) succession of heirs; **that but**: if only.
6. **bank and shoal**: riverbank or sandbank and shallows.
7. **jump**: risk.
8. **judgment**: punishment; **that**: in that.
11. **chalice**: drinking goblet, also used for the celebration of the Eucharist.

Hath borne his faculties so meek, hath been
So clear in his great office, that his virtues
Will plead like angels, trumpet-tongued, against
The deep damnation of his taking-off;   20
And Pity, like a naked newborn babe
Striding the blast, or heaven's cherubim horsed
Upon the sightless couriers of the air,
Shall blow the horrid deed in every eye,
That tears shall drown the wind. I have no spur   25
To prick the sides of my intent, but only
Vaulting ambition, which o'erleaps itself
And falls on th'other—
    Enter LADY MACBETH.
                  How now? What news?
LADY MACBETH   He has almost supped. Why have you left the
   chamber?
MACBETH   Hath he asked for me?
LADY MACBETH   Know you not he has?   30
MACBETH   We will proceed no further in this business.
   He hath honored me of late, and I have bought
   Golden opinions from all sorts of people,
   Which would be worn now in their newest gloss,
   Not cast aside so soon.
LADY MACBETH   Was the hope drunk   35
   Wherein you dressed yourself? Hath it slept since?
   And wakes it now to look so green and pale
   At what it did so freely? From this time
   Such I account thy love. Art thou afeard
   To be the same in thine own act and valor   40
   As thou art in desire? Wouldst thou have that
   Which thou esteem'st the ornament of life,
   And live a coward in thine own esteem,
   Letting "I dare not" wait upon "I would,"
   Like the poor cat i'th' adage?

17. **faculties**: powers.
18. **clear**: blameless.
20. **taking-off**: murder.
22. **Striding the blast**: riding the wind; **cherubim**: an order of angels, sometimes represented as babies, sometimes as huge winged creatures (Ezekiel 10, Psalms 18).
23. **sightless couriers**: invisible messengers, i.e., the winds.
25. **That . . . wind**: so that the resulting tears, thick as rain, shall still the wind.
28. **other**: other side (Ambition overleaps and falls down on the other side of the horse);
   How now: How is it now?
32. **bought**: acquired.
34. **gloss**: luster.
37. **green and pale**: sickly, as if hung over.
42. **ornament of life**: chief acquisition and good, i.e., the crown.
44. **wait upon**: attend.

MACBETH   Prithee, peace!   45
  I dare do all that may become a man;
  Who dares do more is none.
LADY MACBETH   What beast was't, then,
  That made you break this enterprise to me?
  When you durst do it, then you were a man;
  And to be more than what you were, you would   50
  Be so much more the man. Nor time nor place
  Did then adhere, and yet you would make both.
  They have made themselves, and that their fitness now
  Does unmake you. I have given suck and know
  How tender 'tis to love the babe that milks me;   55
  I would, while it was smiling in my face,
  Have plucked my nipple from his boneless gums
  And dashed the brains out, had I so sworn as you
  Have done to this.
MACBETH   If we should fail?
LADY MACBETH   We fail?
  But screw your courage to the sticking-place,   60
  And we'll not fail. When Duncan is asleep—
  Whereto the rather shall his day's hard journey
  Soundly invite him—his two chamberlains
  Will I with wine and wassail so convince
  That memory, the warder of the brain,   65
  Shall be a fume, and the receipt of reason
  A limbeck only. When in swinish sleep
  Their drenchèd natures lies as in a death,

---

45. cat . . . adage: The proverb, "The cat would eat fish but she will not wet her feet" (Dent C144, see Resources), exhorted the idle or timorous to action; **Prithee**: I pray thee, please.
48. break: disclose.
49. durst: dared.
50. to be: if you were to be.
52. adhere: suit; **would make both**: resolved to make time and place suit the deed.
53. that their fitness: the very suitability of time and place (for murder).
58. dashed . . . out: Psalms 137:9, anticipating the destruction of Babylon, may have contributed to this horrific image: "Blessed shall he be that taketh and dasheth thy children against the stones."
59. We fail?: Folio's punctuation ("?") can represent a question mark or exclamation point and the actress must here choose among various inflections and emotions (incredulity, resignation, scorn).
60. But: only; **sticking-place**: the notch or place that holds the string taut on a crossbow or a musical instrument.
62. Whereto the rather: to which all the sooner.
63. Soundly invite him: induce him to sleep deeply; **chamberlains**: bedroom servants.
64. wine and wassail: drink in abundance (a **wassail** is a drink and drinking toast); **convince**: conquer.
65. warder: guardian.
66. fume: vapor; **receipt**: receptacle.
67. limbeck: the cap of a distilling apparatus, which receives the vapors. The elaborate chemical metaphor says that the vapors rising from drink will overpower the memory and subdue the reason.

What cannot you and I perform upon
Th'unguarded Duncan? What not put upon   70
His spongy officers, who shall bear the guilt
Of our great quell?
MACBETH   Bring forth men-children only,
For thy undaunted mettle should compose
Nothing but males. Will it not be received,
When we have marked with blood those sleepy two   75
Of his own chamber and used their very daggers,
That they have done't?
LADY MACBETH   Who dares receive it other,
As we shall make our griefs and clamor roar
Upon his death?
MACBETH   I am settled, and bend up
Each corporal agent to this terrible feat.   80
Away, and mock the time with fairest show;
False face must hide what the false heart doth know.

                                          Exeunt.

                              2.1

         Enter BANQUO *and* FLEANCE, *with a torch before him.*
BANQUO   How goes the night, boy?
FLEANCE   The moon is down; I have not heard the clock.
BANQUO   And she goes down at twelve.
FLEANCE   I take't 'tis later, sir.
BANQUO   Hold, take my sword. There's husbandry in heaven;
Their candles are all out. Take thee that, too.   5
A heavy summons lies like lead upon me,
And yet I would not sleep. Merciful powers,
Restrain in me the cursèd thoughts that nature
Gives way to in repose.
         Enter MACBETH *and a Servant with a torch.*
                    Give me my sword!
—Who's there?   10

---

71. **spongy**: absorbent (having soaked up drink).
72. **quell**: murder.
73. **mettle**: spirit, courage. There is also a pun on "metal" and another on **males** (74) and
    "mails," i.e., armor.
77. **other**: otherwise.
80. **corporal agent**: bodily part.
81. **mock**: delude.
2.1. **Location**: Macbeth's castle or courtyard.
4. **husbandry**: good management, thrift.
5. **candles**: i.e., stars; **that**: perhaps a dagger.
6. **heavy summons**: urge to sleep.
7. **powers**: an order of angels that resists demons.

MACBETH   A friend.
BANQUO   What, sir, not yet at rest? The King's abed.
He hath been in unusual pleasure
And sent forth great largesse to your offices.
This diamond he greets your wife withal,   15
By the name of most kind hostess, and shut up
In measureless content.
            [*He gives a diamond.*]
MACBETH   Being unprepared,
Our will became the servant to defect,
Which else should free have wrought.
BANQUO   All's well.
I dreamt last night of the three weïrd sisters.   20
To you they have showed some truth.
MACBETH   I think not of them.
Yet, when we can entreat an hour to serve,
We would spend it in some words upon that business,
If you would grant the time.
BANQUO   At your kind'st leisure.
MACBETH   If you shall cleave to my consent, when 'tis,   25
It shall make honor for you.
BANQUO   So I lose none
In seeking to augment it, but still keep
My bosom franchised and allegiance clear,
I shall be counseled.
MACBETH   Good repose the while.
BANQUO   Thanks, sir; the like to you.   30
                              Exit BANQUO [*with* FLEANCE].
MACBETH   Go bid thy mistress, when my drink is ready,
She strike upon the bell. Get thee to bed.   *Exit* [*Servant*].
Is this a dagger which I see before me,
The handle toward my hand? Come, let me clutch thee.
I have thee not, and yet I see thee still.   35
Art thou not, fatal vision, sensible

14. **largesse . . . offices**: gifts to your household quarters.
15. **greets . . . withal**: salutes . . . with. He honors her with the diamond and with the title (**name**) of **most kind hostess** (16).
16. **shut up**: (1) concluded (his remarks); (2) went to bed (amidst closed curtains).
18. **will**: good will (to entertain the King); **defect**: deficient means, caused by late notice of the visit.
19. **free**: freely.
22. **entreat . . . serve**: find a suitable time.
25. **cleave . . . consent**: agree with my opinion, i.e., go along with me; **'tis**: (1) it is my leisure; (2) it is achieved (and I am king).
26. **honor**: external honor, i.e., wealth and station. Banquo, however, understands the term to mean internal honor, or virtue.
28. **franchised**: free (from guilt); **clear**: stainless.
36. **sensible**: perceptible.

To feeling as to sight? Or art thou but
A dagger of the mind, a false creation,
Proceeding from the heat-oppressèd brain?
I see thee yet in form as palpable   40
As this which now I draw.
     [*He draws a dagger.*]
Thou marshall'st me the way that I was going,
And such an instrument I was to use.
Mine eyes are made the fools o'th' other senses,
Or else worth all the rest. I see thee still,   45
And on thy blade and dudgeon gouts of blood.
Which was not so before. There's no such thing.
It is the bloody business which informs
Thus to mine eyes. Now o'er the one half world
Nature seems dead, and wicked dreams abuse   50
The curtained sleep. Witchcraft celebrates
Pale Hecate's off'rings, and withered Murder,
Alarumed by his sentinel the wolf,
Whose howl's his watch, thus with his stealthy pace,
With Tarquin's ravishing strides, towards his design   55
Moves like a ghost. Thou sure and firm-set earth,
Hear not my steps, which way they walk, for fear
Thy very stones prate of my whereabout
And take the present horror from the time,
Which now suits with it. Whiles I threat, he lives;   60
Words to the heat of deeds too cold breath gives.
                        A bell rings.
I go, and it is done. The bell invites me.
Hear it not, Duncan, for it is a knell
That summons thee to heaven or to hell.   *Exit.*

42. **marshall'st**: guide.
44–45. **Mine . . . rest**: My eyes are reporting a delusion, unverifiable by the other senses, or else my eyes alone perceive truly.
46. **dudgeon**: handle; **gouts**: drops.
48–49. **informs Thus**: shapes this fantasy.
50. **abuse**: deceive.
52. **Pale Hecate's off'rings**: deeds done by or sacrifices to Hecate, traditionally goddess of sorcery and the moon (thus **pale**), leader of the witches on stage in 3.5 and 4.1.
53. **Alarumed**: signaled.
54. **his watch**: Murder's signal (like the watchman's cry).
55. **Tarquin**: a Roman tyrant who raped Lucrece. Shakespeare dramatized the incident in a narrative poem, *The Rape of Lucrece*.
59–60. **take . . . it**: break the silence appropriate to the horror of the moment.
61. Words are weak and cold substitutes for the heat of real deeds.
63. **knell**: sound of a struck bell.

2.2

Enter LADY MACBETH.

LADY MACBETH   That which hath made them drunk hath made
   me bold;
What hath quenched them hath given me fire.
   [*An owl shrieks.*]
                                                    Hark! Peace!
It was the owl that shrieked, the fatal bellman
Which gives the stern'st good-night. He is about it.
The doors are open, and the surfeited grooms   5
Do mock their charge with snores. I have drugged their possets
That death and nature do contend about them
Whether they live or die.
   Enter MACBETH [*with bloody daggers*].

MACBETH   Who's there? What ho!

LADY MACBETH [*to herself*]   Alack, I am afraid they have awaked,
And 'tis not done. Th'attempt and not the deed   10
Confounds us. Hark! I laid their daggers ready;
He could not miss 'em. Had he not resembled
My father as he slept, I had done't.—My husband?

MACBETH   I have done the deed. Didst thou not hear a noise?

LADY MACBETH   I heard the owl scream and the crickets cry.   15
Did not you speak?

MACBETH   When?

LADY MACBETH   Now.

MACBETH   As I descended?

LADY MACBETH   Ay.   20

MACBETH   Hark, who lies i'th' second chamber?

LADY MACBETH   Donaldbain.

MACBETH   This is a sorry sight.

LADY MACBETH   A foolish thought to say a sorry sight.

MACBETH   There's one did laugh in's sleep, and one cried
   "Murder!"   25
That they did wake each other. I stood and heard them.

2.2. Location: Macbeth's castle.
2. quenched: (1) satisfied their thirst; (2) rendered them unconscious.
2. SD *owl*: a bird of ill omen.
3. bellman: night watchman.
4. Which . . . good-night: i.e., who tolls the bell to announce death.
5. grooms: servants.
6. charge: responsibility (to guard the King); **possets**: drinks made of hot milk, liquor, and spices.
8. SD: Editors usually have Macbeth speak the next line while off-stage, or less frequently from above in the gallery, and move this entrance to 13. But his entrance here, as indicated by the Folio, has them miss each other (visually and auditorily) in the dark while on stage, together but each alone.
11. Confounds: ruins.

But they did say their prayers and addressed them
Again to sleep.
LADY MACBETH   There are two lodged together.
MACBETH   One cried "God bless us!" and "Amen" the other,
As they had seen me with these hangman's hands.   30
List'ning their fear, I could not say "Amen"
When they did say "God bless us!"
LADY MACBETH   Consider it not so deeply.
MACBETH   But wherefore could not I pronounce "Amen"?
I had most need of blessing, and "Amen"   35
Stuck in my throat.
LADY MACBETH   These deeds must not be thought
After these ways; so, it will make us mad.
MACBETH   Methought I heard a voice cry "Sleep no more!
Macbeth does murder sleep"—the innocent sleep,
Sleep that knits up the raveled sleeve of care,   40
The death of each day's life, sore labor's bath,
Balm of hurt minds, great nature's second course,
Chief nourisher in life's feast—
LADY MACBETH   What do you mean?
MACBETH   Still it cried "Sleep no more!" to all the house;
"Glamis hath murdered sleep, and therefore Cawdor   45
Shall sleep no more! Macbeth shall sleep no more!"
LADY MACBETH   Who was it that thus cried? Why, worthy thane,
You do unbend your noble strength to think
So brainsickly of things. Go get some water
And wash this filthy witness from your hand.   50
Why did you bring these daggers from the place?
They must lie there. Go, carry them and smear
The sleepy grooms with blood.
MACBETH   I'll go no more.
I am afraid to think what I have done.
Look on't again I dare not.
LADY MACBETH   Infirm of purpose!   55
Give me the daggers. The sleeping and the dead

---

27. **addressed them**: prepared themselves.
30. **hangman's hands**: executioner's hands, hence bloody from cutting up bodies.
34. **wherefore**: why.
37. **so**: thinking so.
40. **raveled sleeve**: frayed sleeve (the part of a garment that covers the arm and wrist).
    Some prefer "raveled sleave," i.e., a tangled filament or thread, indistinguishable in
    sound but less likely in sense, given the idea of repair by knitting.
42. **second course**: the main course.
48. **unbend**: slacken (as one does a bow).
50. **witness**: evidence, i.e., the blood.

Are but as pictures; 'tis the eye of childhood
That fears a painted devil. If he do bleed,
I'll gild the faces of the grooms withal,
For it must seem their guilt.   *Exit [with the daggers].*
    Knock within.

MACBETH   Whence is that knocking?   60
How is't with me, when every noise appalls me?
What hands are here? Ha, they pluck out mine eyes!
Will all great Neptune's ocean wash this blood
Clean from my hand? No, this my hand will rather
The multitudinous seas incarnadine,   65
Making the green one red.
    Enter LADY MACBETH.

LADY MACBETH   My hands are of your color, but I shame
To wear a heart so white. (*Knock.*) I hear a knocking
At the south entry. Retire we to our chamber.
A little water clears us of this deed.   70
How easy is it then. Your constancy
Hath left you unattended. (*Knock.*) Hark, more knocking.
Get on your nightgown lest occasion call us
And show us to be watchers. Be not lost
So poorly in your thoughts.   75

MACBETH   To know my deed 'twere best not know myself.
    (*Knock.*) Wake Duncan with thy knocking. I would thou couldst!
                         Exeunt.

2.3

Enter a PORTER. *Knocking within.*

PORTER   Here's a knocking indeed! If a man were porter of
hell gate, he should have old turning the key. (*Knock.*)

---

58. **he**: the King. Corpses of victims were thought to bleed in the presence of their
    murderers.
59. **gild**: cover with gold, a synonym for red (see 2.3.106). **Gild** here sets up the pun on
    guilt (60).
60. SD *within*: behind the stage façade (representing the outside of the castle).
60. **Whence**: from where.
63. **Neptune**: Roman god of the ocean.
65. **multitudinous**: many and vast; **incarnadine**: turn red.
66. **green one red**: green color of the oceans a pervasive red.
68. **white**: cowardly.
72. **left you unattended**: deserted you.
74. **watchers**: awake.
75. **poorly**: dejectedly.
76. If I fully admit to this crime, I would be better off if I were someone else. I no longer
    know who I am.
2.3. **Location: the courtyard of Macbeth's castle.**
2. **hell gate**: the door to hell, imagined as a castle; **old**: frequent.

Knock, knock, knock. Who's there, i'th' name of Beelzebub? Here's a farmer that hanged himself on th'expectation of plenty. Come in time! Have napkins enough about you; here you'll sweat for't. (*Knock.*) Knock, knock. Who's there, in th'other devil's name? Faith, here's an equivocator that could swear in both the scales against either scale, who committed treason enough for God's sake, yet could not equivocate to heaven. Oh, come in, equivocator. (*Knock.*) Knock, knock, knock. Who's there? Faith, here's an English tailor come hither for stealing out of a French hose. Come in, tailor. Here you may roast your goose. (*Knock.*) Knock, knock. Never at quiet? What are you? But this place is too cold for hell. I'll devil-porter it no further. I had thought to have let in some of all professions that go the primrose way to th'everlasting bonfire. (*Knock.*) Anon, anon. [*He opens the gate.*]—I pray you, remember the porter. 5

10

15

    Enter MACDUFF *and* LENNOX.

MACDUFF   Was it so late, friend, ere you went to bed,
That you do lie so late? 20

PORTER   Faith, sir, we were carousing till the second cock, and drink, sir, is a great provoker of three things.

MACDUFF   What three things does drink especially provoke?

PORTER   Marry, sir, nose-painting, sleep, and urine. Lechery, sir, it provokes and unprovokes: it provokes the desire but it takes away the performance. Therefore, much drink may be said to be an equivocator with lechery: it makes him and it mars him; it sets him on and it takes him off; it persuades him and disheartens him, makes him stand to and not stand to; in 25

---

3. Beelzebub: the devil.

4–5. farmer . . . plenty: The porter introduces imaginary residents of hell, beginning with the farmer who, expecting plenty but disappointed, hanged himself.

5. Come in time: You have come in good time; **napkins**: handkerchiefs (to wipe away sweat).

7. Faith: in faith (a mild oath); **equivocator**: one who uses deceitful language. Shakespeare alludes to the doctrine of equivocation, associated with Jesuits including Henry Garnet, recently executed (1606) for alleged complicity in the Gunpowder Plot (1605), a plan to blow up Parliament. In his *Treatise on Equivocation* Garnet justifies various types of verbal deceit, including, for example, the telling of a partial truth (see below, 218–19).

8. both . . . scale: argue either side (perhaps with an allusion to the scales of Justice).

11–12. English . . . hose: The tailor has skimped on the fabric when making stylish French leggings or breeches.

13. roast . . . goose: (1) heat your tailor's smoothing iron; (2) have sex with a prostitute; (3) suffer from venereal disease.

16. primrose . . . bonfire: the pleasant path to hell.

17–18. remember: i.e., tip.

21. second cock: 3:00 A.M., when the cock crowed for the second time.

24. Marry: a mild oath ("By the Virgin Mary," originally); **nose-painting**: nose-reddening from excessive drink.

29. stand to: become erect.

conclusion, equivocates him in a sleep and, giving him the lie,   30
  leaves him.
MACDUFF   I believe drink gave thee the lie last night.
PORTER   That it did, sir, i'the very throat on me. But I requited
  him for his lie and, I think, being too strong for him, though
  he took up my legs sometime, yet I made a shift to cast him.   35
MACDUFF   Is thy master stirring?
          Enter MACBETH.
  Our knocking has awaked him. Here he comes.

                                              [PORTER *may exit.*]

LENNOX   Good morrow, noble sir.
MACBETH   Good morrow, both.
MACDUFF   Is the King stirring, worthy thane?
MACBETH   Not yet.
MACDUFF   He did command me to call timely on him.   40
  I have almost slipped the hour.
MACBETH   I'll bring you to him.
MACDUFF   I know this is a joyful trouble to you,
  But yet 'tis one.
MACBETH   The labor we delight in physics pain.
  This is the door.
MACDUFF   I'll make so bold to call,   45
  For 'tis my limited service.   *Exit* MACDUFF.
LENNOX   Goes the King hence today?
MACBETH   He does; he did appoint so.
LENNOX   The night has been unruly. Where we lay,
  Our chimneys were blown down and, as they say,   50
  Lamentings heard i'th' air, strange screams of death,
  And prophesying with accents terrible
  Of dire combustion and confused events,
  New hatched to th'woeful time. The obscure bird
  Clamored the livelong night. Some say the earth   55
  Was feverous and did shake.
MACBETH   'Twas a rough night.

---

30. **equivocates . . . sleep**: tricks him into falling asleep; **giving . . . lie**: (1) deceiving him; (2) making him lie down.
32. **gave . . . lie**: (1) called you a liar; (2) made you sleep.
33. **i' . . . throat**: deeply, egregiously. (Drink accused the porter of serious, deliberate lying.)
35. **took . . . legs**: lifted me (as a wrestler would); **made a shift**: managed; **cast**: (1) toss him as in wrestling; (2) vomit.
40. **timely**: early.
41. **slipped**: let slip.
44. **physics**: relieves.
46. **limited**: appointed.
52. **accents**: utterances.
53. **combustion**: (1) fire; (2) tumult.
54. **obscure bird**: bird of darkness, the owl.
55. **livelong**: long-lived.

LENNOX   My young remembrance cannot parallel
  A fellow to it.
     Enter MACDUFF.
MACDUFF   Oh, horror, horror, horror!
  Tongue nor heart cannot conceive nor name thee!   60
MACBETH *and* LENNOX   What's the matter?
MACDUFF   Confusion now hath made his masterpiece!
  Most sacrilegious murder hath broke ope
  The Lord's anointed temple and stole thence
  The life o'th' building!
MACBETH   What is't you say? The life?   65
LENNOX   Mean you his majesty?
MACDUFF   Approach the chamber and destroy your sight
  With a new Gorgon. Do not bid me speak.
  See, and then speak yourselves.
                  Exeunt MACBETH *and* LENNOX.
                  —Awake, awake!
Ring the alarum bell! Murder and treason!   70
Banquo and Donaldbain, Malcolm, awake!
Shake off this downy sleep, death's counterfeit,
And look on death itself! Up, up, and see
The great doom's image! Malcolm, Banquo,
As from your graves rise up and walk like sprites   75
To countenance this horror!—Ring the bell!
     Bell rings. Enter LADY MACBETH.
LADY MACBETH   What's the business
  That such a hideous trumpet calls to parley
  The sleepers of the house? Speak, speak!
MACDUFF   O gentle lady,   80
  'Tis not for you to hear what I can speak.
  The repetition in a woman's ear
  Would murder as it fell.
     Enter BANQUO.
  —O Banquo, Banquo! Our royal master's murdered!
LADY MACBETH   Woe, alas! What, in our house?   85
BANQUO   Too cruel anywhere.

57–58. parallel A fellow: recall a similar one.
60. The subjects and verbs are out of order (the **tongue** names, the **heart** conceives) to
  suggest the disorder and emotion.
62. Confusion: destruction.
68. Gorgon: a mythical monster whose face turned beholders to stone.
72. counterfeit: likeness.
74. great doom's image: a sight of doomsday, the Last Judgment.
75. On doomsday the spirits (**sprites**) of the dead will rise to be judged; see John 5.28:
  "The hour is coming, in the which all that are in the graves shall hear his voice."
76. countenance: (1) face; (2) act in accordance with.
78. parley: conference, generally between enemies.

Dear Duff, I prithee, contradict thyself,
And say it is not so.
   Enter MACBETH, LENNOX, *and* ROSS.
MACBETH Had I but died an hour before this chance,
 I had lived a blessèd time, for from this instant   90
 There's nothing serious in mortality.
 All is but toys. Renown and grace is dead.
 The wine of life is drawn, and the mere lees
 Is left this vault to brag of.
   Enter MALCOLM *and* DONALDBAIN.
DONALDBAIN What is amiss?
MACBETH   You are and do not know't. 95
 The spring, the head, the fountain of your blood
 Is stopped, the very source of it is stopped.
MACDUFF Your royal father's murdered.
MALCOLM   Oh! By whom?
LENNOX Those of his chamber, as it seemed, had done't.
 Their hands and faces were all badged with blood; 100
 So were their daggers, which unwiped we found
 Upon their pillows. They stared and were distracted;
 No man's life was to be trusted with them.
MACBETH Oh, yet I do repent me of my fury
 That I did kill them.
MACDUFF   Wherefore did you so? 105
MACBETH Who can be wise, amazed, temp'rate and furious,
 Loyal and neutral in a moment? No man.
 Th'expedition of my violent love
 Outran the pauser, reason. Here lay Duncan,
 His silver skin laced with his golden blood, 110
 And his gashed stabs looked like a breach in nature
 For ruin's wasteful entrance; there the murderers,
 Steeped in the colors of their trade, their daggers
 Unmannerly breeched with gore. Who could refrain
 That had a heart to love, and in that heart 115
 Courage to make's love known?
LADY MACBETH [*faints*]   Help me hence, ho!

89. **chance**: occurrence.
91. **mortality**: human life.
93. **lees**: dregs.
94. **vault**: (1) wine cellar; (2) earth, with its vault, the sky.
100. **badged**: marked as if with a badge or emblem.
106. **amazed**: shocked out of one's wits.
108. **expedition**: speedy expression.
109. **pauser**: controller.
110. **golden**: red.
111. **breach**: gap (in fortifications).
114. **Unmannerly . . . gore**: indecently clothed in blood on his thighs (as if wearing red breeches).

MACDUFF Look to the lady!

MALCOLM [*aside to* DONALDBAIN] Why do we hold our tongues,
That most may claim this argument for ours?

DONALDBAIN [*aside to* MALCOLM] What should be spoken here,
  where our fate,
Hid in an auger-hole, may rush and seize us?   120
Let's away. Our tears are not yet brewed.

MALCOLM [*aside to* DONALDBAIN] Nor our strong sorrow upon the
  foot of motion.

BANQUO Look to the lady.

                    [LADY MACBETH *may exit, attended.*]
And when we have our naked frailties hid,
That suffer in exposure, let us meet   125
And question this most bloody piece of work
To know it further. Fears and scruples shake us.
In the great hand of God I stand, and thence
Against the undivulged pretense I fight
Of treasonous malice.

MACDUFF   And so do I.

ALL   So, all!   130

MACBETH Let's briefly put on manly readiness,
And meet i'th' hall together.

ALL   Well contented.
              Exeunt [*all but* MALCOLM *and* DONALDBAIN].

MALCOLM What will you do? Let's not consort with them.
To show an unfelt sorrow is an office
Which the false man does easy. I'll to England.   135

DONALDBAIN To Ireland, I. Our separated fortune
Shall keep us both the safer. Where we are,
There's daggers in men's smiles. The nearer in blood,
The nearer bloody.

MALCOLM   This murderous shaft that's
  shot
Hath not yet lighted, and our safest way   140
Is to avoid the aim. Therefore, to horse,

---

120. **auger-hole**: a hole made by an auger, or carpenter's pointer; here, a place of ambush.
122. **upon . . . motion**: ready to act.
124. **naked frailties**: (1) unclothed bodies; (2) vulnerabilities.
126. **question**: examine.
128. **thence**: from there.
129. **undivulged pretense**: unrevealed purpose (of the traitor).
131. **briefly**: quickly.
134. **office**: function.
138–39. **The nearer . . . bloody**: The nearer one is to Duncan in blood, the closer he is to
    being killed.
140. **lighted**: landed.

And let us not be dainty of leave-taking,
But shift away. There's warrant in that theft
Which steals itself when there's no mercy left.

Exeunt.

2.4

Enter ROSS *with an* OLD MAN.

OLD MAN   Threescore and ten I can remember well,
Within the volume of which time I have seen
Hours dreadful and things strange, but this sore night
Hath trifled former knowings.
ROSS   Ha, good father,
Thou seest the heavens, as troubled with man's act,   5
Threatens his bloody stage. By th'clock 'tis day,
And yet dark night strangles the traveling lamp.
Is't night's predominance or the day's shame
That darkness does the face of earth entomb
When living light should kiss it?
OLD MAN   'Tis unnatural,   10
Even like the deed that's done. On Tuesday last
A falcon, tow'ring in her pride of place,
Was by a mousing owl hawked at and killed.
ROSS   And Duncan's horses—a thing most strange and certain—
Beauteous and swift, the minions of their race,   15
Turned wild in nature, broke their stalls, flung out,
Contending 'gainst obedience, as they would
Make war with mankind.
OLD MAN   'Tis said they ate each other.
ROSS   They did so, to th'amazement of mine eyes
That looked upon't.
        Enter MACDUFF.

142. **dainty of**: particular about.
143. **shift**: leave stealthily; **warrant**: justification.
144. **steals**: steals away.
2.4. **Location: outside Macbeth's castle.**
1. **Threescore and ten**: 70, the biblical allotment of human life; see Psalms 90:10: "The days of our years are threescore years and ten."
3. **sore**: severe, violent.
4. **Hath . . . knowings**: has made other experiences seem trivial; **father**: old man.
6. **stage**: the earth. The metaphor continues the theatrical imagery of **heavens**, the decorated roof over the stage, and **act** (5).
7. **traveling lamp**: the sun.
8. **predominance**: superiority.
12. **tow'ring**: soaring; **pride of place**: pre-eminent position.
13. **mousing owl**: an owl that preys on mice; **hawked at**: attacked in flight.
15. **minions**: darlings.
16. **flung out**: kicked and bucked violently.

                    Here comes the good Macduff.   20
        How goes the world, sir, now?
MACDUFF   Why, see you not?
ROSS   Is't known who did this more than bloody deed?
MACDUFF   Those that Macbeth hath slain.
ROSS   Alas, the day!
        What good could they pretend?
MACDUFF   They were suborned.
        Malcolm and Donaldbain, the King's two sons,   25
        Are stol'n away and fled, which puts upon them
        Suspicion of the deed.
ROSS   'Gainst nature still!
        Thriftless ambition that will ravin up
        Thine own life's means! Then 'tis most like
        The sovereignty will fall upon Macbeth.   30
MACDUFF   He is already named and gone to Scone
        To be invested.
ROSS   Where is Duncan's body?
MACDUFF   Carried to Colmekill,
        The sacred storehouse of his predecessors
        And guardian of their bones.
ROSS   Will you to Scone?   35
MACDUFF   No, cousin, I'll to Fife.
ROSS   Well, I will thither.
MACDUFF   Well may you see things well done there. Adieu,
        Lest our old robes sit easier than our new.
ROSS   Farewell, father.
OLD MAN   God's benison go with you and with those   40
        That would make good of bad and friends of foes.
                                        Exeunt all.

                            3.1

        Enter BANQUO.
BANQUO   Thou hast it now—King, Cawdor, Glamis, all
        As the weïrd women promised, and I fear

---

24. **pretend**: put forward as a pretext; **suborned**: bribed.
28. **Thriftless**: wasteful; **ravin up**: devour hungrily.
31. **Scone**: ancient royal city of Scotland.
32. **invested**: formally crowned and robed as king.
33. **Colmekill**: small island (now Iona) off the West of Scotland, home of St. Columba (see 1.2.63).
34. **storehouse**: burial place.
36. **Fife**: land ruled by Macduff.
40. **benison**: blessing.
3.1. **Location**: Forres. The palace.

Thou play'dst most foully for't. Yet it was said
It should not stand in thy posterity
But that myself should be the root and father   5
Of many kings. If there come truth from them—
As upon thee, Macbeth, their speeches shine—
Why by the verities on thee made good
May they not be my oracles as well
And set me up in hope? But hush, no more.   10

  Sennet sounded. Enter MACBETH *as King,* LADY [MACBETH
  as Queen,] LENNOX, ROSS, LORDS *and Attendants.*

MACBETH Here's our chief guest.
LADY MACBETH   If he had been forgotten,
It had been as a gap in our great feast,
And all-thing unbecoming.
MACBETH Tonight we hold a solemn supper, sir,
And I'll request your presence.
BANQUO   Let your highness   15
Command upon me, to the which my duties
Are with a most indissoluble tie
Forever knit.
MACBETH Ride you this afternoon?
BANQUO Ay, my good lord.
MACBETH We should have else desired your good advice,   20
Which still hath been both grave and prosperous,
In this day's council; but we'll take tomorrow.
Is't far you ride?
BANQUO As far, my lord, as will fill up the time
Twixt this and supper. Go not my horse the better,   25
I must become a borrower of the night
For a dark hour or twain.
MACBETH   Fail not our feast.
BANQUO My lord, I will not.
MACBETH We hear our bloody cousins are bestowed
In England and in Ireland, not confessing   30
Their cruel parricide, filling their hearers

---

4. **stand**: remain.
7. **shine**: shed light (of good fortune).
10. **SD *Sennet***: a distinctive set of notes on a trumpet or cornet signaling a ceremonious
 entrance.
13. **all-thing**: completely.
14. **solemn**: formal.
16. **the which**: which commandments.
21. **still**: always.
22. **take**: take it (Banquo's advice).
25. **Go . . . better**: unless my horse goes faster than I expect.
27. **twain**: two.
29. **bestowed**: lodged.
31. **parricide**: father-killing.

With strange invention. But of that tomorrow,
When therewithal we shall have cause of state
Craving us jointly. Hie you to horse. Adieu,
Till you return at night. Goes Fleance with you?   35
BANQUO   Ay, my good lord. Our time does call upon's.
MACBETH   I wish your horses swift and sure of foot,
And so I do commend you to their backs.
Farewell.   *Exit* BANQUO.
—Let every man be master of his time   40
Till seven at night. To make society
The sweeter welcome, we will keep ourself
Till supper-time alone. While then, God be with you.
          Exeunt Lords [and all but MACBETH *and a* SERVANT].
—Sirrah, a word with you: attend those men
Our pleasure?   45
SERVANT   They are, my lord, without the palace gate.
MACBETH   Bring them before us.   *Exit* SERVANT.
To be thus is nothing, but to be safely thus.
Our fears in Banquo stick deep,
And in his royalty of nature reigns   50
That which would be feared. 'Tis much he dares;
And to that dauntless temper of his mind
He hath a wisdom that doth guide his valor
To act in safety. There is none but he
Whose being I do fear, and under him   55
My genius is rebuked, as it is said
Mark Antony's was by Caesar. He chid the sisters
When first they put the name of king upon me,
And bade them speak to him; then, prophet-like,
They hailed him father to a line of kings.   60
Upon my head they placed a fruitless crown
And put a barren scepter in my grip,
Thence to be wrenched with an unlineal hand.

---

32. invention: falsehood (i.e., that Macbeth killed the King).
33. therewithal: besides that.
33–34. cause . . . jointly: state business requiring our joint attention.
38. commend: entrust.
41. society: company of friends.
43. While: till.
44. Sirrah: a form of address to a social inferior.
48. but: unless.
49. stick deep: pierce deeply.
50. royalty of nature: natural royalty.
52. to: in addition to; **dauntless temper**: fearless temperament.
56. genius: attendant spirit; **rebuked**: abashed.
57. Caesar: Octavius Caesar (Augustus), who eventually defeated Mark Antony in a battle Shakespeare dramatized in *Antony and Cleopatra*.
63. unlineal hand: a descendant from another family line.

No son of mine succeeding. If't be so,
For Banquo's issue have I filed my mind,   65
For them the gracious Duncan have I murdered,
Put rancors in the vessel of my peace
Only for them, and mine eternal jewel
Given to the common enemy of man
To make them kings, the seeds of Banquo kings!   70
Rather than so, come fate into the list,
And champion me to th'utterance!—Who's there!
    Enter SERVANT *and two* MURDERERS.
[*to* SERVANT] Now go to the door, and stay there till we call.
                            Exit SERVANT.
—Was it not yesterday we spoke together?
MURDERERS   It was, so please your highness.
MACBETH   Well, then; now,   75
Have you considered of my speeches? Know
That it was he in the times past which held you
So under fortune, which you thought had been
Our innocent self. This I made good to you
In our last conference, passed in probation with you   80
How you were borne in hand, how crossed, the instruments,
Who wrought with them, and all things else that might
To half a soul and to a notion crazed
Say "Thus did Banquo."
FIRST MURDERER   You made it known to us.
MACBETH   I did so, and went further, which is now   85
Our point of second meeting. Do you find
Your patience so predominant in your nature
That you can let this go? Are you so gospeled
To pray for this good man and for his issue,
Whose heavy hand hath bowed you to the grave   90
And beggared yours for ever?

---

65. **filed**: defiled.
66. **gracious**: virtuous, filled with divine grace.
67. **rancors**: bitter feelings (imagined as poison added to a **vessel**, or cup).
68. **eternal jewel**: immortal soul.
69. **common enemy**: the devil.
71. **list**: combat area, originally, jousting lanes.
72. **champion me**: (1) fight with me; (2) support me; **to th'utterance**: to the end, to death (French *à l'outrance*).
78. **under**: out of favor with.
80. **passed . . . with**: proved to.
81. **borne in hand**: manipulated; **crossed**: thwarted; **instruments**: means.
82. **wrought**: worked.
83. **To . . . crazed**: to a half-wit and unsound mind.
88. **gospeled**: influenced by gospel teachings, especially Matthew 5:44: "But I say unto you, love your enemies, bless them that curse you, do good to them that hate you, and pray for them which despitefully use you, and persecute you."
91. **beggared yours**: made your family poor.

FIRST MURDERER   We are men, my liege.
MACBETH   Ay, in the catalogue ye go for men,
     As hounds and greyhounds, mongrels, spaniels, curs,
     Shoughs, water-rugs, and demi-wolves are clept
     All by the name of dogs. The valued file   95
     Distinguishes the swift, the slow, the subtle,
     The housekeeper, the hunter—every one
     According to the gift which bounteous nature
     Hath in him closed, whereby he does receive
     Particular addition from the bill   100
     That writes them all alike; and so of men.
     Now, if you have a station in the file.
     Not i'th' worst rank of manhood, say't,
     And I will put that business in your bosoms
     Whose execution takes your enemy off,   105
     Grapples you to the heart and love of us,
     Who wear our health but sickly in his life,
     Which in his death were perfect.
SECOND MURDERER   I am one, my liege,
     Whom the vile blows and buffets of the world
     Have so incensed that I am reckless what   110
     I do to spite the world.
FIRST MURDERER   And I another,
     So weary with disasters, tugged with fortune,
     That I would set my life on any chance
     To mend it or be rid on't.
MACBETH   Both of you
     Know Banquo was your enemy.
MURDERERS   True, my lord.   115
MACBETH   So is he mine, and in such bloody distance
     That every minute of his being thrusts

---

92. **catalogue**: list (of human types).
93. **curs**: watch dogs or sheep dogs, sometimes used as a term of contempt.
94. **Shoughs**: lapdogs; **water-rugs**: shaggy water-dogs; **demi-wolves**: dogs that are half
      wolf; **clept**: named.
95. **valued file**: list that records the qualities of each breed.
97. **housekeeper**: watchdog.
99. **closed**: enclosed.
100. **Particular addition**: distinguishing characteristics.
100–101. **the bill . . . alike**: the general qualities common to all dogs.
102. **station . . . file**: place in the list (of humans).
105. **takes . . . off**: removes, kills.
106. **Grapples**: seizes and attaches firmly. Grappling irons held ships to each other dur-
      ing nautical battles.
107. **in his life**: while he (Banquo) lives.
113. **set**: risk.
114. **on't**: of it.
116. **distance**: (1) enmity; (2) striking range.

Against my near'st of life. And though I could
With barefaced power sweep him from my sight
And bid my will avouch it, yet I must not   120
For certain friends that are both his and mine,
Whose loves I may not drop, but wail his fall
Who I myself struck down. And thence it is
That I to your assistance do make love,
Masking the business from the common eye   125
For sundry weighty reasons.
SECOND MURDERER   We shall, my lord,
    Perform what you command us.
FIRST MURDERER   Though our lives—
MACBETH   Your spirits shine through you. Within this hour,
        at most,
    I will advise you where to plant yourselves,
    Acquaint you with the perfect spy o'th' time,   130
    The moment on't, for't must be done tonight,
    And something from the palace, always thought
    That I require a clearness. And with him—
    To leave no rubs nor botches in the work—
    Fleance, his son that keeps him company,   135
    Whose absence is no less material to me
    Than is his father's, must embrace the fate
    Of that dark hour. Resolve yourselves apart.
    I'll come to you anon.
MURDERERS   We are resolved, my lord.
MACBETH   I'll call upon you straight; abide within.   140
                                    Exeunt [MURDERERS].
    It is concluded. Banquo, thy soul's flight,
    If it find heaven, must find it out tonight.   [*Exit.*]

---

118. **near'st of life**: vital organs.
119. **barefaced**: open, without excuses.
120. **And . . . it**: And use my royal will as justification enough for Banquo's murder.
122. **wail**: I must lament.
124. That I request your help.
130. **perfect spy o'th'time**: (1) best time and place for spying; (2) the best spy for the job,
    i.e., the Third Murderer of 3.3.
131. **on't**: for the murder.
132. **something**: some distance; **thought**: borne in mind.
133. **clearness**: freedom from suspicion.
134. **rubs nor botches**: rough spots nor flaws.
136. **material**: important.
138. **Resolve . . . apart**: (1) determine your course of action in private; (2) gather your
    courage in private.

3.2

Enter LADY MACBETH *and a* SERVANT.

LADY MACBETH   Is Banquo gone from court?

SERVANT   Ay, madam, but returns again tonight.

LADY MACBETH   Say to the King I would attend his leisure
For a few words.

SERVANT   Madam, I will.   *Exit.*

LADY MACBETH   Naught's had, all's spent,
Where our desire is got without content.   5
'Tis safer to be that which we destroy
Than by destruction dwell in doubtful joy.
        Enter MACBETH.
How now, my lord? Why do you keep alone,
Of sorriest fancies your companions making,
Using those thoughts which should indeed have died   10
With them they think on? Things without all remedy
Should be without regard. What's done is done.

MACBETH   We have scorched the snake, not killed it.
She'll close and be herself, whilst our poor malice
Remains in danger of her former tooth.   15
But let the frame of things disjoint, both the worlds suffer,
Ere we will eat our meal in fear and sleep
In the affliction of these terrible dreams
That shake us nightly. Better be with the dead,
Whom we, to gain our peace, have sent to peace,   20
Than on the torture of the mind to lie
In restless ecstasy. Duncan is in his grave.
After life's fitful fever he sleeps well.
Treason has done his worst; nor steel, nor poison,
Malice domestic, foreign levy, nothing   25
Can touch him further.

LADY MACBETH   Come on, gentle my lord,
Sleek o'er your rugged looks. Be bright and jovial
Among your guests tonight.

3.2. **Location**: the palace.
4. **Naught**: nothing.
7. **doubtful**: (1) uncertain; (2) worried.
9. **sorriest fancies**: most wretched imaginings.
11. **them . . . on**: the subject of your thoughts, i.e., the murdered King; **all**: any.
13. **scorched**: slashed.
14. **close**: heal; **poor**: weak.
15. **her former tooth**: her fang, just as before.
16. **frame . . . disjoint**: structure of the universe collapse; **both the worlds**: heaven and earth.
22. **ecstasy**: frenzy.
25. **domestic**: civil; **levy**: troops.
26–27. **gentle . . . looks** My noble lord, smooth over your rough look of concern.

[handwritten: look/talk in a certain way] 41

MACBETH   So shall I, love,
And so, I pray, be you. Let your remembrance
Apply to Banquo; present him eminence   30
Both with eye and tongue—unsafe the while that we
Must lave our honors in these flattering streams
And make our faces vizards to our hearts,
Disguising what they are.   *[handwritten: → poisin]*
LADY MACBETH   You must leave this.
MACBETH   Oh, full of scorpions is my mind, dear wife!   35
Thou know'st that Banquo and his Fleance lives.
LADY MACBETH   But in them nature's copy's not eterne. *[handwritten: → Not going to live forever]*
MACBETH   There's comfort yet; they are assailable.
Then be thou jocund. Ere the bat hath flown
His cloistered flight, ere to black Hecate's summons   40
The shard-born beetle with his drowsy hums   *[handwritten: don't]*
Hath rung night's yawning peal, there shall be done *[handwritten: boss/wife tell me to put a happy face on]*
A deed of dreadful note.
LADY MACBETH   What's to be done?
MACBETH   Be innocent of the knowledge, dearest chuck, *[handwritten: yet, until I become king]*
Till thou applaud the deed. Come, seeling night,
Scarf up the tender eye of pitiful day,
And with thy bloody and invisible hand
Cancel and tear to pieces that great bond
Which keeps me pale! Light thickens,
And the crow makes wing to th'rooky wood;   50
Good things of day begin to droop and drowse,
Whiles night's black agents to their preys do rouse.
—Thou marvel'st at my words, but hold thee still.
Things bad begun make strong themselves by ill.
So, prithee, go with me.   55

                                          Exeunt.

---

29. **remembrance**: reminder.
30. **eminence**: favor.
31–32. **unsafe . . . streams**: We are unsafe during this time in which we must cover ourselves with this display of flattering cordiality.
33. **vizards**: masks.
37. **copy**: copyhold, i.e., lease (on life); **eterne**: eternal.
40. **cloistered**: through dark buildings and enclosures.
41. **shard-born**: born in dung.
42. **Hath . . . peal**: has (with its **hums**) announced the arrival of night and sleep. (The image derives from the ringing of the curfew bell.)
43. **note**: notoriety.
44. **chuck**: a term of affection.
45. **seeling**: eye-closing. (Falconers seeled, i.e., stitched shut, the eyes of falcons.)
46. **Scarf up**: blindfold.
48. **bond**: contract (Banquo's lease on life).
49. **thickens**: dims.
50. **rooky**: filled with rooks, i.e., black birds, regarded as ill omens.
52. **rouse**: rouse themselves.

3.3

Enter three MURDERERS.

FIRST MURDERER   But who did bid thee join with us?

THIRD MURDERER   Macbeth.

SECOND MURDERER [*to* FIRST MURDERER]
He needs not our mistrust, since he delivers
Our offices and what we have to do
To the direction just.

FIRST MURDERER [*to* THIRD MURDERER]   Then stand with us.
The west yet glimmers with some streaks of day.   5
Now spurs the lated traveler apace
To gain the timely inn, and near approaches
The subject of our watch.

THIRD MURDERER   Hark, I hear horses.

BANQUO (*within*) Give us a light there, ho!

SECOND MURDERER   Then 'tis he. The rest
That are within the note of expectation   10
Already are i'th' court.

FIRST MURDERER   His horses go about.

THIRD MURDERER   Almost a mile, but he does usually.
So all men do from hence to th'palace gate
Make it their walk.

           Enter BANQUO *and* FLEANCE, *with a torch.*

SECOND MURDERER   A light, a light!   15

THIRD MURDERER   'Tis he.

FIRST MURDERER   Stand to't.

BANQUO   It will be rain tonight.

FIRST MURDERER   Let it come down!
           [*They attack.* FIRST MURDERER *puts out the light.*]

BANQUO   Oh, treachery!
Fly, good Fleance, fly, fly, fly!   20
Thou mayst revenge.—O slave!
           [BANQUO *dies.* FLEANCE *escapes.*]

3.3. Location: outdoors, near the palace.
0.1. SD *three*: The identity of the Third Murderer has caused speculation; some have
    proposed Ross, Macbeth himself in disguise, an allegorical abstraction like Destiny, or,
    most probably, an unnamed extra whom Macbeth sent to make sure the others carry
    out the murder.
2. He: the Third Murderer.
2–3. delivers Our offices: explains our duties.
4. To . . . just: exactly according to Macbeth's instructions.
6. spurs: hurries; lated: belated; apace: quickly.
7. timely: arrived at in good time.
10. note of expectation: list of invited guests.
11. about: another route, being led or ridden to the stable.
17. Stand to't: get ready.
18. It: i.e., the rain and the attack.

THIRD MURDERER   Who did strike out the light?
FIRST MURDERER   Was't not the way?
THIRD MURDERER   There's but one down. The son is fled.
SECOND MURDERER   We have lost best half of our affair.
FIRST MURDERER   Well, let's away and say how much is done.   25
                         Exeunt [with BANQUO's *body].*

3·4

   Banquet prepared. Enter MACBETH, LADY MACBETH, ROSS,
   LENNOX, LORDS, *and Attendants.*

MACBETH   You know your own degrees; sit down.
  At first and last, the hearty welcome.
LORDS   Thanks to your majesty.
MACBETH   Ourself will mingle with society
  And play the humble host.   5
  Our hostess keeps her state, but in best time
  We will require her welcome.
LADY MACBETH   Pronounce it for me, sir, to all our friends,
  For my heart speaks they are welcome.
     Enter FIRST MURDERER [*and stands aside*].
MACBETH   See, they encounter thee with their hearts' thanks.   10
  Both sides are even. Here I'll sit, i'th' midst.
  Be large in mirth; anon we'll drink a measure
  The table round.
     [*He converses apart with the* FIRST MURDERER.]
               There's blood upon thy face.
FIRST MURDERER   'Tis Banquo's, then.
MACBETH   'Tis better thee without than he within.   15
  Is he dispatched?
FIRST MURDERER   My lord, his throat is cut. That I did for him.
MACBETH   Thou art the best o'th' cutthroats.
  Yet he's good that did the like for Fleance;
  If thou didst it, thou art the nonpareil.   20

---

22. **way**: right way to proceed.
3.4. Location: a room in the palace.
1. **degrees**: ranks, and, therefore, places at the table.
2. **At . . . last**: to all.
4. **mingle with society**: mix with the guests (and not remain in his special chair).
6. **keeps her state**: remains in her special chair; **in best time**: at the right time.
10. **encounter**: respond to.
11. **Both . . . even**: (1) Both sides of the table have equal numbers; (2) The guests' grati-
    tude matches Lady Macbeth's welcome.
12. **anon**: straightway.
12–13. **measure . . . round**: toast for the whole table.
15. **thee . . . within**: on you than in him.
20. **nonpareil**: one without equal.

FIRST MURDERER   Most royal sir, Fleance is scaped.
MACBETH   Then comes my fit again. I had else been perfect,
  Whole as the marble, founded as the rock,
  As broad and general as the casing air,
  But now I am cabined, cribbed, confined, bound in   25
  To saucy doubts and fears. But Banquo's safe?
FIRST MURDERER   Ay, my good lord, safe in a ditch he bides,
  With twenty trenchèd gashes on his head,
  The least a death to nature.
MACBETH   Thanks for that.
  There the grown serpent lies; the worm that's fled   30
  Hath nature that in time will venom breed,
  No teeth for th'present. Get thee gone. Tomorrow
  We'll hear ourselves again.   *Exit* FIRST MURDERER.
LADY MACBETH   My royal lord,
  You do not give the cheer. The feast is sold
  That is not often vouched, while 'tis a-making,   35
  'Tis given with welcome. To feed were best at home;
  From thence the sauce to meat is ceremony:
  Meeting were bare without it.
      Enter the Ghost of BANQUO *and sits in* MACBETH's *place.*
MACBETH   Sweet remembrancer.
  —Now, good digestion wait on appetite,
  And health on both.
LENNOX   May't please your highness, sit.   40
MACBETH   Here had we now our country's honor roofed,
  Were the gracèd person of our Banquo present,
  Who may I rather challenge for unkindness
  Than pity for mischance.
ROSS   His absence, sir,
  Lays blame upon his promise. Please't your highness   45
  To grace us with your royal company?
MACBETH [*seeing his place occupied*]   The table's full.

---

23. **founded**: securely established.
24. **broad and general**: free and omnipresent; **casing**: encasing.
25. **cribbed**: enclosed in a narrow space.
26. **saucy**: sharp, insolent.
30. **worm**: small serpent.
31. **nature**: such a nature.
33. **hear ourselves**: converse together.
34–36. **The . . . welcome**: The feast seems a mere duty, as if sold for a price, if not often accompanied with assurances of welcome while the guests are eating.
36. **To . . . home**: Simply eating is best done at home.
37. **From thence**: away from home; **meat**: food; **ceremony**: courtesy.
38. **Meeting were bare**: social gathering would be unadorned.
39. **wait on**: serve, follow.
41. **roofed**: under one roof.
43. **challenge**: rebuke.
45. **Lays blame**: calls into question.

LENNOX   Here is a place reserved, sir.
MACBETH   Where?
LENNOX   Here, my good lord. What is't that moves your highness?
MACBETH   Which of you have done this?
LORDS   What, my good lord?   50
MACBETH [to Ghost]   Thou canst not say I did it. Never shake
   Thy gory locks at me!
ROSS   Gentlemen, rise. His highness is not well.
LADY MACBETH   Sit, worthy friends. My lord is often thus
   And hath been from his youth. Pray you, keep seat.   55
   The fit is momentary; upon a thought
   He will again be well. If much you note him,
   You shall offend him and extend his passion.
   Feed, and regard him not.
      [She converses apart with MACBETH.]
                              Are you a man?
MACBETH   Ay, and a bold one that dare look on that   60
   Which might appall the devil!
LADY MACBETH   Oh, proper stuff!
   This is the very painting of your fear;
   This is the air-drawn dagger which you said
   Led you to Duncan. Oh, these flaws and starts,
   Impostors to true fear, would well become   65
   A woman's story at a winter's fire,
   Authorized by her grandam. Shame itself!
   Why do you make such faces? When all's done,
   You look but on a stool.
MACBETH   Prithee, see there!
   Behold, look, lo! How say you?   70
   Why, what care I? [to Ghost] If thou canst nod, speak too.
   If charnel houses and our graves must send
   Those that we bury back, our monuments
   Shall be the maws of kites.   [Exit Ghost.]
LADY MACBETH   What, quite unmanned in folly?   75
MACBETH   If I stand here, I saw him.

---

49. **moves**: affects (an implied stage direction, as Macbeth recoils at the sight of the Ghost).
52. **gory locks**: bloody hair.
56. **upon a thought**: as quick as a thought.
61. **proper stuff**: nonsense.
63. **air-drawn**: imagined in, or moved through, the air.
64. **flaws**: outbursts of passion; **starts**: sudden nervous movements.
65. **to**: compared to.
67. **Authorized**: originally told and validated.
70. **lo**: look.
71. **nod**: an implicit stage direction for the ghost.
72. **charnel houses**: repositories for bones or corpses.
73–74. **monuments . . . kites**: burial places will be the stomachs of scavenging birds.

LADY MACBETH   Fie, for shame!
MACBETH   Blood hath been shed ere now, i'th' olden time,
   Ere humane statute purged the gentle weal;
   Ay, and since, too, murders have been performed,
   Too terrible for the ear. The times has been   80
   That, when the brains were out, the man would die,
   And there an end. But now they rise again,
   With twenty mortal murders on their crowns,
   And push us from our stools. This is more strange
   Than such a murder is.
LADY MACBETH   My worthy lord,   85
   Your noble friends do lack you.
MACBETH   I do forget.
   —Do not muse at me, my most worthy friends.
   I have a strange infirmity, which is nothing
   To those that know me. Come, love and health to all;
   Then I'll sit down. Give me some wine; fill full.   90
        Enter Ghost.
   I drink to th'general joy o'th' whole table
   And to our dear friend Banquo, whom we miss.
   Would he were here! To all and him we thirst,
   And all to all.
LORDS   Our duties and the pledge.
        [_They drink._]
MACBETH [_to Ghost_]   Avaunt, and quit my sight! Let the
        earth hide thee!   95
   Thy bones are marrowless, thy blood is cold;
   Thou hast no speculation in those eyes
   Which thou dost glare with.
LADY MACBETH   Think of this, good peers,
   But as a thing of custom; 'tis no other,
   Only it spoils the pleasure of the time.   100
MACBETH   What man dare, I dare.
   Approach thou like the rugged Russian bear,
   The armed rhinoceros, or th'Hyrcan tiger!

78. Before law (human and kindly) cleansed and civilized the commonwealth.
80. **times has been**: it used to be.
83. **mortal murders**: deadly wounds; **crowns**: heads.
93. **thirst**: long for.
94. **all to all**: let all drink to all.
94. **Our . . . pledge**: We offer our respect (**duties**) and this toast (**pledge**).
95. **Avaunt**: go away.
97. **speculation**: sight.
99. **thing of custom**: common occurrence.
103. **armed**: armor-plated; **Hyrcan**: Hyrcanian, i.e., an ancient region on the Caspian sea, noted for its wildness.

Take any shape but that, and my firm nerves
Shall never tremble. Or be alive again,   105
And dare me to the desert with thy sword.
If trembling I inhabit then, protest me
The baby of a girl. Hence, horrible shadow,
Unreal mock'ry, hence!   [*Exit Ghost.*]
                    Why, so. Being gone,
I am a man again. —Pray you, sit still.   110

LADY MACBETH   You have displaced the mirth, broke the good
    meeting
With most admired disorder.

MACBETH   Can such things be,
    And overcome us like a summer's cloud,
    Without our special wonder? You make me strange
    Even to the disposition that I owe,   115
    When now I think you can behold such sights
    And keep the natural ruby of your cheeks
    When mine is blanched with fear.

ROSS   What sights, my lord?

LADY MACBETH   I pray you, speak not; he grows worse and worse.
    Question enrages him. At once, good night.   120
    Stand not upon the order of your going,
    But go at once.

LENNOX   Good night, and better health
    Attend his majesty.

LADY MACBETH   A kind good night to all.
                        Exeunt LORDS [*and Attendants*].

MACBETH   It will have blood, they say; blood will have blood.
    Stones have been known to move and trees to speak;   125
    Augurs and understood relations have
    By maggot-pies and choughs and rooks brought forth

---

104. **nerves**: tendons.
107. If I tremble then proclaim me.
108. **baby**: infant or doll.
112. **admired**: amazing.
113. **overcome**: come over.
114–15. **You . . . owe**: You make me feel estranged from my natural courageous self (**owe** means "own").
118. **blanched**: whitened.
121. Don't insist on an orderly, ceremonious exit (cf. the ordered entrance 3.4.1).
124. Macbeth recalls the proverb "Blood will have blood" (Dent B458, see Resources); the idea occurs in Genesis 9:6: "Whoso sheddeth man's blood, by man shall his blood be shed."
126. **Augurs**: predictions; **understood relations**: comprehended correspondences, as between cause and effect, for example.
127. **maggot-pies . . . rooks**: magpies, jackdaws, and crows (three types of birds that mimicked human speech); **brought forth**: revealed.

The secret'st man of blood. What is the night?
LADY MACBETH   Almost at odds with morning, which is which.
MACBETH   How say'st thou that Macduff denies his person   130
    At our great bidding?
LADY MACBETH   Did you send to him, sir?
MACBETH   I hear it by the way, but I will send.
    There's not a one of them but in his house
    I keep a servant fee'd. I will tomorrow—
    And betimes I will—to the weïrd sisters.   135
    More shall they speak, for now I am bent to know
    By the worst means the worst. For mine own good
    All causes shall give way. I am in blood
    Stepped in so far that, should I wade no more,
    Returning were as tedious as go o'er.   140
    Strange things I have in head that will to hand,
    Which must be acted ere they may be scanned.
LADY MACBETH   You lack the season of all natures, sleep.
MACBETH   Come, we'll to sleep. My strange and self-abuse
    Is the initiate fear that wants hard use.   145
    We are yet but young in deed.

                                            Exeunt.

                            3·5

        Thunder. Enter the three WITCHES, *meeting* HECATE.
FIRST WITCH   Why, how now, Hecate? You look angerly.
HECATE   Have I not reason, beldams, as you are
    Saucy and overbold? How did you dare
    To trade and traffic with Macbeth
    In riddles and affairs of death,   5

---

128. **secret'st . . . blood**: best-hidden murderer; **the night**: the time of night.
130. **How sayst thou**: what do you think.
132. **by the way**: casually; **send**: send a messenger.
133. **them**: the Scottish nobles.
134. **fee'd**: paid (to spy).
135. **betimes**: (1) speedily; (2) early in the morning.
136. **bent**: determined.
140. **go o'er**: going all the way over.
141. **will to hand**: demand to be acted out.
142. **scanned**: analyzed.
143. **season**: seasoning, preservative.
144. **strange and self-abuse**: unusual violation of who I am.
145. **initiate**: new; **wants hard use**: lacks experience.
3.5. **Location: a heath**. Most scholars agree that this scene and parts of 4.1 were written by another author, perhaps Thomas Middleton. See below, 295–305.
1. **angerly**: angrily, angry.
2. **beldams**: hags, witches.

And I, the mistress of your charms,
The close contriver of all harms,
Was never called to bear my part,
Or show the glory of our art?
And, which is worse, all you have done   10
Hath been but for a wayward son,
Spiteful and wrathful, who, as others do,
Loves for his own ends, not for you.
But make amends now. Get you gone,
And at the pit of Acheron   15
Meet me i'th' morning. Thither he
Will come to know his destiny.
Your vessels and your spells provide,
Your charms and everything beside.
I am for th'air. This night I'll spend   20
Unto a dismal and a fatal end.
Great business must be wrought ere noon.
Upon the corner of the moon
There hangs a vap'rous drop profound;
I'll catch it ere it come to ground.   25
And that, distilled by magic sleights,
Shall raise such artificial sprites
As by the strength of their illusion
Shall draw him on to his confusion.
He shall spurn fate, scorn death, and bear   30
His hopes 'bove wisdom, grace, and fear.
And you all know security
Is mortals' chiefest enemy.
        Music and a song.
Hark, I am called. My little spirit, see,
Sits in a foggy cloud and stays for me.   [*Exit.*] 35
        Sing within: "Come away, come away," etc.
FIRST WITCH   Come, let's make haste. She'll soon be back again.
                                                    Exeunt.

---

7. **close**: secret.
11. **wayward**: self-willed, disobedient.
15. **Acheron**: a river in Hades.
21 **dismal**: disastrous.
24. **vap'rous drop**: lunar foam, supposedly gathered for enchantments; **profound**: with deep, hidden properties.
26. **sleights**: tricks.
27. **artificial**: constructed by art.
29. **confusion**: destruction.
32. **security**: spiritual overconfidence and complacency.
35. **SD**: For an early text of the song see below, p. 317.

3.6

Enter LENNOX *and another* LORD.

LENNOX   My former speeches have but hit your thoughts,
    Which can interpret farther. Only I say
    Things have been strangely borne. The gracious Duncan
    Was pitied of Macbeth; marry, he was dead.
    And the right valiant Banquo walked too late,   5
    Whom you may say, if't please you, Fleance killed,
    For Fleance fled; men must not walk too late.
    Who cannot want the thought how monstrous
    It was for Malcolm and for Donaldbain
    To kill their gracious father? Damnèd fact,   10
    How it did grieve Macbeth! Did he not straight
    In pious rage the two delinquents tear,
    That were the slaves of drink and thralls of sleep?
    Was not that nobly done? Ay, and wisely, too,
    For 'twould have angered any heart alive   15
    To hear the men deny't. So that I say
    He has borne all things well. And I do think
    That had he Duncan's sons under his key—
    As, an't please heaven, he shall not—they should find
    What 'twere to kill a father. So should Fleance.   20
    But peace. For from broad words and 'cause he failed
    His presence at the tyrant's feast, I hear
    Macduff lives in disgrace. Sir, can you tell
    Where he bestows himself?
LORD   The son of Duncan,
    From whom this tyrant holds the due of birth,   25
    Lives in the English court and is received
    Of the most pious Edward with such grace
    That the malevolence of fortune nothing
    Takes from his high respect. Thither Macduff

3.6. Location: somewhere in Scotland.
1. hit: touched upon.
2. interpret: draw the logical conclusions (without me saying more).
3. borne: (1) endured; (2) represented.
4. of: by.
8. cannot . . . thought: can help thinking.
10. fact: crime.
13. thralls: prisoners.
17. borne: (1) carried out; (2) represented.
18. under his key: in his control.
19. an't: if it.
21. from broad words: for plain speaking.
24. son of Duncan: Malcolm.
27. Edward: Edward the Confessor (King of England, 1042–66).
28–29. nothing Takes: does not detract.

Is gone to pray the holy King, upon his aid,   30
To wake Northumberland and warlike Siward,
That by the help of these, with Him above
To ratify the work, we may again
Give to our tables meat, sleep to our nights,
Free from our feasts and banquets bloody knives,   35
Do faithful homage, and receive free honors—
All which we pine for now. And this report
Hath so exasperate the King that he
Prepares for some attempt of war.
LENNOX   Sent he to Macduff?   40
LORD   He did, and with an absolute "Sir, not I,"
The cloudy messenger turns me his back
And hums, as who should say, "You'll rue the time
That clogs me with this answer."
LENNOX   And that well might
Advise him to a caution, t'hold what distance   45
His wisdom can provide. Some holy angel
Fly to the court of England and unfold
His message ere he come, that a swift blessing
May soon return to this our suff'ring country
Under a hand accursed.
LORD   I'll send my prayers with him.   50

Exeunt.

4.1

Thunder. Enter the three WITCHES.
FIRST WITCH   Thrice the brinded cat hath mewed.

30. upon his aid: with his assistance.
31. Northumberland: an earl, or a northern English county; **Siward**: the family name of some Northumberland earls.
33. ratify: approve.
35. Free our feasts and banquets from bloody knives.
36. free: untainted.
37. this report: (1) news of Macduff's flight (though this is in apparent contradiction with Macbeth's surprise at 4.1.141); (2) news of Malcolm's reception and purpose in England.
38. exasperate the King: exasperated Macbeth. Those who do not emend the Folio's "their" to **the** take "their" to refer to Northumberland's and Siward's King, Edward; in this reading the **report** (37) refers to Malcolm's report of Scotland's troubles to Edward. But the **he** (40) following, which must refer to Macbeth, argues strongly for emendation.
41. absolute: certain, unconditional; **Sir . . . I**: In these words Macduff refuses Macbeth's request (to return?).
42. cloudy: gloomy; **turns me**: turns ("me" is colloquial).
44. clogs: burdens.
45. t'hold: to keep.
47. unfold: reveal.
4.1. Location: an interior space, perhaps a cavern.
1. brinded: streaked or spotted.

SECOND WITCH   Thrice, and once the hedge-pig whined.

THIRD WITCH   Harpier cries, "'Tis time, 'tis time!"

FIRST WITCH   Round about the cauldron go;
In the poisoned entrails throw.   5
Toad, that under cold stone
Days and nights has thirty-one
Sweltered venom sleeping got,
Boil thou first i'th' charmèd pot.

ALL   Double, double, toil and trouble;   10
Fire burn, and cauldron bubble.

SECOND WITCH   Fillet of a fenny snake
In the cauldron boil and bake;
Eye of newt and toe of frog,
Wool of bat and tongue of dog,   15
Adder's fork and blind-worm's sting,
Lizard's leg and owlet's wing,
For a charm of powerful trouble,
Like a hell-broth boil and bubble.

ALL   Double, double, toil and trouble;   20
Fire burn, and cauldron bubble.

[handwritten: creepy — chanting]

THIRD WITCH   Scale of dragon, tooth of wolf,
Witches' mummy, maw and gulf
Of the ravined salt-sea shark,
Root of hemlock digged i'th' dark,   25
Liver of blaspheming Jew,
Gall of goat, and slips of yew
Slivered in the moon's eclipse,
Nose of Turk and Tartar's lips,
Finger of birth-strangled babe   30
Ditch-delivered by a drab,
Make the gruel thick and slab.
Add thereto a tiger's chawdron,
For th'ingredients of our cauldron.

---

2. **hedge-pig**: hedgehog.
3. **Harpier**: perhaps a familiar spirit.
7–8. For thirty-one days and nights has exuded venom like sweat while sleeping.
12. **Fillet**: slice; **fenny**: inhabiting fens or swamps.
16. **fork**: forked tongue; **blind-worm**: a small venomous snake.
17. **owlet**: a small owl.
23. **mummy**: mummified human flesh; **maw and gulf**: throat and stomach.
24. **ravined**: (1) ravenous; (2) glutted with prey.
26. **blaspheming**: Jews were so called for denying Christ's divinity.
27. **slips**: cuttings.
29. **Turk**: In the popular imagination the Turk threatened Europe and Christian civilization and often appeared as a figure of evil; **Tartar**: inhabitants of Central Asia, often considered as Turks or violent pagans.
31. **drab**: whore.
32. **slab**: semi-solid.
33. **chawdron**: entrails.

ALL   Double, double, toil and trouble;   35
   Fire burn, and cauldron bubble.
SECOND WITCH   Cool it with a baboon's blood;
   Then the charm is firm and good.
      Enter HECATE *and the other three* WITCHES.
HECATE   Oh, well done. I commend your pains,
   And every one shall share i'th' gains.   40
   And now about the cauldron sing,
   Live elves and fairies in a ring,
   Enchanting all that you put in.
      Music and a song, "Black spirits," etc.
SECOND WITCH   By the pricking of my thumbs,
   Something wicked this way comes.   45
   Open, locks, whoever knocks!
      Enter MACBETH.
MACBETH   How now, you secret, black, and midnight hags!
   What is't you do?
ALL WITCHES   A deed without a name.
MACBETH   I conjure you by that which you profess,
   Howe'er you come to know it, answer me.   50
   Though you untie the winds and let them fight
   Against the churches, though the yeasty waves
   Confound and swallow navigation up,
   Though bladed corn be lodged and trees blown down,
   Though castles topple on their warders' heads,   55
   Though palaces and pyramids do slope
   Their heads to their foundations, though the treasure
   Of nature's germens tumble all together
   Even till destruction sicken, answer me
   To what I ask you. — *Stichomythia (sharing a line)*
FIRST WITCH   Speak.
SECOND WITCH   Demand.
THIRD WITCH   We'll answer.   60
FIRST WITCH   Say if thou'dst rather hear it from our mouths,
   Or from our masters.
MACBETH   Call 'em; let me see 'em.
FIRST WITCH   Pour in sow's blood that hath eaten

39–43. Most consider these lines non-Shakespearean. For an early text of the song "Black spirits," see p. 317.
49. conjure: invoke.
52. yeasty: frothy.
54. bladed corn: leafed grain (**corn** is a generic term); **lodged:** laid on the ground (by the wind).
55. warders: guards.
56. slope: bend.
58. nature's germens: seeds from which all life springs.
59. sicken: gets sick from excess.

Her nine farrow; grease that's sweaten
From the murderer's gibbet throw   65
Into the flame.

ALL WITCHES   Come high or low,
Thyself and office deftly show!

    Thunder. FIRST APPARITION, *an armed head.*

MACBETH   Tell me, thou unknown power—

FIRST WITCH   He knows thy thought.
Hear his speech, but say thou naught.

FIRST APPARITION   Macbeth, Macbeth, Macbeth. Beware
    Macduff,   70
Beware the Thane of Fife. Dismiss me. Enough.

                            He descends.

MACBETH   Whate'er thou art, for thy good caution, thanks;
Thou hast harped my fear aright. But one word more—

FIRST WITCH   He will not be commanded. Here's another,
More potent than the first.   75

    Thunder. SECOND APPARITION, *a bloody child.*

SECOND APPARITION   Macbeth, Macbeth, Macbeth.

MACBETH   Had I three ears, I'd hear thee.

SECOND APPARITION   Be bloody, bold, and resolute; laugh to scorn
The power of man, for none of woman born
Shall harm Macbeth.   *Descends.* 80

MACBETH   Then live, Macduff. What need I fear of thee?
But yet I'll make assurance double sure
And take a bond of fate. Thou shalt not live,
That I may tell pale-hearted fear it lies
And sleep in spite of thunder.

    Thunder. THIRD APPARITION, *a child crowned, with a tree in*
    his hand.

                   What is this   85
That rises like the issue of a king,
And wears upon his baby brow the round

---

64. **nine farrow**: litter of nine; **sweaten**: sweated (rhymes with **eaten**).
65. **gibbet**: gallows, from which criminals were hanged.
67. **office**: function.
67. SD *armed head*: helmeted head, foreshadowing Macbeth's decapitation by Macduff.
71. SD *descends*: The stage had a trap-door for such effects.
73. **harped**: given voice to; **aright**: exactly.
75. SD *bloody child*: This image suggests the infanticides in the imagery (1.7.54–58) and
    the action (4.2), and also the retribution in the person of Macduff, untimely ripped
    from his mother's womb.
79. **of woman born**: a human being. The phrase echoes biblical pronouncements (see Job
    14:1, 15:14, 25:4).
83. **take . . . fate**: get a guarantee from fate; **Thou**: Macduff.
85. SD *child*: This figure may represent Malcolm, true heir to the throne, or Banquo's
    issue, future heirs. The tree suggests Birnam Wood.
87–88. **round And top**: crown.

And top of sovereignty?
ALL WITCHES   Listen, but speak not to't.
THIRD APPARITION   Be lion-mettled, proud, and take no care
  Who chafes, who frets, or where conspirers are.   90
  Macbeth shall never vanquished be until
  Great Birnam Wood to high Dunsinane Hill
  Shall come against him.   *Descends.*
MACBETH   That will never be.
  Who can impress the forest, bid the tree
  Unfix his earth-bound root? Sweet bodements, good.   95
  Rebellious dead, rise never till the Wood
  Of Birnam rise, and our high-placed Macbeth
  Shall live the lease of nature, pay his breath
  To time and mortal custom. Yet my heart
  Throbs to know one thing: tell me, if your art   100
  Can tell so much, shall Banquo's issue ever
  Reign in this kingdom?
ALL WITCHES   Seek to know no more.
MACBETH   I will be satisfied. Deny me this,
  And an eternal curse fall on you! Let me know.
                  [*The cauldron descends.*] *Hautboys.*
  Why sinks that cauldron? And what noise is this?   105
FIRST WITCH   Show!
SECOND WITCH   Show!
THIRD WITCH   Show!
ALL WITCHES   Show his eyes, and grieve his heart;
  Come like shadows, so depart.   110
     A show of eight Kings, and BANQUO *last;* [*the eighth King*]
     with a glass in his hand.
MACBETH   Thou art too like the spirit of Banquo. Down!
  Thy crown does sear mine eyeballs! And thy heir,
  Thou other gold-bound brow, is like the first.
  A third is like the former. —Filthy hags,
  Why do you show me this? —A fourth! Start, eyes!   115
  What, will the line stretch out to th'crack of doom?

---

89. lion-mettled: as fearless and fierce as a lion.
94. impress: draft into service.
95. bodements: omens, prophecies.
96. Rebellious dead: i.e., Banquo and his ghost.
98. lease of nature: natural lifespan.
99. mortal custom: the custom of mortality.
110. SD: The eight kings represent descendants of Banquo, the ancestors of the Stuart
    line culminating in King James (1603–1625), reigning at the time of the play.
110.2. SD *glass*: mirror.
113. other: second.
115. Start: bulge from eye sockets.
116. crack of doom: thunder at the end of world and Last Judgment.

Another yet? A seventh! I'll see no more.
And yet the eighth appears, who bears a glass
Which shows me many more; and some I see
That two-fold balls and treble scepters carry.   120
Horrible sight! Now, I see 'tis true,
For the blood-boltered Banquo smiles upon me,
And points at them for his.   [*The apparitions vanish.*]
                    What, is this so?
FIRST WITCH   Ay, sir, all this is so. But why
    Stands Macbeth thus amazedly?   125
    Come, sisters, cheer we up his sprites,
    And show the best of our delights.
    I'll charm the air to give a sound,
    While you perform your antic round,
    That this great king may kindly say   130
    Our duties did his welcome pay.
                    Music. The WITCHES *dance and vanish.*
MACBETH   Where are they? Gone? Let this pernicious hour
    Stand aye accursèd in the calendar!
    Come in, without there.
            Enter LENNOX.
LENNOX   What's your grace's will?
MACBETH   Saw you the weïrd sisters?
LENNOX   No, my lord.   135
MACBETH   Came they not by you?
LENNOX   No, indeed, my lord.
MACBETH   Infected be the air whereon they ride,
    And damned all those that trust them! I did hear
    The galloping of horse. Who was't came by?
LENNOX   'Tis two or three, my lord, that bring you word   140
    Macduff is fled to England.
MACBETH   Fled to England?
LENNOX   Ay, my good lord.
MACBETH [*aside*]   Time, thou anticipat'st my dread exploits.
    The flighty purpose never is o'ertook

---

120. **two-fold . . . scepters**: two orbs and three scepters, symbolic accoutrements of
    royalty, perhaps alluding to James I, King of Scotland and Ireland. The three scepters
    may refer to James's assumed authority over Great Britain, France, and Ireland.
122. **blood-boltered**: having hair matted with blood.
124–31. Usually regarded as non-Shakespearean.
129. **antic round**: fantastic circle dance.
133. **aye**: ever.
143. **anticipat'st**: foresee (and thus prevent).
144–45. **The . . . it**: The fleeting resolution to do something never amounts to anything
    unless accompanied by action.

Unless the deed go with it. From this moment   145
The very firstlings of my heart shall be
The firstlings of my hand. And even now,
To crown my thoughts with acts, be it thought and done.
The castle of Macduff I will surprise,
Seize upon Fife, give to th'edge o'th' sword   150
His wife, his babes, and all unfortunate souls
That trace him in his line. No boasting like a fool;
This deed I'll do before this purpose cool.
But no more sights. —Where are these gentlemen?
Come, bring me where they are.   155

Exeunt.

4.2

Enter Macduff's WIFE, *her* SON, *and* ROSS.

WIFE What had he done to make him fly the land?

ROSS You must have patience, madam.

WIFE   He had none;
  His flight was madness. When our actions do not,
  Our fears do make us traitors.

ROSS   You know not
  Whether it was his wisdom or his fear.   5

WIFE Wisdom? To leave his wife, to leave his babes,
  His mansion, and his titles in a place
  From whence himself does fly? He loves us not;
  He wants the natural touch. For the poor wren,
  The most diminutive of birds, will fight,   10
  Her young ones in her nest, against the owl.
  All is the fear and nothing is the love,
  As little is the wisdom, where the flight
  So runs against all reason.

ROSS   My dearest coz,
  I pray you, school yourself. But, for your husband,   15

---

146. **firstlings**: first children. Macbeth promises to turn immediately his impulses to
  deeds.
149. **surprise**: attack unexpectedly.
152. **trace . . . line**: follow him in his family line.
154. **these gentlemen**: the two or three messengers (140).
4.2. **Location**: Fife. Macduff's castle.
3–4. **When . . . traitors**: Even when we commit no acts of treason, our fears can make us
  treasonous or appear treasonous. (By running away, Macduff has betrayed his family
  and country or he has made himself look guilty of treason.)
9. **wants**: lacks.
14. **coz**: cousin, kinswoman (a term of affection).
15. **school**: discipline.

He is noble, wise, judicious, and best knows
The fits o'th' season. I dare not speak much further.
But cruel are the times when we are traitors
And do not know ourselves; when we hold rumor
From what we fear, yet know not what we fear,   20
But float upon a wild and violent sea,
Each way and none. I take my leave of you;
Shall not be long but I'll be here again.
Things at the worst will cease or else climb upward
To what they were before. [to the SON] My pretty cousin,   25
Blessing upon you.

WIFE   Fathered he is, and yet he's fatherless.

ROSS   I am so much a fool, should I stay longer
It would be my disgrace and your discomfort.
I take my leave at once.   *Exit* ROSS.

WIFE   Sirrah, your father's dead.   30
And what will you do now? How will you live?

SON   As birds do, mother.

WIFE   What, with worms and flies?

SON   With what I get, I mean, and so do they.

WIFE   Poor bird, thou'dst never fear the net nor lime,
The pitfall nor the gin.   35

SON   Why should I, mother? Poor birds they are not set for.
My father is not dead, for all your saying.

WIFE   Yes, he is dead. How wilt thou do for a father?

SON   Nay, how will you do for a husband?

WIFE   Why, I can buy me twenty at any market.   40

SON   Then you'll buy 'em to sell again.

WIFE   Thou speak'st with all thy wit, and yet, i'faith, with wit
enough for thee.

SON   Was my father a traitor, mother?

WIFE   Ay, that he was.   45

SON   What is a traitor?

WIFE   Why, one that swears and lies.

SON   And be all traitors that do so?

WIFE   Every one that does so is a traitor and must be hanged.

17. fits . . . season: violent conditions of the time.
19. know ourselves: know ourselves to be such (traitors); hold: believe.
20. About what we fear, though we don't know what we fear exactly.
22. Each . . . none: in every direction at once and in none specifically.
29. My staying (and weeping) would disgrace me and distress you.
30. Sirrah: an affectionate form of address to a child.
34–35. net . . . gin: These are all traps for birds. lime: birdlime, a sticky substance; gin: snare or trap.
36. they: traps. (The traps are set for superior or game birds.)
47. swears and lies: swears an oath to a sovereign (or wife) and breaks it.

SON   And must they all be hanged that swear and lie?   50
WIFE   Every one.
SON   Who must hang them?
WIFE   Why, the honest men.
SON   Then the liars and swearers are fools, for there are liars
and swearers enough to beat the honest men and hang up   55
them.
WIFE   Now, God help thee, poor monkey! But how wilt thou
do for a father?
SON   If he were dead, you'd weep for him; if you would not, it
were a good sign that I should quickly have a new father.   60
WIFE   Poor prattler, how thou talk'st!
        Enter a MESSENGER.
MESSENGER   Bless you, fair dame. I am not to you known,
Though in your state of honor I am perfect.
I doubt some danger does approach you nearly.
If you will take a homely man's advice,   65
Be not found here; hence with your little ones.
To fright you thus, methinks, I am too savage;
To do worse to you were fell cruelty,
Which is too nigh your person. Heaven preserve you.
I dare abide no longer.   *Exit* MESSENGER.
WIFE   Whither should I fly?   70
I have done no harm. But I remember now
I am in this earthly world, where to do harm
Is often laudable, to do good sometime
Accounted dangerous folly. Why, then, alas,
Do I put up that womanly defense,   75
To say I have done no harm?
        Enter MURDERERS.
                          What are these faces?
MURDERER   Where is your husband?
WIFE   I hope in no place so unsanctified
Where such as thou mayst find him.
MURDERER   He's a traitor.
SON   Thou liest, thou shag-haired villain!
MURDERER [*stabbing him*]   What, you egg!   80
Young fry of treachery.

59–60. if . . . father: The son suggests that the mother's lack of tears would indicate a
new love interest.
63. Though I know well your nobility.
64. doubt: fear.
65. homely: plain (speaking).
68. fell: vicious.
69. Which . . . person: such cruelty is too near you now.
81. fry: offspring (of fish).

SON   He has killed me, mother.
  Run away, I pray you! [*He dies.*]

                              Exit [WIFE] *crying* "Murder!"
                  [*followed by* MURDERERS *with* SON's *body*].

4·3

  Enter MALCOLM *and* MACDUFF.

MALCOLM   Let us seek out some desolate shade and there
  Weep our sad bosoms empty.

MACDUFF   Let us rather
  Hold fast the mortal sword and like good men
  Bestride our downfall birthdom. Each new morn
  New widows howl, new orphans cry, new sorrows   5
  Strike heaven on the face, that it resounds
  As if it felt with Scotland and yelled out
  Like syllable of dolor.

MALCOLM   What I believe, I'll wail;
  What know, believe; and what I can, redress;
  As I shall find the time to friend, I will.   10
  What you have spoke, it may be so, perchance.
  This tyrant, whose sole name blisters our tongues,
  Was once thought honest. You have loved him well;
  He hath not touched you yet. I am young, but something
  You may deserve of him through me, and wisdom   15
  To offer up a weak, poor, innocent lamb
  T'appease an angry god.

MACDUFF   I am not treacherous.

MALCOLM   But Macbeth is.
  A good and virtuous nature may recoil
  In an imperial charge. But I shall crave your pardon. 20
  That which you are my thoughts cannot transpose;
  Angels are bright still though the brightest fell.

4.3. Location: England. Before King Edward's palace.
3. **mortal**: deadly.
4. **Bestride . . . birthdom**: stand over and protect our fallen native land.
6. **that**: so that.
8. **Like . . . dolor**: the same cry of pain.
10. **friend**: befriend me, be favorable.
12. **sole**: mere.
15. **deserve . . . me**: get from him as a reward for betraying me; **wisdom**: it is wise.
19–20. **recoil . . . charge**: give way, or go in a reverse motion, because of imperial force
  or command. (The image is of a gun springing back by force of the firing.)
21. **transpose**: transform.
22. **the brightest**: i.e., Lucifer.

Though all things foul would wear the brows of grace,
Yet grace must still look so.
MACDUFF   I have lost my hopes.
MALCOLM   Perchance even there where I did find my doubts.   25
   Why in that rawness left you wife and child,
   Those precious motives, those strong knots of love,
   Without leave-taking? I pray you,
   Let not my jealousies be your dishonors
   But mine own safeties. You may be rightly just,   30
   Whatever I shall think.
MACDUFF   Bleed, bleed, poor country!
   Great tyranny, lay thou thy basis sure,
   For goodness dare not check thee; wear thou thy wrongs,
   The title is affeered.—Fare thee well, lord.
   I would not be the villain that thou think'st   35
   For the whole space that's in the tyrant's grasp
   And the rich East to boot.
MALCOLM   Be not offended.
   I speak not as in absolute fear of you.
   I think our country sinks beneath the yoke;
   It weeps, it bleeds, and each new day a gash   40
   Is added to her wounds. I think withal
   There would be hands uplifted in my right,
   And here from gracious England have I offer
   Of goodly thousands. But, for all this,
   When I shall tread upon the tyrant's head   45
   Or wear it on my sword, yet my poor country
   Shall have more vices than it had before,
   More suffer and more sundry ways than ever,
   By him that shall succeed.
MACDUFF   What should he be?
MALCOLM   It is myself I mean, in whom I know   50

---

23. **brows**: appearance.
24. **look so**: like grace. Though foul things put on good appearances, good things must
   still appear good and may be trusted.
25. **there**: in the general climate of suspicion and fear.
26. **rawness**: (1) vulnerable position; (2) rudeness (referring to Macduff's abrupt
   departure).
29–30. **Let . . . safeties**: Assume that I voice my suspicions not for your dishonor but for
   my safety.
32. **basis sure**: foundation securely.
33. **check**: restrain, rebuke; **wear**: display (as on a heraldic shield).
34. **title is affeered**: Tyranny is confirmed.
38. **absolute fear**: complete mistrust.
41. **withal**: in addition.
42. **in my right**: in support of my claim to the throne.
43. **England**: the King of England.
44. **goodly**: considerable in respect to size.
49. **succeed**: follow as king.

All the particulars of vice so grafted
That, when they shall be opened, black Macbeth
Will seem as pure as snow, and the poor state
Esteem him as a lamb, being compared
With my confineless harms.

MACDUFF   Not in the legions   55
Of horrid hell can come a devil more damned
In evils to top Macbeth.

MALCOLM   I grant him bloody,
Luxurious, avaricious, false, deceitful,
Sudden, malicious, smacking of every sin
That has a name. But there's no bottom, none,   60
In my voluptuousness: your wives, your daughters,
Your matrons, and your maids could not fill up
The cistern of my lust, and my desire
All continent impediments would o'erbear
That did oppose my will. Better Macbeth   65
Than such an one to reign.

MACDUFF   Boundless intemperance
In nature is a tyranny. It hath been
Th'untimely emptying of the happy throne
And fall of many kings. But fear not yet
To take upon you what is yours. You may   70
Convey your pleasures in a spacious plenty
And yet seem cold; the time you may so hoodwink.
We have willing dames enough. There cannot be
That vulture in you to devour so many
As will to greatness dedicate themselves,   75
Finding it so inclined.

MALCOLM   With this there grows
In my most ill-composed affection such
A stanchless avarice that, were I king,
I should cut off the nobles for their lands,
Desire his jewels and this other's house,   80

51. **grafted**: implanted into his character.
52. **opened**: revealed (as a bud opens).
55. **confineless**: limitless.
58. **Luxurious**: lecherous.
59. **Sudden**: rash, impetuous.
63. **cistern**: water tank.
64. **continent**: containing, restraining.
65. **will**: lust.
67. **nature**: human nature.
69. **yet**: nevertheless.
71. **Convey**: manage in secret.
72. **cold**: chaste; **hoodwink** blindfold, deceive.
77. **ill-composed affection**: (1) evil disposition; (2) poorly managed passion.
78. **stanchless**: insatiable.
80. **his**: one man's.

And my more-having would be as a sauce
To make me hunger more, that I should forge
Quarrels unjust against the good and loyal,
Destroying them for wealth.

MACDUFF   This avarice
Sticks deeper, grows with more pernicious root   85
Than summer-seeming lust, and it hath been
The sword of our slain kings. Yet do not fear;
Scotland hath foisons to fill up your will
Of your mere own. All these are portable,
With other graces weighed.   90

MALCOLM   But I have none. The king-becoming graces—
As justice, verity, temp'rance, stableness,
Bounty, perseverance, mercy, lowliness,
Devotion, patience, courage, fortitude—
I have no relish of them, but abound   95
In the division of each several crime,
Acting it many ways. Nay, had I power, I should
Pour the sweet milk of concord into hell,
Uproar the universal peace, confound
All unity on earth.

MACDUFF   O Scotland, Scotland!   100

MALCOLM   If such a one be fit to govern, speak.
I am as I have spoken.

MACDUFF   Fit to govern?
No, not to live. O nation miserable,
With an untitled tyrant, bloody-sceptered!
When shalt thou see thy wholesome days again,   105
Since that the truest issue of thy throne
By his own interdiction stands accused
And does blaspheme his breed? Thy royal father
Was a most sainted king; the queen that bore thee,
Oft'ner upon her knees than on her feet,   110

81. **more-having**: gains and greed for more.
85. **pernicious**: evil, destructive.
86. **summer-seeming**: (1) seeming like summer, i.e., hot and transitory; (2) summer beseeming, i.e., appropriate to youth.
87. **sword . . . slain**: sword that slew our.
88. **foisons**: resources.
89. **Of . . . own**: from your royal supplies alone; **portable**: endurable.
90. **graces weighed**: virtues considered.
91. **king-becoming graces**: virtues suitable to a king.
93. **lowliness**: humility.
95. **relish**: enjoyment of the taste.
96. **division**: variations; **several**: distinct.
99. **Uproar**: throw into confusion.
104. **untitled**: usurping.
107. **interdiction**: declaration of incompetency.
108. **blaspheme**: slander.

Died every day she lived. Fare thee well.
These evils thou repeat'st upon thyself
Hath banished me from Scotland.—O my breast,
Thy hope ends here.

MALCOLM   Macduff, this noble passion,
    Child of integrity, hath from my soul   115
    Wiped the black scruples, reconciled my thoughts
    To thy good truth and honor. Devilish Macbeth
    By many of these trains hath sought to win me
    Into his power, and modest wisdom plucks me
    From over-credulous haste. But God above   120
    Deal between thee and me. For even now
    I put myself to thy direction and
    Unspeak mine own detraction, here abjure
    The taints and blames I laid upon myself
    For strangers to my nature. I am yet   125
    Unknown to woman, never was forsworn,
    Scarcely have coveted what was mine own,
    At no time broke my faith, would not betray
    The devil to his fellow, and delight
    No less in truth than life. My first false speaking   130
    Was this upon myself. What I am truly
    Is thine and my poor country's to command,
    Whither, indeed, before thy here-approach,
    Old Siward with ten thousand warlike men
    Already at a point was setting forth.   135
    Now we'll together, and the chance of goodness
    Be like our warranted quarrel. Why are you silent?

MACDUFF   Such welcome and unwelcome things at once
    'Tis hard to reconcile.

             Enter a DOCTOR.

MALCOLM   Well, more anon, [*to the* DOCTOR] Comes the King
    forth, I pray you?   140

---

111. **Died . . . lived**: died to this world by daily religious practices.
112. **repeat'st upon**: declare against.
113. **banished me**: made it impossible for me to return (with you).
116. **scruples**: doubts.
118. **trains**: tricks.
119. **plucks**: restrains.
123. **mine own detraction**: my former self-condemnation.
125. **For**: as.
126. **Unknown to women**: a virgin.
131. **this upon**: this false witness against.
133. **Whither**: to which place; **here-approach**: arrival here.
134. **warlike**: armed.
135. **at a point**: prepared.
136. **we'll**: we'll go; **the . . . goodness**: may the chance of our success.
137. **Be . . . quarrel**: match the justice of our cause.

DOCTOR   Ay, sir. There are a crew of wretched souls
   That stay his cure. Their malady convinces
   The great assay of art, but at his touch—
   Such sanctity hath heaven given his hand—
   They presently amend.
MALCOLM   I thank you, Doctor.   *Exit*   145
                                                 [DOCTOR].

MACDUFF   What's the disease he means?
MALCOLM   'Tis called the Evil.
   A most miraculous work in this good King,
   Which often since my here-remain in England
   I have seen him do. How he solicits heaven
   Himself best knows; but strangely-visited people,   150
   All swoll'n and ulcerous, pitiful to the eye,
   The mere despair of surgery, he cures,
   Hanging a golden stamp about their necks,
   Put on with holy prayers; and, 'tis spoken,
   To the succeeding royalty he leaves   155
   The healing benediction. With this strange virtue,
   He hath a heavenly gift of prophecy,
   And sundry blessings hang about his throne
   That speak him full of grace.
       Enter ROSS.
MACDUFF   See who comes here.
MALCOLM   My countryman, but yet I know him not.   160
MACDUFF   My ever gentle cousin, welcome hither.
MALCOLM   I know him now. Good God, betimes remove
   The means that makes us strangers.
ROSS   Sir, amen.
MACDUFF   Stands Scotland where it did?
ROSS   Alas, poor country,
   Almost afraid to know itself. It cannot   165
   Be called our mother but our grave, where nothing

142. **stay**: await; **convinces**: conquers.
143. **assay of art**: attempts of medical science.
146. **Evil**: scrofula, the chronic enlargement of the lymphatic glands and ulcers, supposedly cured by the royal touch.
148. **here-remain**: stay.
150. **visited**: afflicted.
152. **mere**: absolute.
153. **stamp**: coin. (Elizabeth and James gave a gold coin to those they touched.)
154. **Put on with**: accompanied by.
155. **succeeding royalty**: following monarchs.
156. **healing benediction**: this power to heal; **virtue**: power.
159. **speak him**: declare him to be.
160. **countryman**: Malcolm recognizes Ross as a Scot by his dress.
162. **betimes**: immediately.
163. **means . . . strangers**: cause of our separation, i.e., Macbeth.
166. **nothing**: nobody.

But who knows nothing is once seen to smile;
Where sighs and groans and shrieks that rend the air
Are made, not marked; where violent sorrow seems
A modern ecstasy. The deadman's knell   170
Is there scarce asked for who, and good men's lives
Expire before the flowers in their caps,
Dying or ere they sicken.
MACDUFF   Oh, relation
Too nice and yet too true!
MALCOLM   What's the newest grief?
ROSS   That of an hour's age doth hiss the speaker;   175
Each minute teems a new one.
MACDUFF   How does my wife?
ROSS   Why, well.
MACDUFF   And all my children?
ROSS   Well too.
MACDUFF   The tyrant has not battered at their peace?
ROSS   No, they were well at peace when I did leave 'em.
MACDUFF   Be not a niggard of your speech. How goes't?   180
ROSS   When I came hither to transport the tidings
Which I have heavily borne, there ran a rumor
Of many worthy fellows that were out,
Which was to my belief witnessed the rather
For that I saw the tyrant's power afoot.   185
Now is the time of help, [to MALCOLM] Your eye in Scotland
Would create soldiers, make our women fight
To doff their dire distresses.
MALCOLM   Be't their comfort
We are coming thither. Gracious England hath
Lent us good Siward and ten thousand men—   190
An older and a better soldier none

---

167. **who**: one who; **once**: ever.
169. **marked**: noticed.
170. **modern ecstasy**: common frenzy.
170–171. **The deadman's . . . who**: No one in Scotland bothers to ask who died when the
      funeral bell tolls (because death is so common).
173. **or . . . sicken**: before they become ill; **relation**: report.
174. **nice**: precise.
175. A report only one hour old is hissed as old news.
176. **teems**: brings forth.
180. **niggard**: miser.
183. **out**: in the field, in arms.
184. **witnessed the rather**: made more credible.
185. **power afoot**: army mobilized for action.
186. **eye**: person, i.e., yourself.
188. **doff**: take off (like clothing).
189. **England**: King Edward.
191. **none**: is no one.

That Christendom gives out.

ROSS   Would I could answer
This comfort with the like. But I have words
That would be howled out in the desert air,
Where hearing should not latch them.

MACDUFF   What concern they?   195
The general cause, or is it a fee-grief
Due to some single breast?

ROSS   No mind that's honest
But in it shares some woe, though the main part
Pertains to you alone.

MACDUFF   If it be mine,
Keep it not from me; quickly let me have it.   200

ROSS   Let not your ears despise my tongue forever,
Which shall possess them with the heaviest sound
That ever yet they heard.

MACDUFF   Hum—I guess at it.

ROSS   Your castle is surprised, your wife and babes
Savagely slaughtered. To relate the manner   205
Were, on the quarry of these murdered deer,
To add the death of you.

MALCOLM   Merciful heaven!
What, man, ne'er pull your hat upon your brows.
Give sorrow words. The grief that does not speak
Whispers the o'er-fraught heart and bids it break.   210

MACDUFF   My children too?

ROSS   Wife, children, servants—
All that could be found.

MACDUFF   And I must be from thence?
My wife killed too?

ROSS   I have said.

MALCOLM   Be comforted.
Let's make us med'cines of our great revenge
To cure this deadly grief.   215

MACDUFF   He has no children. All my pretty ones?
Did you say all? Oh, hell-kite! All?

192. **gives out**: tells of.
195. **latch**: catch.
196–97. **fee-grief . . . breast**: grief belonging to a particular person. (The phrase derives from legal language about property inheritance.)
206. **Were**: would be; **quarry**: heap of slaughtered deer (with a pun on "dear").
210. **Whispers**: whispers to; **o'er-fraught**: overburdened.
212. **from thence**: away from home.
216. **He . . . children**: 1) Macbeth has no children (and therefore cannot suffer a fitting retribution); 2) Malcolm has no children (and therefore cannot understand this pain).
217. **hell-kite**: kite (bird of prey) from hell.

What, all my pretty chickens and their dam
At one fell swoop?
MALCOLM   Dispute it like a man.
MACDUFF   I shall do so.   220
   But I must also feel it as a man.
   I cannot but remember such things were
   That were most precious to me. Did heaven look on
   And would not take their part? Sinful Macduff,
   They were all struck for thee. Naught that I am,   225
   Not for their own demerits but for mine
   Fell slaughter on their souls. Heaven rest them now.
MALCOLM   Be this the whetstone of your sword. Let grief
   Convert to anger; blunt not the heart, enrage it.
MACDUFF   Oh, I could play the woman with mine eyes   230
   And braggart with my tongue. But, gentle heavens,
   Cut short all intermission. Front to front
   Bring thou this fiend of Scotland and myself.
   Within my sword's length set him. If he scape,
   Heaven forgive him too.
MALCOLM   This tune goes manly.   235
   Come, go we to the King. Our power is ready;
   Our lack is nothing but our leave. Macbeth
   Is ripe for shaking, and the powers above
   Put on their instruments. Receive what cheer you may;
   The night is long that never finds the day.   240

                                            Exeunt.

5.1

Enter a DOCTOR *of physic and a waiting* GENTLEWOMAN.
DOCTOR   I have two nights watched with you but can perceive
   no truth in your report. When was it she last walked?
GENTLEWOMAN   Since his majesty went into the field, I have
   seen her rise from her bed, throw her nightgown upon her,
   unlock her closet, take forth paper, fold it, write upon't, read   5

218. **dam**: mother.
219. **Dispute**: fight against.
225. **Naught**: wicked man.
226. **demerits**: faults.
228. **whetstone**: sharpening stone.
230. **play . . . eyes**: weep.
232. **intermission**: delay; **Front to front**: face to face.
237. **Our . . . leave**: We have only to take leave of the English King.
239. **Put . . . instruments**: (1) arm themselves for action; (2) take us as their agents.
5.1. **Location: Dunsinane Hill. Macbeth's castle.**
0.1. SD *physic*: medicine; *waiting* GENTLEWOMAN: personal servant.
5. **closet**: cabinet.

it, afterwards seal it, and again return to bed, yet all this while in a most fast sleep.

DOCTOR   A great perturbation in nature, to receive at once the benefit of sleep and do the effects of watching. In this slumb'ry agitation, besides her walking and other actual performances, 10 what at any time have you heard her say?

GENTLEWOMAN   That, sir, which I will not report after her.

DOCTOR   You may to me, and 'tis most meet you should.

GENTLEWOMAN   Neither to you nor anyone, having no witness to confirm my speech.   15

    Enter LADY MACBETH *with a taper.*

Lo, you, here she comes. This is her very guise and, upon my life, fast asleep. Observe her; stand close.

DOCTOR   How came she by that light?

GENTLEWOMAN   Why, it stood by her. She has light by her continually; 'tis her command.   20

DOCTOR   You see her eyes are open.

GENTLEWOMAN   Ay, but their sense are shut.

DOCTOR   What is it she does now? Look how she rubs her hands.

GENTLEWOMAN   It is an accustomed action with her to seem thus washing her hands. I have known her continue in this a 25 quarter of an hour.

LADY MACBETH   Yet here's a spot.

DOCTOR   Hark, she speaks. I will set down what comes from her to satisfy my remembrance the more strongly.

LADY MACBETH   Out, damned spot! Out, I say! One, two, why, 30 then, 'tis time to do't. Hell is murky. Fie, my lord, fie, a soldier and afeard?   *irratic*

What need we fear? Who knows it when none can call our power to account? Yet who would have thought the old man to have had so much blood in him?   *Why are we afraid*35

DOCTOR   Do you mark that?

LADY MACBETH   The Thane of Fife had a wife. Where is she now? What, will these hands ne'er be clean? No more o'that, my lord, no more o'that. You mar all with this starting.   40

---

7. **fast**: deep.
9. **do . . . watching**: act as if she were awake.
13. **meet**: fitting.
15. **SD** *taper*: candle.
16. **very guise**: exact manner or conduct.
17. **close**: concealed.
22. **their . . . shut**: they are unseeing.
28. **set**: write.
29. **satisfy**: confirm.
37. **Thane of Fife**: Macduff.
40. **starting**: flinching.

Asides on what LMc is saying (handwritten margin note)

DOCTOR   Go to, go to. You have known what you should not.

GENTLEWOMAN   She has spoke what she should not, I am sure of that. Heaven knows what she has known.

LADY MACBETH   Here's the smell of the blood still. All the perfumes of Arabia will not sweeten this little hand. Oh, 45 oh, oh!

DOCTOR   What a sigh is there! The heart is sorely charged.

GENTLEWOMAN   I would not have such a heart in my bosom for the dignity of the whole body.

DOCTOR   Well, well, well.   50

GENTLEWOMAN   Pray God it be, sir.

DOCTOR   This disease is beyond my practice. Yet I have known those which have walked in their sleep who have died holily in their beds.

LADY MACBETH   Wash your hands, put on your nightgown, 55 look not so pale. I tell you yet again, Banquo's buried; he cannot come out on's grave.

DOCTOR   Even so?

LADY MACBETH   To bed, to bed. There's knocking at the gate. Come, come, come, come, give me your hand. What's done 60 cannot be undone. To bed, to bed, to bed.

                         Exit LADY MACBETH.

DOCTOR   Will she go now to bed?

GENTLEWOMAN   Directly.

DOCTOR   Foul whisp'rings are abroad. Unnatural deeds
Do breed unnatural troubles. Infected minds   65
To their deaf pillows will discharge their secrets.
More needs she the divine than the physician.
God, God, forgive us all. Look after her;
Remove from her the means of all annoyance,
And still keep eyes upon her. So, good night.   70
My mind she has mated, and amazed my sight.
I think but dare not speak.

GENTLEWOMAN   Good night, good Doctor.

                            Exeunt.

---

41. **Go to**: come on (a mild reprimand).
45. **Arabia**: exotic land known for its spices.
49. **dignity**: high rank (as queen).
57. **on's**: of his.
67. **divine**: clergyman.
69. **annoyance**: harm. (The Doctor seeks to prevent suicide.)
71. **mated**: stupefied.

5.2

Drum and colors. Enter MENTEITH, CAITHNESS,
    ANGUS, LENNOX, *Soldiers.*

MENTEITH   The English power is near, led on by Malcolm,
  His uncle Siward, and the good Macduff.
  Revenges burn in them, for their dear causes
  Would to the bleeding and the grim alarm
  Excite the mortified man.

ANGUS   Near Birnam Wood   5
  Shall we well meet them; that way are they coming.

CAITHNESS   Who knows if Donaldbain be with his brother?

LENNOX   For certain, sir, he is not. I have a file
  Of all the gentry. There is Siward's son
  And many unrough youths that even now   10
  Protest their first of manhood.

MENTEITH   What does the tyrant?

CAITHNESS   Great Dunsinane he strongly fortifies.
  Some say he's mad; others that lesser hate him
  Do call it valiant fury, but for certain
  He cannot buckle his distempered cause   15
  Within the belt of rule.

ANGUS   Now does he feel
  His secret murders sticking on his hands;
  Now minutely revolts upbraid his faith-breach.
  Those he commands move only in command,
  Nothing in love. Now does he feel his title   20
  Hang loose about him, like a giant's robe
  Upon a dwarfish thief.

MENTEITH   Who then shall blame
  His pestered senses to recoil and start,
  When all that is within him does condemn

5.2. Location: country near Dunsinane Hill.
0.1. SD *Drum and colors*: Drummers and flag-carriers.
3. **dear**: deeply felt.
4–5. **Would . . . man**: would stir a dead (**mortified**) man to bloody (**bleeding**) and grim
    battle.
8. **file**: list.
10. **unrough**: unbearded, young.
11. **Protest**: assert publicly; **first**: first evidence.
15. **distempered**: diseased and swollen. (The image of failing to buckle a belt around a
    bloated stomach suggests that Macbeth cannot legally or morally justify his disordered
    regime.)
18. **minutely**: every minute; **upbraid**: rebuke; **faith-breach**: violation of faith and trust.
19. **in command**: out of obligation.
23. **pestered**: tormented.
24. **all . . . him**: Macbeth's conscience.

Itself for being there?

CAITHNESS   Well, march we on   25
To give obedience where 'tis truly owed.
Meet we the med'cine of the sickly weal,
And with him pour we in our country's purge
Each drop of us.
LENNOX   Or so much as it needs
To dew the sovereign flower and drown the weeds.   30
Make we our march towards Birnam.   *Exeunt, marching.*

5.3

Enter MACBETH, DOCTOR, *and Attendants.*
MACBETH   Bring me no more reports. Let them fly all.
Till Birnam Wood remove to Dunsinane
I cannot taint with fear. What's the boy Malcolm?
Was he not born of woman? The spirits that know
All mortal consequences have pronounced me thus: 5
"Fear not, Macbeth. No man that's born of woman
Shall e'er have power upon thee." Then fly, false thanes,
And mingle with the English epicures!
The mind I sway by and the heart I bear
Shall never sag with doubt nor shake with fear.   10
        Enter SERVANT.
The devil damn thee black, thou cream-faced loon!
Where gott'st thou that goose look?
SERVANT   There is ten thousand—
MACBETH   Geese, villain?
SERVANT   Soldiers, sir.
MACBETH   Go prick thy face and over-red thy fear,
Thou lily-livered boy. What soldiers, patch?   15

---

25. **there**: illegitimately in power.
27. **weal**: commonweal.
28. **him**: Malcolm (the medicine for sick Scotland); **pour we**: we pour ourselves (as part of the bloodletting, or **purge** of the country).
30. **sovereign** (1) royal; (2) curative. Malcolm is the **sovereign flower.**
5.3. **Location: Dunsinane Hill. Macbeth's castle.**
1. **them**: deserting thanes.
3. **taint**: become weak.
5. **mortal consequences**: human eventualities.
8. **epicures**: soft lovers of pleasure.
9. **sway**: rule.
11. **black**: the color of damned souls; **loon**: idler.
12. **goose**: stupid.
14. **over-red**: redden over. The servant is pale with fear (**cream-faced**, 11; having **linen cheeks**, 16).
15. **lily-livered**: cowardly. Blood has vacated the servant's liver, seat of passions like courage; **patch**: fool.

Death of thy soul! Those linen cheeks of thine
Are counselors to fear. What soldiers, whey-face?
SERVANT   The English force, so please you.
MACBETH   Take thy face hence.   [*Exit* SERVANT.]
                                    —Seyton! —I am sick at heart,
When I behold—Seyton, I say!—This push   20
Will cheer me ever or disseat me now.
I have lived long enough. My way of life
Is fall'n into the sere, the yellow leaf,
And that which should accompany old age,
As honor, love, obedience, troops of friends,   25
I must not look to have, but in their stead
Curses, not loud but deep, mouth-honor, breath,
Which the poor heart would fain deny and dare not.
—Seyton!
          Enter SEYTON.
SEYTON   What's your gracious pleasure?
MACBETH   What news more?   30
SEYTON   All is confirmed, my lord, which was reported.
MACBETH   I'll fight till from my bones my flesh be hacked.
Give me my armor.
SEYTON   'Tis not needed yet.
MACBETH   I'll put it on.
Send out more horses, skirr the country round,   35
Hang those that talk of fear. Give me mine armor.
—How does your patient, doctor?
DOCTOR   Not so sick, my lord,
As she is troubled with thick-coming fancies
That keep her from her rest.
MACBETH   Cure her of that.
Canst thou not minister to a mind diseased,   40
Pluck from the memory a rooted sorrow,
Raze out the written troubles of the brain,
And with some sweet oblivious antidote
Cleanse the stuffed bosom of that perilous stuff
Which weighs upon the heart?
DOCTOR   Therein the patient   45

16. **of thy**: on thy.
17. **Are . . . fear**: advise others to fear; **whey**: pale (as milk).
20. **behold**: Macbeth does not finish this thought; **push**: enemy advance.
21. **disseat**: dethrone.
23. **sere**: withered.
27. **mouth-honor**: honors given only with the mouth (and not the heart).
28. **fain**: gladly.
35. **skirr**: scour.
42. **Raze out**: erase.
43. **oblivious**: causing forgetfulness.

Must minister to himself.

MACBETH   Throw physic to the dogs! I'll none of it.
   —Come, put mine armor on; give me my staff.
   —Seyton, send out. —Doctor, the thanes fly from me.
   —Come, sir, dispatch. —If thou couldst, Doctor, cast   50
   The water of my land, find her disease,
   And purge it to a sound and pristine health,
   I would applaud thee to the very echo
   That should applaud again. —Pull't off, I say.
   —What rhubarb, senna, or what purgative drug   55
   Would scour these English hence? Hear'st thou of them?
DOCTOR   Ay, my good lord. Your royal preparation
   Makes us hear something.
MACBETH   —Bring it after me.
   I will not be afraid of death and bane
   Till Birnam forest come to Dunsinane.   60
                               Exeunt [all but the DOCTOR].
DOCTOR   Were I from Dunsinane away and clear,
   Profit again should hardly draw me here.   [*Exit.*]

5·4

Drum and colors. Enter MALCOLM, SIWARD, MACDUFF, YOUNG
SIWARD, MENTEITH, CAITHNESS, ANGUS, *and* SOLDIERS,
marching.

MALCOLM   Cousins, I hope the days are near at hand
   That chambers will be safe.
MENTEITH   We doubt it nothing.
SIWARD   What wood is this before us?
MENTEITH   The Wood of Birnam.
MALCOLM   Let every soldier hew him down a bough
   And bear't before him. Thereby shall we shadow   5
   The numbers of our host and make discovery
   Err in report of us.
SOLDIER   It shall be done.

47. **physic**: medicine.
50. **dispatch**: hurry, finish the job (of arming me).
50–51. **cast . . . land**: discover the disease of Scotland. To "cast water" was to diagnose
   by the inspection of urine.
55. **rhubarb, senna**: medicinal plants.
56. **scour**: clear out, purge.
58. **it**: the armor, not yet put on.
59. **bane**: destruction.
5.4. **Location: country near Birnam Wood.**
2. **chambers**: bedchambers, i.e., the homes of citizens; **nothing**: not at all.
5. **shadow**: conceal.
6. **discovery**: scouting information.

SIWARD We learn no other but the confident tyrant
  Keeps still in Dunsinane and will endure
  Our setting down before't.
MALCOLM   'Tis his main hope.   10
  For where there is advantage to be given,
  Both more and less have given him the revolt,
  And none serve with him but constrainèd things
  Whose hearts are absent too.
MACDUFF   Let our just censures
  Attend the true event, and put we on   15
  Industrious soldiership.
SIWARD   The time approaches
  That will with due decision make us know
  What we shall say we have and what we owe.
  Thoughts speculative their unsure hopes relate,
  But certain issue strokes must arbitrate—   20
  Towards which, advance the war.   *Exeunt, marching.*

5·5

  Enter MACBETH, SEYTON, *and Soldiers, with drum and colors.*
MACBETH Hang out our banners on the outward walls.
  The cry is still, "They come!" Our castle's strength
  Will laugh a siege to scorn. Here let them lie
  Till famine and the ague eat them up.
  Were they not forced with those that should be ours,   5
  We might have met them dareful, beard to beard,
  And beat them backward home.
      A cry within of women.
                    What is that noise?
SEYTON It is the cry of women, my good lord.
                                        [*Exit.*]

MACBETH I have almost forgot the taste of fears.
  The time has been my senses would have cooled   10

8. **other**: other news.
9. **Keeps still**: remains yet.
10. **setting down before't**: besieging the castle.
11. **advantage . . . given**: opportunity (to escape).
12. **more and less**: soldiers higher and lower in rank.
14–15. **Let . . . event**: Let our impartial judgment await the actual outcome.
18. What is truly ours and what we owe to another.
19–20. Thoughts now can relate only our hopes; blows must decide the real outcome.
21. **war**: army.
5.5. Location: **Dunsinane Hill. Macbeth's castle.**
4. **ague**: fever.
5. **forced**: reinforced.
6. **dareful**: boldly.
10. **my . . . cooled**: I would have felt cold fear.

To hear a night-shriek, and my fell of hair
Would at a dismal treatise rouse and stir
As life were in't. I have supped full with horrors.
Direness, familiar to my slaughterous thoughts,
Cannot once start me.
     [SEYTON *re-enters.*]
                            Wherefore was that cry?   15
SEYTON   The Queen, my lord, is dead.
MACBETH   She should have died hereafter;
  There would have been a time for such a word.
  Tomorrow and tomorrow and tomorrow
  Creeps in this petty pace from day to day   20
  To the last syllable of recorded time,
  And all our yesterdays have lighted fools
  The way to dusty death. Out, out, brief candle.
  Life's but a walking shadow, a poor player
  That struts and frets his hour upon the stage   25
  And then is heard no more. It is a tale
  Told by an idiot, full of sound and fury,
  Signifying nothing.
      Enter a MESSENGER.
Thou com'st to use thy tongue; thy story quickly.
MESSENGER   Gracious my lord,   30
  I should report that which I say I saw,
  But know not how to do't.
MACBETH   Well, say, sir.
MESSENGER   As I did stand my watch upon the hill,
  I looked toward Birnam, and anon methought
  The wood began to move.
MACBETH   Liar and slave!   35
MESSENGER   Let me endure your wrath if't be not so.
  Within this three mile may you see it coming,
  I say, a moving grove.
MACBETH   If thou speak'st false,

---

11. **fell**: covering, i.e., the hair on my head.
12. **dismal treatise**: dreadful story.
14. **Direness**: horror.
15. **start**: startle; **Wherefore**: why.
17. **should have**: (1) ought to have (at some better time); (2) would have (anyway).
21. **syllable**: bit; **recorded time**: recordable time.
23. **dusty death**: perhaps echoing Genesis 3:19: "for dust thou art, and unto dust shalt thou return"; **candle**: a traditional symbol of life (see Job 18:6, 21:17; Dent CC1, Resources).
24. **Life's . . . shadow**: There are many classical and biblical precedents for the idea, including Job 8.9: "We are but of yesterday and know nothing because our days upon earth are a shadow" (see Dent L249.1, Resources).
25. **stage**: The world as stage is another common metaphor; **frets**: (1) worries; (2) wears out; (3) consumes.

Upon the next tree shall thou hang alive
Till famine cling thee; if thy speech be sooth,   40
I care not if thou dost for me as much.
I pull in resolution and begin
To doubt th'equivocation of the fiend
That lies like truth. "Fear not, till Birnam Wood
Do come to Dunsinane" —and now a wood   45
Comes toward Dunsinane. Arm, arm, and out!
If this which he avouches does appear,
There is nor flying hence nor tarrying here.
I 'gin to be aweary of the sun,
And wish th'estate o'th' world were now undone.   50
Ring the alarum bell! Blow, wind, come, wrack!
At least we'll die with harness on our back.

                                            Exeunt.

5.6

Drum and colors. Enter MALCOLM, SIWARD, MACDUFF, *and
their army, with boughs.*

MALCOLM   Now near enough. Your leafy screens throw down
And show like those you are. You, worthy uncle,
Shall with my cousin, your right noble son,
Lead our first battle. Worthy Macduff and we
Shall take upon's what else remains to do,   5
According to our order.
SIWARD   Fare you well.
Do we but find the tyrant's power tonight,
Let us be beaten if we cannot fight.
MACDUFF   Make all our trumpets speak. Give them all breath,
Those clamorous harbingers of blood and death!   10
                        Exeunt. Alarums continued.

40. **cling**: shrivel; **sooth**: truth.
42. **pull in**: rein in.
47. **avouches**: reports.
49. **'gin**: begin.
50. **estate**: order.
51. **wrack**: ruin.
52. **harness**: armor.
5.6. Location: Dunsinane Hill. Before Macbeth's castle.
2. **show**: show yourselves; **uncle**: Siward (a term of respect).
4. **battle**: battalion.
6. **order**: battle plan.
7. **power**: army.
10. **harbingers**: forerunners.

5·7

Enter MACBETH.

MACBETH   They have tied me to a stake. I cannot fly,
But bear-like I must fight the course. What's he
That was not born of woman? Such a one
Am I to fear, or none.
                    Enter YOUNG SIWARD.

YOUNG SIWARD   What is thy name?

MACBETH   Thou'lt be afraid to hear it.   5

YOUNG SIWARD   No, though thou call'st thyself a hotter name
Than any is in hell.

MACBETH   My name's Macbeth.

YOUNG SIWARD   The devil himself could not pronounce a title
More hateful to mine ear.

MACBETH   No, nor more fearful.

YOUNG SIWARD   Thou liest, abhorrèd tyrant! With my sword   10
I'll prove the lie thou speak'st.
                    Fight, and YOUNG SIWARD *slain.*

MACBETH   Thou wast born of woman.
But swords I smile at, weapons laugh to scorn,
Brandished by man that's of a woman born.
                                        Exit [with the body].
                    Alarums. Enter MACDUFF.

MACDUFF   That way the noise is. Tyrant, show thy face!   15
If thou beest slain and with no stroke of mine,
My wife and children's ghosts will haunt me still.
I cannot strike at wretched kerns, whose arms
Are hired to bear their staves. Either thou, Macbeth,
Or else my sword with an unbattered edge   20
I sheathe again, undeeded. There thou shouldst be;
By this great clatter one of greatest note
Seems bruited. Let me find him, Fortune,
And more I beg not.   *Exit. Alarums.*
                    Enter MALCOLM *and* SIWARD.

SIWARD   This way, my lord. The castle's gently rendered.   25

5.7. Location: Dunsinane Hill. Before Macbeth's castle.
2. **course**: a round in bearbaiting, the blood sport wherein dogs attacked a bear tied to a
    stake (1).
11. **prove . . . speak'st**: prove that you speak a lie.
17. **still**: ever.
18. **kerns**: light-armed foot soldiers.
19. **staves**: lances.
21. **undeeded**: having done nothing.
22. **note**: reputation.
23. **bruited**: noised, indicated.
25. **rendered**: surrendered.

The tyrant's people on both sides do fight;
The noble thanes do bravely in the war;
The day almost itself professes yours,
And little is to do.
MALCOLM   We have met with foes
That strike beside us.
    SIWARD   Enter, sir, the castle.   30

Exeunt. Alarums.

Enter MACBETH.
MACBETH   Why should I play the Roman fool and die
On mine own sword? Whiles I see lives, the gashes
Do better upon them.

Enter MACDUFF.

MACDUFF   Turn, hellhound, turn!
MACBETH   Of all men else I have avoided thee.
But get thee back. My soul is too much charged   35
With blood of thine already.
MACDUFF   I have no words.
My voice is in my sword, thou bloodier villain
Than terms can give thee out!

Fight. Alarums.

MACBETH   Thou losest labor.
As easy mayst thou the intrenchant air
With thy keen sword impress as make me bleed.   40
Let fall thy blade on vulnerable crests.
I bear a charmèd life which must not yield
To one of woman born.
MACDUFF   Despair thy charm,
And let the angel whom thou still hast served
Tell thee, Macduff was from his mother's womb   45
Untimely ripped.
MACBETH   Accursèd be that tongue that tells me so.
For it hath cowed my better part of man.

28. **itself professes**: proclaims itself.
30. **strike beside**: (1) fight on our side; (2) miss intentionally.
30. **SD**: The action is continuous but the cleared stage has led editors to indicate a change
    in scene, perhaps to another part of the battlefield or to a place within the castle.
31. **play . . . fool**: imitate those foolish Romans who commit suicide to avoid dishonor.
32. **lives**: living enemies.
35. **charged**: (1) burdened; (2) accused.
38. **terms**: words; **give . . . out**: describe.
39. **intrenchant**: incapable of being cut.
40. **impress**: leave a mark on.
41. **crests**: heads.
43. **charm**: magic.
44. **angel**: evil spirit (said ironically).
46. **Untimely**: prematurely, by Caesarean section.
48. **better . . . man**: courage.

And be these juggling fiends no more believed,
That palter with us in a double sense,   50
That keep the word of promise to our ear
And break it to our hope. I'll not fight with thee.
MACDUFF   Then yield thee, coward,
And live to be the show and gaze o'th' time.
We'll have thee, as our rarer monsters are,   55
Painted upon a pole and underwrit,
"Here may you see the tyrant."
MACBETH   I will not yield,
To kiss the ground before young Malcolm's feet,
And to be baited with the rabble's curse.
Though Birnam Wood be come to Dunsinane,   60
And thou opposed, being of no woman born,
Yet I will try the last. Before my body
I throw my warlike shield. Lay on, Macduff,
And damned be him that first cries, "Hold, enough!' "
                               Exeunt fighting. Alarums.
         Enter [MACBETH and MACDUFF] fighting, and Macbeth slain.
                    [*Exit MACDUFF with MACBETH's body.*]
         Retreat and flourish. Enter, with drum and colors,
         MALCOLM, SIWARD, ROSS, *Thanes, and Soldiers.*
MALCOLM   I would the friends we miss were safe arrived.   65
SIWARD   Some must go off; and yet, by these I see
So great a day as this is cheaply bought.
MALCOLM   Macduff is missing, and your noble son.
ROSS   Your son, my lord, has paid a soldier's debt.
He only lived but till he was a man,   70
The which no sooner had his prowess confirmed
In the unshrinking station where he fought,
But like a man he died.
SIWARD   Then he is dead?
ROSS   Ay, and brought off the field. Your cause of sorrow

---

49. **juggling**: deceiving.
50. **palter**: equivocate.
51–52. **to . . . hope**: verbally but not in deed.
54. **gaze**: spectacle.
56. Macbeth's picture will be painted on a pole and displayed with an accompanying
description.
59. **baited**: attacked (as by dogs).
62. **last**: (1) my last reserves of strength and courage; (2) the last battle.
64.4. **SD**: The *Retreat* is a sound from a trumpet or drum signaling the concluding stage
of battle. Some editors indicate a new scene here.
66. **go off**: die; **these**: the survivors present.
71. **prowess**: courage.
72. **unshrinking station**: place where he refused to back down.

Must not be measured by his worth, for then   75
  It hath no end.
SIWARD   Had he his hurts before?
ROSS   Ay, on the front.
SIWARD   Why, then, God's soldier be he.
  Had I as many sons as I have hairs,
  I would not wish them to a fairer death.
  And so, his knell is knolled.
MALCOLM   He's worth more sorrow,   80
  And that I'll spend for him.
SIWARD   He's worth no more.
  They say he parted well and paid his score,
  And so, God be with him. Here comes newer comfort.
     Enter MACDUFF *with* MACBETH's *head.*
MACDUFF   Hail, King, for so thou art. Behold where stands
  Th'usurper's cursèd head. The time is free.   85
  I see thee compassed with thy kingdom's pearl,
  That speak my salutation in their minds,
  Whose voices I desire aloud with mine:
  Hail, King of Scotland!
ALL   Hail, King of Scotland!
     Flourish.
MALCOLM   We shall not spend a large expense of time   90
  Before we reckon with your several loves
  And make us even with you. My thanes and kinsmen,
  Henceforth be earls, the first that ever Scotland
  In such an honor named. What's more to do,
  Which would be planted newly with the time,   95
  As calling home our exiled friends abroad
  That fled the snares of watchful tyranny,
  Producing forth the cruel ministers
  Of this dead butcher and his fiend-like queen—
  Who, as 'tis thought, by self and violent hands   100
  Took off her life—this, and what needful else
  That calls upon us, by the grace of grace,

---

76. **before**: on his front (from facing the enemy).
80. **knolled**: rung.
82. **score**: reckoning.
85. **time is free**: a proclamation of liberty from tyranny and the restoration of order in Scotland.
86. **compassed . . . pearl**: surrounded by the treasures of your kingdom, the Scottish nobles.
91. **reckon**: settle accounts.
95. **planted . . . time**: established in this new age.
98. **Producing forth**: leading to justice; **ministers**: agents.
100. **self and violent**: her own violent.
102. **grace of grace**: favor of divine grace.

We will perform in measure, time, and place.
So, thanks to all at once and to each one
Whom we invite to see us crowned at Scone.   105

> *Flourish. Exeunt all.*

Finis.

---

103. **measure**: due proportion.

Textual Notes

These notes record substantive departures from the copy text, i.e., the First Folio (1623). They do not (1) present an historical collation, (2) record correction of obvious typographical errors, (3) document minor movements of stage directions, and (4) indicate changes in lineation and punctuation. The Act and Scene division in this edition follows the Folio. The reading adopted for this Norton Critical Edition appears in boldface below, followed by the rejected reading from the Folio.

Abbreviations used: F the First Folio; SD stage direction; SP speech prefix; *uncorr.* uncorrected

1.1.1 [*and elsewhere*] **SP**: 1.   3 [*and elsewhere*] **SP**: 2.   5 [*and elsewhere*] **SP**: 3.
1.2.13 **galloglasses**: Gallowgrosses
1.3.33 [*and elsewhere*] **weïrd**: weyward [*sometimes* "weyard"]
40 **Forres**: Soris   58 **rapt**: wrapt   72 **Finel's**: *Sinells*   98 **hail**: Tale   99 **Came**: Can
1.5.1 **SP** [*and elsewhere*]: Lady [*sometimes* "*Wife*"].   15 **human**: humane
45 **it**: hit
1.6.4 **martlet**: Barlet   13 **God 'ield**: God-eyld
1.7.6 **shoal**: Schoole   28 **other—**: other.   47 **do**: no
2.1.55 **strides**: sides   56 **sure**: sowre   57 **way they**: they may
2.2.66 **green one red**: Greene one, Red
2.3.138 **nearer**: neere
2.4.18 **ate**: eat   41 [*and elsewhere*] **SD** *all*: *omnes*
3.1.10. **SD** LADY [MACBETH *as Queen,*] LENNOX: *Lady Lenox*   74 [*and elsewhere*] **SP**: *Murth.*   94 **clept**: clipt
3.3.1 [*and elsewhere*] **SP**: 1. 2 [*and elsewhere*] **SP**: 3. 3. [*and elsewhere*] **SP**: 2.
7 **and**: end
3.4.14 [*and elsewhere*] **SP**: *Mur.* 123 **SD** *Exeunt*: *Exit* 146 **in deed**: indeed
3.6.24 **son**: Sonnes 38 **the**: their
4.1.48 [*and elsewhere*] **SP**: *All.* 58 **germens**: Germaine 58 **all together**: altogether 92 **Dunsinane**: Dunsmane 93 **SD**: *Descend.* 112 **heir**: haire 118 **eighth**: eight 129 **antic**: Antique
4.2.22 **none**: moue 70 **Whither**: Whether 80 **shag-haired**: shagge-ear'd
4.3.15 **deserve**: discerne 34 **affeered**: affear'd 34 **Fare**: Far 107 **accused**: accust 133 **thy**: they 154 **on with**: on my with [F *uncorr.*] 160 **not**: nor 168 **rend**: rent 213 **SP** ROSS: Roffe [F *uncorr.*] 235 **tune**: time
5.3.39 **Cure her**: Cure 55 **senna**: Cyme
5.4.0.1–2 [*and elsewhere*] **SD** YOUNG SIWARD: *Seywards Sonne* 3 [*and elsewhere*] **SP**: *Syew.* [*sometimes* "*Syw.*" *and* "*Sey.*"]
5.7.30 [*and elsewhere*] **SD** *Alarums*: *Alarum*

THE ACTORS' GALLERY

DAVID GARRICK

Letter (1762)†

"Shakes so my single" [1.3.142]

If I stop at the last word ["single"], it is a glaring fault for the sense is imperfect; but my idea of that passage is this: Macbeth is absorbed in thought and struck with the horror of the murder, though but in idea ("fantastical"), and it naturally gives him a slow, tremulous under-tone of voice; and though it might appear that I stopped at every word in the line more than usual, yet my intention was far from dividing the substantive ["state"] from its adjective ["single"], but to paint the horror of Macbeth's mind and keep the voice suspended a little, which it will naturally be in such a situation.

* * *

My notions, as well as execution of the lines in the second appearance of Banquo, are, I fear, opposite to your opinion. Should Macbeth sink into pusillanimity, I imagine that it would hurt the character and be contrary to the intentions of Shakespeare—the first appearance of the Spirit overpowers him more than the second; but even before it vanishes at first, Macbeth gains strength: "If thou canst nod, speak too" [3.4.71] must be spoke with horror, but with a recovering mind; and in the next speech with him, he cannot pronounce "Avaunt, and quit my sight!" [95] without a stronger exertion of his powers, under the circumstance of horror. The "Why so, being gone" [109] &c., means in my opinion, "I am a man again, or returning to my senses, which were before mad and inflamed with what I had seen." I make a great difference between a mind sunk by guilt into cowardice, and one rising with horror to acts of madness and desperation, which last I take to be the case of Macbeth. I certainly (as you say) recollect a degree of resolution, but I never advance an inch, for notwithstanding my agitation, my feet are immovable.

* * *

† From *The Private Correspondence of David Garrick*, ed. James Boaden, 2 vols. (London: H. Colburn and R. Bentley, 1831–32), 1: 135–37. Book collector, editor, adapter, actor, and bardolator, David Garrick (1717–1779) first played *Macbeth* in 1744. He created a new acting text based on the Folio and tried for a more realistic acting style to portray Macbeth as a heroic man who succumbs to ambition and guilt. This is his reply to a letter discussing his performance from H. H., perhaps Hall Harson, a contemporary poet and dramatist.

David Garrick and Hannah Pritchard in *Lady Macbeth Seizing the Daggers* by Henry Fuseli (1812). Courtesy of akg-images/De Agostini Picture Library.

I quite agree with you about "Out, out, brief candle" [5.5.23], but surely I must have spoke those words quite the reverse of my own ideas, if I did not express with them the most contemptuous indifference of life.

THOMAS DAVIES

From Dramatic Miscellanies (1783)[†]

"Is this a dagger which I see before me!" [2.1.33]

Many stage critics suppose this to be one of the most difficult situations in acting. The sudden start on seeing the dagger in the air, the endeavour of the actor to seize it, the disappointment, the suggestion of its being only a vision of the disturbed fancy, the seeing

[†] From *Dramatic Micellanies: Consisting of Critical Observations on Several Plays of Shakespeare*, 3 vols. (Dublin, 1783–84), 2: 88, 92–94, 105–106. Thomas Davies (1712–1785) wrote a biography of Garrick and critical observations on the theater of his day. Here he recalls Garrick's sensitive Macbeth and the fierce Lady Macbeth of Hannah Pritchard (1711–1768).

it still in form most palpable, with the reasoning upon it—these are difficulties which the mind of Garrick was capable of encountering and subduing. So happy did he think himself in the exhibition of this scene, that, when he was in Italy, and requested by the duke of Parma to give a proof of his skill in action,[1] to the admiration of that prince, he at once threw himself into the attitude of Macbeth's seeing the air-drawn dagger. The duke desired no farther proof of Garrick's great excellence in his profession, being perfectly convinced, by this specimen, that he was an absolute master of it.

* * *

"To know my deed 'twere best not know myself." [2.2.76]

"Whilst I am conscious of having committed this murder, I cannot but be miserable; I have no remedy but in the total forgetfulness of the deed, or, to speak more plainly, in the loss of my senses."

The merit of this scene transcends all panegyric. Amongst the many discourses which, from the earliest time to the present hour, have been composed on the subject of murder, it will be difficult to find so powerful a dissuasive or dehortation[2] from that dreadful crime as the tragedy of Macbeth exhibits. In drawing the principal character of the play, the author has deviated somewhat from history; but by abating the fierceness of Macbeth's disposition he has rendered him a fitter subject for the drama. The rational and severe delight which the spectator feels from the representation of this piece proceeds in a great measure from the sensibility of the murderer, from his remorse and agonies, and from the torments he suffers in the midst of his successful villainy.

The representation of this terrible part of the play by Garrick and Mrs. Pritchard can no more be described than I believe it can be equalled. I will not separate these performers for the merits of both were transcendent. His distraction of mind and agonizing horrors were finely contrasted by her seeming apathy, tranquillity, and confidence. The beginning of the scene after the murder was conducted in terrifying whispers. Their looks and action supplied the place of words. You heard what they spoke, but you learned more from the agitation of mind displayed in their action and deportment. The poet here gives only an outline to the consummate actor. "I have done the deed!—Didst thou not hear a noise?—When?— Did you not speak?" [2.2.14ff.]. The dark colouring given by the actor to these abrupt speeches makes the scene awful and tremendous to the auditors! The wonderful expression of heartful horror,

1. Acting.
2. Argument against.

which Garrick felt when he showed his bloody hands, can only be
conceived and described by those who saw him!

*　*　*

This admirable scene [3.4] was greatly supported by the speaking
terrors of Garrick's look and action. Mrs. Pritchard showed admirable art in endeavouring to hide Macbeth's frenzy from the observation of the guests by drawing their attention to conviviality. She
smiled on one, whispered to another, and distantly saluted a third;
in short, she practiced every possible artifice to hide the transaction
that passed between her husband and the vision his disturbed
imagination had raised. Her reproving and angry looks, which
glanced toward Macbeth, at the same time were mixed with marks
of inward vexation and uneasiness. When, at last, as if unable to
support her feelings any longer, she rose from her seat and seized
his arm and with a half-whisper of terror said, "Are you a man!"
[59], she assumed a look of such anger, indignation, and contempt
as cannot be surpassed.

DAVID GARRICK

Garrick's *Macbeth* (1761)†

'Tis done! The scene of life will quickly close.
Ambition's vain, delusive dreams are fled,
And now I wake to darkness, guilt and horror.
I cannot bear it! Let me shake it off.
'Twa not be; my soul is clogged with blood.
And cannot rise! I dare not ask for mercy!
It is too late, hell drags me down. I sink,
I sink! Oh, my soul's lost forever! (*Dies*).

† From *The Historical Tragedy of Macbeth* (Dublin, 1761), sig. L2. Garrick's acting edition
dispensed with most of Davenant's additions to the text of *Macbeth* but also gave Macbeth this final speech on the perils of ambition. One observer commented: "The
approach of death showed each instant on his face; his eyes became dim, his voice
could not support the efforts he made to speak his thoughts . . . his legs gave way under
him, his face lengthened, his pale and livid features bore the signs of suffering and
repentance. At last, he fell; . . . His plight made the audience shudder, he clawed the
ground and seemed to be digging his own grave . . . The death rattle and the convulsive
movement of the features, arms and breast, gave the final touch to this terrible picture," Jean Georges Noverre, *Letters on Dancing and Ballets*, trans. Cyril W. Beaumont
(Brooklyn: Dance Horizons, 1966), 84–85.

SARAH SIDDONS

[On Playing Lady Macbeth] (1834)†

It was my custom to study my characters at night, when all the domestic cares and business of the day were over. On the night preceding that in which I was to appear in this part for the first time, I shut myself up, as usual, when all the family were retired, and commenced my study of Lady Macbeth. As the character is very short, I thought I should soon accomplish it. Being then only twenty years of age, I believed, as many others do believe, that little more was necessary than to get the words into my head; for the necessity of discrimination and the development of character at that time of my life had scarcely entered into my imagination. But, to proceed. I went on with tolerable composure, in the silence of the night (a night I never can forget) till I came to the assassination scene, when the horrors of the scene rose to a degree that made it impossible for me to get farther. I snatched up my candle and hurried out of the room in a paroxysm of terror. My dress was of silk and the rustling of it as I ascended the stairs to go to bed seemed to my panic-struck fancy like the movement of a spectre pursuing me. At last I reached my chamber, where I found my husband fast asleep. I clapt my candlestick down upon the table, without the power of putting the candle out, and I threw myself on my bed, without daring to stay even to take off my clothes. At peep of day I rose to resume my task; but so little did I know of my part when I appeared in it at night that my shame and confusion cured me of procrastinating my business for the remainder of my life.

About six years afterwards I was called upon to act the same character in London. By this time I had perceived the difficulty of assuming a personage with whom no one feeling of common general nature was congenial or assistant. One's own heart could prompt one to express with some degree of truth the sentiments of a mother, a daughter, a wife, a lover, a sister, &c., but, to adopt this character must be an effort of the judgment alone.

Therefore it was with the utmost diffidence, nay terror, that I undertook it, and with the additional fear of Mrs. Pritchard's[1]

---

† From Thomas Campbell, *The Life of Mrs. Siddons*, 2 vols. (London: Effingham Wilson, 1834), 2: 35–39, 10–12, 15–16, 20–21, 31–33. Perhaps the most celebrated Lady Macbeth, the statuesque Sarah Siddons (1755–1831) acted the role from 1781 to 1817, portraying both fragile femininity and brutal power.

1. Hannah Pritchard (1711–1768), whose angry and imposing Lady Macbeth won great admiration previously (see Davies' account above, 88–90).

Mrs. Siddons as the Tragic Muse by Joshua Reynolds (1783).

reputation in it before my eyes. The dreaded first night at length arrived, when, just as I had finished my toilette, and was pondering with fearfulness my first appearance in the grand fiendish part, comes Mr. Sheridan,[2] knocking at my door and insisting, in spite of all my entreaties not to be interrupted at this to me tremendous moment, to be admitted. He would not be denied admittance, for he protested he must speak to me on a circumstance which so deeply concerned my own interest that it was of the most serious nature. Well, after much squabbling, I was compelled to admit him that I might dismiss him the sooner and compose myself before the play began. But, what was my distress and astonishment when I found that he wanted me, even at this moment of anxiety and terror, to adopt another mode of acting the sleeping scene. He told me he had heard with the greatest surprise and concern that I meant to act it without holding the candle in my hand; and when I urged the impracticability of washing out that "damned spot" with the vehemence that was certainly implied by both her own words and by those of her gentlewoman, he insisted that if I did put the candle out of my hand, it would be thought a presumptuous innovation, as Mrs. Pritchard had always retained it in hers. My mind, however, was made up, and it was then too late to make me alter it; for I was too agitated to adopt another method. My deference for Mr. Sheridan's taste and judgment was, however, so great that, had he proposed the alteration whilst it was possible for me to change my own plan, I should have yielded to his suggestion; though, even then, it would have been against my own opinion and my observation of the accuracy with which somnambulists perform all the acts of waking persons. The scene, of course, was acted as I had myself conceived it, and the innovation, as Mr. Sheridan called it, was received with approbation.[3] Mr. Sheridan himself came to me after the play and most ingenuously congratulated me on my obstinacy. When he was gone out of the room I began to undress, and, while standing up before my glass, and taking off my mantle, a diverting circumstance occurred, to chase away the feelings of this anxious night; for while I was repeating and endeavouring to call to mind the appropriate tone and action to the following words, "Here's the smell of blood still!" [5.1.44], my dresser innocently exclaimed, "Dear me, ma'am, how very hysterical you are tonight; I protest and vow, ma'am, it was not blood but rose-pink[4] and water, for I saw the property-man mix it up with my own eyes."

2. Richard Brinsley Sheridan (1751–1816), actor, statesman, dramatist (*The Rivals, The School for Scandal*) and manager of Drury Lane Theater.
3. Siddons's portrayal of Lady Macbeth in this scene has influenced many other actresses.
4. Pink or red pigment used for stage effects.

Remarks on the Character of Lady Macbeth

In this astonishing creature one sees a woman in whose bosom the passion of ambition has almost obliterated all the characteristics of human nature; in whose composition are associated all the sub-jugating powers of intellect and all the charms and graces of personal beauty. You will probably not agree with me as to the character of that beauty; yet, perhaps, this difference of opinion will be entirely attributable to the difficulty of your imagination disengaging itself from that idea of the person of her representative which you have been so long accustomed to contemplate.[5] According to my notion, it is of that character which I believe is generally allowed to be most captivating to the other sex—fair, feminine, nay, perhaps, even fragile—

> Fair as the forms that, wove in Fancy's loom,
> Float in light visions round the poet's head.[6]

Such a combination only, respectable in energy and strength of mind, and captivating in feminine loveliness, could have composed a charm of such potency as to fascinate the mind of a hero so dauntless, a character so amiable, so honourable as Macbeth, to seduce him to brave all the dangers of the present and all the terrors of a future world; and we are constrained, even whilst we abhor his crimes, to pity the infatuated victim of such a thralldom. His letters, which have informed her of the predictions of those preternatural beings who accosted him on the heath, have lighted up into daring and desperate determinations all those pernicious slumbering fires which the enemy of man is ever watchful to awaken in the bosoms of his unwary victims. To his direful suggestions she is so far from offering the least opposition, as not only to yield up her soul to them, but moreover to invoke the sightless ministers of remorseless cruelty to extinguish in her breast all those compunctious visitings of nature which otherwise might have been mercifully interposed to counteract, and perhaps eventually to overcome, their unholy instigations. But having impiously delivered herself up to the excitements of hell, the pitifulness of heaven itself is withdrawn from her, and she is abandoned to the guidance of the demons whom she has invoked.

*   *   *

It is very remarkable that Macbeth is frequent in expressions of tenderness to his wife, while she never betrays one symptom of affection towards him, till, in the fiery furnace of affliction her

---

5. Pritchard, whom Siddons purposefully plays against.
6. From William Mason, "Elegy V: On the Death of a Lady" (1760).

iron heart is melted down to softness. For the present she flies to welcome the venerable gracious Duncan with such a show of eagerness as if allegiance in her bosom sat crowned with devotion and gratitude.

* * *

In the tremendous suspense of these moments [2.2], while she recollects her habitual humanity, one trait of tender feeling is expressed, "Had he not resembled my father as he slept, I had done it" [12–13]. Her humanity vanishes, however, in the same instant; for when she observes that Macbeth, in the terror and confusion of his faculties, has brought the daggers from the place where they had agreed they should remain for the crimination of the grooms, she exhorts him to return with them to that place and to smear those attendants of the sovereign with blood. He, shuddering, exclaims, "I'll go no more! I am affear'd to think of what I have done. Look on't again I dare not" [53–55].

Then instantaneously the solitary particle of her human feeling is swallowed up in her remorseless ambition, and, wrenching the daggers from the feeble grasp of her husband, she finishes the act which the infirm of purpose had not courage to complete, and calmly and steadily returns to her accomplice with the fiend-like boast,

> My hands are of your colour;
> But I would scorn to wear a heart so white. [67–68]

A knocking at the gate interrupts this terrific[7] dialogue; and all that now occupies her mind is urging him to wash his hands and put on his nightgown, "lest occasion call," says she, "and show us to be the watchers" [73–74]. In a deplorable depravation of all rational knowledge, and lost to every recollection except that of his enormous guilt, she hurries him away to their own chamber.

* * *

Now, it is not possible that she should hear all these ambiguous hints about Banquo [3.2.35ff.] without being too well aware that a sudden, lamentable fate awaits him. Yet, so far from offering any opposition to Macbeth's murderous designs, she even hints, I think, at the facility, if not the expediency, of destroying both Banquo and his equally unoffending child, when she observes that, "in them Nature's copy is not eterne" [37]. Having, therefore, now filled the measure of her crimes, I have imagined that the last appearance of Banquo's ghost became no less visible to her eyes than it became to

---

7. Terrifying.

those of her husband. Yes, the spirit of the noble Banquo has smil-
ingly filled up, even to overflowing, and now commends to her own
lips the ingredients of her poisoned chalice.

The Fifth Act

Behold her now, with wasted form, with wan and haggard countenance, her starry eyes glazed with the ever-burning fever of remorse,
and on their lids the shadows of death. Her ever-restless spirit wanders in troubled dreams about her dismal apartment; and, whether
waking or asleep, the smell of innocent blood incessantly haunts
her imagination:

> Here's the smell of the blood still. All the perfumes of Arabia
> will not sweeten this little hand. [5.1.43–44]

How beautifully contrasted is this exclamation with the bolder
image of Macbeth in expressing the same feeling!

> Will all great Neptune's ocean wash the blood
> Clean from this hand? [2.2.63–64]

And how appropriately either sex illustrates the same idea!

During this appalling scene [5.1], which, to my sense, is the most
so of them all, the wretched creature, in imagination, acts over
again the accumulated horrors of her whole conduct. These dreadful images, accompanied with the agitations they have induced,
have obviously accelerated her untimely end; for in a few moments
the tidings of her death are brought to her unhappy husband. It is
conjectured that she died by her own hand. Too certain it is that she
dies and makes no sign. I have now to account to you for the weakness which I have, a few lines back, ascribed to Macbeth; and I am
not quite without hope that the following observations will bear me
out in my opinion. Please to observe, that he (I must think pusillani-
mously, when I compare his conduct to her forbearance) has been
continually pouring out his miseries to his wife. His heart has therefore been eased from time to time by unloading its weight of woe,
while she, on the contrary, has perseveringly endured in silence the
uttermost anguish of a wounded spirit.

> The grief that does not speak
> Whispers the o'erfraught heart, and bids it break.
> [4.3.209–10]

Her feminine nature, her delicate structure, it is too evident, are
soon overwhelmed by the enormous pressure of her crimes. Yet it
will be granted that she gives proofs of a naturally higher toned
mind than that of Macbeth. The different physical powers of the

two sexes are finely delineated in the different effects which their mutual crimes produce. Her frailer frame and keener feelings have now sunk under the struggle—his robust and less sensitive constitution has not only resisted it, but bears him on to deeper wickedness, and to experience the fatal fecundity of crime.

G. J. BELL

Notes on Siddons's Lady Macbeth (1809)[†]

When you see Mrs. Siddons play this part you scarcely can believe that any acting could make her part subordinate. Her turbulent and inhuman strength of spirit does all. She turns Macbeth to her purpose, makes him her mere instrument, guides, directs, and inspires the whole plot. Like Macbeth's evil genius she hurries him on in the mad career of ambition and cruelty from which his nature would have shrunk. The flagging of her spirit, the melancholy and dismal blank[1] beginning to steal upon her, is one of the finest lessons of the drama.

> O, never\ . . .
> (never) Shall sun that morrow see.\! [1.5.58–59]

"O never\." A long pause, turned from him, her eye steadfast. Strong dwelling emphasis on "never," with deep downward inflection, "never shall sun that morrow see!" Low, very slow sustained voice, her eye and her mind occupied steadfastly in the contemplation of her horrible purpose, pronunciation almost syllabic, not unvaried. Her self-collected solemn energy, her fixed posture, her determined eye and full deep voice of fixed resolve never should be forgot, cannot be conceived nor described.

> We fail.\ [1.7.59]

Not surprise, strong downward inflection, bowing with her hands down, the palm upward.[2] Then voice of strong assurance, "When

---

[†] G. J. Bell, professor of Scottish law in Edinburgh, wrote down observations on Siddons's performances, even marking the rise (/) and fall (\) of her voice. I quote Bell as preserved by H. C. Fleeming Jenkin, "Sarah Siddons as Lady Macbeth and Queen Katherine, with an introduction by Brander Matthews," *Publications of the Dramatic Museum of Columbia University*, 2nd Series, *Papers on Acting* 3 (New York: Corlies, Macy and Co., 1915), 35–36, 43, 48–49.

1. Vacancy.

2. "Her celebrated delivery of 'We fail' (*Macbeth*) was in opposition to the opinion of all the actors of that day. It had been usual, when Macbeth said, 'What if we fail?' to reply, 'We fail?' as scouting the possibility of a failure. But Mrs. Siddons's reading expressed the calm mildness of a mind prepared for the worst; why, then, 'We fail,' and there an end," *Famous Actors: Biographies and Portraits reprinted and reproduced from Oxberry's "Dramatic Biography"* [1825–26] (Edinburgh: W. H. White and Co., 1894), 127.

Duncan," &c. This spoken near to him, and in a low earnest whisper of discovery she discloses her plans.

A limbeck only. [1.7.67]

Pauses as if trying the effect on him. Then renews her plan more earnestly, low still, but with increasing confidence. Throughout this scene she feels her way, observes the wavering of his mind, suits her earnestness and whole manner to it. With contempt, affection, reason, the conviction of her well-concerted plan, the assurance of success which her wonderful tones inspire, she turns him to her purpose with an art in which the player shares largely in the poet's praise.

EDWIN FORREST

Letters (1849, 1860)[†]

[New York] 11 May 1849
My Dear Oakes,[1]

I cannot sufficiently thank you for the generous proffer which you have made and, should occasion require, I shall most gratefully accept your services. If you have read the succeeding number of the print to which you refer, you will perceive that the creature who penned the falsehood has eaten his own words.[2] I most sincerely regret to say that last night, the

---

† Letters to James Oakes (1849–1872), folder one (1849–63), Princeton University Special Collections, C0721. Reprinted with permission of Princeton University Press. The rivalry between American Edwin Forrest and the English Shakespearean William Macready culminated on one fateful night in New York, May 10, 1849, when an Anglophobe mob attacked the Astor Place Theatre where Macready was performing Macbeth. (Earlier in the week enthusiastic partisans had applauded Forrest's Macbeth on Broadway.) In the ensuing melee between twenty-six and thirty were killed and many more wounded. Nigel Cliff admirably explicates the many factors behind the riot: "A personal, a local, and an international feud had all converged in one fraught moment. Macready's determination to make the theatre respectable had made him the archetype of the Victorian Englishman. Forrest's frontier populism had made him the hero of the new America. The theatre's central place in both British and American culture had thrust the two actors onto an international stage, the competitiveness of their profession had fostered a jealous rivalry, and years of being stars had excised a sense of proportion from both men. English abuse had worn America's patience thin, and American expansionism and indebtedness had raised England's hackles. The wealth of New York's elite had incensed its increasingly impoverished workers, and the power of the gangs had made organized violence a demonstrable threat. Even Forrest's marital troubles and the election of an inexperienced Whig mayor had added to the crisis. Not least of all, America's conflicted relationship with its heritage had split the nation into two opposing camps, and both were determined to claim Shakespeare as their own," *The Shakespeare Riots* (New York: Random House, 2007), 208.
1. James Oakes, Boston merchant, lifelong friend and correspondent of Forrest.
2. The *Courier* newspaper named Forrest as the instigator of the week's earlier demonstration (May 7, 1849) against Macready, where audiences pelted his Macbeth with eggs and rotten vegetables. Forrest's lawyer threatened a libel suit and the paper quickly retracted the charge.

military fired upon the people who were standing outside the Astor House Theatre and several were killed and many wounded. This blood will rest on the heads of the Committee[3] who insisted that Mr. Macready should perform in despite of the known wishes of the people to the contrary,[4] and on the hands of the public authorities who were requested by many of the citizens to close the house and thereby prevent any further demonstration.

I shall have a bed for you at Font Hill in the course of a few weeks, when I shall send you a formal invitation to pass some days with me at the place.

I shall not perform in Boston during the present seasons.

> With feelings of sincerest friendship I am yours,
> Edwin Forrest

Baltimore, 29 August 1860
My Dear Oakes,

I have received your letter and you say right. Friendship is as much prostituted as art. My heart is sick and I grow aweary of life.[5]

> Truly Yours,
> Edwin Forrest

WILLIAM MACREADY

From Reminiscences (1849)[†]

New York, May 7. "Rehearsed with much care. . . . Rested. Went to [Astor Place] theatre, dressed. My hairdresser told me there would be a good house, for there was—an unusual sight—a great crowd outside. My call came; I heard immense applause and three cheers for Mr [C. W.] Clarke in Macduff [In the acting version used by Macready, Macduff spoke Ross's lines in Act I, scene ii.]. I smiled and said to myself, 'They mistake him for me.' I went on—the greatest applause, as it seemed, from the whole house. I bowed

---

3. After the May 7 debacle, the Committee, a group of forty-eight prominent New Yorkers, including Washington Irving and Herman Melville, petitioned Macready to continue his performances.
4. Most of the people in the theatre were Macready supporters; demagogic opponents, however, had bought blocks of tickets for gang members and instructed them to show their patriotism by disrupting the performance.
5. Compare *Macbeth*: "I 'gin to be aweary of the sun" (5.5.49).
† From *Macready's Reminiscences and Selections from his Diaries and Letters*, ed. Sir Frederick Pollock (New York: Macmillan and Co., 1875), 614–20. Bracketed material in the text is by Sir Frederick Pollock.

respectfully, repeatedly. It still kept on. I bowed, as it were, emphatically (to coin an expression for a bow), rather significantly that I was touched by such a demonstration; it continued. I thought, 'This is becoming too much.' It did not cease, and I began to distinguish howlings from the right corner of the parquet. Still, I thought, it is only like the Western shriek—a climax of their applause. At length I became sensible there was opposition, and that the prolongation of the applause was the struggle against it; I then waited for its subsidence, but no cessation; I at last walked forward to address them, intending to say—'I felt pain and shame, which the intelligent and respectable must feel for their country's reputation, and that I would instantly resign my engagement rather than encounter such disgraceful conduct.'

"They would not let me speak. They hung out placards—'You have been proved a liar,' etc., flung a rotten egg close to me. I pointed it to the audience and smiled with contempt, persisting in my endeavour to be heard. I could not have been less than a quarter of an hour on the stage altogether, with perfect *sang-froid* and good humour reposing in my consciousness of my own truth. At last there as nothing for it and I said, 'Go on,' and the play *Macbeth* proceeded in dumb show, I hurrying the players on. Copper cents were thrown, some struck me, four or five eggs, a great many apples, nearly, if not quite, a peck of potatoes, lemons, pieces of wood, a bottle of asafoetida[1] which splashed my own dress, smelling, of course, most horribly. The first act, at least in my scenes, with these accompaniments, passed in dumb show; I looking directly at these men as they committed these outrages, and no way moved by them. Behind the scenes some attempted to exhibit sympathy which I received very loftily, observing, 'My concern was for the disgrace such people inflicted on the character of the country.' The second act closed in exactly the same way. I dressed for the third and went on; the tumult was the same, the missiles growing thicker. At last a chair was thrown from the gallery on the stage, something heavy was thrown into the orchestra (a chair), which made the remaining musicians move out. Another chair was hurled by the same man, whom I saw deliberately throw it, then wrench up another, and throw it too. I bowed to the audience, and going up to Mr Chippendale, observed that I thought 'I had quite fulfilled my obligation to Messrs Niblo and Hackett, and that I should now remain no longer.'

"I accordingly went down and undressed; Colden was there, and seemed to apprehend danger out of doors; I did not. However, I

---

1. a pungent herb reduction.

took my dirk,[2] but thinking it unworthy to carry it, threw it down again. Colden (who made too much of it), Tallmadge [Recorder of New York], and Emmett walked back home with me [This was Robert Emmett, nephew of the Irish patriot of the same name.]; there was no sign of any attempt in the back street, but there was a crowd at the front door, which Colden had not been able to penetrate, and which the Chief of the Police [G. W. Matsell] informed me afterwards, made the strongest efforts to break into the house."

*   *   *

[Macready decided not to act that night and was disinclined to appear again. But a petition signed by forty-seven leading New Yorkers (including David Colden, Washington Irving, and Herman Melville) urged him to stay; eventually he agreed to repeat Macbeth on 10 May. That morning hand-bills throughout New York asked simply: "Working men! Shall Americans or English rule in this city?" and went on: "The crew of the English steamer has threatened all Americans who shall dare to express their opinion this night at the English Aristocratic Opera House! We advocate no violence, but a free expression of opinion to all public men!" This was signed "American Committee," here used as a cover not only for supporters of Forrest but also for various fanatical societies advocating "America for the Americans."]

10 May. "The Recorder called, Mr. Tallmadge, and assured me that every measure should be taken to insure the tranquillity of the house tonight, etc. . . . I was going to the theatre to rehearsal; went there; saw the performers, all in good spirits; ran through the scenes of Macbeth for fear the excitement of Monday night might have put the business from their memories. Spoke with Messrs Sefton and Chippendale, expressing my own opinion that there would not be the slightest demonstration of opposition. They thought there might be a hiss or perhaps two at the beginning, but that it could be instantly silenced. . . . [William Henry Chippendale, 1801–1888, who acted in America between 1836 and 1853. On his return to London he spent nearly two decades at the Haymarket.]

"I went gaily, I may say, to the theatre, and on my way, looking down Astor Place, saw one of the Harlem cars on the railroad stop and discharge a full load of policemen; there seemed to be others at the door of the theatre. I observed to myself, 'This is a good precaution.' I went to my dressing-room, and proceeded with the evening's business. The hairdresser was very late and my equanimity was disturbed. I was ruffled and nervous from fear of being late, but soon

2. dagger.

composed myself. The managers were delaying the beginning, and I was unwilling to be behind the exact hour.

"The play began; there was some applause for Mr. Clarke (I write of what I could hear in my room below). I was called, and at my cue went on with full assurance, confidence, and cheerfulness. My reception was very enthusiastic, but I soon discovered that there was opposition, though less numerously manned than on Monday. I went right on when I found that it would not instantly be quelled, looking at the wretched creatures in the parquet, who shook their fists violently at me, and called out to me in savage fury. I laughed at them, pointing them out with my truncheon to the police, who, I feared, were about to repeat the inertia of the previous evening. A blackboard with white letters was leaned against the side of the proscenium: 'The friends of order will remain silent.' This had some effect in making the rioters more conspicuous.

"My first, second, third scenes passed over rapidly and unheard; at the end of the fourth one of the officers gave a signal, the police rushed in at the two sides of the parquet, closed in upon the scoundrels occupying the central seats and furiously vociferating and gesticulating, and seemed to lift them or bundle them in a body out of the centre of the house, amid the cheers of the audience. I was in the act of making my exit with Lady Macbeth, and stopped to witness this clever manoeuvre, which, like a *coup de main*, swept the place clear at once. As well as I can remember, the bombardment outside now began. Stones were hurled against the windows in Eighth Street, smashing many. The work of destruction became then more systematic. The volleys of stones flew without intermission, battering and smashing all before them; the Gallery and Upper Gallery still kept up the din within, aided by the crashing of glass and boarding without. The second act passed, the noise and violence without increasing, the contest within becoming feebler. Mr. Povey, as I was going to my raised seat in the banquet scene, came up to me and, in an undertone and much frightened, urged me to cut out some part of the play and bring it to a close. I turned round upon him very sharply and said that I had consented to do this thing, to place myself here, and whatever the consequence I must go through with it, it must be done, that I could not cut out. The audience had paid for so much and the law compelled me to give it; they would have cause for riot if it were not all properly done. I was angry, and spoke very sharply to the above effect.

"The banquet scene was partially heard and applauded. I went down to change my dress, the battering at the building, doors, and windows growing, like the fiends at Old Woman of Berkeley's burial,[3] louder and louder. Water was running down fast from the ceiling to the floor of my room and making a pool there. I inquired; the stones hurled in had broken some of the pipes. The fourth act passed; louder and more fierce waxed the furious noises against the building and from without; for whenever a missile did effectual mischief in its discharge it was hailed with shouts outside; stones came in through the windows and one struck the chandelier; the audience removed for protection behind the walls; the house was considerably thinned, gaps of unoccupied seats appearing in the audience part.

"The fifth act was heard, and in the very spirit of resistance I flung my whole soul into every word I uttered, acting my very best and exciting the audience to a sympathy even with the glowing words of fiction, whilst these dreadful deeds of real crime and outrage were roaring at intervals in our ears and rising to madness all round us. The death of Macbeth was loudly cheered, and on being lifted up and told that I was called, I went on, and with action earnestly and most emphatically expressive of my sympathy with them and my feelings of gratefulness to them, I quitted the New York stage among the acclamations of those before me.

"Going to my room I began without loss of time to undress, but with no feeling of fear or apprehension. When washed and half dressed, people came into my room—consternation on the faces of some, fear, anxiety, and distress on those of others. 'The mob were getting stronger; why were not the military sent for?' 'They were here.' 'Where?' 'Why did they not act?' 'They were not here; they were drawn up in the Bowery.' 'Of what use were they there?' Other arrivals. 'The military had come upon the ground.' [Soldiers of the Seventh Regiment, cavalry and infantry, more than two hundred in all] 'Why did they not disperse the mob there?' These questions and answers, with many others, were passed to and fro among the persons round me whilst I was finishing my hasty toilet, I occasionally putting in a question or remark. Suddenly we heard a volley of musketry: 'Hark, what's that?' I asked. 'The soldiers have fired.' 'My God!' I exclaimed. Another volley and another! The question among those surrounding me . . . was which way was I to go out? News came that several were killed; I was really insensible to the degree of danger in which I stood, and saw at once—there being no avoidance—there was nothing for it but to meet the worst with dignity, and so I stood prepared.

[Outside, though the Sheriff of New York had given a solemn warning, the mob, mostly youths, pressed in upon the police; the

3. an allusion to a poem by Robert Southey.

cavalrymen, their horses restive and almost unmanageable, had to retire, and the remaining soldiers were penned in a crowd of twenty thousand people on a night of thickening darkness, the street lamps out. Ultimately, firing was imperative; General Hall ordered his men—seventy were left, in front of the theatre—to fire above the heads of the crowd and against a blank wall. The noise carried off his order; soldiers, mishearing, fired straight into the crowd. In spite of casualties, the crowd—believing that blanks were used—still surged forward. This time the soldiers fired low and several men fell. When the rioters attacked again, now in two sections, the troops fired obliquely, one half to the right, one to the left, volleys that caused much of the carnage. At length a space about the theatre was freed; two brass cannon, charged with grape, were brought on, to command Broadway and the Bowery; and slowly the mob began to disperse.]

"They sent some one to reconnoitre, and urged the necessity of a change in my appearance. I was confident that people did not know my person, and repeated this belief. They overbore all objections, and took the drab surtout[4] of the performer of Malcolm, he taking my black one; they insisted, too, that I must not wear my hat; I said, 'Very well; lend me a cap.' Mr Sefton gave me his, which was all cut up the back to go upon my head. Thus equipped I went out, following Robert Emmett to the stage door; here we were stopped, not being allowed to pass. The 'friend' was to follow us as a sort of aide, but we soon lost him. We crossed the stage, descended into the orchestra, got over into the parquet, and passing into the centre passage, went along with the thin stream of the audience moving out. We went right on, down the flight of stairs and out of the door into Eighth Street. All was clear in front—kept so by two cordons or lines of police at either end of the building, stretched right across. We passed the line near Broadway, and went on threading the excited crowd, twice or three times muttering in Emmett's ear, 'You are walking too fast.' We crossed Broadway, still through a scattered crowd, and walked on along Clinton Place till we passed the street leading down to the New York Hotel. . . .

"I sat down in the drawing-room, talking of the facts about us, and wondering at myself and my condition, secretly preparing myself for the worst result, viz., falling into the hands of these sanguinary ruffians. A son of Emmett's was there, Robert; in about a quarter of an hour Colden came in. Several men had been killed, how many not certainly known yet. 'You must leave the city at once; you must not stay here!' It was then a consultation between these excellent friends, I putting in an occasional opinion objecting or suggesting

4. military frock coat.

upon the safest course to pursue. At length it was decided, and Robert was sent out to find Richard, another son, probably at the Racket Club, to put the plan in execution. . . . An omnibus drove furiously down the street, followed by a shouting crowd. We asked Richard, when he came in, what it was; he said, 'Merely an omnibus,' but next morning he told me that he asked the men pursuing 'What was the matter?' and one answered, 'Macready's in that omnibus; they've killed twenty of us, and by G— we'll kill him!' Well, all was settled; it was believed that twenty had perished.

"Robert went to bed to his wife. Emmett went upstairs to lie down, which I declined to do, and with Richard went down into the comfortable office below before a good fire, and, by the help of a cigar, to count the slow hours until four o'clock. We talked, and he dozed, and I listened to the sounds of the night and thought of home, and what would be the anguish of hearts there if I fell in this brutal outbreak; but I resolved to do what was right and becoming. The clock struck four; we were on the move; Emmett came down; sent Richard to look after the carriage. All was still in the dawn of morning; but we waited some ten minutes—an age of suspense—the carriage arrived. I shook the hand of my preserver and friend—my heart responded to my parting prayer of 'God bless him!'—and stepping into the carriage, a covered phaeton,[5] we turned up Fifth Avenue and were on our way to safety. Thank God.

ADELAIDE RISTORI

[On Lady Macbeth] (1888)[†]

With me, the close investigation of this character, produced the conviction that with Lady Macbeth affection for her husband was the last factor actuating her deeds—that she was animated only by her excessive ambition to reign with him, and that, knowing his inferiority of mind, his weak nature, which was not able even to move the greed for possession which burned in his veins and in his brain to action—she used her affection for him as a means to satisfy her ambition. Being conscious of the fascination that she exercised over him, she took advantage of it for the purpose of instilling

---

5. an open carriage drawn by a horse or pair.

† Adelaide Ristori, *Memoirs and Artistic Studies*, trans. G. Mantellini (New York: Doubleday, 1907), 161, 164, 165–66, 168–74. In 1847 Ristori (1822–1906), Italy's greatest tragic actress, traveled to London to play Lady Macbeth in Giulio Carcano's Italian verse translation of the play. In 1887 she returned to London to perform the role in English. Critics admired her portrayal of Lady Macbeth's control over herself and her husband.

into his mind the virus of crime, putting it in the most natural light and with the most insinuating and persuasive reasonings.

* * *

I resolved to read that missive [1.5] straight down as if I had already read the first words of it while I was entering the stage, only stopping at the places where the strange knowledge of what has happened is in accord with what the regulating destiny of all the events had long before led her to foresee.

For instance my expression would portray a superstitious wonder on reading that the fatal sisters "made themselves air, into which they vanished" [1.5.4–5] after the prophecy they had cast at him, addressing him: "Hail, king that shalt be" [8].

Having ended the reading I make a long pause, as if analysing the fatal content of that missive, which was in accordance with what I had anticipated. Then, for a moment I remain sadly steeped in thought, gloomy, considering and fearing on account of the weak nature of my husband; then reflecting on the most striking passages of the missive, I say: "Glamis thou art, and Cawdor, and shalt be / What thou art promised" [13–14]. And to that "shalt be" I would give a supernatural force of expression.

* * *

The frightful soliloquy [1.5.36ff.] in the scene which follows the departure of the messenger, reveals all the diabolical perfidy and cruelty of this monster in human likeness, and this inhuman power with which she is armed in order to succeed in leading her husband to become the instrument of her ambition. In a word, she becomes the Satanic spirit of the body of Macbeth. He has a hard struggle between the "wishing and not wishing"; that woman, that serpent, becomes absolute mistress of this man, entwines him in her grasp, and no human power can ever tear him from it. Consequently, the first words of this monologue I pronounced in a cavernous voice, with my eyes bloodshot, with the accent of a spirit which comes from the abyss, and I ended it with a *crescendo* of thundering voice, which changed into an exaggerated expression of joy on beholding my husband enter.

During this first scene with Macbeth I show a cold, reserved and patient demureness, not minding at all the weak denials of my husband in his endeavour not to listen to my criminal insinuations. I make it apparent that he will have to yield to my influence. I therefore imagined a counter-scene at the exit of the *personae*, in order to portray the powerful fascination that this woman exercised upon her husband. I fancy that Macbeth wished to interrogate me again and ask of me further explanations. For the purpose of preventing him, I had the thought of inducing him to pass his left arm around my waist. In that attitude I take his right hand and placing his index finger upon my lips I charge him to be silent; in the meanwhile I am slowly pushing him behind the wings, his back turned to them. All this was executed with a mingling of sentiments and magnetising glances, which fascinations Macbeth could not very well resist.

* * *

It is in this act [Three] that one can plainly see the skill of Shakespeare. Lady Macbeth must—not only with words but with her "stage business"—either diminish or enlarge a great many of the striking episodes of the drama. Such considerations led me to make a logical, analytical study of this part. For instance, I did not allow to pass unobserved the entrance of the hired assassin, who comes in to announce to Macbeth the accomplishment of the murder of Banquo, and the failure of the attempt against Fleance's life. This news, which causes two very different forms of emotion, should not escape a watching eye like that of Lady Macbeth. And then again, at the sight of the hired murderer who presents himself in the banquet hall, she must be the only person to see that man speaking in a whisper to her husband, and to notice his excited gestures, never losing sight of him for a moment. She fears some imprudence on his part, remembering that Macbeth has told her shortly before "that a great deed would be accomplished to cause her wonder" [3.2.45].

I have taken into consideration that during this scene Lady Macbeth must show her fear, lest the guests may notice this strange conversation between Macbeth and the murderer, in that place and at that moment, and suspect some wrongdoing against themselves. I found it, therefore, necessary to play a double part, a dramatic one with Macbeth and a graceful one with my guests. While taking part in the conversation and the toasts that the guests are making who remain seated upon their stools, I cast at intervals fearful and investigating glances toward my husband and the hired murderer; and in order to draw Macbeth's attention to me and warn him of the danger he runs of betraying himself by some imprudence, I say in a vibrant tone of voice, and with ostentatious joviality,

> My royal lord,
> You do not give the cheer; the feast is sold
> That is not often vouch'd, while 'tis a-making,
> 'T is given with welcome: to feed were best at home;
> From thence the sauce to meat is ceremony:
> Meeting were bare without it. [3.4.33–38]

With the same "scenic business," but with a more marked accentuation than before, in a reproachful tone, half-serious, half-jesting, I give him the following warning: "My worthy lord. / Your noble friends do lack you" [85–86]. I utter these words so that Macbeth alone could understand my object in calling his attention. This is apparently justified by the fear that Macbeth should fail to be courteous, and neglect his guests. I would show great agitation and great fright at the incomprehensible and furious visions of Macbeth, seeing that he is on the verge of revealing the secret of our guilt. Though the reproach is a bitter one, Lady Macbeth, by speaking to her guests, should keep up her pretended gaiety with her facial expression, and apologise for the eccentricities of her husband by attributing them to an old infirmity of his.

In the end, finding that all her efforts at repressing the strange horrors of Macbeth have proved vain, the noble lady sees herself forced to take leave of the guests in an excited manner, in order to be alone with Macbeth and put an end to a situation which becomes dangerous.

After the guests' departure, I thought it best to begin to indicate the state of prostration of Lady Macbeth, by imagining a counter-scene showing distress and failing power, making manifest my painful conviction that it is useless to struggle against the adverse destiny which has suddenly risen before me. I show how remorse begins to torment me, and in showing the beginning of those terrible sufferings I found it necessary for its justification to render realistic the impending end of that great criminal.

At the end of the act, at the moment of leaving, I make it apparent that I am penetrated with a deep sense of pity for Macbeth who for my sake has become the most miserable of men, and tell him, "You lack the season of all natures, sleep" [143].

I take hold of his left hand with my right and place it over my right shoulder, then painfully bending my head in deep reflection and turning toward my husband with a look filled with the remorse which is agitating my mind, I drag him toward our chamber in the same manner that one leads an insane person. When reaching the limit of the stage Macbeth, frightened by the tail of his cloak trailing at my feet, again shudders suddenly. Then, with a quick turn, I pass on the other side of him, and try to master the terror with which I am also seized in spite of myself. Using a little violence I succeed in pushing him behind the wings, while quieting him with affectionate gestures.

*   *   *

This woman, this colossus of both physical and moral force, who with one single word had the faculty of imaging and causing the execution of deeds of hellish character—there she is, now reduced to her own shadow which, like the bony carcass left bare by a vulture, is eaten up by the remorse preying on her mind. In her trouble she becomes so thoroughly unconscious of herself as to reveal in her sleep her tremendous, wicked secret. But what do I say "in her sleep"? It is like a fever which, rising to her brain, softens it. The physical suffering taking hold of her mind with the recollection of the evil of which she has been the cause masters and regulates all her actions, causing her, spasmodically, to give different directions to her thoughts. . . .

I enter the stage with the looks of an automaton, dragging my feet as if they wore leaden shoes. I mechanically place my lamp upon the table, taking care that all my movements are slow and intercepted by my chilled nerves. With a fixed eye which looks but does not see, my eyelids wide open, a difficult mode of breathing, I constantly show the nervous agitation produced by the derangement of my brain. It was necessary to clearly express that Lady Macbeth was a woman in the grasp of a moral disease whose effects and whose manifestations were moved by a terrible cause.

Having placed the lamp upon the table, I advance as far as the footlights, pretending to see on my hands still some spots of blood, and while rubbing them I make the motion of one who takes in the palms of his hands a certain quantity of water in order to wash them. I am very careful with this motion, which I repeat at various moments. After this I say, "Yet here's a spot. Out damned spot! Out, I say!" [5.1.30]. Then, listening, I say softly "One: two: why, then 't is time to do't" [30–31]. Then, as if answering "Hell is murky!—Fie, my Lord, fie! a soldier, and afraid? What need you fear? Who knows it, when none can call our power to account" [31–34]. And at this place, returning to the cause of my delirium, "Yet who would have thought the old man to have had so much blood in him?" [34–35]. And I show here that I am struck by the colour of blood in which it seems to me as if I had dipped my hands. Returning to my manifestation of delirium, I add, "The Thane of Fife had a wife: where is she now?" [37–38]. And looking again at my hands with an expression between rage and sadness: "What, will these hands ne'er be clean?" [38]. With a convulsive motion I rub them again. Then, always a prey to my delirium, in a bitter tone, and speaking excitedly, I pretend to whisper in Macbeth's ear, "No more o' that, my lord, no more o' that; you mar all with this starting" [38–40]. Then coming back to my first idea, I smell my hands, pretending they smell of blood, and I break forth with passion: "Here's the smell of the blood still: all the perfumes of Arabia will not sweeten this little hand. Oh! oh, oh!" [44–46]. And I make these exclamations as if an internal shudder convulsed my heart and caused me to breathe with difficulty, after which I remain with my head thrown back, breathing slowly, as if in a deep lethargy.

During the short dialogue between the gentlewoman and the doctor, I pretend in my delirium to be taken to the scene of the murder of Duncan, and, as if the object of my regard were the chamber of the king, bending my body, advancing slowly and mysteriously toward my right side where I imagine the murder has taken place, I pretend that I hear the quick step of my husband and anxiously inclining my ear in the posture of one who waits I express how Macbeth is coming to confirm to me the accomplishment of the deed. Then, with an outburst of joy, as if I saw him appear and announce the deed, feeling very much agitated, I say, "Wash your hands, put on your nightgown; look not so pale. I tell you yet again, Banquo's buried; he cannot come out on's grave" [55–57]. I took much care never to forget that the woman who spoke was in troubled sleep; and during this scene, between one thought and another, I would emit a long, deep and painful sigh.

The following verses: "To bed, to bed! There's knocking at the gate: Come, come, come, come, give me your hand. What's done cannot be undone. To bed, to bed, to bed!" [59–61]. I speak these words in an insistent tone, as if it were a thing that should be done quickly; then, frightened, fancying that they knock at the door of the castle and come to surprise us, I show great emotion, a greater fear, as if I found it necessary to hide ourselves quickly in our own rooms. I start in that direction, inviting Macbeth to follow me, saying in a very imperative and furious tone, "Come, come, come!" Then, simulating the act of grasping his hand, I show that I am dragging him with great pain, and disappear from the sight of the audience, saying in a suffocating voice: "To bed, to bed, to bed!"

* * *

Though I flatter myself that I entered into the spirit of this character in the best way I could, I trust this analysis of mine—the interpretation of the part of Lady Macbeth—to the appreciation of the critic. From what I have stated it must be clearly evident what an amount of strenuous study and how much mental labour such an interpretation cost me.

ORSON WELLES

[On the 1936 Voodoo Production and the 1948 *Macbeth* Film]†

Richard Marienstras When you presented *Macbeth* in Harlem [1936], there was a certain agitation among the blacks. Was it really the first Shakespeare play performed by blacks?

Orson Welles There were others, I think; but it was the first important production. In any case it was the most chic premiere of my whole career. I'd never seen anything like it. The Lafayette Theatre, this enormous theater, was filled with anyone who was anyone in Harlem and in New York, dressed in suits with white ties, standing because there was no more room. It was the most chic, elegant and lively atmosphere I've ever seen. And at the end of the play there were so many curtain calls that we finally left the curtain open and the audience came onto the stage.

Richard Marienstras At the time, the play was acclaimed by militant blacks. I found this clipping from critic King Otley: "The black actor is tired of bearing the burden of the black face assigned to him by whites. In *Macbeth*, he finally has the opportunity to play a universal character. The Harlem community attended a production in which the Black was neither taunted nor ridiculed. We attended the production of *Macbeth*, happy to know that the show would not once again give us the odious feeling of being dirty Negroes" [Amsterdam News, 18 April 1845]. This is extraordinary, because it was a precocious manifestation of . . .

Orson Welles It was. It was a great political event.

Richard Marienstras There were riots in Harlem . . .

Orson Welles And also a riot that night! The police were everywhere because a large portion of the black community thought we were ridiculing blacks by having them perform Shakespeare and that the public had come to mock them. So there were

† From Richard Marienstras, "Orson Welles: Shakespeare, Welles, and Moles," *Orson Welles: Interviews*, ed. Mark W. Estrin (Jackson: University Press of Mississippi, 2002), 154–55, 150–53. Director, producer, and actor, celebrated for achievements on stage and screen, Orson Welles produced the famous "Voodoo *Macbeth*" in Harlem, which featured a black cast, a Haitian setting, African witches and sorcerers, and a Macbeth modeled on the Haitian tyrant, Henri Christophe. Welles also directed and starred in a film production (1948) that pitted ancient forces of paganism (represented by the witches) against Christianity (represented by ubiquitous Celtic crosses and a priest added to the play).

Orson Welles as Macbeth, film (1948). Courtesy of the Everett Collection.

hundreds of policemen to stop people from throwing bricks. There was a rumor that it was a kind of burlesque show. But it was just the opposite. The rehearsals lasted a very long time. I've never rehearsed a play so long: three months. And during all these rehearsals, I never once suggested an intonation to the actors. The blacks invented the whole diction of Shakespeare. It was very interesting and very beautiful. I didn't suggest anything about Shakespearean tradition or the white way of reciting Shakespeare. But their sense of rhythm and music is so great and their diction so good that they found their own way of reciting Shakespeare. It was astonishing!

Richard Marienstras   Apparently there was a real sorcerer in
Macbeth.

Orson Welles   Fourteen! We brought them from Dahomey—we
couldn't find any in the Antilles—and while we prepared, they
killed goats on the stage and made the sorcerer's tom-toms.[1]

Richard Marienstras   You had a large number of actors.

Orson Welles Yes, an enormous cast. The scenery was very ugly,
but the rest extraordinary.[2]

※   ※   ※

Orson Welles   Let's take *Macbeth.* In Shakespeare's times, Macbeth wore an Elizabethan costume, with a fraise[3] and all that.
And for two hundred years, he was dressed as a romantic: that's
the romantic visual tradition, which has become prehistoric! If
I find a way of creating a primitivism which moves the public,
which communicates with them without touching the play, at
least the little part that I am able to understand, why not do it?
Macbeth poses a particularly interesting problem: no actor in
the history of theater has ever been a great Macbeth. Why?
Because there has never been an actor who could perform the
first and second parts of the play. For this play has a great
defect, an imperfection: the Macbeth who is the victim of Lady
Macbeth is not the one who then becomes king. No actor has
ever been able to play both parts equally well. The actor must be
brutally simple and completely natural to play the first part, and
extremely cerebral to play the second part. In other words, Laurence Olivier would have to play in the first part, and John Gielgud in the second.

1. Like Davenant before him, Welles expanded the supernatural elements in the play,
particularly the character of Hecate (played by Eric Burroughs), here a male voodoo
master who bids Macbeth to kill Macduff's children, joins in the murder of Banquo,
and closes the play shrieking, "Peace! The charm's wound up," *Orson Welles on Shakespeare: The WPA and Mercury Theatre Playscripts,* ed. Richard France (New York:
Routledge, 2001). Inspired by his father's performance, Norris Burroughs has produced
a graphic novel entitled *Voodoo Macbeth.*
2. James Baldwin, age twelve or thirteen, later recalls attending the production, his
first play: "[B]efore the curtain rose, I knew the play by heart. . . . I knew enough to
know that the actress (the colored lady!) who played Lady Macbeth might very well be
a janitor, or a janitor's wife, when the play closed, or when the curtain came down.
Macbeth was a nigger, just like me, and I saw the witches in church, every Sunday,
and all up and down the block, all week long, and Banquo's face was a familiar face.
At the same time, the majesty and torment on that stage were real: indeed they
revealed the play, *Macbeth.* They *were* those people and that torment was a torment I
recognized. . . . For, they were themselves, these actors—these people were themselves. They could *be* Macbeth only because they were themselves," *The Devil Finds
Work,* 1976, *James Baldwin: Collected Essays,* ed. Toni Morrison (New York: Library
of America, 1998), 499, 504.
3. ornate collar.

Richard Marienstras In your film [1948], you modified certain things, like the relation between the witches.

Orson Welles I was making a film!

Richard Marienstras One has the impression that Macbeth is an instrument in the hands of the witches. The witches mold a little clay figure in the image of Macbeth, and there seems to be a sort of magic at work, and from that moment he acts like a man hallucinating, like a pure instrument of evil.

Orson Welles Not like a pure instrument of evil, because he's a Christian. The forces of evil are fighting to win him over, but the battle isn't won at the beginning of the film, nor is it won at the end. Even at the end, Macbeth remains a member of the Christian world and continues to fight to save his integrity. The fact that he's destroyed by evil doesn't mean that he is its plaything, as the forces of evil wanted him to be. Finally he falls, he collapses. His wife, because of her ambitions for him, also uses him. Everyone uses him. It's the same Christian conscience that Shakespeare gives to his villains. When Hamlet's uncle, the king, says, "O, my offense is rank . . . It hath the primal eldest curse upon't, a brother's murder," this is absolutely part of the Christian tradition which Shakespeare, I think, whether he was a believer or not, belonged to by virtue of his culture. So scoundrels had to speak and act like this, and all the way through the play Macbeth acts like a man of conscience.

Richard Marienstras From the beginning to the end of the film, then, you think of him as a man possessed of his free will . . .

Orson Welles And who is trying to use it, but forces more powerful than he—a woman endowed with a stronger personality, historic forces and everything else—get the better of him. But he's not a mere instrument of evil going to his downfall.

Richard Marienstras One has the impression that from one end to the other, he is possessed, he is hallucinating.

Orson Welles He is hallucinating, of course, but it's the hallucination of a member of the Christian community. And the forces of evil, according to me—not according to me in general, but my specific design for this film—are not necessarily evil. They represent ancient religion, paganism. Just as ambition is not necessarily evil. And his wife represents evil.

Richard Marienstras In this specific case, ambition is an evil.

Orson Welles Let's consider it in the historical context. What is ambition? Take the story of William the Conqueror at an earlier era, or the story of Henry II [who ordered the murder of Thomas Becket] and men like him who were assassins. If Richard III had found a horse at Bosworth, the Plantaganets would still be reigning in England and Richard would not be a villain because Thomas More would not have written the bitter pamphlet against him! [This unfinished history served as a source for Shakespeare.]

Richard Marienstras Yes, but in this particular kind of evildoing do you only see a sort of literary creation? Or do you think it goes farther than that? In the play, the portrait of Richard III is an act of propaganda against a defeated monarchy, but isn't Richard also the incarnation of evil?

Orson Welles *Richard III* isn't really a play about evil. It's a play about a delicious villain. It has a marvelous role for a great actor, that of the fascinating felon. The role of Macbeth is very different. It's the story of a weak man. This is why Macbeth has never been the great role of a great actor. To play it requires an actor of great physical and intellectual power, capable of incarnating a weakling. However you interpret Lady Macbeth or the witches—and there are thirty ways to do it—Macbeth is always a weakling. The nature of his weakness remains to be found. He's not a strong man who is defeated and collapses. He's sick from the outset.

Richard Marienstras But at the beginning of the play, when he appears as a glorious general who just defeated a rebel, he doesn't give that impression.

Orson Welles He's not as glorious as all that. These battles which were waged so often, at intervals of a few weeks, were a sort of permanent guerilla war and not very glorious. Yes, Macbeth brought home a victory. But he's not glorious like a Coriolanus, or a Julius Caesar, or a Mark Antony. There's not a single line in the play which gives him this kind of seductiveness. He simply won a battle, and that's all that can be said.

Richard Marienstras And the witches immediately tempted him?

Orson Welles They put an idea into his head. And he's so stupid that it wouldn't have come to him otherwise! As I often say, most of Shakespeare's heroes are noble and stupendous, grandiose, and imbeciles! Hamlet, Richard II . . .

IAN McKELLEN

[On the 1976 Trevor Nunn *Macbeth*]†

Julian Curry   Why do you suppose you have such an affinity with these Shakespearean villains?

Ian McKellen   Well, I suspect it's because those are the parts that Shakespeare wrote best, or made most entertaining or of most interest to the audience. It's unexpected, isn't it, that the greatest playwright who ever lived should have written about monsters as successfully as he wrote about heroes and heroines. *Macbeth* is an extremely popular play. In fact it was the first Shakespeare play I saw, in an amateur production at the Wigan Little Theatre when I was pre-teens. It's short, which I think helps the audience. The story doesn't have a subplot, so it's relatively easy to realise what's going on. Particularly as Macbeth keeps telling the audience what's going on, at least inside his head. And if the actor can convincingly convey, with the immediacy of Shakespeare's language, what he's thinking and worrying about and suffering, agonizing over, then the audience can't help being engaged. The result of his decisions is appalling, and one has the privilege of being inside the head of someone whose behaviour, if read about in the newspaper, would be dismissed as that of an "Evil Monster." But I think Shakespeare's message is that those sort of words aren't helpful in explaining human behaviour, because they don't explain it, they just give it a label. Therefore I didn't think of Macbeth as a terrible man, any more than I did Iago. I thought of each of them as a man with a problem, and in both cases that problem is shared with the audience.

It was enormously helpful that our production was first put on in The Other Place, which only seated a hundred people. I'd seen *King Lear* done there very successfully, in a Buzz Goodbody production. It's riveting to be so close to the actors when they're not having to project their performance, either vocally or emotionally. Or indeed to select from it what they want the audience to receive. It's part of our job to let them know what's going on,

† From Julian Curry, *Shakespeare on Stage: Thirteen Leading Actors on Thirteen Key Roles* (London: Nick Hern Books, 2010), 145–47, 149, 151–53, 155, 162–63, 167–69. In 1976 Ian McKellen and Judi Dench starred in the now-legendary *Macbeth*, directed by Trevor Nunn of the Royal Shakespeare Company. On the dark, bare stage of the small Stratford-upon-Avon theater, The Other Place, the play unfolded as an intense and riveting psychological drama. There is a film version of the production (1979). Reprinted by permission of Nick Hern Books.

but if you're working in a big theatre you can't let them know everything, and they're not close enough to glimpse it for themselves. So they're relying on the actor carrying the character on his back, as it were. But in The Other Place, the actor and the character can become much closer together. The level of speaking can be conversational and the audience can see not only the eyes, but perhaps what's behind the eyes. A play like *Macbeth* is about the psychology of the person. You have to be very close to the subject to be of any help. So that was all set up in my favour: (a) it's a popular play, it's one that people want to see; and (b) we had the right circumstances for plugging into what is special about the play, what's needed if it's going to come across.

* * *

Once you put *Macbeth* into a large theatre, a Victorian theatre, let's say, the actors get betrayed into doing things that are just not helpful to the play. And the designer too: "Oh, God, Where's Scotland?" Scotland is the least interesting feature of *Macbeth*, I think, the real Scotland. In John Napier's design for our production there was no sense of Scotland. We were actors on a stage, and the play began with us coming in and sitting on fruit boxes, round a rough white circle painted on the floor of the stage. We could be seen doing the sound effects. At one point I was in charge of the thunder machine. You could see Macbeth and Lady Macbeth putting the blood on their hands in the wings. I don't think this was an attempt to be Brechtian in any sense, but just to say this is a group of people telling a story, and it'll be just as riveting and frightening and exciting as if we were in a large theatre trying to convince you that we were in medieval Scotland, which is no help whatsoever. That's one thing that Trevor Nunn solved. The second thing he solved, which again can go wrong in a big theatre, is the magic. What do you do about heads coming, not the heads, the, er . . .

Julian Curry   Apparitions?

Ian McKellen   The apparitions. In an earlier production with Nicol Williamson, Trevor had a puppet show of some sort, and we were left over with a couple of the puppets. But ours was happening inside Macbeth's head, where, as I said, so much of the play takes place. So the idea was that he had been drugged and laid on the floor and told these things were happening to him, even though they weren't. I thought that was much more plausible in the twentieth century. The witches were very clearly ordinary— well, not *ordinary* but they were, believably, people going about their business. And they had a relationship that Trevor worked out between the grandmother, the daughter and her daughter. They were a little family of people who were in touch with things beyond themselves. Hecate was cut. So the magic was solved. And the third difficulty of *Macbeth*, which is, I think, the least understood, is that the fifth act isn't very good. Well, it's not very good if you're telling the story of the leading part, because so much of it is about other characters. You've had the long scene with Macduff and Malcolm in England [4.3]—very welcome!—as a result of which they decide to come back and invade Scotland where Macbeth's holed up in his castle. But you've no sooner got to Macbeth in his castle, and he's saying something riveting about how he feels, than Shakespeare cuts to the boring old English troops with their rhododendron leaves and all that. And when you stage that, as you feel you have to in a big theatre, the audience is constantly frustrated. And time and again in the reviews you will see "The amazing Mr. So-and-So as Macbeth unfortunately couldn't bring off the fifth act." But it's not his fault, it's the play's fault. And what Trevor did brilliantly was to cut down the number of lines of the invading army, which are much less interesting than Macbeth's dilemma. He kept Macbeth in the centre of the magic circle the whole time, while the words of the invading army were spoken by the actors standing round observing Macbeth, so the focus never left him. So that was Trevor giving me the chance to bring off the fifth act. It was his awareness that there was a weakness there.

*   *   *

Julian Curry   There are various possible reasons for the murder of Duncan. . . .

Ian McKellen   It's the same story for Macbeth, as I observed later when I was doing Richard III, exactly the same story. With Richard, Shakespeare is beginning to imagine Macbeth—it's astonishing. They both come back hugely successful, they've both been germane in bringing about the end of a civil war. (Well, in Macbeth's case, it's fighting the Norwegian sledded somebody or other.) And it's not enough for them. Similarly, it's not enough to be Coriolanus, single-handedly defeating a town. By his breeding and his temperament, he wants to run the country. Richard III wants to *own* the country and will do anything to get it. He's totally conscienceless until that last amazing speech after his nightmare in which he asks himself, is he doing the right thing? Is he a monster or not? And he speaks in language worthy of Beckett, it's quite extraordinary. It's more modern than even you get in *Macbeth*. Then he writes *Macbeth*, and instead of bringing the conscience in right at the end of the play, he thinks, "Of course, I must put it in at the beginning!" And that's what he's exploring—that Macbeth should be ambitious for civilian power, wants to be King.

* * *

Julian Curry   One reviewer, talking about you and Judi, describes you as "an ostensibly nice and reasonable pair." He also talks about you as having "a certain courtliness, even wit. He can regard his downfall as an inexorable joke."

Ian McKellen   Yes, I cottoned on to that early on—that Macbeth's got a very good sense of humour and is always cracking gags. I think his first line indicates that: "So foul and fair a day I have not seen" [1.3.39]. Isn't that a witty thing to say? And yet isn't it totally germane to his problem? He sees both sides. Anybody who sees both sides can laugh. And "If it were done when 'tis done" [1.7.1]—you know—"If I do this, then that . . . If I do that, then the other." There's almost a chuckle as he's saying it. It's funny. And laughter releases you. Later he gets more and more bound up. But even "She should have died hereafter" [5.5.17] is within calling distance of wit. And the courtliness, yes, he's a warrior whom everybody loves and admires. He's clearly "a man's man," they all adore him, everybody thinks he's fantastic. And it's a great shock as it dawns on them that he's dreadful. Lady Macbeth too, she's the perfect hostess. When we were rehearsing it was not long after Watergate, and I said "Well, of course, they're the Nixons, aren't they?" And Trevor Nunn said "No, no, they're not the Nixons, they're the Kennedys." They're the golden couple, the couple everybody wants to be with, whose house everybody wants to visit, including the King, a couple we all admire. There the comparison with the Kennedys ends, presumably. But that's the sort they are. We're privileged to see inside their lives, and when we do we find they are dissatisfied, and want more. I should imagine they have great parties. It's against that background of people with social graces and great strengths that people admire, that the horror of the banquet is even more intense [3.4]. Because normally these people do it superbly.

* * *

Julian Curry   When she says "What beast was't, then, / That made you break this enterprise to me?" [1.7.47–48], she could be referring to his letter, after talking to the witches. It doesn't necessarily mean they've talked about it before the play begins, does it?

Ian McKellen   No, no. I think they're highly attuned in their marriage, deeply in love and dependent upon each other, or have been in the past. It's later on that they get rather out of sync. Macbeth behaves like a general who says, "We have to plot this out, we have to write these things down. Now, 'if it were done when 'tis done,' we have to do it quickly." But Lady Macbeth says "God, what's the matter with you? Get on with it! I thought you were the man who just went out and killed people!" But no. He's a commander who works out the best place—"What would happen if I do that," he thinks. He works things through in his mind, Macbeth, as well as his imagination. She can't see any problems, she's not a man of action, she's not a great organiser of armies, she's a hostess.

Julian Curry   What was your physicality like with Judi?

Ian McKellen   As far as possible we were never out of each other's arms. Certainly what she can give him, which nobody else in the world can, is her love and her passion and her sex. I always felt that I was a husband coming back to my beloved, to my wife, my sweetheart, the only woman that I cared about in the world, coming back from the long, desperate life elsewhere and hardship with the men. And she immediately wants to talk about killing the King. No wonder he's a bit put off. And yes, I think the story of their progression is of them getting separated from the bliss of that union.

Julian Curry   It can be played, can't it, with her emasculating him—diminishing his manhood at several moments in those scenes early on, in order to challenge him.

Ian McKellen   Well, she thinks that's how to get at him. And she's right, because he's very proud. So she says "You're not being yourself." It's not that she wants to be Queen and have a consort at her side, she wants him to be King. He's her man. These are very, very private conversations. She's not trying to change Macbeth, but make him more like himself. She can't understand, she doesn't understand the problems. That's why quite soon afterwards, she's not privy to the problems. He doesn't include her because she doesn't understand. He's on his own. And of course he's not at his best when he's on his own.

*   *   *

I mean, when you're acting with Judi Dench, you're not up against a great analytic mind that has sourced everything within herself and within the other works of Shakespeare, in order to speak his lines exactly as they were meant to be delivered. What you get with Judi, and with the best actors, is a pumping heart and blood coursing through the veins, living in the moment, terrified or ecstatic, whatever is required. And able to turn on the emotions as easily as a tap. That's not given to many of us. What she doesn't do is give a running commentary on the character, as I tended to do in the past.

* * *

Julian Curry   How was Banquo's ghost done in the banquet scene [3.4]?

Ian McKellen   It was done the right way, the only way that makes sense, which is that he didn't exist. The text says: *"Enter the Ghost of Banquo"* [3.4.38 sd]. Well, maybe that's how it was done originally, but the only person who sees the ghost is Macbeth. Nobody else does. If you want to have the ghost appearing onstage, everybody has to act that they can't see him. But we in the audience can see him, so what's wrong with all those people, are they mad? Macbeth then becomes the only sane, sensible person in the room. It's the absolute reverse of the situation. In fact there's no ghost, just as there was no dagger, they're in his imagination. Poor old Tony Hopkins had to have a dagger, there was one floating round the stage in that Michael Blakemore production. It was projected onto the scenery, and he followed it around trying to catch it. Well, there you go, how far can you get from the reality of the situation! No, the ghost is not there.

* * *

Julian Curry   Then, "Tomorrow and tomorrow" [5.5.19] . . . Where does all that come from?

Ian McKellen   Well, that's his future. What is the future? It's "Tomorrow and tomorrow and tomorrow." I used to think when I was saying it, if you repeat a word often enough—"tomorrow, tomorrow, tomorrow, tomorrow, tomorrow"—does it stop having any meaning? It must have been the first rap song! It "creeps in this petty pace from day to day" and I used to think "Tomorrow, today, and all our yesterdays." So it's about the future and the present and the past. And all our *future* tomorrows, todays and yesterdays—all in advance of the certainty that we're going to die. And the poor players strutting and fretting our hour upon the stage. I've analysed it into the ground, this speech. But the way I think it actually hits home to the audience, which makes it such an unbelievable speech, is this: what other writer would dare, at the moment of trying to understand the complexity of the character's fictional life, to remind the audience that there are such things as poor players that strut and fret their hour upon the stage? You'd think that's the last thing we should be considering. But no, because the actor can say it with total conviction. He knows what it's like to strut and fret his hour upon the stage and then be heard no more. And talking to the audience, I can say that with total conviction as Ian McKellen. If they're not buying the story of Macbeth, at least they cannot avoid the certainty that the man who's speaking these lines knows and feels what he's talking about. It's a complicated thing going on. It just seems that with her death (the woman he loved, who's been his prop and best friend and everything), he can't cope with life. Life is death. That's what it seems like at that point.

Julian Curry On "I 'gin to be a-weary of the sun" [5.5.49] you had a naked light bulb which swung around your head.

Ian McKellen It was just on a wire, and I used to tap it so it would go to and fro, or sometimes it went round, depending on how I tapped it. That being the only light, it sent shadows and flashed into the audience's eyes as it did in Macbeth's eyes, so they had the sort of experience he was having.

*   *   *

Julian Curry Would you like to say more?

Ian McKellen Shakespeare's writing about a believable society of civil servants and soldiers and royalty, and if you think it's just about a man in a kilt who doesn't get on with his wife, you're missing the point. The play is much more resonant than that. Imagine the despair at the end when young Malcolm stood there and said what he was going to do, with such clarity and lack of passion. This was the man who lied so convincingly to Macduff in the England scene, when he said he was acquainted with all the evils of the flesh [4.3]. He could describe them, he could imagine them vividly. And you think "Oh gosh, here he comes, Mr. Innocent, what are *his* demons like? What's the inside of *his* head like?" Macbeth is no more, but Malcolm's going to replace him. I think you feel that at the end of *Richard III*, in a way you don't feel at the end of *King Lear*. At the end of *King Lear* something has happened to those people. "We that are young / Shall never see so much, nor live so long" [5.3.331–32]. A suffering has taken place which is beneficial somehow. I don't think there's an optimistic ending to Macbeth at all. It's chilling. There's a chilling pause while you're just invited to look at these frail human beings and think "Oh, Christ."

HIRA MIKIJIRÔ AND YUKIO NINAGAWA

[On the 1980 Ninagawa *Macbeth*]†

Minami   It is *Ninagawa Macbeth* to which the foreign reader may feel the greatest affinity, and it was you who played Macbeth in that unique production. How do you feel about his ideas?

Hira   Well, first of all, I felt closer to Macbeth on account of the production's Japanese style. Ninagawa's setting of the play within a Butsudan [Buddhist home altar] didn't come as a surprise.

Anzai   Were you conscious of the influence of *Throne of Blood*?[1]

Hira   I certainly felt that Ninagawa was under the influence of Kurosawa's work, but we never talked about it because I thought it better not to. Kurosawa's *Macbeth* was presented in a black and white, austere world. On the other hand, *Ninagawa Macbeth* was gorgeous and splendid, using rich, showy colors. I just took care to keep Macbeth a somber and weighty personality in such a magnificent setting, even though I admit I was dragged in a little. When I work with Ninagawa, I always try not to be caught up too much in his world. It's very seductive, you know! If I didn't have any concepts of my own that can offer resistance, I could never create my role. My approach may have made *Ninagawa Macbeth* rather heavy, but I believed it was necessary in order to keep Ninagawa's world from being merely magnificent.

Matsuoka   At the end of some speeches, you seemed to strike beautifully articulated Kabuki-style *mie* freezes.[2] If you had worn western clothes, you wouldn't have struck such flamboyant poses, would you?

Hira   No, it would have looked too theatrical. By stylizing my way of acting, it was possible to go beyond a realist *Macbeth*, but there were some risks involved. Striking flamboyant poses increases the possibility of *Ninagawa Macbeth* being seen as merely a pastiche

---

† "Interview with Hira Mikijirô," *Performing Shakespeare in Japan*, ed. Minami Ryuta, Ian Carruthers, John Gillies (Cambridge: Cambridge Univ. Press, 2001), 234–35; "Interview with Yukio Ninagawa," Ibid., 212–13. Hira Mikijirô played Macbeth in Yukio Ninagawa's Japanese adaptation (1980), which enjoyed successful runs in Edinburgh, London, the United States, Canada, and elsewhere (1985–90). Two aged crones, this play's version of the witches, hovered about the action, which featured Japanese symbolism and the stylized acting and costuming of Japanese theater with the *Pie Jesu* from the *Requiem*, and selections from Barber and Brahms. Reprinted with permission of Cambridge University Press.
1. Akira Kurosawa's celebrated 1957 film adaptation of *Macbeth*, set in feudal Japan, originally titled, *Kumonosu-jô*, "The Castle of the Spider's Web."
2. Kabuki is a highly stylized and colorful drama consisting of recognizable plots, songs, and dances, featuring *mie* poses, i.e., recognizable body configurations, held in stillness to convey heightened emotion.

Hira Mikijirô as Macbeth and Shinobu Otake as Lady Macbeth in Yukio Ninagawa's 1980 production.

of Kabuki. I think it can sometimes weaken a performance. In short, style is a double-edged sword. If I strike a flamboyant pose superficially, it will convey nothing to the audience. And, if I give emotion and significance to such *mie*-style poses, it will sometimes seem too serious to the audience. When I perform, I need to find a balance, but it's very hard for me because I didn't study Japanese classical plays or dance very much. I want to strike a skilful *mie* pose, but can't do so without any classical training. And if I can do it with ease, it may appear to lack seriousness and depth of emotion.

Anzai   An important point. When I go to Kabuki, I look forward to seeing the beauty of the style. One of the pleasures of seeing Kabuki is the pure theatricality of the *kata* (forms). On the other hand, we also find realism in Kabuki. Neither theatricalism nor realism is satisfactory by itself.

Hira   When I performed in *Macbeth* and *Double Suicide*, creating mental exaltation while being realistic was indispensable to achieving a style. When you try to go beyond realism while retaining a sense of realism at the same time, some styles or *kata* are created anew, just as in the case of the suicide scene in *Double Suicide* and some of the murder scenes in *Macbeth*.[3]

3. Ronnie Mulryne observes that "Macduff's sword makes its whistling whip-like descent to cleave Macbeth in one blow, and the stage lighting simultaneously and immediately

Matsuoka   Ninagawa always visualizes his *mise-en-scène*[4] vividly, and is a recognized master of both realism and stylization. Did his direction of *Macbeth* help you bring your Macbeth to such an intensity as to create a style of *kata*?

Hira   Ninagawa not only accepted my way of acting, but also stirred up my passions with music and extravagant visual effects such as snowstorms.[5] He stimulated me with the most magnificent *mise-en-scène*, and expected me to challenge him with my acting, again and again. (*Translated by Chiba Shôko.*)

From the interview with Yukio Ninagawa

Nakane[6]   *Macbeth* was the first play in which you transposed the setting completely to Japan. I first had the idea of setting the play in Azuchi castle. I thought the setting would be good for *Macbeth* because it was created by Oda Nobunaga (the first warlord to reunify Japan in the late sixteenth century).

Ninagawa   But when I went back home and opened up our family Butsudan (Buddhist home altar) to light a candle and pray for my father, at that moment, I thought, "this is the right image." I had two overlapping complex ideas: ordinary people watching *Macbeth*, and a Japanese audience looking at the stage and seeing through it to our ancestors.

When I was in front of the Butsudan, my thoughts were racing. It was like I was having a conversation with my ancestors. When I thought of *Macbeth* in this way, I thought of him appearing in the Butsudan where we consecrate dead ancestors. Then we could change the setting when the witches appear, as in the Japanese expression, "To be tempted by time." We could create a setting like dusk, neither night nor day, when, according to a Japanese tradition, one often meets with demonic beings.

I was thinking about the scene of Birnam wood too. In that scene, they carry Kadomatsu-like tree-branches (New Year's gate decoration of pine sprigs), which looks a bit funny. I thought I could change the setting to a lot of cherry blossoms moving, suggesting that the season is changing. As spring arrives, the whole scene would change, and the doors of the Butsudan would turn into the

---

switches from rose to cold. The emotional climax follows, into the silence, and the gradual swelling of Fauré's *Sanctus*." He quotes Ninagawa on this moment: "Macbeth is slain against the huge orange moon on the backcloth with a grim smile of emotional emptiness, which seems to show he has given up the fight. . . . [He] slowly becomes a foetus as if he acquired peace of mind for the first time," "From text to foreign stage: Yukio Ninagawa's Cultural Translation of *Macbeth*," *Shakespeare from Text to Stage*, ed. Patricia Kennan and Mariangela Tempera (Bologna: Clueb, 1992), 131–43 (140).
4. visual design in theater or film.
5. In addition to the snowstorm, the stage also featured a blossoming cherry tree.
6. Tadao Nakane, Ninagawa's producer.

great gates of a castle, and the shelves within the Butsudan would turn into its stately staircase. Everything would connect together in this way. I thought the Butsudan idea should be the *leitmotif* of the play, and, as I was wondering about it, we received an advertisement for Butsudans at home. So I thought it was a divine blessing. (*Translated by Yoshida Masako, Ian Carruthers, and Anzai Tetsuo.*)

ANTONY SHER AND HARRIET WALTER

Interviews (2001)[†]

Antony Sher   I began this whole venture with a very false impression about Macbeth, which I think hangs over all the great parts. You think you know what they are, and in this case it was really kind of pride before a fall. It was me thinking, "Oh, he's one of Shakespeare's villains. I've done those. He's a tortured soul. Oh, yes, I can do all that." It is without question the hardest part I've ever played and I think it's because what I gradually discovered was that the part is all about his mind, his brain. It's one of the thinking parts. I remember early on in rehearsal saying, "I've never played anyone who thinks so much."

The journey towards Macbeth, and I suppose this applies to any role with Shakespeare, is that you have to start getting whatever clues you can from the text. It's very painstaking work. First of all, you have to understand the text, translate it into ordinary English. Shakespeare, because he writes so well, writes lots of contradictions, because as human beings we are tremendously contradictory, and Shakespeare writes all of that into his great roles. At first these contradictions can seem baffling, and then as you start to understand it, you embrace the contradiction. I'll give you an example. He's a soldier, a tremendous soldier, whose behavior on the battlefield seems to go beyond the call of duty. He's unseaming people "from the naves to the chaps" [1.2.22], and he's trying to "memorize another Golgotha" [1.2.40]. We emphasized this by the first entrance, very, very kind of war crazy; we brought him on on the shoulders of his men, everyone chanting and screaming, and they've just had a victory—that real kind of war power, macho, crazy kind of state that they're in. Now

† *Macbeth*, Illuminations Media, DVD (2001), Extras Interviews, Antony Sher and Harriet Walter. Sir Antony Sher, an associate actor of the Royal Shakespeare Company, played Macbeth in Gregory Doran's production at the Swan Theatre in Stratford (1999–2000), and in the subsequent national and international tour. His Macbeth combined black humor and brutal courage, while Harriet Walter's Lady Macbeth embodied repressed emotion and sexual energy in a bleak, modern, militarized setting. Used with permission of Illuminations Media.

Antony Sher as Macbeth and Harriet Walter as Lady Macbeth in
Gregory Doran's 1999 Royal Shakespeare Company stage production.
© Robbie Jack/Corbis.

the same incredible soldier cannot murder one old man in his own
home and Lady Macbeth mocks him at one stage and says, "What,
a soldier and afeared?" [5.1.31–32]. And when eventually he does
murder Duncan he completely messes it up. He panics, he forgets to leave the daggers at the scene of the crime. He behaves
not like a top soldier but he behaves like you or I would if we
committed a murder. That's brilliant writing because everyone in
that audience watching the play goes, "Yes, of course, I would
panic in the sight of blood, it upset me." It's fantastic writing, but
at the beginning, contradictions like that seem baffling. Eventually, as I say, you kind of work through them.

I think something that helped me closer to the character was, as
part of my research for this, I went to meet two men who'd actually
committed murder, who had done their sentences, were now back
in the community. I met them on two separate occasions. And I
think they're among the most extraordinary, moving, and disturbing encounters of my life. Oddly enough, they were both Scottish
and they had both committed knife murders, which is just pure
coincidence. The first guy was a very haunting character. He'd had
a gambling addiction problem and ended up murdering a really
close friend rather than admit what had happened to fifty pounds
that should have been spent on the electricity bill. He was a very
sensitive, very articulate man, and took me through in grisly detail
the whole process and he said, "You wouldn't believe how long it

takes to kill somebody." And halfway through the stabbing, the victim cried out, "I don't want to die." And he describes waking up, the murderer, realizing what he was doing, walking to the door to get an ambulance, standing on the threshold, thinking, "Oh no, no, of course I can't take this option," coming back and finishing it. Extraordinary character and very, very haunted by the experience.

The second guy was a Glasgow hard man, who, you feel, if he hadn't been caught, wouldn't have given it a second thought. It was a suspected grass [informer], he'd gone around to, in his words, "give him a hiding" [beating], and it had got completely out of control. He'd killed the guy in the most savage way. He'd been caught, and for him, he was haunted not by the crime but by the punishment. He hated being in prison, he fought the system, he added five years to his sentence. And by meeting these two—the one man haunted by the crime, the other by the punishment, it brought Macbeth immediately into clearer focus because he is absolutely haunted by the crime. Even before he commits the crime, he is haunted by it; he knows he shouldn't do it. He is so much like the first man that I met because Macbeth is a sensitive, articulate, imaginative man—he has the most astonishing imagination. In fact, Lady Macbeth is a little bit more like the second murderer I met in that she'd be happy if she didn't get caught. She doesn't imagine the consequences.

[Macbeth's] always watching himself. People talk about him going mad. I don't believe he goes mad. I think that he retains a gruesome sanity so that he keeps seeing, and this mind, this brain, this great imagination—. Later in the play he will say, "Oh, full of scorpions is my mind, dear wife" [3.2.35]; and right towards the end of the play he will say to the doctor, "Can'st thou not minister to a mind diseased?" [5.3.40]. Don't you have a pill that helps my mind? His journey is from a man whose imagination soars in the early part of the play, even if it soars on fairly terrifying images, to a man whose brain is literally hurting by the end of the play because of his conscience, because of knowing that he has committed the ultimate sin. And then what Shakespeare does, of course, is give him the "Tomorrow and tomorrow" speech, significantly, after he's just heard the news of the death of Lady Macbeth, And there Shakespeare goes on to quite another level, because not only is it the bleakest, most nihilistic speech imaginable, but he goes to,

> Life's but a walking shadow, a poor player
> That struts and frets his hour upon the stage,
> And then is heard no more. It is a tale
> Told by an idiot, full of sound and fury,
> Signifying nothing. [5.5.24–28]

Shakespeare virtually makes the actor lean out of the action and say, "What are we all doing here? I'm just a not-very-good actor who's strutting around here. The story that the playwright has written could be told by an idiot. It signifies nothing. What are you all sitting here watching me [for]?" It's so nihilistic that he actually goes out of the action of the play. Indeed, in the stage version I got off the stage at that point and briefly aborted the action. We sort of played a little trick on the audience as though the actor really had just got pissed off and climbed off the stage and said, "This is just not worth carrying on with." But it's brilliant writing, it's so modern in a way, isn't it, that he can actually break through his own action and talk about, "We're on a stage here, this is all pointless." It goes beyond just Macbeth's despair into a really sort of existential despair.

*   *   *

Harriet Walter   I had played Lady Macbeth on the radio a couple of times, and I had been asked to play her in a couple of other productions, I think that's right in saying, and that's what happens, sometimes a part just keeps nagging at you until the formula becomes perfect. And it was a very tempting formula, Tony Sher and Greg Doran and the Swan. And other than that we knew nothing. I just took it on those grounds. What I did say was that I found it was very necessary to—I think in my first conversation with Greg—I said, "Is Tony prepared to look as though he needs me?" Because if your Macbeth doesn't need, if you get an actor, because I think that it had happened to me before, and if you get a Macbeth who thinks it's all about Macbeth, then Lady Macbeth gets sidelined and feels pretty impotent, the actress. And of course from that sentence onwards, I needn't had worried because that was what all of us found very rich, the dynamics of the couple, and how that shed light on the whole play. It wasn't doing me a favor, making my time as an actress better, it was actually, it's how the play's written, it's how it has to be.

It's so hard to know where to begin when you're groping towards a character. With Shakespeare it is almost incantation of the words so that they go into your bloodstream. I went on wild winter walks—actually they were summer walks, winter would have been more appropriate—but I went on to try to contact something very elemental in the character, because she doesn't have the sort of data that you have with other characters—you know, age 42, twice divorced, red-haired, and dresses in tweeds, or whatever it is. You don't have that kind of character breakdown. And Shakespeare gives her no back-story really, and no companion to whom she can confide what's going on in her heart. She does soliloquize but she doesn't confess in soliloquy. She has about five lines when she actually bares her heart. So she doesn't release her secrets very easily and it's as though she came ready made, as a package into Shakespeare's head, and he wasn't interested in what she does behind the scenes or when she's not on stage. She's a real theater invention. And there are other characters you play who you can sort of imagine what they're like in other situations, where they've just come from, where they're going to, what's their favorite color. With her all that's irrelevant, really. It's only what she does in the moment on stage and how she affects Macbeth. And so there's very little you can do in preparation before you get into rehearsal with your counterpart. But what I did do is just incant these frightening words—they're frightening, they still frighten me—the rhythms and the murkiness of the language, "Hell is murky" [5.1.31]. I mean it is just the spooky words. And it helped get me out of me and into some foreign territory.

There are several often asked and never quite satisfactorily answered questions about the Macbeths. One is, "Have they had children? If so, where are they? Did they die? When she says, 'I have given suck' [1.7.54], is she talking about Macbeth's child or did she have another child?" Historically, she had another child but that's not really the most fruitful way of looking at it theatrically.

The rehearsals were very much about uncovering these mysteries at the heart of the characters. We had some wonderfully revelatory moments where something that was an acting problem or a puzzle—I think in both cases in Tony's head, where he said, "How do I get from this point to this point"—would unearth through discussion something much deeper than had it been acted more facilely. There was this question of when Macbeth gets cold feet at the banquet and just dashes out, and she follows him and says, "What the hell's going on?" and he says, "I'm not going through with it," and within a space of five pages, not five pages depending, a very short space of time, he has flipped to, "Ok, I'll do it." And there's a burden on the actress to find what is it about my argument or my personality or my charisma or my power that manages to turn him round when he's got such good arguments against it. And for the actor it's equally, why, if I've got this conscience about doing this, am I so easily swayed by this woman? And so we both had the problem and we both found the heart of the matter round this issue of the child, because it's almost as though she brings up as an emotional last dart she can get him on. We used it as an emotional blackmail—that they were both in great pain about a child who they'd lost. And I argued in my own head that there were more than one, that she was one of these women who could never quite bring a child to fruition, and that it was a great source of personal agony to both of them, and that it was a very intimate, unspoken, coded, awful chasm.[1] And if you take it that far then somehow everything suddenly got solved. He has to go through with it because he feels terribly sorry for her, and their marriage suddenly finds a way of finding a purpose again, having lost it. It's a barren marriage and yet somehow this business of going for the crown could give them a new lease of life. It's better than going to Relate [relationship counseling organization]; they found this really good, mutually beneficial kind of cause.

She didn't put the thought in his head, that's very, very important, that is often a misconception. She did not put the thought in his head, she knew the thought was there, and there's masses of proof in the text that that's the case. She's gone down in history as the one who put the idea in his head and that's inaccurate. Her cleverness was to know that it was in his head already and to give him the courage to do it. She was full of steel at the beginning because she didn't really know what she was talking about. She knew Macbeth had ambition in him, she knew he had all sorts of qualities that she could bring out of him and harness, but she didn't know he was quite the monster he turns out to be. Nor did he know he was quite the monster he turned out to be.

PATRICK STEWART AND KATE FLEETWOOD

Stewart Interview (2010)[†]

Paula Zahn   This is a very contemporary interpretation of Shakespeare, and I have to say it is very shocking at times, in a visual

---

1. Director Gregory Doran commented: "When Lady Macbeth welcomes Duncan to Dunsinane, we had Macduff there with his wife and their children. As Lady Macduff, this fecund woman with all her pretty children, passed Lady Macbeth, Harriet gave her a very wan smile, and you could tell that children were something she desperately wanted, but that now, somehow because of her dead child, was unable to have" (ed. Bate and Rasmussen, 2009, 155).

† "Macbeth: A conversation with Sir Patrick Stewart," Public Broadcasting Service, October 6, 2010. Used with permission of PBS. Patrick Stewart discusses his Macbeth in the acclaimed Rupert Goold production, which opened in Chichester (2007), toured London and New York, and became a television film in 2009, now available in DVD and online http://video.pbs.org/video/1604122998/. Set in a post World-War II Soviet Russia or Eastern European country, the action took place in a sinister basement, which became a military hospital with attending religious nurses (who shockingly revealed themselves to be witches), served by an industrial elevator with sliding metal doors that only reinforced the sense of intensity and entrapment. After the murder of Banquo, which occurs in a simulated train carriage, filled with desperate fugitives from Macbeth, the passengers rise and rearrange the stage into the Banquet scene. After the following interval, the audience sees the Banquet scene again, this time with a pantomime version of Macbeth's conversation with the Murderers and with only a shaft of light replacing Banquo's bloody ghost. The sleepwalking Lady Macbeth tries to wash her hands in a bare sink that eerily gushes forth red blood.

sense and emotionally. And I was curious if it was that contemporary interpretation that drew you to the production in the first place.

Patrick Stewart   It was the role that drew me to the production. You know if you're at all a serious classical actor, a Shakespearean actor, there are certain roles that you have to pencil in for the future and Macbeth was one of them but I thought too much time had passed because there has been a fashion current the last fifteen, twenty years of casting the Macbeths younger and younger and I'd begun to think that I was now too long in the tooth for the role. But I had just worked with Rupert Goold, our director, on a most unusual production of *The Tempest*, and working with him had been such a treat. He has—it might be almost like a split vision of seeing something either profoundly in focus or ever so slightly out of focus, which shifts the content of the material. I'll give you an instance: there's a very long scene in the middle of the play which is known as "The Murderers' Scene" [3.1]; it's when Macbeth corrupts two men into killing Banquo and Banquo's child; it's a savage and dark and unsettling scene but it's long and there's a lot of exposition. And one day in rehearsals I said, "Rupert, oh, we stand here and we talk, talk, talk, talk, talk. I wish I had an action, something, something." And he said, "Why don't you make a sandwich?" This idea of taking something everyday, commonplace, absurdly incongruous, like buttering a slice of bread, putting on ham, and then sharing it with the murderers while the main objective of the scene being to corrupt them, seemed to give an added horror to what was happening. This was a classic example of how Rupert can perceive a traditional scene and just put a little twist on it.

Paula Zahn   Yes, it betrayed such a coldness and such a sense of depravity.

Patrick Stewart   Yes.

Paula Zahn   Yes, and that's what you wanted, isn't it?

Patrick Stewart   Well, it was necessary to emerge, both of us, Kate and myself, all the whole company, into this violent, cruel, and completely psychotic world. The approach we took to the play was one in which I began in quite a muted manner, a little introspective, insecure, uncertain of what he really wanted, delighted to be promoted by the king, and because we haven't talked about this, the wife who was generations younger and hungry for the absolute power, for the ultimate power, and it had always been my conception that Macbeth should be enthralled by her.

Paula Zahn   So was it your idea to cast Lady Macbeth generations younger than you?

Patrick Stewart This was the one concept I took to Rupert at the very beginning, yes.

Paula Zahn And it just so happened he happened to be married to the gorgeous woman who would later become Lady Macbeth?

Patrick Stewart Was that at all strange!

Paula Zahn She's extraordinary.

Patrick Stewart First of all I have to say that she is one of the most delightful people, actresses, I have ever known, and we became the greatest of friends, true buddies during the life of that production and we still are. But when I was on stage with her there were times when she scared me witless. Her reentrance after she has gone back to the murder scene [2.2] was something that in a year, over a year, I never got used to. For me there was a significant turning point in the play when Macbeth decides to embrace the darkness totally and not to look back and no longer to have a conscience, to banish his conscience. But someone has said that his problem was that he had too much imagination. And that's what finally unseats him, he cannot be ultimately a truly possessed, psychotic, lost individual because even towards the end of the play, there are little murmurs of remorse, little murmurs of what he has done, and it never, ever quite leaves him. So in other words, he [Shakespeare] makes him human.

Paula Zahn What did it mean to you when Ian McKellen told you during the "Tomorrow and tomorrow" soliloquy, you should think about the word "and"? Is that true, that that happened?

Patrick Stewart It is true and I'll tell you how it happened. I had had to pay a visit to the Royal Shakespeare Company rehearsal room in Clapham, in South London, and it just so happened that Trevor Nunn was directing Ian McKellen in *Lear*. They were in rehearsal, and Ian had gone missing. I went into the rehearsal room and they said, "We've lost him. We're in the middle of a run-through and he's disappeared." So I was on the sidewalk outside when I saw in the distance coming up the street Sir Ian, munching away on a piece of cake that he'd been out and bought; and so we talked about the *Lear*. And he said, "If I may, can I, one thing about—because he of course is a famous Macbeth—and he said, "Just one thing, if I may—." And I said, "Yes, what is it?" feeling a little bit defensive. And he said, "'Tomorrow and tomorrow and tomorrow'—the important word is 'and.'" And it was like a light went off in my head because I got it instantly, instantly, even though we hadn't even started rehearsals.

Paula Zahn Give me an example of what he meant.

Patrick Stewart Well, conventionally, you might think of that line as being "**Tomorrow** and **tomorrow** and **tomorrow**" [stressing "tomorrow"]. What Ian was suggesting, that it might read,

"Tomorrow **and** tomorrow **and** tomorrow" [stressing "and"] and then you get the sense of weight of time and the relentless nature of time and it's never going to stop, and every day will be awful, awful. And it was thrilling, so every single night when we got to that, there was a little quiet, "Thank you, Sir Ian, for that one note."

Paula Zahn I am curious if you ended up calibrating your film performance any differently than what you did on stage.

Patrick Stewart Calibrating, yes, and perhaps it is about calibrating most of all, because you're not having to communicate a complex thought or a complex idea or a phrase across twenty-five rows. It can be done very, very intimately.

Paula Zahn Oh, and it's so intensely personal because you're looking straight into that close-up lens. And I imagine that everybody watching the film adaptation would feel like I did, "He's talking to me."

Patrick Stewart I hope so. I hope so. The early experience of rehearsing and performing a play I think had very much prepared us for being in front of a camera and what actors have now for decades discovered is that Shakespeare was a screenwriter, that his language, his imagery, his verse, but most importantly, his characters translate into images that close [hands frame head as a close up shot]. And because there is such truthfulness, such profound reality, in the way that he creates these characters that there is no sense of strain about being in front of a camera. On the contrary, you know, if stage acting is about action and film acting is about thinking, what better playwright than Shakespeare to have thoughts photographed?

Fleetwood Interview (2011)[†]

I try not to have too many fixed ideas before I get into the rehearsal room, because that's where the rich pickings take place. You're in a room with lots of people, and you're collaborating, and the acting, and being in a show, is a big form of collaboration. But you have to wait until you're in the room and see what's going to spark your imagination. You also have and see what the chemistry is going to be like between you and the actor playing Macbeth. And also, particularly, because our show was quite concept heavy, that's going to just take you in all sorts of different directions. If you have too much in your bank, if you like, before you start, that can hold you back in a way.

---

† *Macbeth*, Illuminations Media, DVD (2011), Extras Interview. Used with permission of Illuminations Media.

When Rupert suggested to me about the domestic side of her, the Nigella Lawson[1] side of her, that started to ring really big bells for me, and I don't know whether that's because we're married, that may have had some sort of subconscious effect on his interpretation— that is, to always see me in a kitchen. But that side of it, the domestic side, seeing her as a hostess, that was a great way in. Because then you get the flip side of her—dark, the elemental, dark, spiritual side of her.

What's funny about playing Lady Macbeth is that she's a very strong color, and I think as an actor you always want to play three-dimensional characters, obviously, and that's what you hope to bring. But I remember quite early on in the rehearsal process Rupert said to me—maybe he could say this to me because we're married—but he said look don't try too hard in shaping her, two, three dimensionally, because she is an incredibly strong color, and she has to act on that axis. If you start embellishing it with too much back-story then in the moment it's not going to serve the narrative. So you have to trust what Shakespeare's doing.

In rehearsals as well you're working together all the time. There's a lot of banter, there's a lot of collaboration, there's a lot of ideas sparking around the room. And even when you're working just in a dialogue with Patrick, there's a lot of fun and play, but in performance you realize that she's incredibly isolated. There's only one scene where they seem to be happy, which is at the top of the play, where she says, "To beguile the time, look like the time" [1.5.61–62]—even though she's still sort of motivating him. From that point on they split, and she's only ever trying to get him to do something that he's uneasy about. And so, actually in performance you spend a lot of time alone in your thoughts when you're playing Lady Macbeth, and it's very different than in the rehearsal room.

There was a moment—I don't know whether it was because there's a big age gap, though that never affected us as a friendship. We're very close and we had, really, a lovely time together, and we're still very good friends, and also having my husband mediating this relationship, as Lady Macbeth and Macbeth, was also quite interesting, though fine, and not an issue at all. There was a moment where I had to abandon any issue of age between Patrick and I, and also my relationship with the director. It was when he comes back and I see him for the first time, and I think it was the first time we kissed in rehearsal, and we both had to just sort of go for it, and from that moment on, I think Patrick and I had our own intimacy.

Because, I think in our show, not only is she ambitious and also younger than him, and a trophy wife, but I think it does come from

1. English journalist, television personality, and food writer.

love, it comes from a point of passion from her. And so once that moment had been galvanised between us, then the relationship could then take on a more complex route of being married. So we had the passionate embrace and the kiss and the earthiness of their relationship, the sexuality of their relationship, and then you see the domestic to-ings and fro-ings, and comings and goings—his impatience with her, her terrible impatience with him, his long-sufferingness with her, her anger at him, and it became very much like a marriage. So that's how that developed.

I mean I am talking mostly, I suppose, and I'm thinking about this in the first half of the play. I certainly played Lady Macbeth—having talked a lot about it with Patrick and Rupert—that she starts from a strength. I know there are detractors from that theory—"Then why would she summon the spirits?" [1.5.38ff.]. And I think she dares, she dares herself to summon the spirits. That was my point of view. I can understand not having that point of view, but for me and in this pro- duction, this particular production, she had to dare it in herself. I mean that's the steel that she has. And so when I talk about the rela- tionship [with Macbeth] there comes a point in the play where that scale completely tips.

So if it was a graph, she would start like this [left hand high] and he starts like this [right hand low], and it does this [left hand comes down, right hand goes up]. And there's a moment in the play where she realizes that she really should've been careful about what she wished for, the enormity of this. But I think she glazes over that when she hears [Macduff at] the door, and she has to go into practi- cal mode again. But the moment where it tips for us is when Ban- quo leaves, and Macbeth holds the gun and he says, "God be with you" [3.1.43] to her, dismissing her. Quite often I think in produc- tions that "God be with you" would be to Lennox or whatever, but he [Stewart] says it to her, and he dismisses her, and at that moment she says, "I don't know you anymore" or, "I fear, I don't know you. What is happening?" It's a very, very small moment, but it's abso- lutely important for me as an actor to have that as a pivotal moment. That moment is when the scales tip.[2]

When you play Shakespeare there are so many opportunities for a back-story, and quite often they are important and necessary, but for some reason on this one, every time they came up, those

2. Patrick Stewart concurs: "One of the things that I so admired about Kate's performance, although she was strong and passionate, there was a brittleness about her that made you feel that aspects of her personality were being held together with sticky tape. And, of course, the collapse in her, when it happened, was mirrored by the increasing confi- dence of Macbeth and no better example than the lines about "I am in blood stepped in so far" [3.4.138–39], that going back is just as meaningless as going forward. One of the most potently cynical and dark, demonish-like lines that I know in anywhere in dra- matic literature," Patrick Stewart interview on the Illuminations DVD.

questions appeared in rehearsal—When did she have this baby? When did they decide to kill Duncan? And how long have they been married? Was she married before? And had he been married before? Who was her father?—all of these questions that obviously come up, inevitably, we would just sort of hit a kind of—, well we'd investigate them, but they never really mattered.

To answer those questions, they sort of don't matter, it doesn't mean you don't have any awareness of what that might be saying to the audience, and neither does it not vibrate, but it doesn't always help to answer those questions. Particularly I believe, in Shakespeare. Shakespeare writes what he wants you to know. Now that's not to say when you're playing those lines ["I have given suck," 1.7.54ff.], you're not imagining having a child or what that could be, but in that moment you're not thinking, "Oh, I had that child then, with that person, it looked like that, it made me feel like that." You're thinking, "I had a child, and I would be happy to kill it." So it's very much in the moment. That's why it's difficult, it can be a bit of a red herring, to answer those questions.[3]

Of course, it's an entirely different process when you're putting it on camera. You have to think the thought rather than show the thought; you don't have to communicate to the back of a two-thousand seater. What was interesting about the journey of this particular piece is that we went from a small studio space in Chichester, seating three hundred people, and it was basically in the round, to then playing the Gielgud Theatre, which is an eighteen-hundred seater pros-arch.[4] Then we went to BAM [Brooklyn Academy of Music] in Brooklyn, which is like playing in an airplane hanger, it's enormous, then to a small space on Broadway, smaller space on Broadway, pros-arch again.

In the language of our playing we'd always had this mobility in shifting it, and changing its focus of size, if you like, for want of a

---

3. In his interview on the Illuminations DVD Patrick Stewart has an entirely different perspective: "I think in the case of this play and this relationship a back-story is critical. I don't know how you can play the first and second scenes that they have, if you have not agreed between you what their history has been. In terms of class, perhaps, Lady Macbeth was of a more aristocratic background than was Macbeth who had, literally, fought his way to the top, made his own way up. A powerful, strong and virile individual attractive to this perhaps rather fragile, disappointed, somewhat more aristocratic woman, who wanted from this man all the things that she felt life had not given her. There is the whole question of, "How many children did Lady Macbeth have?" We know she had one, that's for certain. We wavered between her having had a child of another marriage. I think that's where we finally settled; that the child had not been Macbeth's child, but the death of the child was something that he knew was a very sensitive area for her. Not just sensitive but one which there were signs of instability about her, and that when she first mentions the child, "I have given suck" [1.7.54], that instantly Macbeth's instinct is to comfort her, reassure her. . . . And then the very important detail in the back-story, which was that they probably had a lively and creative sex life."
4. Proscaeniuin arch, a rectangular or curved frame that separates the stage from the auditorium in a conventional theater.

Kate Fleetwood as Lady Macbeth in Rupert Goold's 2007 production.
© Manuel Harlan.

better phrase. So I think as a company we were always ready to change it and shift it, and so going from the stage to the camera was probably less of journey for us as a company, than maybe if we'd only played it in one space. So that was helpful. But, of course, technically it's a very different ballgame; on camera, it wasn't just a one-location show, so we were playing in more real spaces, which obviously lends itself to your imagination.

I remember [during the filming] doing the same space, doing "Come, you spirits" in the same space as the sleepwalking. Now "Come, you spirits" always used to have quite a big impact on stage, and I think the sleepwalking has more impact than it did on stage on screen, and I'm really glad that that story has come across. Because I think going back to playing the part, the main thing you feel, you want, ought, to feel about Lady Macbeth, by the end, is pity, not hatred.

When you hear her scream, it's like hearing someone—I remember Rupert giving me a really, really good note about it, which was, "Imagine you're being buried alive, and there's nothing you can do."[5] And that harrowing scream you might hear from somebody, so that the audience should feel not hatred but deep pity. And so, I'm really, really pleased that in the sleepwalking scene you can see a little more into, a bit more of that detail on camera.

---

5. In an interview with *New York Magazine* (April 9, 2008) Fleetwood describes her preparation for the sleepwalking scene: "I was thinking about the Hyrcan tiger that Macbeth mentions [3.4.103] and imagining it ripping my arm off. Okay? Also, there's a really nasty conveyor belt suspending the lift. It's really ugly and industrial, and sometimes I imagine I'm lying on it and being thrown in the horrible motor. It's Gothic! But the language requires you to be in the moment. It's very muscular." See www.vulture.com /2008/04/how_to_play_lady_macbeth_imagi.html

SOURCES AND
CONTEXTS

Sources

N-TOWN CYCLE

[The Slaughter of the Holy Innocents and the Death of Herod] (fourteenth century)†

[*Enter* KING HEROD, STEWARD, SOLDIERS.]
Then, looking back, the Steward goes to Herod and speaks.
STEWARD   Lord, I have walked by dale and hill,
   And waited as it is your will.
   The kings three steal away full still
   Through Bethlehem land.
   They will never, so may I the,[1]
   Come in the land of Galilee
   For to see your fair city,
   Nor deeds of your hand.
KING HEROD   I ride on my rowel,[2] rich in my reign,
   Ribs full red with rape[3] shall I rend!
   Poppets and pap-hawks[4] I shall put in pain,
   With my spear proven pichen and to-pend.[5]
   The gomes with gold crowns ne get never again![6]
   To seek those sots, sondes[7] shall I send.

---

† From *Ludus Coventriae: or The Plaie called Corpus Christi, Cotton MS Vespasian D. VIII*, ed. K. S. Block (London: Oxford University Press, 1922), 169–77. The editor of this Norton Critical Edition has supplied footnotes and modernized spelling and punctuation. The popular medieval cycle plays, presenting Biblical scenes in lively Middle English verse, influenced much later drama. The ranting, murderous Herod, for example, lurks behind the tyrants of Elizabethan drama, including Macbeth. Both Herod and Macbeth boast, kill children, throw a feast, and suddenly face death. Perceiving a threat to his power, Herod sends the three kings to search for the child, but they do not return. Herod then orders all the male children around Bethlehem killed, the Slaughter of the Holy Innocents (Matthew 2.7–18).
1. thrive.
2. spur.
3. blows.
4. children and suckling infants.
5. to thrust and to stab.
6. The gold-crowned children will never thrive again. (Here and in the next line Herod may refer to the children or the three kings.)
7. messengers, i.e., soldiers; *sots*: fools.

Do owlet hoot, hoberd and hein,
When her bairns bleed under cradle-band?[8]
Sharply I shall them shend![9]
The knave[1] children that be
In all Israel country,
They shall have bloody blee[2]
For one I called unkind.[3]
It is told in Gru[4]
His name should be Jesu
Ifound.[5]
To have him, you gone,[6]
Hew the flesh with the bone,
And give him wound!
Now keen knights, kithe[7] your crafts,
And killeth knave children and casteth them in clay!
Showeth on your shoulders shields and shafts,
Shapeth among scheltrownys a shrilling shray![8]
Doth rounces run with raking raftes[9]
Till ribs be to-rent with a red array![1]
Let no bairn be left unbeat baftes[2]
Till a beggar bleed by beasts' bay.[3]
Mahound, that best may![4]
I warn you, my knights,
A bairn is born, I plights,[5]
Would climb[6] king and knights,
And let my lordly lay.[7]
Knights wise,
Chosen, full choice,[8]
Arise, arise,

8. Does the screech owl hoot, clown and rascal, when her babes bleed in their swaddling clothes? (The owl refers metaphorically to the bereaved mothers of the slaughtered Holy Innocents.)
9. destroy.
1. male.
2. complexion.
3. wicked (i.e., Jesus Christ).
4. Greek.
5. found to be.
6. go.
7. show.
8. Raise among troops a shrill outcry!
9. Let horses run with thrusting spears.
1. torn in pieces and covered in blood.
2. behind.
3. stall. (The beggar is Christ in the stable.)
4. Mahound, who best can (an oath). Mahound (Mahomet, Mohammed), is considered a devil or false god in English mystery cycles.
5. swear.
6. climb above.
7. diminish my rule.
8. excellent.

And take your toll!
And every page,[9]
Of two-year age,
Ere ever you swage,[1]
Slayeth ilk a fool![2]
One of them all
Was born in stall;
Fools him call
King in crown!
With bitter gall
He shall down fall!
My might in hall
Shall never go down!

FIRST SOLDIER   I shall slay churls,
And queans with thirls;[3]
Her knave-girls[4]
I shall stick!
Forth will I speed
To do[5] them bleed.
Though girls grede,[6]
We shall be wreak![7]

SECOND SOLDIER   For swords sharp
As an harp[8]
Queans shall carp,[9]
And of sorrow sing.
Bairns young,
They shall be stung!
Through liver and lung,
We shall them sting!   [*Exeunt all.*]

        [*Enter* ANGEL, JOSEPH, MARY *with* BABY JESUS.]

ANGEL   Awake, Joseph, and take thy wife,
Thy child also—ride belife![1]
For King Herod with sharp knife,
His knights he doth send.
The Father of Heaven hath to thee sent[2]

---

9. boy.
1. cease.
2. kill every baby.
3. whores with piercings.
4. their male children.
5. make.
6. children cry out.
7. avenged.
8. grappling hook (shortened form of *arpago*).
9. whores will wail.
1. at once.
2. commanded.

Into Egypt that thou be bent,[3]
For cruel knights thy child have meant
With sword to slay and shend![4]
JOSEPH   Awake, good wife, out of your sleep,
And of your child taketh good keep,[5]
While I your clothes lay on heap,[6]
And truss[7] them on the ass.
King Herod the child will slay,
Therefore to Egypt must we go—
An angel of God said me so,
And therefore let us pass.   [*Exeunt all.*]
    [*Enter* SOLDIERS, *and* WOMEN *carrying babies.*]
    Then the soldiers will go to kill the boys and the First
    Woman will speak.
FIRST WOMAN   Long lulling have I lorn![8]
Alas, why was my bairn born?
With swapping[9] sword now is he shorn
The head right from the neck!
Shank and shoulder is all to-torn.[1]
Sorrow I see behind and before,
Both midnight, midday, and at morn.
Of my life I not reck.[2]
SECOND WOMAN   Certainly I say the same,
Gone is all my good game![3]
My little child lieth all lame,
That lulled on my paps.[4]
My forty weeks' groaning
Hath sent me seven-year sorrowing.
Mickle[5] is my mourning,
And right hard are mine haps![6]
FIRST SOLDIER   Lord in throne,
Maketh no moan!
Queans 'gin groan
In world about.
Upon my spear

3. headed.
4. destroy.
5. care.
6. gather.
7. tie.
8. Long singing of lullabyes have I lost.
9. smiting.
1. torn to pieces.
2. do not care.
3. joy.
4. slept peacefully on my breasts.
5. much.
6. misfortunes.

A girl[7] I bear,
I dare well swear,
Let mothers hoot!   [*Exeunt all.*]
   [*Enter* KING HEROD, SOLDIERS.]
SECOND SOLDIER   Lord, we have sped
As you bade:
Bairns been bled,
And lie in ditch,
Flesh and vein
Have tholed[8] pain,
And you shall reign
Evermore rich.
KING HEROD   You shall have steeds
To your meeds,[9]
Lands and ledes,[1]
Frith and fee.[2]
Well have you wrought,
My foe is sought,
To death is he brought,
Now come up to me!
In scat now am I set as king of mights most;
All this world for their love to me shall they lout,[3]
Both of heaven and of earth, and of hell coast.
For digne of my dignity they have of me doubt![4]
There is no lord like on life to me worth a toast,[5]
Neither king nor kaiser[6] in all this world about!
If any briber do brag or blow against[7] my boast,
I shall rap those ribalds and rake them on rout[8]
With my bright brond![9]
There shall be neither kaiser nor king
But that I shall them down ding,[1]
Less than[2] he at my bidding
Be buxom[3] to mine hand.

---

7. baby.
8. suffered.
9. for your rewards.
1. people.
2. property and goods.
3. bow.
4. fear; **digne**: out of respect.
5. alive compared to me worth a piece of toast.
6. emperor (from Caesar).
7. scoundrel brags or contradicts.
8. smite those rogues and destroy them all together.
9. sword.
1. strike them down.
2. unless.
3. obedient.

Now my gentle and courteous knights, hark to me this stound.[4]
Good time soon, methinketh, at dinner that we were.
Smartly, therefore, set a table anon here full sound,
Covered with a curious[5] cloth and with rich, worthy fare,
Service for the loveliest lord that living is on ground.
Best meats and worthiest wines look that you none spare,
Though that a little pint should cost a thousand pound!
Bring always of the best; for cost take you no care.
Anon that it be done!

    [*A table is set. Enter* STEWARD, *a* MINSTREL.]

STEWARD   My lord, the table is ready dight,[6]
Here is water; now wash forthright.
Now blow up,[7] minstrel, with all your might!
The service[8] cometh in soon.

    [*Herod and the soldiers sit at table; food is served.*]

KING HEROD   Now am I set at meat
And worthily served at my degree.[9]
Come forth, knights, sit down and eat,
And be as merry as you can be!

FIRST SOLDIER   Lord, at your bidding we take our seat,
With hearty[1] will obey we thee.
There is no lord of might so great,
Through all this world in no country,
In worship to abide.[2]

KING HEROD   I was never merrier herebeforn,[3]
Sith[4] that I was first born,
Than I am now right in this morn.
In joy I 'gin to glide.[5]

    [*Enter* DEATH *in tattered garments, covered with worms.*][6]

DEATH   Ow! I heard a page make praising of pride![7]
All princes he passeth, he weeneth, of pousty.[8]
He weeneth to be the worthiest of all this world wide;

---

4. listen to me now.
5. elaborate.
6. prepared.
7. sound the fanfare.
8. meal.
9. as befits my station.
1. heartfelt.
2. who lives in such honor.
3. before now.
4. since the time.
5. into joy I begin to pass.
6. Death may be present all along, an ominous figure at the feast silently undercutting
Herod's pride and boasts.
7. servant make proud boasts.
8. surpasses, he thinks, in power.

King over all kings, that page weeneth to be.
He sent into Bethlehem to seek on every side
Christ for to quell,[9] if they might him see.
But of his wicked will, lurdan,[1] yet he lied.
God's Son doth live; there is no lord but he.
Over all lords he is king.
I am Death, God's messenger.
Almighty God hath sent me here
Yon lurdan to slay, without dwere,[2]
For his wicked working.
I am sent from God. Death is my name.
All thing that is on ground I wield at my will:
Both man and beast, and birds, wild and tame.
When that I come them to, with death I do them kill;
Herb, grass, and trees strong, take them all in same.[3]
Yea, the great, mighty oaks with my dent I spill.[4]
What man that I wrestle with, he shall right soon have shame;
I give him such a trippet[5] he shall evermore lie still,
For Death kan[6] no sport!
Where I smite there is no grace,
For after my stroke man hath no space
To make amends for his trespass,
But[7] God him grant comfort.
Ow, see how proudly yon caitiff[8] sits at meat!
Of death hath he no doubt;[9] he weeneth to live evermore.
To him will I go and give him such an heat[1]
That all the leeches[2] of the land his life shall never restore.
Against my dreadful dents it vaileth[3] never to plead.
Ere I him part from, I shall him make full poor.
All the blood of his body I shall him out-sweat,[4]
For now I go to slay him with strokes sad[5] and sore,
This tide,[6]

9. kill.
1. rogue.
2. doubt.
3. I take them all together.
4. with my blow I kill.
5. tripping up.
6. knows.
7. unless.
8. scoundrel.
9. fear.
1. fever. The word **hete** also could mean "hit" or "blow."
2. doctors.
3. against my dreadful blows it avails.
4. sweat out of him.
5. heavy.
6. time.

Both him and his knights all,
I shall them make to me but thrall;[7]
With my spear slay them I shall,
And so cast down his pride!

KING HEROD   Now, kind[8] knights, be merry and glad;
With all good diligence show now some mirth,
For, by gracious Mahound, more mirth never I had,
Nor never more joy was in[9] from time of my birth.
For now my foe is dead and prended as a pad.[1]
Above me is no king, on ground nor on garth,[2]
Mirths, therefore, make you and be right nothing[3] sad!
Spare neither meat nor drink, and spare for no dearth
Of wine nor of bread.
For now am I a king alone.
So worthy as I, may there be none.
Therefore, knights be merry each one,
For now my foe is dead.

FIRST SOLDIER   When the boys sprawled at my spear's end,
By Satan, our sire, it was a goodly sight!
A good game it was that boy for to shend,[4]
That would have been our king and put you from your right.

SECOND SOLDIER   Now truly, my lord the King, we had been
    unhende[5]
And never none of us able for to be a knight,
If that any of us to them had been a friend,
And a-saved any life against thy mickle[6] might,
From death them to flyte.[7]

KING HEROD   Amongst all that great rout
He is dead, I have no doubt.
Therefore, minstrel, round about,
Blow up a merry fit![8]

> *Here, while they play trumpets, let Death kill Herod and
> two soldiers immediately, and let the Devil [emerging from
> hell-mouth] receive them.*

DEVIL   All ours! all ours! This chattel[9] is mine!

---

7. slaves.
8. noble.
9. in me.
1. taken as a toad.
2. in open or enclosed space, i.e., anywhere.
3. not at all.
4. destroy.
5. discourteous.
6. great; **a-saved**: had saved.
7. deliver.
8. tune.
9. property.

I shall them bring unto my cell,
I shall them teach plays[1] fine,
And show such mirth as is in hell.
It were more better amongst swine,
That evermore stink thereby to dwell!
For in our lodge[2] is so great pain
That no earthly tongue can tell.
[*To the victims*] With you I go my way.
I shall you bear forth with me,
And show you sports of our glee.
Of our mirths now shall you see,
And ever sing "Wellaway!"[3]

      [*The Devil in a dance of death takes their souls to hell.*]

DEATH   Of King Herod all men beware,
That hath rejoiced in pomp and pride.
For all his boast of bliss full bare,[4]
He lieth now dead here on his side.
For when I come I cannot spare,
From me no wight may him[5] hide.
Now is he dead and cast in care,[6]
In hell pit ever to abide;
His lordship is all lorn.[7]
Now is he as poor as I,
Worms' meat is his body;
His soul in hell full painfully
Of devils is all to-torn.[8]
All men dwelling upon the ground,
Beware of me, by mine counsel,
For faint fellowship in me is found.
I kan[9] no courtesy, as I you tell,
For be a man never so sound,
Of health in heart never so well,
I come suddenly within a stound.[1]
Me withstand may no castle!
My journey will I speed.[2]

1. games.
2. prison.
3. an exclamation of sorrow.
4. absolute bliss.
5. person may himself.
6. lament.
7. lost.
8. torn to pieces.
9. know.
1. moment.
2. accomplish.

Of my coming no man is ware,[3]
For when men make most merry fare,
Then suddenly I cast them in care,
And slay them even in deed!
Though I be naked and poor of array,
And worms gnaw me all about,
Yet look you dread me night and day,
For when Death cometh you stand in doubt.
Even like to me, as I you say,
Shall all you be here in this rout.[4]
When I you challenge, at my day,
I shall you make right low to lout,[5]
And naked for to be.
Amongst worms, as I you tell,
Under the earth shall you dwell,
And they shall eat both flesh and fell,[6]
As they have done me.   [*Exeunt all.*]

SENECA

Medea (first century, trans. 1581)[†]

Medea: Then at the altars of the gods my children shall be slain,
With crimson-colored blood of babes their altars will I stain,
Through[1] livers, lungs, the lights,[2] and heart, through every gut and
    gall,[3]
For vengeance break away, perforce, and spare no blood at all,
If any lusty life as yet within thy soul do rest,
If aught of ancient courage still do dwell within my breast,
Exile all foolish female fear and pity from thy mind,
And as th'untamed tigers use to rage and rave unkind,

3. aware.
4. crowd.
5. bow.
6. skin.
† From *Seneca His Tenne Tragedies, Translated into Englysh*, ed. Thomas Newton (London, 1581), sigs. R2v, D2v, C4, D3v, D4–D4v, T8–T8v. *Medea* is translated by John Studley. Footnotes are by the editor of this Norton Critical Edition. Spelling and punctuation have been modernized by the editor. A Stoic philosopher, Lucius Annaeus Seneca (4?B.C.E–65 C.E.) wrote plays that served as models of tragic language and action for Elizabethans. In this first selection the witch Medea rouses herself to a terrible revenge on her unfaithful husband by murdering their children. Compare Lady Macbeth (1.5.38–52) urging herself to *scelus*, "crime," in a highly charged monologue of self-creation.
1. by means of. Medea uses her children's vital organs as the beast entrails of a sacrifice.
2. eyes.
3. liver, here used generically for internal organ.

Judith Anderson and Zoe Caldwell in *Medea* (1983). Courtesy of
Photofest.

That haunt the croaking, cumbrous caves and clumpered[4] frozen
      climes,
And craggy rocks of Caucasus,[5] whose bitter cold deprives
The soil of all inhabitors, permit to lodge and rest
Such savage, brutish tyranny within thy brazen breast.
Whatever hurly-burly wrought doth Phasis[6] understand,
What mighty, monstrous, bloody feat I wrought by sea or land,
The like in Corinth[7] shall be seen in most outrageous guise,
Most hideous, hateful, horrible to hear or see with eyes,
Most devilish, desperate, dreadful deed, yet never known
      before,
Whose rage shall force heaven, earth, and hell to quake and tremble
      sore.
My burning breast that rolls in wrath and doth in rancor boil,
Sore thirsteth after blood and wounds with slaughter, death, and
      spoil,
By renting[8] racked limbs from limbs to drive them down to
      grave.

4. congealed (with ice); cumbrous: difficult to access.
5. mountain range between the Black and Caspian seas, a symbol of remoteness and
   desolation.
6. Whatever disturbance has occurred near Phasis, a river in Colchis, Medea's homeland
   (present-day Russia).
7. ancient Greek city, home of Medea's husband Jason, and scene of the present tragedy.
8. tearing.

Tush, these be but as flea-bitings that mentionèd I have;
As weighty things as these I did in greener girlish age.
Now sorrow's smart doth rub the gall[9] and frets with sharper rage.
But sith my womb hath yielded fruit, it doth me well behove,[1]
The strength and parlous puissance[2] of weightier ills to prove.
Be ready, Wrath, with all thy might that fury kindle may,
Thy foes to their destruction be ready to assay.[3]

Hercules Furens (first century, trans. 1581)[†]

Theseus: In one appointed judgment place is Gnossian Minos hard,
And in another, Rhadamanth; this crime doth Aeac hear.[1]
What each man once hath done he feels, and guilt to th'author there
Returns,[2] and th'hurtful with their own example punished be.
The bloody, cruel captains I in prison shut did see,
And back of tyrant impotent even with his people's hand
All torn and cut. What man of might with favor leads his land,
And, of his own life lord, reserves his hurtless hands to good,[3]
And gently doth his empire guide without the thirst of blood,
And spares his soul, he, having long led forth the ling'ring days
Of happy age, at length to heaven doth either find the ways,
Or joyful, happy places else of fair Elysius wood.[4]

⁂

Hercules:[5] Take mercy, father; lo, I lift to thee my humble hands.
What meaneth this? My hand fleeth back. Some privy[6] guilt there
    stands.
Whence comes this blood? Or what doth mean, flowing with death
    of child,

---

9. chafe the wound.
1. behoove, suit.
2. dangerous power.
3. attempt (to bring about).
† Translated by Jasper Heywood. Recalling his journey to Hades in the first passage from
    Hercules Furens, Theseus articulates a pagan conception of justice and the afterlife
    important to Elizabethan tragedy and Shakespeare.
1. Minos, Rhadamanthus, and Aecus, the three judges in Hades.
2. a popular Senecan sentence, *auctorem scelus / repetit* (735–36), "crime returns to its
    own author"; compare *Macbeth*, 1.7.8–12.
3. and, though is lord of life (*dominusque vitae*, 740), uses his harmless hands only to do
    good.
4. the abode of the blessed and virtuous.
5. The next selections feature the hero of the tragedy, Hercules, realizing that he has
    slain his own children in a mad rage set upon him by the goddess Juno. His anguished
    rhetoric of recognition and remorse echoes through Shakespeare's great tragedies; the
    imagery of blood-stained hands is especially important for *Macbeth* (see 2.2.62–66).
6. private.

The shaft imbrued with slaughter once of Lerney monster killed?[7]
I see my weapons now; the hand I seek no more to wit.[8]
Whose hand could bend this bow but mine? Or what right arm but it
Could string the bow that unto me even scantly[9] doth obey?
To you I turn: O father dear, is this my guilt,[1] I pray?
They held their peace,[2] is mine own.

            *   *   *

Hercules: Wherefore I longer should[3] sustain my life yet in this light
And linger here, no cause there is; all good lost have I quite—
My mind, my weapons, my renown, my wife, my sons, my hands,
And fury too; no man may heal and loose from guilty bands
My mind defiled.

            *   *   *

Hercules: What place shall I seek, runagate,[4] for rest?
Where shall I hide myself? Or in what land myself engrave?[5]
What Tanais, or what Nilus else, or with his Persian wave
What Tigris violent of stream, or what fierce Rhenus flood,
Or Tagus troublesome that flows with Iber's treasures good,
May my right hand now wash from guilt? Although Maeotis cold[6]
The waves of all the northern sea on me shed out now would,
And all the water thereof should now pass by my two hands,
Yet will the mischief deep remain. Alas, into what lands
Wilt thou, O wicked man, resort? To east or western coast?
Each were well known; all place I have of banishment quite lost.

Agamemnon (first century, trans. 1581)[†]

Chorus: O Fortune, that dost fail[1] the great estate[2] of kings,
On slippery, sliding seat thou placest lofty things,

---

7. the arrow stained formerly with the slaughter of the Lernaean Hydra (a monster Hercules slew as one of his labors).
8. know.
9. hardly.
1. with a pun on "gilt," a gold or red covering.
2. His father and Theseus kept silent.
3. Why I should longer. Compare *Macbeth* 5.3.22–28.
4. fugitive.
5. bury myself in.
6. The exotic waters include the Tanais, a river of ancient Scythia (Southern Russia); the Nile river in Egypt; the Tigris river (in present-day Turkey and Iraq); the Rhine river in Western Europe; the Tagus river of golden sands in Spain (Iber); and Lake Maeotis in ancient Scythia. (Compare *Macbeth* 2.2.63–66.)
† Translated by John Studley. This Choral song about Fortune's power and sleeplessness echoes throughout *Macbeth* (see 2.2.38–43; 5.5.17–28).
1. make fail.
2. power and position.

And setst on tott'ring sort,[3] where perils do abound.
Yet never kingdom calm nor quiet could be found;
No day to scepters sure doth shine,[4] that they might say,
"Tomorrow shall we rule as we have done today."
One clod of crooked care another bringeth in,
One hurly-burly[5] done, another doth begin.

*   *   *

O how doth Fortune toss and tumble in her wheel[6]
The stagg'ring states of kings that ready be to reel!
Fain[7] would they dreaded be, and yet not settled so,[8]
When as they fearèd are, they fear and live in woe.
The silent lady, Night, so sweet to man and beast,
Cannot bestow on them her safe and quiet rest;
Sleep that doth overcome and break the bonds of grief,
It cannot ease their hearts nor minister relief.
What castle strongly built, what bulwark, tower, or town,
Is not by mischief's means brought topsy-turvy down?
What rampart[9] walls are not made weak by wicked war?
From stately courts of kings doth justice fly afar;
In princely places, of honesty the lore,
And wedlock vow devout, is set by little store.[1]
The bloody Bellon[2] those doth haunt with gory hand,
Whose light and vain conceit[3] in painted pomp doth stand.

RAPHAEL HOLINSHED

[Duff and Duncan] (1587)[†]

Duff

Amongst them there were also certain young gentlemen, right
beautiful and goodly personages, being near of kin unto Donwald,

---

3. set in motion wavering fate.
4. No day shines surely to rulers.
5. commotion.
6. Fortune was often depicted as a wheel upon which all rose and fell in ceaseless motion.
7. gladly.
8. They are not settled, or content, when they are feared (*metui cupiunt / metuique timent*, 72–73, "they want to be feared, they dread to be feared").
9. fortified.
1. The doctrine (lore) of honesty and marital fidelity are little valued at court.
2. Bellona, Roman goddess of war.
3. self-conception.
† From Raphael Holinshed; *The First and Second Volumes of Chronicles* (London, 1587), vol. 2, *The History of Scotland*, fols. 150–52, 168–76. Footnotes are by the editor of this Norton Critical Edition. Spelling and punctuation have been modernized by the editor. Raphael Holinshed (d. 1580) gathered various legends and accounts into a bulky

captain of the castle, and had been persuaded to be partakers with the other rebels more through the fraudulent counsel of divers wicked persons than of their own accord. Whereupon the foresaid Donwald, lamenting their case, made earnest labor and suit to the King to have begged their pardon; but having a plain denial, he conceived such an inward malice towards the King (though he showed it not outwardly at the first) that the same continued still boiling in his stomach and ceased not till, through setting on of his wife[1] and in revenge of such unthankfulness, he found means to murder the King within the foresaid castle of Forres where he used to sojourn. For the King, being in that country, was accustomed to lie most commonly within the same castle, having a special trust in Donwald as a man whom he never suspected.

But Donwald, not forgetting the reproach which his lineage[2] had sustained by the execution of those his kinsmen whom the King for a spectacle to the people had caused to be hanged, could not but show manifest tokens of great grief at home amongst his family, which his wife, perceiving, ceased not to travail[3] with him till she understood what the cause was of his displeasure. Which at length when she had learned by his own relation, she, as one that bare no less malice in her heart towards the King for the like cause on her behalf than her husband did for his friends', counseled him (sith[4] the King oftentimes used to lodge in his house without any guard about him other than the garrison of the castle, which was wholly at his commandment) to make him away,[5] and showed him the means whereby he might soonest accomplish it.

Donwald, thus being the more kindled in wrath by the words of his wife, determined to follow her advice in the execution of so heinous an act. Whereupon, devising with himself for a while which way he might best accomplish his cursed intent, at length gat[6] opportunity and sped his purpose as followeth. It chanced that the King, upon the day before he purposed to depart forth of the castle, was long in his oratory[7] at his prayers and there continued till it was late in the night. At the last, coming forth, he called such afore him

chronicle of England, Scotland, and Ireland (1577, 1587), which became the main source of Shakespeare's English history plays. In *Macbeth* Shakespeare combines the assassinations of Duff and Duncan from the *Chronicles*, greatly expanding the supernatural elements and the role of Lady Macbeth. He alters Holinshed's Banquo, a conspirator, and his Duncan, a weak ruler, and suppresses all mention of Macbeth's ten years of good rule. Shakespeare makes his greatest changes to Macbeth himself, endowing Holinshed's cruel tyrant with a voice of moral sensibility, poetic self-consciousness, and regret.

1. because of his wife's encouragement.
2. family.
3. labor.
4. since.
5. to kill him.
6. got.
7. chapel.

as had faithfully served him in pursuit and apprehension of the rebels, and, giving the hearty thanks, he bestowed sundry honorable gifts amongst them, of the which number Donwald was one, as he that had been ever accounted a most faithful servant to the King.

At length, having talked with them a long time, he got him[8] into his privy chamber only with two of his chamberlains[9] who, having brought him to bed, came forth again and then fell to banqueting with Donwald and his wife, who had prepared divers delicate dishes and sundry sorts of drinks for their rear supper or collation[1] whereat they sat up so long till they had charged their stomachs with such full gorges[2] that their heads were no sooner got to the pillow but asleep they were so fast that a man might have removed the chamber over them sooner than to have awaked them out of their drunken sleep.

Then Donwald, though he abhorred the act greatly in heart, yet through instigation of his wife he called four of his servants unto him, whom he had made privy to his wicked intent before and framed[3] to his purpose with large gifts, and now declaring unto them after what sort[4] they should work the feat, they gladly obeyed his instructions. And speedily going about the murder, they enter[ed] the chamber in which the King lay a little before cock's crow, where they secretly cut his throat as he lay sleeping, without any buskling[5] at all. And immediately, by a postern[6] gate, they carried forth the dead body into the fields, and, throwing it upon an horse there provided ready for that purpose, they convey[ed] it unto a place about two miles distant from the castle, where they stayed and gat certain laborers to help them to turn the course of a little river running through the fields there; and digging a deep hole in the channel, they burie[d] the body in the same, ramming it up with stones and gravel so closely that, setting the water in the right course again, no man could perceive that anything had been newly digged there. This they did by order appointed them by Donwald (as is reported), for that the body should not be found and, by bleeding when Donwald should be present, declare him to be guilty of the murder. For such an opinion men have that the dead corpse of any man, being slain, will bleed abundantly if the murderer be present. But for what consideration soever they buried him there, they had

8. himself.
9. personal servants.
1. final meal of the day.
2. large ingestions.
3. shaped.
4. in what manner.
5. scuffling, commotion.
6. back.

no sooner finished the work but that they slew them whose help they used herein and straightways thereupon fled into Orkney.

Donwald, about the time that the murder was in doing, got him amongst them that kept the watch and so continued in company with them all the residue of the night. But in the morning, when the noise was raised in the King's chamber how the King was slain, his body conveyed away, and the bed all berayed[7] with blood, he with the watch ran thither as though he had known nothing of the matter and, breaking into the chamber and finding cakes[8] of blood in the bed and on the floor about the sides of it, he forthwith slew the chamberlains as guilty of that heinous murder. And then, like a madman, running to and fro, he ransacked every corner within the castle as though it had been to have seen if he might have found either the body or any of the murderers hid in any privy[9] place. But at length coming to the postern gate and finding it open, he burdened the chamberlains whom he had slain with all the fault, they having the keys of the gates committed to their keeping all the night, and therefore it could not be otherwise (said he) but that they were of counsel[1] in the committing of that most detestable murder.

Finally, such was his over-earnest diligence in the severe inquisition and trial of the offenders herein that some of the lords began to mislike the matter and to smell forth shrewd tokens[2] that he should not be altogether clear himself. But forsomuch as they were in that country where he had the whole rule, what by reason of his friends and authority together, they doubted[3] to utter what they thought till time and place should better serve thereunto, and hereupon got them away, every man to his home. For the space of six months together after this heinous murder thus committed, there appeared no sun by day nor moon by night in any part of the realm, but still[4] was the sky covered with continual clouds, and sometimes such outrageous winds arose, with lightnings and tempests, that the people were in great fear of present destruction.

In the meantime, Culain, Prince of Cumberland, the son (as I have said) of King Indulph, accompanied with a great number of lords and nobles of the realm, came unto Scone, there to receive the crown according to the manner. But at his coming thither he demanded of the bishops what the cause should be of such untemperate weather. Who made answer that undoubtedly almighty God showed himself thereby to be offended most highly for that wicked

7. befouled.
8. clots.
9. private.
1. agreed.
2. detect ominous signs.
3. feared.
4. continually.

murder of King Duff, and, surely, unless the offenders were tried forth and punished for that deed, the realm should feel the just indignation of the divine judgement for omitting such punishment as was due for so grievous an offense.

* * *

Monstrous sights also that were seen within the Scottish kingdom that year were these: Horses in Lothian, being of singular beauty and swiftness, did eat their own flesh and would in no wise taste any other meat. In Angus there was a gentlewoman brought forth a child without eyes, nose, hand, or foot. There was a sparhawk[5] also strangled by an owl. Neither was it any less wonder that the sun, as before is said, was continually covered with clouds for six months' space. But all men understood that the abominable murder of King Duff was the cause hereof, which being revenged by the death of the authors (in manner as before is said), Cullen was crowned as lawful successor to the same Duff at Scone, with all due honor and solemnity, in the year of our Lord 972.

* * *

Duncan

After Malcolm, succeeded his nephew[6] Duncan, the son of his daughter Beatrice. For Malcolm had two daughters; the one, which was this Beatrice, being given in marriage unto one Abbanath Crinen, a man of great nobility and thane of the Isles and west parts of Scotland, bare of that marriage the foresaid Duncan. The other, called Doada, was married unto Sinel, the Thane of Glamis, by whom she had issue one Macbeth, a valiant gentleman and one that, if he had not been somewhat cruel of nature, might have been thought most worthy the government of a realm. On the other part, Duncan was so soft and gentle of nature that the people wished the inclinations and manners of these two cousins to have been so tempered[7] and interchangeably bestowed betwixt them that, where the one had too much of clemency and the other of cruelty, the mean virtue betwixt these two extremities might have reigned by indifferent partition[8] in them both; so should Duncan have proved a worthy king and Macbeth an excellent captain. The beginning of Duncan's reign was very quiet and peaceable, without any notable trouble; but after it was perceived how negligent he was in punishing offenders, many misruled[9]

5. sparrow-hawk.
6. grandson.
7. mixed.
8. equal distribution.
9. disorderly.

persons took occasion thereof to trouble the peace and quiet state of the commonwealth by seditious commotions which first had their beginnings in this wise.

Banquo, the Thane of Lochaber, of whom the House of the Stuarts[1] is descended, the which by order of lineage hath now for a long time enjoyed the crown of Scotland even till these our days, as he gathered the finances due to the King and further punished somewhat sharply such as were notorious offenders, being assailed by a number of rebels inhabiting in that country and spoiled[2] of the money and all other things, had much ado to get away with life after he had received sundry grievous wounds amongst them. Yet, escaping their hands, after he was somewhat recovered of his hurts and was able to ride, he repaired[3] to the court, where, making his complaint to the King in most earnest wise, he purchased[4] at length that the offenders were sent for by a sergeant-at-arms to appear to make answer unto such matters as should be laid to their charge. But they, augmenting their mischievous act with a more wicked deed, after they had misused the messenger with sundry kinds of reproaches, they finally slew him also.

Then, doubting not but for such contemptuous demeanor against the King's regal authority they should be invaded with all the power[5] the King could make, Macdowald, one of great estimation among them, making first a confederacy with his nearest friends and kinsmen, took upon him to be chief captain of all such rebels as would stand against the King in maintenance of their grievous offenses lately committed against him. Many slanderous words also and railing taunts this Macdowald uttered against his prince, calling him a fainthearted milksop more meet to govern a sort[6] of idle monks in some cloister than to have the rule of such valiant and hardy men of war as the Scots were. He used also such subtle persuasions and forged allurements that in a small time he had gotten together a mighty power of men; for out of the Western Isles there came unto him a great multitude of people offering themselves to assist him in that rebellious quarrel, and out of Ireland in hope of the spoil came no small number of kerns and galloglasses,[7] offering gladly to serve under him whither it should please him to lead them.

Macdowald, thus having a mighty puissance[8] about him, encountered with such of the King's people as were, sent against him into

1. royal family governing England from the time of King James I (1603–1625) to 1688.
2. robbed.
3. returned.
4. arranged.
5. army.
6. bunch.
7. light-armed Irish foot soldiers and soldiers on horse with axes.
8. power.

Lochaber and, discomfiting them, by mere[9] force took their captain Malcolm and after the end of the battle smote off his head. This overthrow, being notified to the King, did put him in wonderful[1] fear by reason of his small skill in warlike affairs. Calling therefore his nobles to a council, he asked of them their best advice for the subduing of Macdowald and other the rebels. Here in sundry heads (as ever it happeneth) were sundry opinions, which they uttered according to every man his skill. At length Macbeth, speaking much against the King's softness and overmuch slackness in punishing offenders, whereby they had such time to assemble together, he promised, notwithstanding, if the charge were committed unto him and unto Banquo, so to order the matter that the rebels should be shortly vanquished and quite put down, and that not so much as one of them should be found to make resistance within the country.[2]

*   *   *

Shortly after happened a strange and uncouth[3] wonder, which afterward was the cause of much trouble in the realm of Scotland, as ye shall after hear. It fortuned, as Macbeth and Banquo journeyed toward Forres where the King then lay, they went sporting[4] by the way together without other company save only themselves, passing thorough the woods and fields, when suddenly, in the midst of a laund,[5] there met them three women in strange and wild apparel, resembling creatures of elder worlds,[6] whom when they attentively beheld, wondering much at the sight, the first of them spake and said, "All hail, Macbeth, Thane of Glamis!" (for he had lately entered into that dignity and office by the death of his father Sinel). The second of them said, "Hail, Macbeth, Thane of Cawdor!" But the third said, "All hail, Macbeth, that hereafter shalt be King of Scotland!"

Then Banquo: "What manner of women," saith he, "are you, that seem so little favorable unto me, whereas to my fellow here, besides high offices, ye assign also the kingdom, appointing forth nothing for me at all?" "Yes," saith the first of them, "we promise greater benefits unto thee than unto him, for he shall reign indeed, but with an unlucky end; neither shall he leave any issue behind him to succeed in his place. Where, contrarily, thou in deed shalt not reign

9. sheer.
1. great.
2. Macbeth and Banquo put down the rebellion, then vanquish the invading Sueno, king of Norway, and an accompanying force from Denmark.
3. uncommon.
4. for amusement.
5. glade, an open space in the woods.
6. ancient times.

at all, but of thee those shall be born which shall govern the Scottish kingdom by long order of continual descent." Herewith the foresaid women vanished immediately out of their sight. This was reputed at the first but some vain fantastical illusion by Macbeth and Banquo, insomuch that Banquo would call Macbeth, in jest, King of Scotland, and Macbeth again would call him in sport likewise the father of many kings. But afterwards the common opinion was that these women were either the Weird Sisters, that is (as ye would say), the goddesses of destiny, or else some nymphs or fairies endued with knowledge of prophecy by their necromantical science,[7] because everything came to pass as they had spoken. For shortly after, the Thane of Cawdor being condemned at Forres of treason against the King committed, his lands, livings, and offices were given of[8] the King's liberality to Macbeth.

The same night after at supper Banquo jested with him and said, "Now Macbeth, thou hast obtained those things which the two former sisters prophesied; there remaineth only for thee to purchase[9] that which the third said should come to pass." Whereupon Macbeth, revolving the thing in his mind, began even then to devise how he might attain to the kingdom. But yet he thought with himself that he must tarry a time which should advance him thereto by the divine providence, as it had come to pass in his former preferment.[1] But shortly after it chanced that King Duncan, having two sons by his wife (which was the daughter of Siward, Earl of Northumberland), he made the elder of them called Malcolm, Prince of Cumberland, as it were thereby to appoint him his successor in the kingdom immediately after his decease. Macbeth, sore troubled herewith for that he saw by this means his hope sore hindered (where, by the old laws of the realm, the ordinance was that if he that should succeed were not of able age to take the charge upon himself, he that was next of blood unto him should be admitted), he began to take counsel how he might usurp the kingdom by force, having a just quarrel so to do, as he took[2] the matter, for that Duncan did what in him lay[3] to defraud him of all manner of title and claim which he might in time to come pretend[4] unto the crown.

The words of the three Weird Sisters also (of whom before ye have heard) greatly encouraged him hereunto; but specially his wife lay sore upon him[5] to attempt the thing, as she that was very ambitious,

---

7. occult knowledge, perhaps gained from communication with the dead.
8. through.
9. obtain.
1. appointment (as Thane of Cawdor).
2. understood.
3. whatever he could.
4. present as a claim.
5. pressed him vigorously.

burning in unquenchable desire to bear the name of a queen. At length, therefore, communicating his purposed intent with his trusty friends, amongst whom Banquo was the chiefest, upon confidence of their promised aid he slew the King at Inverness or (as some say) at Bothgowanan in the sixth year of his reign. Then, having a company about him of such as he had made privy to his enterprise, he caused himself to be proclaimed king and forthwith went unto Scone, where by common consent he received the investure[6] of the kingdom according to the accustomed manner. The body of Duncan was first conveyed unto Elgin and there buried in kingly wise; but afterwards it was removed and conveyed unto Colmekill and there laid in a sepulture amongst his predecessors in the year after the birth of our Saviour 1046.

Malcolm Cammore and Donald Bane, the sons of King Duncan, for fear of their lives (which they might well know that Macbeth would seek to bring to end for his more sure confirmation in the estate), fled into Cumberland, where Malcolm remained till time that Saint Edward, the son of Ethelred, recovered the dominion of England from the Danish power; the which Edward received Malcolm by way of most friendly entertainment. But Donald passed over into Ireland where he was tenderly cherished by the king of that land. Macbeth, after the departure thus of Duncan's sons, used great liberality towards the nobles of the realm, thereby to win their favor. And when he saw that no man went about to trouble him, he set his whole intention to maintain justice and to punish all enormities and abuses which had chanced through the feeble and slothful administration of Duncan. * * * Macbeth, showing himself thus a most diligent punisher of all injuries and wrongs attempted by any disordered persons within realm, was accounted the sure defense and buckler[7] of innocent people; and hereto he also applied his whole endeavor to cause young men to exercise themselves in virtuous manners, and men of the Church to attend their divine service according to their vocations.

He caused to be slain sundry thanes, as of Caithness, Sutherland, Stranaverne, and Ross, because through them and their seditious attempts much trouble daily rose in the realm. He appeased the troubled state of Galloway, and slew one Magill, a tyrant who had many years before passed nothing of[8] the regal authority or power. To be brief, such were the worthy doings and princely acts of this Macbeth in the administration of the realm that if he had attained thereunto by rightful means and continued in uprightness

6. investiture, the reception of the ceremonial robes and symbols of rule.
7. shield.
8. respected not.

of justice, as he began, till the end of his reign, he might well have been numbered amongst the most noble princes that anywhere had reigned. He made many wholesome laws and statutes for the public weal of his subjects.[9]

*   *   *

These and the like commendable laws Macbeth caused to be put as then in use, governing the realm for the space of ten years in equal justice. But this was but a counterfeit zeal of equity[1] showed by him, partly against his natural inclination, to purchase thereby the favor of the people. Shortly after, he began to show what he was, instead of equity practicing cruelty. For the prick of conscience (as it chanceth[2] ever in tyrants and such as attain to any estate by unrighteous means) caused him ever to fear lest he should be served of the same cup as he had ministered to his predecessor. The words also of the three Weird Sisters would not out of his mind, which, as they promised him the kingdom, so likewise did they promise it at the same time unto the posterity of Banquo. He willed therefore the same Banquo, with his son named Fleance, to come to a supper that he had prepared for them; which was indeed, as he had devised, present[3] death at the hands of certain murderers whom he hired to execute that deed, appointing them to meet with the same Banquo and his son without[4] the palace as they returned to their lodgings and there to slay them, so that he would not have his house[5] slandered, but that in time to come he might clear himself if anything were laid to his charge upon any suspicion that might arise.

It chanced yet by the benefit of the dark night that though the father were slain, the son yet by the help of almighty God reserving him to better fortune, escaped that danger; and afterwards having some inkling, by the admonition of some friends which he had in the court, how his life was sought no less than his father's (who was slain not by chance-medley,[6] as by the handling of the matter Macbeth would have had it to appear) but even upon a prepensed device,[7] whereupon, to avoid further peril he fled into Wales.[8]

*   *   *

9. There follows a list of laws made by Macbeth.
1. false enthusiasm for justice.
2. happens.
3. immediate.
4. outside.
5. royal house or lineage.
6. the accidental killing of a man though with some culpability for the murderer (a legal term).
7. premeditated plot.
8. Holinshed next traces the line of Scottish kings from Fleance to James VI of Scotland, i.e., James I of England (1603–1625).

But to return unto Macbeth in continuing the history and to begin where I left, ye shall understand that after the contrived slaughter of Banquo, nothing prospered with the foresaid Macbeth. For in manner[9] every man began to doubt his own life and durst uneath[1] appear in the King's presence; and even as there were many that stood in fear of him, so likewise stood he in fear of many, in such sort that he began to make those away by one surmised cavillation[2] or other whom he thought most able to work him any displeasure.

At length he found such sweetness by putting his nobles thus to death that his earnest thirst after blood in this behalf might in no wise be satisfied. For ye must consider he won double profit (as he thought) hereby: for first they were rid out of the way whom he feared; and then again his coffers were enriched by their goods which were forfeited to his use, whereby he might better maintain a guard of armed men about him to defend his person from injury of them whom he had in any suspicion. Further, to the end he might the more cruelly oppress his subjects with all tyrantlike wrongs, he builded a strong castle on the top of an high hill called Dunsinane, situate in Gowrie, ten miles from Perth, on such a proud height that, standing there aloft, a man might behold well near all the countries of Angus, Fife, Stormont, and Earndale as it were lying underneath him. This castle, then, being founded on the top of that high hill, put the realm to great charges before it was finished, for all the stuff necessary to the building could not be brought up without much toil and business. But Macbeth, being once determined to have the work go forward, caused the thanes of each shire within the realm to come and help towards that building, each man his course about.[3]

At the last, when the turn fell unto Macduff, Thane of Fife, to build his part, he sent workmen with all needful provision and commanded them to show such diligence in every behalf that no occasion might be given for the King to find fault with him in that he came not himself, as other had done, which he refused to do for doubt[4] lest the King, bearing him (as he partly understood) no great good will, would lay violent hands upon him as he had done upon divers other. Shortly after, Macbeth coming to behold how the work went forward and because he found not Macduff there, he was sore offended and said, "I perceive this man will never obey my commandments till he be ridden with a snaffle,[5] but I shall provide well

---

9. in some way.
1. dared only with difficulty.
2. phony technicality.
3. taking his turn.
4. fear.
5. bridle.

enough for him." Neither could he afterwards abide to look upon the said Macduff, either for that he thought his puissance overgreat, either else for that he had learned of certain wizards in whose words he put great confidence (for that the prophecy had happened so right which the three fairies or Weird Sisters had declared unto him) how that he ought to take heed of Macduff, who in time to come should seek to destroy him.

And surely hereupon had he put Macduff to death but that a certain witch, whom he had in great trust, had told that he should never be slain with man born of any woman nor vanquished till the wood of Birnam came to the castle of Dunsinane. By this prophecy Macbeth put all fear out of his heart, supposing he might do what he would, without any fear to be punished for the same; for by the one prophecy he believed it was unpossible for any man to vanquish him, and by the other unpossible to slay him. This vain hope caused him to do many outrageous things, to the grievous oppression of his subjects. At length Macduff, to avoid peril of life, purposed with himself[6] to pass into England to procure[7] Malcolm Cammore to claim the crown of Scotland. But this was not so secretly devised by Macduff but that Macbeth had knowledge given him thereof, for kings (as is said) have sharp sight like unto Lynx[8] and long ears like unto Midas.[9] For Macbeth had in every nobleman's house one sly fellow or other in fee with him[1] to reveal all that was said or done within the same, by which sleight he oppressed the most part of the nobles of his realm.

Immediately, then, being advertised[2] whereabout Macduff went, he came hastily with a great power into Fife and forthwith besieged the castle where Macduff dwelled, trusting to have found him therein. They that kept the house without any resistance opened the gates and suffered him to enter, mistrusting none evil. But, nevertheless, Macbeth most cruelly caused the wife and children of Macduff, with all other whom he found in that castle, to be slain. Also, he confiscated the goods of Macduff, proclaimed him traitor, and confined[3] him out of all the parts of his realm. But Macduff was already escaped out of danger and gotten into England unto Malcolm Cammore, to try what purchase[4] he might make by means of his support to revenge the slaughter so cruelly executed on his

6. decided.
7. induce.
8. Lynceus, who could see through the earth.
9. a king who had ass's ears.
1. in his payment.
2. informed.
3. banished.
4. gain.

wife, his children, and other friends. At his coming unto Malcolm he declared into what great misery the estate of Scotland was brought by the detestable cruelties exercised by the tyrant Macbeth, having committed many horrible slaughters and murders both as well of the nobles as commons, for the which he was hated right mortally of all his liege people,[5] desiring nothing more than to be delivered of that intolerable and most heavy yoke of thralldom[6] which they sustained at such a caitiff's[7] hands.

Malcolm, hearing Macduff's words which he uttered in very lamentable sort, for mere compassion and very ruth[8] that pierced his sorrowful heart bewailing the miserable state of his country, he fetched a deep sigh, which Macduff, perceiving, began to fall most earnestly in hand with him to enterprise the delivering of the Scottish people out of the hands of so cruel and bloody a tyrant as Macbeth by too many plain experiments[9] did show himself to be. Which was an easy matter for him to bring to pass, considering not only the good title he had but also the earnest desire of the people to have some occasion ministered whereby they might be revenged of those notable injuries which they daily sustained by the outrageous cruelty of Macbeth's misgovernance. Though Malcolm was very sorrowful for the oppression of his countrymen, the Scots, in manner as Macduff had declared, yet doubting whether he were come as one that meant unfeignedly as he spake or else as sent from Macbeth to betray him, he thought to have some further trial. And thereupon dissembling his mind[1] at the first, he answered as followeth: "I am truly very sorry for the misery chanced to my country of Scotland, but though I have never so great affection to relieve the same, yet by reason of certain incurable vices which reign in me I am nothing meet thereto.[2] First, such immoderate lust and voluptuous sensuality (the abominable fountain of all vices) followeth me that, if I were made King of Scots, I should seek to deflower your maids and matrons in such wise that mine intemperancy should be more importable[3] unto you than the bloody tyranny of Macbeth now is." Hereunto Macduff answered, "This surely is a very evil fault, for many noble princes and kings have lost both lives and kingdoms for the same. Nevertheless there are women enough in Scotland, and therefore follow my counsel. Make thyself king, and I shall convey

5. subjects.
6. captivity.
7. villain's.
8. pity.
9. trials.
1. hiding his thoughts.
2. not at all fit for that.
3. unbearable.

the matter so wisely that thou shalt be so satisfied at thy pleasure in such secret wise[4] that no man shall be aware thereof."

Then said Malcolm, "I am also the most avaricious creature on the earth, so that if I were king I should seek so many ways to get lands and goods that I would slay the most part of all the nobles of Scotland by surmised[5] accusations to the end I might enjoy their lands, goods, and possessions. And, therefore, to show you what mischief may ensue on you through mine unsatiable covetousness, I will rehearse unto you a fable. There was a fox having a sore place on h[er] overset with a swarm of flies that continually sucked out her blood. And when one that came by and saw this manner demanded whether she would have the flies driven before her, she answered: 'No, for if these flies that are already full and by reason thereof suck not very eagerly should be chased away, other that are empty and felly anhungered[6] should light in their places and suck out the residue of my blood far more to my grievance than these, which now being satisfied, do not much annoy me.' Therefore," saith Malcolm, "suffer me to remain where I am, lest if I attain to the regiment of your realm, mine unquenchable avarice may prove such that ye would think the displeasures which now grieve you should seem easy in respect of the unmeasurable outrage which might ensue through my coming amongst you."

Macduff to this made answer how it was a far worse fault than the other. "For avarice is the root of all mischief, and for that crime the most part of our kings have been slain and brought to their final end. Yet, notwithstanding, follow my counsel and take upon thee the crown. There is gold and riches enough in Scotland to satisfy thy greedy desire." Then said Malcolm again, "I am, furthermore, inclined to dissimulation, telling of leasings,[7] and all other kinds of deceit, so that I naturally rejoice in nothing so much as to betray and deceive such as put any trust or confidence in my words. Then, sith there is nothing that more becometh a prince than constancy, verity, truth, and justice, with the other laudable fellowship of those fair and noble virtues which are comprehended only in sooth-fastness[8] and that lying utterly overthroweth the same, you see how unable I am to govern any province or region; and, therefore, sith you have remedies to cloak and hide all the rest of my other vices, I pray you find shift to cloak this vice amongst the residue."

4. manner.
5. false.
6. cruelly starving.
7. lies.
8. truthfulness.

Then said Macduff, "This yet is the worst of all and there I leave thee and therefore say: 'O ye unhappy and miserable Scottishmen, which are thus scourged with so many and sundry calamities, each one above other! Ye have one cursed and wicked tyrant that now reigneth over you without any right or title, oppressing you with his most bloody cruelty. This other that hath the right to the crown is so replete with the inconstant behavior and manifest vices of Englishmen that he is nothing worthy to enjoy it; for by his own confession he is not only avaricious and given to unsatiable lust but so false a traitor withal[9] that no trust is to be had unto any word he speaketh. Adieu, Scotland, for now I account myself a banished man forever, without comfort or consolation.'" And with those words the brackish tears trickled down his cheeks very abundantly.

At the last, when he was ready to depart, Malcolm took him by the sleeve and said, "Be of good comfort, Macduff, for I have none of these vices before remembered, but have jested with thee in this manner only to prove[1] thy mind, for divers times heretofore hath Macbeth sought by this manner of means to bring me into his hands; but the more slow I have showed myself to condescend to thy motion and request, the more diligence shall I use in accomplishing the same." Incontinently[2] hereupon they embraced each other and, promising to be faithful the one to the other, they fell in consultation how they might best provide for all their business to bring the same to good effect. Soon after, Macduff, repairing to the borders of Scotland, addressed his letters with secret dispatch unto the nobles of the realm, declaring how Malcolm was confederate with him to come hastily into Scotland to claim the crown; and therefore he required them, sith he was right inheritor thereto, to assist him with their powers to recover the same out of the hands of the wrongful usurper.

In the meantime, Malcolm purchased such favor at King Edward's hands that old Siward, Earl of Northumberland, was appointed with ten thousand men to go with him into Scotland to support him in this enterprise for recovery of his right. After these news were spread abroad in Scotland, the nobles drew into two several[3] factions, the one taking part with Macbeth and the other with Malcolm. Hereupon ensued oftentimes sundry bickerings and divers light skirmishes, for those that were of Malcolm's side would not jeopard[4] to join with their enemies in a pight field[5] till his coming

9. in addition.
1. test.
2. immediately.
3. separate.
4. risk.
5. prepared battleground.

out of England to their support. But after that Macbeth perceived his enemies' power to increase by such aid as came to them forth of England with his adversary Malcolm, he recoiled back into Fife, there purposing to abide in camp fortified at the castle of Dunsinane and to fight with his enemies if they meant to pursue him. Howbeit, some of his friends advised him that it should be best for him either to make some agreement with Malcolm or else to flee with all speed into the Isles, and to take his treasure with him, to the end he might wage[6] sundry great princes of the realm to take his part, and retain strangers in whom he might better trust than in his own subjects, which stole daily from him. But he had such confidence in his prophecies that he believed he should never be vanquished till Birnam Wood were brought to Dunsinane, nor yet to be slain with any man that should be or was born of any woman.

Malcolm, following hastily after Macbeth, came the night before the battle unto Birnam Wood; and when his army had rested awhile there to refresh them, he commanded every man to get a bough of some tree or other of that wood in his hand, as big as he might bear, and to march forth therewith in such wise that on the next morrow they might come closely and without sight in this manner within view of his enemies. On the morrow, when Macbeth beheld them coming in this sort, he first marveled what the matter meant, but in the end remembered himself that the prophecy which he had heard long before that time of the coming of Birnam Wood to Dunsinane Castle was likely to be now fulfilled. Nevertheless, he brought his men in order of battle and exhorted them to do valiantly. Howbeit, his enemies had scarcely cast from them their boughs when Macbeth, perceiving their numbers, betook him straight to flight; whom Macduff pursued with great hatred even till he came unto Lunfannaine, where Macbeth, perceiving that Macduff was hard at his back, leapt beside[7] his horse, saying, "Thou traitor, what meaneth it that thou shouldst thus in vain follow me that am not appointed to be slain by any creature that is born of a woman? Come on, therefore, and receive thy reward which thou hast deserved for thy pains!" And therewithal he lifted up his sword, thinking to have slain him.

But Macduff, quickly avoiding[8] from his horse ere he came at him, answered with his naked sword in his hand, saying, "It is true, Macbeth, and now shall thine insatiable cruelty have an end, for I am even he that thy wizards have told thee of, who was never born of my mother but ripped out of her womb." Therewithal he stepped unto him and slew him in the place. Then, cutting his head from his

6. hire.
7. dismounted from.
8. dismounting.

shoulders, he set it upon a pole and brought it unto Malcolm. This was the end of Macbeth, after he had reigned seventeen years over the Scottishmen. In the beginning of his reign he accomplished many worthy acts, very profitable to the commonwealth as ye have heard; but afterward, by illusion of the devil, he defamed[9] the same with most terrible cruelty. He was slain in the year of the Incarnation 1057, and in the sixteenth year of King Edward's reign over the Englishmen.

9. discredited.

Contexts

Debate on Free Will and Predestination

MARTIN LUTHER

[An Attack on Free Will] (1520/21)[†]

After sin free will exists in name only and when it does what in it lies it sins mortally.

Unhappy free will! When a just man does a good deed, he sins mortally, as we have seen, and free will boasts that before justification it is something and can do something. Oh, wretched are they who condemn my article, which rests on the first sentence of chapter 4 in Augustine's *Concerning the Spirit and the Letter:* 'Free will without grace can do nothing but sin.' I ask you, what sort of freedom is it that can choose only one alternative, and that the worse one? Does freedom mean to be able to do nothing but sin? But let us say I don't believe Augustine. Let us listen to Scripture. In John 15[:5] Christ says: 'Without me you can do nothing.' What is this 'nothing' which free will does without Christ? It prepares itself for grace, they say, by morally good works. But here Christ calls these nothing; therefore it prepares itself by nothing. A marvelous preparation that is accomplished by nothing!

But he goes on to explain what this 'nothing' is, saying: 'If anyone does not dwell in me, he will be thrown out like a branch and he

† From *Collected Works of Erasmus,* vol. 76: *Controversies,* ed. Charles Trinkaus *et al.* Selection trans. Charles H. Miller (Toronto: University of Toronto Press, 1999), 301–10. Reprinted by permission of University of Toronto Press. All bracketed material in the text is Miller's. Footnotes are by the editor of this Norton Critical Edition, unless otherwise indicated. Martin Luther protested against perceived abuses in the church and initiated the Protestant Reformation. In response Pope Leo X's bull, *Exsurge, Domine* (June 15, 1520), condemned Luther for error and heresy in forty-one articles. Luther replied in his *Assertio omnium articulorum* (1520/21), from which this section affirms the doctrine of predestination and denies free will. Luther argues that the human will is enslaved to sin and that justification, the freeing from sin, occurs solely by God's election and grace. His argument and Erasmus's defense of free will (see the excerpt on pp. 181–89 in this edition) provide one theological context for the choices, actions, and consequences portrayed in *Macbeth.*

173

withers and they gather him up and throw him on the fire and he burns' [John 16:6]. I beg you, most holy Vicar of Christ, how can you have the meretricious effrontery to dare to contradict your Lord in this way? You say that free will can prepare itself to proceed to grace. On the other hand, Christ says that it is thrown out, so that it is further away from grace. How beautifully your bull harmonizes with the gospel! Let us listen, then, to Christ, who posits five steps in the perdition of the pruned branch, showing that it can not only not prepare itself for doing good but necessarily grows worse. The first is that it is thrown out and therefore not brought in; it is given over to the power of Satan, who does not allow it to attempt anything good. For what else can it mean to be thrown out? Secondly, it withers; that is, left to itself, it grows worse every day, and these are the two works of free will: namely, to sin and to persevere and grow worse in sinning, to be thrown out and to wither. For if free will can do anything else, Christ is certainly a liar. There are three punishments after that: they gather it up, that is, for judgment, so that it may be convicted together with the others. Then, when the sentence has been handed down, they throw it into eternal fire, where it finally does nothing but burn, that is, suffers eternal punishment. Therefore, that free will can do nothing does not mean, as they pretend, that it can do nothing meritorious, but that it is thrown out and withers. The pruned branch does not prepare itself for the vine, nor can it do so, but it becomes more removed from the vine and comes closer and closer to perishing: so too free will or a wicked person.

Genesis 6[:5] and 8[:21]: 'The understanding and every thought of the human heart is inclined to evil at all times.' I beg you, if someone says that every thought of the heart is evil, and is so at all times, what good thought does he leave which can prepare for grace? Does evil dispose someone to good? Nor can anyone escape from this authority by saying that a person can sometimes repress his evil thought. For a thought which does this, actively or passively, is good in either case, but it will not be included among those which are said to be all thoughts. If a single good thought can be there, Moses is a liar because he affirms that they are all evil. Moreover, we may represent the Hebrew text as follows: 'Because whatever the human heart desires and thinks is only evil every day'; to 'evil' it adds an exclusive particle which our translation did not render. It also did not render 'desires,' and the translation 'thought' does not fully render 'thinks.' For Moses intended to include not only idle and spontaneous thoughts but also thoughts conceived by the mind and thoughts by which a person deliberately intends to do something, and he also says that they are evil without exception, so that these Pelagians[1] have no way of attributing to free will the power to do something good, if it works hard enough at it.

Again Genesis 6[:3]: 'My spirit does not remain in mankind, because it is flesh.' If mankind is flesh, what progress can it make towards good? Do we not know the works proper to the flesh in Galatians 5[:19–20], which are fornication, impurity, lewdness, anger, envy, murder, etc.? These are the things free will does when it does what in it lies; and these are all mortal sins. For Romans 8[:7] says: 'For the prudence of the flesh is death and an enemy to God.' How can death lead to life? How does enmity dispose itself to grace? For if the Spirit is not in mankind, it is dead before God. But a dead person necessarily does the works of death, not of life, and the work of death does not dispose to life. Therefore everything that has been treated in so many books about the preparation of free will for grace is mere fiction.

*   *   *

Isaiah says the same thing in the same place.[2] 'All flesh is grass and all its glory is like the flower of the grass. The grass is withered and the flower has fallen, because the Spirit of the Lord has blown upon it. But the word of the Lord remains forever' [Isaiah 40:6–8]. Explain the grass and the flower. Is it not the flesh, man, or free will and whatever man has? Its flower and glory, is that not the power, wisdom, and justice of free will, which enable it to glory in the fact that it is something and can do something. What is the reason, then, that when the Spirit blows it is withered and falls and perishes, whereas the word remains? Is the Spirit not grace, by which you said free will is assisted and its preparation fulfilled? Why then does he say here that even the best parts of the flesh are withered and fall? Do you not see that the Spirit and free will are opposed to one another? For when the one blows the other falls and does not remain with the word. And it would not have fallen and perished if it had been fit and prepared for the breath of the Spirit and of the word.

Also Jeremiah in chapter 10 [verse 23] says as follows: 'I know, Lord, that a person's path is not his own and that a man does not have the power to direct his own steps.' What statement could be clearer? If a person's path and his steps are not in his power, how

1. followers of Pelagius, fifth-century heretic who denied the Catholic doctrine of original sin and asserted that the human will is capable of good without the benefit of divine grace.
2. The 'same place' is Isaiah 40:2, 'She has received at the Lord's hand double measure for all her sins'; Luther glosses this verse with the explanation that 'grace is not given by the Lord except for sins, that is, for evil deeds.'

can God's path and God's steps be in his power? A person's path is
what they call the natural power of doing what in him lies. See now
that this is not in man's choice or free will. What, then, is free will
but a thing in name only? How can it prepare itself for the good
when it does not even have the power to make its own paths evil?
For God does even bad deeds in the wicked, as Proverbs 16[:4] says:
'The Lord made everything for his own sake, even the wicked for
the evil day.' And Rom 1[:28]: 'God gave them up to their own
depraved perception so that they do what is not fitting.' And in
chapter 9 [verse 18]: 'He hardens as he wishes; he has mercy as he
wishes.' Just as Exodus 9[:16] says about Pharaoh: 'For this very
purpose I aroused you, that I might show my power in you.' For that
is why God is terrible in his judgments and his deeds.

Again, Proverbs 16[:1] says this: 'It is man's part to prepare his
heart, but it is the Lord's to govern his tongue.' That is, a man usually proposes many things, when in fact his deeds are so little in his
control that he does not even have within his power the words for
this deed of his but rather is forced by the marvelous providence of
God both to speak and to act differently from what he had in mind,
as was shown in Balaam (Numbers 24[:5–27]).[3] And Psalm 138[:4]:
'My tongue has no speech.' And even more clearly further on in
Proverbs 16[:9]: 'The heart of a man thinks of his own path and the
Lord directs his steps.' See, the path of a man does not proceed as
he thinks, but as the Lord ordains. For that reason chapter 21[:1]
says: 'Like water divided into channels, so the heart of the king is in
the hand of the Lord; he will turn it wherever he wishes.' Where,
then, is free will? It is completely fictitious.

And if Scripture did not show this, we would have abundant evidence of its truth from all histories, and everyone would see it from
his own life. For who is there who always carried out everything he
wanted to? Indeed, who is there who has not often had it in mind
to do something and then suddenly changed his mind so as to do
something else, not knowing how he changed it? Who would dare
to deny that even in evil works he has been forced to do something
different from what he had in mind? Don't you think the authors of
this bull applied the sum total of their power of free will to the task
of speaking in their favour and against Luther? And see how this
thought and its execution did not lie in their choice! For they did
everything against themselves and brought it all down on their own
heads, so that I have never read of any persons who disgraced
themselves more foully and more abominably, and out of blindness
and ignorance they cast themselves quite openly into the shameful
depths of error, heresy, and malice—so little control of himself

3. Balaam blesses instead of curses Israel.

does a person have, even when he conceives and executes evil deeds. And Paul spoke the truth in Ephesians 1[:11]: 'God works all things in all persons.'[4]

Here, then, that 'general influence'[5] disappears by which, according to their babble, we have it in our power to perform natural operations. The experience of everyone shows that this is not the case. And see how stupid we are: we know that the root of our works, namely our life, which is the source of all our works, is never for a single moment under our control, and do we dare to say that any intention is under our control? Could we say anything more absurd than that? Did God, who kept our life under his control, place our motions and works under our control? Far from it. Hence there can be no doubt that the teaching of Satan brought this phrase 'free will' into the church in order to seduce men away from God's path into his own paths. The brothers of Joseph fully intended to kill him, and lo and behold! they had so little choice about that very intention that they even changed it immediately to something entirely different, as he said, 'You intended to do me harm, but God changed it to something good' [Gen 50:20].

Have you got anything, miserable pope, to snarl against this? Hence it is also necessary to revoke this article. For I misspoke when I said that free will before grace exists in name only; rather I should have simply said 'free will is a fiction among real things, a name with no reality.' For no one has it within his control to intend anything, good or evil, but rather, as was rightly taught by the article of Wyclif[6] which was condemned at Constance, all things occur by absolute necessity. That was what the poet meant when he said, 'All things are settled by a fixed law' [Vergil, *Aeneid* 2:324]. And Christ in Matt. 10[:29–30]: 'The leaf of a tree does not fall to the earth apart from the will of your Father who is in heaven, and the hairs of your head are all numbered.'[7] And Isaiah 41[:23] taunts them: 'Do good also or evil, if you can!'

Hence, as Elijah exhorted the prophets of Baal [3 Kings 18:25–27], I egg on these proponents of free will: 'Come on, be men, do what in you lies, at least for once put to the test what you teach, prepare yourselves for grace, and obtain what you want, since you say God does not deny anything if you do what free will can do. It is a dreadful disgrace that you cannot bring forward a single example of your teaching and you yourselves cannot provide a single work so

---

4. 1 Cor 12:6, actually. [Miller's note.]
5. *Influentia generalis*, a technical term, denoting the cooperation of first cause (God) with the second cause (the creature). Luther denies the existence of such cooperation.
6. Proposition of John Wyclif (fourteenth century), whom Catholics considered a heretic, Protestants, an early reformer.
7. Luther adapts this verse, substituting 'leaf' for 'sparrow.' [Miller's note.]

that your wisdom consists merely in words.' But these efforts of theirs are a pretext for supporting Pelagius. For what does it matter if you deny that grace comes from our works if you nevertheless teach that it is given through our works? The meaning remains equally impious, since grace is believed to be given not gratuitously but because of our works. For the works which the Pelagians taught and performed and because of which they held that grace is given are not different from the ones you teach and perform. They are works of the same free will and of the same bodily members, but you gave them one name and they gave them another: fasting, prayer, alms-giving were the same things, but you said they are fitting for grace and they claimed they are worthy of grace, but everywhere the same Pelagius carried on triumphantly.

These miserable people are deceived by the inconstancy or (as they call it) the contingency of human affairs. They fix their stupid eyes on things in themselves and the actions of things and never lift them up to the sight of God so that they might recognize in God the things above things. For when we look at things here below they seem to be fortuitous and subject to choice but when we look upward all things are necessary, because we all live, act, and suffer every-thing not as we wish but as he wills. The free will which seems to bear on us and temporal things has no bearing on God, for in him, as James says, there is no variation or shadow of change [James 1:17], but here all things change and vary. And we are so stupid we measure the divine by the temporal, so that we presume to get ahead of God by free will and to wrest grace from him while he is asleep, as it were, whenever we please, as if he were able to change together with us and as if he willed something that at one time he did not will, and all by the working and willing of our free choice. Oh, monstrous madness beyond all madness!

And Paul in Ephesians 2[:3] says: 'We too were by nature sons of wrath like the rest.' If everyone apart from grace is a son of wrath by his very nature, then free will is also a son of wrath by its very nature; if it is so by its very nature, it is much more so by all its works. And how can someone be a son of wrath by his nature except because everything he does is evil, preparing not for grace but for wrath, indeed meriting wrath? Go on now, you Pelagians, and prepare your-selves for grace by your works, since Paul says here that by them no one merits anything except wrath. It would have been milder if he had said only 'We were sons of wrath,' but by adding 'by nature' he wanted it to be understood that everything we are and do by our nature mer-its wrath and not at all grace. You could hardly find a briefer, clearer, or more emphatic statement against free will in Scripture.

Why should we go on at length? From what has been said above, it is abundantly clear to us that even the just struggle mightily against their flesh in order to do good and that free will and the prudence of the flesh resist them; the flesh yearns with all its power against the spirit, despising whatever belongs to the Spirit and the law of God. And how could it be possible that by its own nature and without the Spirit it could yearn for the Spirit or prepare itself for the Spirit by doing what in it lies? While it was in a state of grace, its nature was such that it fought fiercely against grace, and apart from grace can its nature be such that it assists the spirit? Could you imagine anything crazier than that? For such an unheard-of monstrosity would be as if someone who could not control an untamed wild animal while it was tied up should be mad enough to boast that before it was tied up or without being tied up it is so tame and gentle that it willingly tames itself or makes an effort to be tame. Stop being so crazy, I beg you, you miserable Pelagians! If free will in a state of grace sins and rages against grace, as we are all forced to recognize and as the Apostle and all the saints complain, certainly it goes against all common sense that it should be upright apart from grace or prepare itself for grace when it is absent, since it hates and persecutes grace when it is present.

It follows necessarily, then, that whatever is taught and done before grace in order to obtain grace is sheer fabrication and hypocrisy, for it is necessary that we should be preceded by the mercy of God even to wish for it, just as Augustine, writing against the epistles of Pelagius, says that God converts the reluctant and unwilling, as he demonstrated in the case of Paul, whom he converted when he was set against grace and at the height of his burning rage to persecute; and Peter did not look back at the Lord, so as to remember the words Jesus had said to him, but rather Jesus looked back at Peter, in the midst and at the very height of the business, and so Peter remembered the words and wept bitterly.

And so we see in the meaning of this article how deceptively Satan works in teaching this error. For since they cannot deny that we must be saved through the grace of God and cannot avoid this truth, impiety takes another path to avoid it, pretending that if our role is not to save ourselves, nevertheless it is our role to be prepared to be saved by the grace of God. What glory, I beg you, is left for God if we can do so much to be saved by his grace? Is such power a small thing if someone who does not have grace has enough power to be able to have grace whenever he wishes? What difference does it make if you do [not][8] say that we are saved without grace, as the Pelagians do, since you place the grace of God within the choice of men? You seem to me worse than Pelagius when you place the necessary grace of God, which he completely denied was

---

8. Miller adds a 'not' here, as Luther argues that his opponents are worse than Pelagians.

necessary, within the power of men. It seems less impious, I say, to deny grace completely than to say it is prepared by our effort and work and to give us, as it were, control over it. And nevertheless the working of this error has prevailed because it is specious and pleasing to nature and free will, so that it is difficult to confute it, especially when dealing with ignorant and crude minds.

We could put up with the frivolity and stupidity of the pope and his minions in the other articles about the papacy, councils, indulgences, and other unnecessary nonsense, but in this article, which is the best of all and the sum and substance of my case, we must deplore and lament that these wretches are so insane. For I believe the heavens will fall down before the pope and his disciples will ever understand a single jot about this mystery of God's grace. The truth of this article cannot coexist with the church of the pope, no more than Belial with Christ or light with darkness. For if the church of the pope had not taught and sold good works or had sincerely taught that we are justified by grace alone, it would not have grown so full of pompous display and, if by some chance it had done so, it would not have remained that way for a single hour. For this theology which condemns whatever the pope approves of and makes martyrs is based on the cross. That is why the best part of the church and almost all of it flourished when the period of the martyrs came to an end. Soon pleasure took the place of the cross, poverty was replaced by opulence, ignominy by glory, until what is now called the church has become more worldly than the world, so to speak, and more fleshly than the flesh itself. And I have no more powerful argument against the reign of the pope than that he reigns without the cross. His whole aim is not to suffer at all but rather to abound and to exult in all things, and he has not been cheated of his desire. He has what he wanted, and the faithful city has become a whore and truly the kingdom of the true Antichrist.

In this section my prolixity was necessitated by the subject itself, which has been repressed and extinguished not only by this bull (which I consider to be not worth the paper it's written on) but also by almost all teachers in the schools for more than thirteen hundred years. For on this point everyone writes against grace, not for it, so that no point needs to be handled as much as this one, and I have often wished to handle it, leaving aside that trivial papistical nonsense and matters which do not pertain to the church at all except to destroy it; but by length of time and widespread prevalence, the working of Satan has fixed itself so firmly in men's hearts and has used this error to blunt their minds so badly that I do not see anyone who is fit to understand it or even to dispute with me about it. Scripture is abundant on this subject but it has been so ravaged by our Nebuchadnezzar[9] that the very form and knowledge of the letters is gone, and we need some new Esdras[1] who will discover new letters and recover the Bible for us once more, which I hope is now being done as the Hebrew and Greek languages are flourishing all over the world. Amen.

DESIDERIUS ERASMUS

[A Defense of Free Will] (1524)[†]

By 'free will' here we understand a power of the human will by which man be able to direct himself towards, or turn away from, what leads to eternal salvation.

* * *

[Scriptural exhortations are meaningless if we have no power to comply.]

But what point is there in quoting a few passages of this kind when all Holy Scripture is full of exhortations like this: 'Turn back to me with all your heart' [Joel 2:12]; 'Let every man turn from his evil way' [John 3:8]; 'Come back to your senses, you transgressors' [Isa 46:8]; 'Let everyone turn from his evil way, and I will repent the ill that I have thought to do them on account of the evil of their endeavours'; and 'If you will not listen to me, to walk in my law' [Jer 26:3–4]. Nearly the whole of Scripture speaks of nothing but conversion, endeavour, and striving to improve. All this would become meaningless once it was accepted that doing good or evil was a matter of necessity; and so too would all the promises, threats, complaints, reproaches, entreaties, blessings, and curses directed towards those who have amended their ways, or those who have refused to change: 'As soon as a sinner groans at his sin' [Ezek 18:21; Isa 30:15]; 'I have seen that this is a stubborn people' [Exod 32:9]; 'Oh my people, what have I done to you?' [Mic 6:3]; and 'They have rejected

---

9. powerful Babylonian king.
1. Esdras or Ezra, famous Hebrew scribe and priest, edited and corrected the Hebrew Scriptures and wrote the books of Chronicles, Ezra, Nehemiah, and perhaps others.
† From *Collected Works of Erasmus*, vol. 76: *Controversies*, ed. Charles Trinkaus *et al.* Selection trans. Peter Macardle, (Toronto: University of Toronto Press, 1999), 21, 36–38, 59–62, 75–80. Reprinted by permission of University of Toronto Press. All bracketed material in the text is Macardle's. Footnotes are by the editor of this Norton Critical Edition, unless otherwise indicated. Learned Dutch humanist, biblical and Patristics scholar, Desiderius Erasmus (1466?–1536) refuted Luther (see the excerpt on pp. 173–81 in this edition) in *De Libero Arbitrio* (1524). Erasmus argues that the doctrine of predestination makes Scriptural exhortation meaningless and that human will (a secondary cause) cooperates with divine grace (the primary cause) in acts of virtue or vice.

my laws' [Ezek 20:13]; 'Oh, that my people had listened to me, that Israel had walked in my ways!' [Ps 80:14]; 'He who wishes to see good days, let him keep his tongue from evil' [Ps 33:13–14]. The phrase 'he who wishes to see' speaks of free will.

Since such phrases are frequently encountered, does it not immediately occur to the reader to ask, 'why promise conditionally what is entirely dependent on your will? Why complain of my behaviour, when all my actions, good or bad, are performed by you in me regardless of my will? Why reproach me, when I have no power to preserve the good you have given me, or keep out the evil you put into me? Why entreat me, when everything depends on you, and happens as it pleases you? Why bless me, as though I had done my duty, when whatever happens is your work? Why curse me, when I sinned through necessity?' What is the purpose of such a vast number of commandments if not a single person has it at all in his power to do what is commanded? For there are some who believe that man, albeit justified by the gift of faith and charity, cannot fulfill any of God's commandments, but rather that all good works, because they are done 'in the flesh,' would lead to damnation were not God in his mercy to pardon them on account of the merit of our faith.

Yet the word spoken by God through Moses in Deuteronomy, chapter 30[:11–14], shows that what he commands is not merely within our power, but that it demands little effort. He says: 'The commandment that I lay upon you this day is not beyond you, nor is it far away. It is not in heaven, that you might say, "Which one of us is strong enough to go up to heaven and bring it back to us, that we may hear and fulfill it?" Neither is it beyond the sea, that you should make excuses, and say, "Who among us can cross the sea and bring it back to us, that we may hear what is commanded?" No, the word is very near to you, on your lips and in your heart, that you may do it.'

Yet here he is speaking of the greatest commandment of all: 'that you turn back to the Lord your God with all your heart and with all your soul.' And what is the meaning of 'but if you will listen,' 'if you will keep the commandments,' 'if you will turn back' [Deut 30:10], if none of this is in our power at all? I will not attempt to quote an extensive selection of such texts, for the books of both testaments are so full of them wherever you look that anyone attempting to search them out would simply be 'looking for water in the sea,' as the saying goes. And so, as I said, a considerable amount of Holy Scripture will obviously become meaningless if you accept the last opinion discussed above, or the previous one.

*   *   *

[*Passages from the New Testament supporting free will;
Gospel exhortations are meaningless if we have
no power to comply.*]

The quotations so far have come from the Old Testament; this
might be cause for objection, had they not been of the kind which
the light of the Gospel not only fails to efface, but actually endows
with new force. And so let us turn to the books of the New Testament. First we come across that place in the Gospel where Christ,
weeping over the destruction of the city of Jerusalem, says: 'Jerusalem, Jerusalem, city that murders the prophets and stones those
who are sent to you, how often I have wanted to gather you together,
as a hen gathers her chicks under her wings, and you refused!'
[Matt 22:37]. If everything happens by necessity, could Jerusalem
not rightly reply to the Lord's lament, 'Why torment yourself with
pointless weeping? If it was your will that we should not listen to
the prophets, why did you send them? Why blame us for something
that you did voluntarily, and we by necessity? You wanted to gather
us together, and yet in us you did not want to: for in us you brought
it about that we refused.' Yet in our Lord's words, it is not necessity
working in the Jews that is blamed, but their wicked, rebellious
will: 'I wanted to gather you together; you refused.'

Again, elsewhere we find, 'If you want to enter into life, keep the
commandments' [Matt 19:7]. How on earth could one say 'if you
want to' to someone whose will was not free? Or, 'If you want to be
perfect, go and sell what you have' [Matt 19:21] or Luke 9[:23], 'If
anyone wants to come after me, let him deny himself, and take up
his cross, and follow me.' Though the commandment is very difficult, our will is nevertheless mentioned. And shortly afterwards we
find, 'Whoever wants to save his life shall lose it' [Luke 9:24]. Are
not all Christ's excellent commandments emptied of their meaning
if nothing is attributed to human will? 'But I tell you, but I tell you
etc.' [Matt 5:22, 28]; and 'If you love me, keep my commandments'
[John 14:15]. How greatly John stresses the commandments! How
poorly the conjunction 'if' agrees with absolute necessity: 'If you
remain in me, and my words remain in you' [John 15:7]; 'If you want
to be perfect' [Matt 19:21].

Now, when good and bad deeds are mentioned so frequently, as
is reward, I fail to see how there can be any room at all for absolute
necessity: nature and necessity deserve no reward. And yet in Matthew 5[:12] our Lord Jesus says, 'rejoice and be glad, for your
reward is great in heaven.' What is the sense of the parable of the
hired labourers in the vineyard [Matt 20:1–16]? Can they be labourers, if their labour achieves nothing? As agreed, they receive one
penny as reward for their labour. Someone will say that it is called

a reward because it is in some sense owed by God, who has given his word to man if he will believe in God's promises. But this very act of believing is one in which free will plays some part, turning itself towards, or away from, faith. Why is the servant who increased his master's fortune by his own efforts praised, and why is the lazy good-for-nothing condemned [Matt 25:14–30], unless we have some responsibility in such a case? And again, in Matthew, chapter 25, when Christ invites everyone to a share in his eternal kingdom, he refers not to necessity but to people's charitable deeds: 'You gave food and drink'; 'you took in the stranger'; 'you clothed the naked, etc.' [Matt 25:35–36]; speaking to the goats on his left he reproaches not necessity, but their voluntary failures to perform good works: 'You saw the hungry, you were given an opportunity to do good, but you gave no food, etc.' [Matt 25:42]. Are not all the gospel writings in fact full of exhortations?

* * *

[Passages cited by Luther to deny the existence of free will; limited application of Genesis 6:3 and 8:21 and Isaiah 40:6–8.]

Now let us try the strength of the scriptural proofs which Martin Luther quotes to undermine the power of free will. He cites verses from Genesis 6[:3] and 8[:21]. 'My spirit will not remain in man forever, for he is flesh.' In this verse Scripture does not use 'flesh' simply in the sense of 'a wicked desire,' as Paul sometimes does, when he orders us to 'mortify the works of the flesh' [Rom 8:13], but in the sense of the weakness of our nature with its tendency to sinning, as Paul calls the Corinthians 'fleshly' because they were not yet ready to receive teaching in the form of solid food, being still (as it were) babes in Christ [1 Cor 3:1–2]. And in *Questions about the Hebrew* Jerome says that the Hebrew text reads differently from ours, namely, 'My spirit will not pass judgment on those men eternally, for they are flesh.' These words speak not of God's severity, but of his clemency: for by 'flesh' he means men naturally weak, prone to evil, and by 'spirit' he means wrath; and so he is saying that he will not save these people up for eternal punishment, but in his mercy will exact punishment from them in this life. And these words do not even apply to the entire human race, but only to the men of that age, whose heinous vices had utterly corrupted them; and so he says, 'those men.' And it does not even apply to all the men of that time, given that Noah is praised as a righteous man, pleasing to God [Gen 6:8–9].

In the same way it is possible to dismiss his quotations from chapter 8[:21] of the same book, 'For the thought and imagination of man's heart are inclined to evil from his youth on', and from chapter 6[:5], 'The heart's every thought is directed towards evil at all times.' Even if the tendency to evil in most men cannot be overcome without the help of God's grace, it does not remove the freedom of the will completely, for if no aspect of repentance depends on the will, but everything is controlled by God through a kind of necessity, then why are men given time for repentance in this very passage: 'His days will be one hundred and twenty years' [Gen 6:3]? For in *Questions about the Hebrew*, Jerome considers that this verse refers not to the length of human life, but to the interval before the Flood; a time conceded to humans during which to change their ways if they wish, and if not, to be shown to deserve divine condemnation for having disdained God's leniency.

* * *

As for his quotation of Isaiah 40[:6–8]—'All flesh is grass, and all its glory is as the flower of the grass. The grass is withered and the flower has fallen because the Spirit of the Lord has blown upon it, but the word of the Lord abides for ever'—Luther, I feel, twists this somewhat violently to apply to grace and free will. For here Jerome understands 'spirit' as meaning divine wrath, 'flesh' as man's natural weakness, which is powerless against God, and 'flower' as the vainglory aroused by material good fortune. The Jews gloried in the temple, in circumcision, in sacrifices; the Greeks gloried in their wisdom: but now that the wrath of God has been revealed from heaven by the gospel, all that glory has withered.

Yet not every human inclination is 'flesh': there is 'soul' and there is 'spirit,' by which we strive towards goodness. This part of the psyche is called reason or the ruling principle—or was there not a single one of the pagan philosophers who strove for goodness, though they taught that we should a thousand times more readily go to our death than commit an evil action, even if we knew that it would be unknown to men and pardoned by God? Corrupt reason, it is true, often has poor judgment. 'You do not know,' said the Lord, 'to what spirit you belong': the disciples were mistakenly seeking vengeance, referring to the time long before when fire had come down from heaven in answer to Elijah's prayers and burned up the captains with their companies of fifty men [Luke 9:54–55]. In Romans 8[:16] Paul states that even in good people the human spirit is distinct from the spirit of God: 'for that spirit [of God] witnesses to our spirit that we are children of God.' And so, if anyone maintains that the highest powers of human nature are nothing but flesh, that is, evil inclinations, I will gladly agree—if he can demonstrate his assertion with proofs from Holy Scripture!

'What is born of the flesh is flesh, and what is born of the spirit is spirit' [John 3:6]. John further teaches that those who believe in the gospel are born of God and become children of God and even gods [John 1:12, 10:34–36]; and Paul distinguishes the fleshly man, who does not understand the things that are of God, from the spiritual man, who can judge all things, and elsewhere he calls him a new creation in Christ [1 Cor 2:14–15]. If the whole man, even though reborn through faith, is still nothing but flesh, where is the 'spirit born of the spirit'? Where is the 'child of God'? Where is the 'new creation'? I would like instruction on these points; until then I will take full advantage of the authority of the ancients, who teach that there are certain seeds of goodness planted in men's minds,[1] with the help of which they can to some extent see and strive after the good, though there are also baser tendencies which tug them in the opposite direction. Furthermore, choice means the ability of the will to turn in either direction; and although the will is perhaps more inclined to evil than to good, on account of the tendency to sin left in us, yet no one is compelled to sin unless he actually wills it.

*   *   *

[To assert necessity to the exclusion of free will makes God cruel and unjust.]

First, how can you constantly read that holy people, full of good works, 'did justice' [2 Kings 8:15], 'walked righteously in the sight of God' [1 Kings 2:4], 'turned neither to the left nor to the right' [Deut 5:32], if everything that even the godliest do is a sin, and such a sin that without the intervention of God's mercy someone for whom Christ died would be cast into hell? How can you constantly read of a 'reward' where there is absolutely no merit? How can the obedience of those who complied with God's commandments conceivably be praised, and the disobedience of those who did not be condemned? Why is judgment constantly mentioned in the Scriptures if merits are not weighed at all? Why are we made to appear before the judgment-seat if we have done nothing through our own will, but everything has been done in us by absolute necessity?

There is the further objection: what need is there of the many admonitions, commands, threats, exhortations, and remonstrances in the Scriptures if we do nothing, but God works everything in us, the deed as well as the will, in accordance with his immutable will? God requires us to pray without ceasing, to stay vigilant, to struggle, to contend for the prize of eternal life. Why does he want to be constantly asked for something which he has already decided

---

1. Erasmus is here alluding to a central idea of the Stoics, which he encountered in the Fathers, especially Jerome. [Macardle's note.] The Stoics were ancient Greek and Roman philosophers who advocated the rule of reason, the following of nature in moderation, indifference to fortune, and resistance to all passions.

whether or not to give, seeing that his decisions cannot be changed, since he himself is unchangeable? Why does he tell us to labour to obtain what he has decided to bestow on us as a free gift? We suffer affliction, rejection, ridicule, torture, and death; thus God's grace fights, wins, and triumphs in us. A martyr undergoes such torments, yet no merit is credited to him for doing so—indeed he is said to have sinned in having exposed his body to suffering in the hope of heavenly life. But why did the all-merciful God wish to work in the martyrs in this way? A man would seem cruel if he had decided to make a friend a free gift of something, but would not give it to him until he had been tortured to the point of despair.

* * *

[Faith must not be exalted to the exclusion of free will: free will cooperates with grace.]

We listen with equanimity, however, to our opponents' boundlessly exalting faith in, and love of, God, for we are of the opinion that the corruption of Christian life everywhere by so many sins has no other cause than the coldness and drowsiness of our faith, which gives us a merest verbal belief in God: a faith on the lips only, whereas according to Paul 'man is justified by believing from the heart' [Rom 10:10]. Nor will I particularly take issue with those who refer all things to faith as their ultimate source, even though I believe that faith is born from and nurtured by charity, and charity in turn born from and nurtured by faith. Charity certainly feeds faith, just as the light in a lantern is fed by oil, for we more readily trust the person we ardently love: and there is no dearth of people who contend that faith is the beginning, rather than the completion, of salvation. But our argument does not concern these matters.[2]

Yet here we should beware of being so absorbed in enlarging on the praises of faith that we subvert the freedom of the will; and once it has been denied I do not see how the problem of the justice and mercy of God can be resolved. When the ancient authors found they could not extricate themselves from these difficulties, some were forced to posit two Gods: one of the Old Testament who they argued was only just, not good; and one of the New Testament who they argued was only good, not just. Tertullian[3] adequately refuted their wicked fabrication. Manichaeus,[4] as we said, dreamed up the

---

2. Tangentially and briefly Erasmus expresses his reservations about Luther's doctrine of salvation *ex fide sola*, by faith alone. [Macardle's note.]
3. Tertullian (ca. 155–220), an important early Christian theologian and polemicist, refuted this heresy in *Adversus Marcionem*.
4. actually Mani (216–277), whose followers were Manicheans. He taught that two opposing principles, one of light and goodness, the other of darkness and evil, struggled against each other in the universe and in human life.

notion of two natures in man, one which could not avoid sinning and one which could not avoid doing good. Pelagius,[5] concerned for God's justice, attributed too much to free will. There is little difference between him and those who attribute so much to human will as to say that through our natural powers, by morally good works, it can merit the supreme grace by which we are justified. They seem to me to have wanted to urge man to moral effort by holding out a good hope of obtaining salvation, just as Cornelius, because of his prayers and almsgiving, deserved to be taught by Peter, and the eunuch by Philip [Acts 10:1–43; 8:26–38], and Saint Augustine, who assiduously sought Christ in Paul's letters, deserved to find him. Here we can placate those who believe that man cannot do any good deed which he does not owe to God by saying that the whole work is no less due to God, without whom we could achieve nothing; that the contribution of free will is very small indeed; and that our very ability to direct our mind to the things that pertain to salvation, or to cooperate with grace, is itself a gift of God. As a result of the controversy with Pelagius, Augustine reached a less favourable view of free will than he had previously held. In the opposite way Luther, who previously attributed something to free will, has been carried so far by the heat of his defence as to remove it altogether. Yet I believe that among the Greeks Lycurgus is blamed for having had the vines cut down because he hated drunkenness, whereas by bringing the sources of water closer he could have prevented drunkenness without abolishing wine-drinking.

In my opinion free will could have been established in such a way as to avoid that trust in our own merits and the other harmful consequences which Luther avoids, as well as those which we mentioned above, yet so as not to destroy the benefits which Luther admires. This I believe is achieved by the opinion of those who ascribe entirely to grace the impetus by which the mind is first aroused, and only in the succeeding process attribute something to human will in that it does not resist the grace of God. Since there are three parts to everything—beginning, continuation, and completion—they ascribe the first and last to grace and allow that free will has an effect only in the continuation, in so far as in a single, indivisible act there are two causes, divine grace and human will, working together. However, grace is the principal cause and will the secondary cause, unable to do anything without the principal cause, whereas the principal cause is sufficient in itself. Just so the power inherent in fire burns, yet the principal cause is God

---

5. fifth-century heretic who denied the Catholic doctrine of original sin and asserted that the human will is capable of good without the benefit of divine grace.

acting at the same time through the fire, a cause which would be sufficient in itself, and without which fire would have no effect if that cause were to withdraw itself.

On this moderate view man must ascribe his salvation entirely to the grace of God; for what free will accomplishes in this is very insignificant indeed, and what it can accomplish is itself due to divine grace, which first created free will, then freed and healed it. And this will appease (if they can be appeased) those who believe that there is no good in man which he does not owe to God. Owe it he does, but in a different way and for a different reason, as an inheritance falling to children in equal shares is not called benevolence, since it comes to them all in the ordinary course of law. (It is called liberality if one or other of them has been given something over and above his legal due.) Yet children are indebted to their parents even on account of an inheritance.

DEBATE ON WITCHCRAFT

REGINALD SCOT

From The Discovery of Witchcraft (1584)[†]

Book I, Chapter 1: *An impeachment of witches' power in meteors and elementary bodies, tending to the rebuke of such as attribute too much unto them.*

The fables of witchcraft have taken so fast hold and deep root in the heart of man that few or none can nowadays with patience endure the hand and correction of God. For if any adversity, grief, sickness, loss of children, corn, cattle, or liberty happen unto them, by and by they exclaim upon witches. As though there were no God in Israel that ordereth all things according to his will, punishing both just and unjust with grief, plagues, and afflictions in manner and form as he thinketh good, but that certain old women here on earth, called witches, must needs be the contrivers of all men's

---

† From Reginald Scot, *The Dicouerie of Witchcraft* (London, 1584), sigs. ci–cviv. Footnotes are by the editor of this Norton Critical Edition. Spelling and punctuation have been modernized by the editor. Attacking Jacob Sprenger and Heinrich Krämer's seminal treatise on witchcraft, *Malleus Maleficarum* (1486), Reginald Scot (1538–1599) argued that God ruled the world and, therefore, that current beliefs in witchcraft resulted merely from ignorance, superstition, and deceit. Scot associated belief in witchcraft with Catholic practices and idolatry. King James I, a firm believer in devils and witches, responded (see the excerpts on pp. 197–207 in this edition) and their debate provides an interesting context for the witches of *Macbeth*.

calamities, and as though they themselves were innocents and had deserved no such punishments. Insomuch as they stick[1] not to ride and go to such as either are injuriously termed witches, or else are willing so to be accounted, seeking at their hands comfort and remedy in time of their tribulation, contrary to God's will and commandment in that behalf, who bids us resort to Him in all our necessities.

Such faithless people, I say, are also persuaded that neither hail nor snow, thunder nor lightning, rain nor tempestuous winds come from the heavens at the commandment of God, but are raised by the cunning and power of witches and conjurers. Insomuch as a clap of thunder, or a gale of wind is no sooner heard, but either they run to ring bells, or cry out to burn witches, or else burn consecrated things, hoping by the smoke thereof to drive the devil out of the air, as though spirits could be frayed[2] away with such external toys, howbeit these are right enchantments,[3] as Brentius[4] affirmeth.

But certainly it is neither a witch, nor devil, but a glorious God that maketh the thunder. I have read in the scriptures that God maketh the blustering tempests and whirlwinds, and I find that it is the Lord that altogether dealeth with them, and that they blow according to his will. But let me see any of them all rebuke and still the sea in time of tempest, as Christ did, or raise the stormy wind as God did with his word, and I will believe in them. Hath any witch or conjurer or any creature entered into "the treasures of the snow, or seen the secret places of the hail" (Job 38:22), which God hath prepared against the day of trouble, battle, and war? I, for my part, also think with Jesus Sirach[5] that at God's only commandment the snow falleth, and that the wind bloweth according to his will who only maketh all storms to cease and who, if we keep his ordinances, will send us rain in due season, and make the land to bring forth her increase, and the trees of the field to give their fruit (Sirach 43).

But little think our witchmongers that the Lord commandeth the clouds above or openeth the doors of heaven, as David (Psalms 78:23) affirmeth, or that the Lord goeth forth in the tempests and storms, as the Prophet Nahum (Nahum 3) reporteth, but rather that witches and conjurers are then about their business.

The Marcionists[6] acknowledged one God the author of good things, and another the ordainer of evil; but these make the devil a whole god, to create things of nothing, to know men's cogitations,

---

1. hesitate.
2. frightened.
3. proper rituals.
4. Johann Brenz (1499–1570), Lutheran minister and author.
5. author of *Sirach* (also known as *Ecclesiasticus*), a book of the Bible.
6. followers of the second-century heretic Marcion.

and to do that which God never did, as to transubstantiate men into beasts, etc. Which thing if devils could do, yet followeth it not that witches have such power. But if all the devils in hell were dead and all the witches in England burnt or hanged, I warrant you we should not fail to have rain, hail, and tempests, as now we have, according to the appointment and will of God, and according to the constitution of the elements and the course of the planets, wherein God hath set a perfect and perpetual order.

I am also well assured that if all the old women in the world were witches and all the priests conjurers, we should not have a drop of rain, nor a blast of wind the more or the less for them. For the Lord hath bound the waters in the clouds and hath set bounds about the waters until the day and night come to an end. Yea, it is God that raiseth the winds and stilleth them, and he saith to the rain and snow "Be upon the earth," and it falleth. The wind of the Lord and not the wind of witches shall destroy the treasures of their pleasant vessels and dry up the fountains, saith Hosea (Hosea 13:15). Let us also learn and confess with the prophet David (Psalms 39) that we ourselves are the causes of our afflictions, and not exclaim upon witches when we should call upon God for mercy.

* * *

Finally, if witches could accomplish these things, what needed it seem so strange to the people when Christ by miracle commanded both seas and winds, etc. For it is written, "Who is this, for both wind and sea obey him?" (Mark 4:41).

Book I, Chapter 3: *Who they be that are called witches, with a manifest declaration of the cause that moveth men so commonly to think, and witches themselves to believe, that they can hurt children, cattle, etc., with words and imaginations; and of cozening[7] witches.*

One sort of such as are said to be witches are women which be commonly old, lame, blear-eyed, pale, foul, and full of wrinkles, poor, sullen, superstitious, and papists, or such as know no religion, in whose drowsy minds the devil hath gotten a fine seat; so as what mischief, mischance, calamity, or slaughter is brought to pass, they are easily persuaded the same is done by themselves, imprinting in their minds an earnest and constant imagination hereof. They are lean and deformed, showing melancholy in their faces to the horror of all that see them. They are doting, scolds, mad, devilish, and not much differing from them that are thought to be possessed with

7. deceiving.

The three witches in the opening scene of Roman Polanski's film (1971). Courtesy of the Everett Collection.

spirits, so firm and steadfast in their opinions, as whosoever shall only have respect to the constancy of their words uttered would easily believe they were true indeed.

These miserable wretches are so odious unto all their neighbors and so feared, as few dare offend them or deny them anything they ask; whereby they take upon them, yea, and sometimes think that they can do such things as are beyond the ability of human nature. These go from house to house and from door to door for a pot full of milk, yeast, drink, pottage,[8] or some such relief, without the which they could hardly live, neither obtaining for their service and pains, nor by their art, nor yet at the devil's hands (with whom they are said to make a perfect and visible bargain) either beauty, money, promotion, wealth, worship, pleasure, honor, knowledge, learning, or any other benefit whatsoever.

It falleth out many times that neither their necessities nor their expectation is answered or served in those places where they beg or borrow, but rather their lewdness is by their neighbors reproved. And, further, in tract of time the witch waxeth odious and tedious to her neighbors and they again are despised and despited[9] of her,

8. stew or soup.
9. held in contempt.

so as sometimes she curseth one, and sometimes another, and that from the master of the house, his wife, children, cattle, etc., to the little pig that lieth in the sty. Thus in process of time they have all displeased her, and she hath wished evil luck unto them all, perhaps with curses and imprecations made in form. Doubtless, at length, some of her neighbors die or fall sick, or some of their children are visited with diseases that vex them strangely, as apoplexies, epilepsies, convulsions, hot fevers, worms, etc., which by ignorant parents are supposed to be the vengeance of witches. Yea, and their opinions and conceits are confirmed and maintained by unskillful physicians according to the common saying, *Inscitiae pallium maleficium et incantatio*, "Witchcraft and enchantment is the cloak of ignorance"; whereas, indeed, evil humors[1] and not strange words, witches, or spirits are the causes of such diseases. Also some of their cattle perish either by disease or mischance. Then they, upon whom such adversities fall, weighing the fame that goeth upon this woman (her words, displeasure, and curses meeting so justly with their misfortune) do not only conceive but also are resolved that all their mishaps are brought to pass by her only means.

The witch, on the other side, expecting her neighbors' mischances and seeing things sometimes come to pass according to her wishes, curses, and incantations (for Bodin[2] himself confesseth that not above two in a hundred of their witchings or wishings take effect), being called before a Justice, by due examination of the circumstances is driven to see her imprecations and desires and her neighbors' harms and losses to concur and, as it were, to take effect, and so confesseth that she (as a goddess) hath brought such things to pass. Wherein not only she but the accuser and also the Justice are foully deceived and abused, as being through her confession and other circumstances persuaded (to the injury of God's glory) that she hath done or can do that which is proper only to God Himself.

Another sort of witches there are which be absolutely cozeners. These take upon them either for glory, fame, or gain, to do anything which God or the devil can do, either for foretelling of things to come, bewraying[3] of secrets, curing of maladies, or working of miracles. But of these I will talk more at large hereafter.

---

1. Ancient and medieval medical theory held that bodies consisted of four fluids (blood, phlegm, choler or bile, and melancholy or black bile), called humors, and that an excess or deficiency of any one caused ill health.
2. Jean Bodin, an important Catholic political thinker, urged severe punishments for witches in *De la demonologie* (1580).
3. revealing.

Book 1, Chapter 4: *What miraculous actions are imputed to witches by witchmongers, papists, and poets.*

Although it be quite against the hair,[4] and contrary to the devil's will, contrary to the witches' oath, promise, and homage, and contrary to all reason that witches should help anything that is bewitched, but rather set forward their master's businesses, yet we read in *Malleus Maleficarum* of three sorts of witches, and the same is affirmed by all the writers hereupon, new and old. One sort, they say, can hurt and not help; the second can help and not hurt; the third can both help and hurt. And among the hurtful witches he saith there is one sort more beastly than any kind of beasts saving wolves, for these usually devour and eat young children and infants of their own kind. These be they, saith he, that raise hail, tempests, and hurtful weather, as lightning, thunder, etc. These be they that procure barrenness in man, woman, and beast. These can throw children into waters as they walk with their mothers, and not be seen. These can make horses kick till they cast the riders. These can pass from place to place in the air invisible. These can so alter the mind of judges that they can have no power to hurt them. These can procure to themselves and to others taciturnity and insensibility in their torments. These can bring trembling to the hands and strike terror into the minds of them that apprehend them. These can manifest unto others things hidden and lost, and foreshow things to come, and see them as though they were present. These can alter men's minds to inordinate love or hate. These can kill whom they list with lightning and thunder. These can take away man's courage and the power of generation. These can make a woman miscarry in childbirth and destroy the child in the mother's womb, without any sensible means either inwardly or outwardly applied. These can with their looks kill either man or beast.

*   *   *

And first Ovid (*Met.* 7) affirmeth that they can raise and suppress lightning and thunder, rain and hail, clouds and winds, tempests and earthquakes. Others do write that they can pull down the moon and the stars. Some write that with wishing they can send needles into the livers of their enemies; some, that they can transfer corn in the blade from one place to another; some, that they can cure diseases supernaturally, fly in the air, and dance with devils. Some write that they can play the part of succubus, and contract

---

4. contrary to the natural inclination, against the grain.

themselves to incubus,[5] and so young prophets are upon them begotten, etc. Some say they can transubstantiate themselves and others, and take the forms and shapes of asses, wolves, ferrets, cows, apes, horses, dogs, etc. Some say they can keep devils and spirits in the likeness of toads and cats.

They can raise spirits, as others affirm, dry up springs, turn the course of running waters, inhibit the sun, and stay both day and night, changing the one into the other. They can go in and out at auger-holes,[6] and sail in an eggshell, a cockle,[7] or mussel shell, through and under the tempestuous seas. They can go invisible, and deprive men of their privities,[8] and otherwise of the act and use of venery.[9] They can bring souls out of the graves. They can tear snakes in pieces with words, and with looks kill lambs. But in this case a man may say, that *miranda canunt sed non credenda poetae*, ["poets sing of marvelous, but not credible, things"].[1] They can also bring to pass that churn as long as you list, your butter will not come; especially, if either the maids have eaten up the cream or the goodwife have sold the butter before in the market. Whereof I have had some trial, although there may be true and natural causes to hinder the common course thereof; as for example, put a little soap or sugar into your churn of cream, and there will never come any butter, churn as long as you list. But *Malleus Maleficarum* saith, that there is not so little a village where many women are not that bewitch, infect, and kill kine,[2] and dry up the milk, alleging for the strengthening of that assertion the saying of the apostle, *numquid deo cura est de bobus?* "Doth God take any care of oxen?" (1 Cor. 9:9).

> Book I, Chapter 5: *A confutation of the common conceived opinion of witches and witchcraft, and how detestable a sin it is to repair to them for counsel or help in time of affliction.*

But whatsoever is reported or conceived of such manner of witchcrafts I dare avow to be false and fabulous, cozenage, dotage,[3] and poisoning excepted; neither is there any mention made of these kinds of witches in the Bible. If Christ had known them, he would not have pretermitted[4] to inveigh against their presumption in taking upon them his office, as to heal and cure diseases, and to work

---

5. A succubus is a demon believed to have carnal intercourse with men during sleep; an incubus, with women.
6. holes made by an auger, or carpenter's manual drill.
7. sea shell.
8. genitals.
9. sexual intercourse.
1. a proverb attributed to Dionysius Cato, Latin moralist.
2. cows.
3. trickery, senility.
4. omitted.

such miraculous and supernatural things as whereby he himself
was specially known, believed, and published to be God, his actions
and cures consisting (in order and effect) according to the power by
our witchmongers imputed to witches. Howbeit, if there be any in
these days afflicted in such strange sort as Christ's cures and
patients are described in the New Testament to have been, we fly
from trusting in God to trusting in witches, who do not only in
their cozening art take on them the office of Christ in this behalf,
but use his very phrase of speech to such idolaters as come to seek
divine assistance at their hands, saying, "Go thy ways, thy son or
thy daughter, etc., shall do well, and be whole" (Mark 5:34).

It will not suffice to dissuade a witchmonger from his credulity
that he seeth the sequel and event to fall out many times contrary
to their assertion; but in such case to his greater condemnation he
seeketh further to witches of greater fame. If all fail, he will
rather think he came an hour too late than that he went a mile too
far. Truly, I for my part cannot perceive what is to go a-whoring
after strange gods, if this be not. He that looketh upon his neigh-
bor's wife and lusteth after her hath committed adultery. And,
truly, he that in heart and by argument maintaineth the sacrifice
of the mass to be propitiatory for the quick and the dead is an
idolater; as also he that alloweth and commendeth creeping to the
cross[5] and such like idolatrous actions, although he bend not his
corporal knees.

In like manner, I say, he that attributeth to a witch such divine
power as duly and only appertaineth unto God (which all witchmongers do) is in heart a blasphemer, an idolater, and full of gross
impiety, although he neither go nor send to her for assistance.

Book 8, Chapter 2: *That the gift of prophecy is ceased.*

That witches, nor the woman of Endor,[6] nor yet her familiar or devil, can tell what is to come, may plainly appear by the words of the
prophet who saith, "Show what things are to come, and we will say
you are gods, indeed" (Isaiah 41:23). According to that which Solomon saith, "Who can tell a man what shall happen him under the
sun?" "Marry, that can I," saith the witch of Endor to Saul (1 Samuel 28). But I will rather believe Paul and Peter, which say that
prophecy is the gift of God, and no worldly thing (1 Cor. 12:10; 2
Peter 1:21).

*   *   *

5. Catholic practice of advancing to the cross on knees and with bare feet on Good Friday;
   the act was a frequent target of Protestant ridicule.
6. In 1 Samuel 28, Saul in disguise has the witch of Endor raise the spirit of the prophet
   Samuel, who angrily predicts his defeat.

Indeed, we read that Samuel could tell where things lost were strayed, etc.; but we see that gift also ceased by the coming of Christ, according to the saying of Paul: "At sundry times and in divers manners God spoke in the old times by our fathers the prophets; in these last days he hath spoken unto us by his son," etc. (Hebrews 1:1–2). And, therefore, I say that gift of prophecy, wherewith God in times past endued[7] his people, is also ceased, and counterfeits and cozeners are come in their place according to this saying of Peter: "There were false prophets among the people even as there shall be false teachers among you," etc. (2 Peter 2:1). And think not that so notable a gift should be taken from the beloved and elect people of God, and committed to Mother Bungie,[8] and such like of her profession.

KING JAMES I OF ENGLAND
(JAMES VI OF SCOTLAND)

From News from Scotland (1591)[†]

God by his omnipotent power hath at all times and daily doth take such care, and is so vigilant for the weal[1] and preservation of his own, that thereby He disappointeth the wicked practices and evil intents of all such as by any means whatsoever seek indirectly to conspire any thing contrary to his holy will. Yea, and by the same power He hath lately overthrown and hindered the intentions and wicked dealings of a great number of ungodly creatures, no better than devils, who, suffering themselves to be allured and enticed by the Devil whom they served and to whom they were privately sworn, entered into the detestable art of witchcraft. Which they studied and practiced so long time that in the end they had seduced by their sorcery a number of others to be as bad as themselves, dwelling in the bounds of Lothian, which is a principal shire or part of Scotland, where the King's Majesty useth to make his chiefest residence or abode. And to the end that their detestable wickedness, which they privily[2] had pretended against the King's

---

7. endowed.
8. a legendary witch of Rochester in Kent.
† From *Newes from Scotland*, (London, 1592; 2nd ed.), sigs. Aiv–Ci(v), Diii. Footnotes are by the editor of this Norton Critical Edition. Spelling and punctuation have been modernized by the editor. In *Newes from Scotland* (1591), James VI of Scotland (1566–1625), later James I of England from 1603 to 1625, relates his own experiences with witchcraft, both as a potential victim and as a judicial examiner. The excerpts illustrate the lurid mix of black magic, superstition, eroticism, and sensational crime that characterizes the witch literature of the day.
1. welfare.
2. privately.

Majesty, the commonweal of that country, with the nobility and subjects of the same, should come to light, God of his unspeakable goodness did reveal and lay it open in very strange sort,[3] thereby to make known unto the world that their actions were contrary to the law of God and the natural affection which we ought generally to bear one to another; the manner of the revealing whereof was as followeth:

Within the town of Tranent in the kingdom of Scotland there dwelleth one David Seaton, who, being deputy bailiff[4] in the said town, had a maidservant called Gillis Duncan, who used secretly to be absent and to lie forth of her master's house every other night. This Gillis Duncan took in hand to help all such as were troubled or grieved with any kind of sickness or infirmity, and in short space did perform many matters most miraculous; which things, forasmuch as she began to do them upon a sudden, having never done the like before, made her master and others to be in great admiration,[5] and wondered thereat. By means whereof the said David Seaton had his maid in some great suspicion that she did not those things by natural and lawful ways, but rather supposed it to be done by some extraordinary and unlawful means.

Whereupon her Master began to grow very inquisitive and examined her which way and by what means she were able to perform matters of so great importance; whereat she gave him no answer. Nevertheless, her master, to the intent that he might the better try and find out the truth of the same, did with the help of others torment her with the torture of the pilliwinks[6] upon her fingers, which is a grievous torture, and binding or wrenching her head with a cord or rope, which is a most cruel torment also. Yet would she not confess anything. Whereupon they, suspecting that she had been marked by the Devil (as commonly witches are), made diligent search about her, and found the enemy's mark to be in her forecrag, or forepart of her throat; which being found, she confessed that all her doings was done by the wicked allurements and enticements of the Devil and that she did them by witchcraft.

After this her confession, she was committed to prison, where she continued for a season, where immediately she accused these persons following to be notorious witches, and caused them forthwith to be apprehended one after another, viz., Agnes Sampson, the eldest witch of them all, dwelling in Haddington; Agnes Tompson of Edinburgh; Doctor Fian, alias John Cunningham, master of the school at Saltpans in Lothian, of whose life and strange acts you

---

3. manner.
4. an officer under a sheriff, who executes writs and processes.
5. astonishment.
6. a device for crushing fingers.

shall hear more largely in the end of this discourse. These were by the said Gillis Duncan accused, as also George Mott's wife dwelling in Saltpans, Robert Grierson, skipper, and Janet Bandilandis, with the porter's wife of Seaton, the smith at the Bridge Halls, with innumerable others in that parts, and dwelling in those bounds aforesaid. Of whom some are already executed; the rest remain in prison to receive the doom of judgment at the King's Majesty's will and pleasure.

The said Gillis Duncan also caused Euphemia MacCalrean to be apprehended, who conspired and performed the death of her godfather, and who used her art upon a gentleman, being one of the lords and justices of the Session,[7] for bearing good will to her daughter. She also caused to be apprehended one Barbara Napier, for bewitching to death Archibald, last Earl of Angus, who languished to death by witchcraft and yet the same was not suspected, but that he died of so strange a disease as the physician knew not how to cure or remedy the same. But of all, other the said witches these two last before recited[8] were reputed for as civil honest women as any that dwelled within the city of Edinburgh, before they were apprehended. Many other besides were taken dwelling in Leith, who are detained in prison until His Majesty's further will and pleasure be known, of whose wicked doings you shall particularly hear, which was as followeth:

This aforesaid Agnes Sampson, which was the elder witch, was taken and brought to Holyrood House[9] before the King's Majesty and sundry other of the nobility of Scotland, where she was straitly[1] examined. But all the persuasions which the King's Majesty used to her with the rest of his Council might not provoke or induce her to confess anything, but stood stiffly in the denial of all that was laid to her charge. Whereupon they caused her to be conveyed away to prison, there to receive such torture as hath been lately provided for witches in that country. And forasmuch as by due examination of witchcraft and witches in Scotland, it hath lately been found that the Devil doth generally mark them with a privy mark, by reason the witches have confessed themselves that the Devil doth lick them with his tongue in some privy part of their body before he doth receive them to be his servants; which mark commonly is given them under the hair in some part of their body, whereby it may not easily be found out or seen, although they be searched. And generally so long as the mark is not seen to those which search

7. the Scottish law court. An illustration (sig. Bi[v]) shows two magistrates watching a man raise a stick over four kneeling women.
8. the other witches noted before these last two (MacCalrean and Napier).
9. the royal palace in Edinburgh.
1. strictly.

them, so long the parties that hath the mark will never confess any-thing. Therefore, by special commandment this Agnes Sampson had all her hair shaven off, in each part of her body, and her head thrawen[2] with a rope according to the custom of that country, being a pain most grievous, which she continued almost an hour, during which time she would not confess anything until the Devil's mark was found upon her privities.[3] Then she immediately con-fessed whatsoever was demanded of her, and justifying those per-sons aforesaid to be notorious witches.

Item,[4] the said Agnes Tompson was after brought again before the King's Majesty and his council, and being examined of the meetings and detestable dealings of those witches, she confessed that upon the night of All Hallow's Even[5] last, she was accompa-nied as well with the persons aforesaid, as also with a great many other witches to the number of two hundred, and that all they together went by sea, each one in a riddle or sieve,[6] and went in the same very substantially with flagons[7] of wine, making merry and drinking by the way in the same riddles or sieves to the kirk[8] of North Berwick in Lothian, and that after they had landed, took hands on the land and danced this reel[9] or short dance, singing all with one voice:

Comer,[1] go ye before, comer, go ye,
If ye will not go before, comer, let me.

At which time she confessed that this Gillis Duncan did go before them playing this reel or dance upon a small trump, called a Jew's trump,[2] until they entered into the Kirk of North Berwick.

These confessions made the King in a wonderful admiration, and sent for the said Gillis Duncan, who upon the like trump did play the said dance before the King's Majesty, who in respect of the strangeness of these matters took great delight to be present at their examinations.

Item, the said Agnes Tompson confessed that the Devil, being then at North Berwick Kirk attending their coming in the habit or likeness of a man, and seeing that they tarried over long, he at their coming enjoined them all to a penance, which was that they should

2. twisted.
3. genitals.
4. likewise.
5. Halloween (October 31).
6. A riddle is a coarse-meshed sieve. Sailing in a sieve was a traditional means of travel for witches.
7. in substance (i.e., corporeally) with large bottles.
8. church.
9. lively Scottish dance, usually performed by facing couples.
1. one who comes or arrives.
2. a Jew's harp, an instrument held between the teeth, consisting of a frame and a pro-jecting tongue that is struck with the finger.

kiss his buttocks in sign of duty to him; which, being put over the pulpit bare, everyone did as he had enjoined them. And having made his ungodly exhortations, wherein he did greatly inveigh against the King of Scotland, he received their oaths for their good and true service towards him and departed; which done, they returned to sea and so home again.

At which time the witches demanded of the Devil why he did bear such hatred to the King, who answered, by reason the King is the greatest enemy he hath in the world; all which their confessions and depositions are still extant upon record.

Item, the said Agnes Sampson confessed before the King's Majesty sundry things which were so miraculous and strange, as that His Majesty said they were all extreme liars; whereat she answered, she would not wish His Majesty to suppose her words to be false, but rather to believe them, in that she would discover such matter unto him as His Majesty should not any way doubt of.

And thereupon taking His Majesty a little aside, she declared unto him the very words which passed between the King's Majesty and his Queen at Oslo in Norway the first night of their marriage, with their answer each to other; whereat the King's Majesty wondered greatly, and swore by the living God that he believed that all the devils in hell could not have discovered the same, acknowledging her words to be most true and, therefore, gave the more credit to the rest which is before declared.

Touching this Agnes Tompson, she is the only woman who by the Devil's persuasion should have intended and put in execution the King's Majesty's death in this manner:

She confessed that she took a black toad, and did hang the same up by the heels three days, and collected and gathered the venom as it dropped and fell from it in an oyster shell, and kept the same venom close covered, until she should obtain any part or piece of foul linen cloth that had appertained to the King's Majesty, as shirt, handkercher, napkin or any other thing; which she practiced[3] to obtain by means of one John Kers, who being attendant in His Majesty's chamber, desired him for old acquaintance between them to help her to one or a piece of such a cloth as is aforesaid; which thing the said John Kers denied to help her to, saying he could not help her to it.

And the said Agnes Tompson by her depositions since her apprehension saith that if she had obtained any one piece of linen cloth which the King had worn and fouled, she had bewitched him to death, and put him to such extraordinary pains, as if he had been lying upon sharp thorns and ends of needles.

___

3. contrived.

Moreover she confessed that at the time when His Majesty was in Denmark, she being accompanied with the parties before specially named, took a cat and christened it, and afterward bound to each part of that cat the chiefest parts of a dead man and several joints of his body, and that in the night following the said cat was conveyed into the midst of the sea by all these witches sailing in their riddles or sieves, as is aforesaid, and so left the said cat right before the town of Leith in Scotland. This done, there did arise such a tempest in the sea, as a greater hath not been seen. Which tempest was the cause of the perishing of a boat or vessel coming over from the town of Brunt Island to the town of Leith, wherein was sundry jewels and rich gifts, which should have been presented to the now Queen of Scotland at Her Majesty's coming to Leith.

Again it is confessed that the said christened cat was the cause that the King's Majesty's ship at his coming forth of Denmark had a contrary wind to the rest of his ships then being in his company; which thing was most strange and true, as the King's Majesty acknowledgeth, for when the rest of the ships had a fair and good wind, then was the wind contrary and altogether against His Majesty. And further the said witch declared that His Majesty had never come safely from the sea if his faith had not prevailed above their intentions.

Moreover, the said witches being demanded how the Devil would use them when he was in their company, they confessed that when the Devil did receive them for his servants, and that they had vowed themselves unto him, then he would carnally use them, albeit to their little pleasure in respect of his cold nature, and would do the like at sundry other times.

* * *

This strange discourse before recited may perhaps give some occasion of doubt to such as shall happen to read the same, and thereby conjecture that the King's Majesty would not hazard himself in the presence of such notorious witches, lest thereby might have ensued great danger to his person and the general state of the land, which thing in truth might well have been feared. But to answer generally to such, let this suffice: that first it is well known that the King is the child and servant of God, and they but servants to the Devil; he is the Lord's anointed, and they but vessels of God's wrath; he is a true Christian and trusteth in God, they worse than infidels, for they only trust in the Devil, who daily serve[s] them till he have brought them to utter destruction. But hereby it seemeth that His Highness carried a magnanimous and undaunted mind, not feared with their enchantments, but resolute in this: that so long as God is with him, he feareth not who is against him. And

truly the whole scope of this treatise doth so plainly lay open the
wonderful providence of the Almighty, that if he had not been
defended by his omnipotence and power, His Highness had never
returned alive in his voyage from Denmark; so that there is no
doubt but God would as well defend him on the land as on the sea,
where they pretended[4] their damnable practice.

From Daemonology (1597)[†]

Philomathes: These witches, on the other part, being enticed either
for the desire of revenge or of worldly riches, their whole practices
are either to hurt men and their goods or what they possess, for
satisfying of their cruel minds in the former, or else by the wrack in
whatsoever sort of any whom God will permit them to have power
of, to satisfy their greedy desire in the last point.

Epistemon: In two parts their actions may be divided: the actions
of their own persons, and the actions proceeding from them towards
any other. And this division being well understood will easily resolve
you what is possible to them to do. For although all that they confess
is no lie upon their part, yet, doubtlessly, in my opinion a part of it
is not, indeed, according as they take it to be; and in this I mean by
the actions of their own persons. For as I said before, speaking of
magi,[1] that the Devil illudes[2] the senses of these scholars of his in
many things, so say I the like of these witches.

Philomathes: Then I pray you first to speak of that part of their
own persons, and syne[3] ye may come next to their actions towards
others.

Epistemon: To the effect that they may perform such services of
their false master, as he employs them in, the Devil as God's ape[4]
counterfeits in his servants this service and form of adoration that
God prescribed and made his servants to practice. For as the servants of God publicly use to convene for serving of him, so makes
he them in great numbers to convene (though publicly they dare
not) for his service. As none convenes to the adoration and worship-
ping of God except they be marked with his seal, the sacrament of
baptism, so none serves Satan and convenes to the adoring of him
that are not marked with that mark whereof I already spake. As the

---

4. presented.
† From *Daemonologie* (Edinburgh, 1597), sigs. F2–3, G2–3, G4–H1. James I wrote *Daemonologie* against Reginald Scot and Johann Weyer to prove that witchcraft existed
   and that it originated in Satan.
1. practitioners of forbidden, occult arts.
2. deceives.
3. next (Scottish).
4. God's clumsy imitator.

minister sent by God teacheth plainly at the time of their public conventions how to serve him in spirit and truth, so that unclean spirit in his own person teacheth his disciples at the time of their convening how to work all kind of mischief and craves 'count[5] of all their horrible and detestable proceedings passed for advancement of his service. Yea, that he may the more vilely counterfeit and scorn God he oft times makes his slaves to convene in these very places which are destinate[6] and ordained for the convening of the servants of God (I mean by churches). But this far, which I have yet said, I not only take it to be true in their opinions, but even so to be indeed. For the form that he used in counterfeiting God amongst the Gentiles makes me so to think: as God spake by his oracles, spake he not so by his? As God had as well bloody sacrifices as others without blood, had not he the like? As God had churches sanctified to his service with altars, priests, sacrifices, ceremonies, and prayers, had he not the like polluted to his service? As God gave responses by Urim and Thummim,[7] gave he not his responses by the entrails of beasts, by the singing of fowls, and by their actions in the air? As God by visions, dreams, and ecstasies revealed what was to come and what was his will unto his servants, used he not the like means to forewarn his slaves of things to come? Yea, even as God loved cleanness, hated vice and impurity, and appointed punishments therefore, used he not the like (though falsely, I grant, and but in eschewing the less inconvenient to draw them upon a greater) yet dissimuled[8] he not, I say, so far as to appoint his priests to keep their bodies clean and undefiled before their asking responses of him? And feigned he not God to be a protector of every virtue and a just revenger of the contrary?

* * *

Epistemon: In their [witches'] actions used towards others three things ought to be considered: first, the manner of their consulting thereupon; next, their part as instruments; and last, their master's part, who puts the same in execution. As to their consultations thereupon, they use them oftest[9] in the churches where they convene for adoring; at what time their master, inquiring at them what they would be at, every one of them propones[1] unto him what wicked turn they would have done either for obtaining of riches, or for revenging them upon any whom they have malice at. Who, granting their

5. account.
6. destined.
7. the sacred rite by which Hebrews discovered God's will.
8. dissembled.
9. most often.
1. proposes.

demand, as no doubt willingly he will since it is to do evil he teacheth them the means whereby they may do the same. As for little trifling turns that women have ado with, he causeth them to joint[2] dead corpses and to make powders thereof, mixing such other things there amongst as he gives unto them.

Philomathes: But before ye go further, permit me, I pray you, to interrupt you one word, which ye have put me in memory of by speaking of women. What can be the cause that there are twenty women given to that craft, where there is one man?

Epistemon: The reason is easy for as that sex is frailer than man is so is it easier to be entrapped in these gross snares of the Devil, as was over well proved to be true by the serpent's deceiving of Eva at the beginning, which makes him the homelier with that sex sensine.[3]

Philomathes: Return now where ye left.

Epistemon: To some others at these times he teacheth how to make pictures of wax or clay, that by the roasting thereof the persons that they bear the name of may be continually melted or dried away by continual sickness. To some he give such stones or powders as will help to cure or cast on[4] diseases. And to some he teacheth kinds of uncouth poisons which mediciners[5] understands not (for he is far cunninger than man in the knowledge of all the occult properties of nature) not that any of these means which he teacheth them (except the poisons which are composed of things natural) can of themselves help anything to these turns that they are employed in, but only being God's ape as well in that as in all other things. Even as God by his sacraments, which are earthly of themselves, works a heavenly effect, though no ways by any cooperation in them. And as Christ by clay and spittle wrought together opened the eyes of the blind man (John, 9), suppose there was no virtue in that which he outwardly applied; so the Devil will have his outward means to be shows, as it were, of his doing, which hath no part of cooperation in his turns with him, how far that ever the ignorants[6] be abused in the contrary. And as to the effects of these two former parts, to wit, the consultations and the outward means, they are so wonderful as I dare not allege any of them without joining a sufficient reason of the possibility thereof. For leaving all the small trifles among wives and to speak of the principal points of their craft, for the common trifles thereof they can do without converting well enough by themselves; these principal points, I say, are these: they can make men or women to love or hate other, which may be very

2. dismember.
3. the more familiar with that sex since then.
4. inflict.
5. apothecaries (i.e., pharmacists) or physicians.
6. ignorant persons.

possible to the Devil to effectuate, seeing he being a subtle spirit, knows well enough how to persuade the corrupted affection of them whom God will permit him so to deal with. They can lay the sickness of one upon another, which likewise is very possible unto him. For since by God's permission he laid sickness upon Job, why may he not far easier lay it upon any other. For as an old practition[7] he knows well enough what humor domines[8] most in any of us, and as a spirit he can subtly waken up the same, making it peccant or to abound,[9] as he thinks meet for troubling of us, when God will so permit him.

*   *   *

Philomathes: But will God permit these wicked instruments by the power of the Devil their master to trouble by any of these means any that believes in him?

Epistemon: No doubt, for there are three kinds of folks whom God will permit so to be tempted or troubled: the wicked for their horrible sins, to punish them in the like measure; the godly that are sleeping in any great sins or infirmities and weakness in faith, to waken them up the faster by such an uncouth form; and even some of the best, that their patience may be tried before the world as Job's was. For why may not God use any kind of extraordinary punishment when it pleases him, as well as the ordinary rods of sickness or other adversities?

Philomathes: Who then may be free from these devilish practices?

Epistemon: No man ought to presume so far as to promise any impunity to himself, for God hath before all beginnings preordinated as well the particular sorts of plagues as of benefits for every man, which in the own time he ordains them to be visited with. And yet ought we not to be the more afraid for that of anything that the Devil and his wicked instruments can do against us. For we daily fight against the Devil in a hundred other ways. And, therefore, as a valiant captain, affrays[1] no more being at the combat, nor stays from his purpose for the rummishing shot of a cannon nor the small clack of a pistolet,[2] suppose he be not certain what may light upon him. Even so ought we boldly to go forward in fighting against the Devil without any greater terror for these his rarest weapons nor for the ordinary whereof we have daily the proof.

Philomathes: Is it not lawful then by the help of some other witch to cure the disease that is casten[3] on by that craft?

---

7. deceiver.
8. which essential body fluid (humor) dominates.
9. corrupt (peccant) or excessive (thus causing disease).
1. fears.
2. the roaring shot of a cannon or the noise of a small pistol.
3. cast.

Epistemon: No ways lawful, for I gave you the reason thereof in that axiom of theology[4] which was the last words I spoke of magi.

Philomathes: How then may these diseases be lawfully cured?

Epistemon: Only by earnest prayer to God, by amendment of their lives, and by sharp pursuing every one, according to his calling, of these instruments of Satan, whose punishment to the death will be a salutary sacrifice for the patient. And this is not only the lawful way but likewise the most sure. For by the Devil's means can never the Devil be casten out (Mark 3), as Christ saith. And when such a cure is used, it may well serve for a short time, but at the last it will doubtlessly tend to the utter perdition of the patient both in body and soul.

DEBATE ON TYRANNICIDE

CHURCH OF ENGLAND

From An Homily against Disobedience and Willful Rebellion (1570)[†]

As God, the creator and Lord of all things, appointed his angels and heavenly creatures in all obedience to serve and to honor his majesty, so was it his will that man, his chief creature upon the earth, should live under the obedience of his creator and Lord. And for that cause, God, as soon as he had created man, gave unto him a certain precept and law, which he, being yet in the state of innocency and remaining in paradise, should observe as a pledge and token of his due and bounden[1] obedience, with denunciation of death if he did transgress and break the said law and commandment. And as God would have man to be his obedient subject, so did he make all earthly creatures subject unto man, who kept their

---

4. *Numquam faciendum est malum ut bonum inde eveniat* (sig. Ei[v]), "Evil must never be done so that good may result."

† From *An Homilie agaynst disobedience and wylful rebellion* (London, 1570), sigs. Ai–Ai(v), Bii–Biv, Cii(v)–Di, Fi–Fi(v). Footnotes are by the editor of this Norton Critical Edition. Spelling and punctuation have been modernized by the editor. This homily, commissioned by Elizabeth in response to the Northern Rebellion of Catholics (1568), condemns all rebellion and urges instead humble obedience and patient endurance. Those who raise a hand against the Lord's anointed, the preacher argues, re-enact the Fall as well as Lucifer's rebellion and deserve eternal damnation. The arguments from Roman history and from the biblical story of King Saul and David directly oppose Juan de Mariana's reading of the classical and scriptural precedents. Together, this homily and Mariana's treatise (see the excerpt on pp. 214–18 in this edition) provide a polemical context for the killings of both Duncan and Macbeth.

1. obligated.

due obedience unto man so long as man remained in his obedience unto God. In the which obedience if man had continued still, there had been no poverty, no diseases, no sickness, no death, nor other miseries wherewith mankind is now infinitely and most miserably afflicted and oppressed. So here appeareth the original kingdom of God over angels and man and universally over all things, and of man over earthly creatures which God had made subject unto him, and withal[2] the felicity and blessed state which angels, man, and all creatures had remained in, had they continued in due obedience unto God their king. For as long as in this first kingdom the subjects continued in due obedience to God their king, so long did God embrace all his subjects with his love, favor, and grace, which to enjoy is perfect felicity. Whereby it is evident that obedience is the principal virtue of all virtues and indeed the very root of all virtues and the cause of all felicity. But as all felicity and blessedness should have continued with the continuance of obedience, so with the breach of obedience and breaking in of rebellion, all vices and miseries did withal break in and overwhelm the world. The first author of which rebellion, the root of all vices and mother of all mischiefs was Lucifer, first God's most excellent creature and most bounden subject, who, by rebelling against the majesty of God, of the brightest and most glorious angel is become the blackest and most foulest fiend and devil, and from the height of heaven is fallen into the pit and bottom of hell.

*   *   *

But what if the prince be undiscreet[3] and evil in deed, and it also evident to all men's eyes that he so is? I ask again, what if it belong of the wickedness of the subjects that the prince is undiscreet or evil? Shall the subjects both by their wickedness provoke God for their deserved punishment to give them an undiscreet or evil prince, and also rebel against him and withal against God, who for the punishment of their sins did give them such a prince? Will you hear the Scriptures concerning this point? God (say the Holy Scriptures) maketh a wicked man to reign for the sins of the people. Again, God giveth a prince in his anger (meaning an evil one) and taketh away a prince in his displeasure (meaning specially when he taketh away a good prince for the sins of the people); as in our memory he took away our good Josias, King Edward, in his young and good years for our wickedness.[4] And, contrarily, the Scriptures do teach that God giveth wisdom unto princes, and maketh a wise

2. in addition.
3. without sound judgment.
4. Protestants often compared King Edward VI (1537–1553) to the youthful reformer Josias (2 Kings 22–23; 2 Chron. 34–35).

and good king to reign over that people whom he loveth and who loveth him. Again, "If the people obey God, both they and their king shall prosper and be safe, else both shall perish," saith God by the mouth of Samuel (1 Sam. 12:14–15, 25).

Here you see that God placeth as well evil princes as good, and for what cause he doth both. If we, therefore, will have a good prince either to be given us or to continue now we have such a one, let us by our obedience to God and to our prince move God thereunto. If we will have an evil prince (when God shall send such a one) taken away, and a good in his place, let us take away our wickedness, which provoketh God to place such a one over us, and God will either displace him or of an evil prince make him a good prince, so that we first will change our evil into good. For will you hear the Scriptures? "The heart of the prince is in God's hand; which way soever it shall please him, he turneth it" (Prov. 21:1). Thus say the Scriptures. Wherefore let us turn from our sins unto the Lord with all our hearts, and he will turn the heart of the prince unto our quiet and wealth. Else for subjects to deserve through their sins to have an evil prince, and then to rebel against him, were double and treble evil by provoking God more to plague them. Nay, let us either deserve to have a good prince, or let us patiently suffer and obey such as we deserve.

And whether the prince be good or evil, let us, according to the counsel of the Holy Scriptures pray for the prince—for his continuance and increase in goodness if he be good, and for his amendment if he be evil. Will you hear the Scriptures concerning this most necessary point? "I exhort, therefore," saith Saint Paul, "that above all things prayers, supplications, intercessions, and giving of thanks be had for all men, for kings, and all that are in authority, that we may live a quiet and peaceable life with all godliness, for that is good and acceptable in the sight of God our Saviour, etc." (1 Tim. 2:1–3). This is Saint Paul's counsel. And who, I pray you, was prince over the most part of Christians when God's holy spirit by Saint Paul's pen gave them this lesson? Forsooth, Caligula, Claudius, or Nero, who were not only no Christians, but pagans, and also either foolish rulers or most cruel tyrants. Will you yet hear the word of God to the Jews when they were prisoners under Nebuchadnezzar, King of Babylon, after he had slain their king, nobles, parents, children and kinfolks, burned their country, cities, yea, Jerusalem itself, and the holy temple, and had carried the residue remaining alive captives with him unto Babylon? Will you hear yet what the prophet Baruch saith unto God's people being in this captivity? "Pray you," saith the prophet, "for the life of Nebuchadnezzar, King of Babylon, and for the life of Balthasar, his son, that their days may be as the days of heaven upon the earth, that God also may give us strength and lighten our eyes that we may live under the defense of Nebuchadnezzar, King of Babylon, and under the protection of Balthasar, his son, that we may long do them service and find favor in their sight. Pray for us also unto the Lord our God, for we have sinned against the Lord our God" (1 Bar. 1:11–13). Thus far the prophet Baruch his words, which are spoken by him unto the people of God of that king who was a heathen, a tyrant, and cruel oppressor of them, and had been a murderer of many thousands of their nation and a destroyer of their country, with a confession that their sins had deserved such a prince to reign over them.

And shall the old Christians, by Saint Paul's exhortation, pray for Caligula, Claudius or Nero, shall the Jews pray for Nebuchadnezzar—these emperors and kings being strangers unto them, being pagans and infidels, being murderers, tyrants, and cruel oppressors of them, and the destroyers of their country, countrymen, and kinsmen, the burners of their villages, towns, cities and temples? And shall not we pray for the long, prosperous, and godly reign of our natural prince, no stranger (which is observed as a great blessing in the Scriptures), of our Christian, our most gracious Sovereign, no heathen, nor pagan prince?

* * *

As in the first part of this treaty[5] of obedience of subjects to their princes and against disobedience and rebellion I have alleged divers sentences out of the Holy Scriptures for proof, so shall it be good for the better both declaration and confirmation of the said wholesome doctrine to allege one example or two out of the same Holy Scriptures of the obedience of subjects, not only unto their good and gracious governors, but also unto their evil and unkind princes.

As King Saul was not of the best, but rather of the worst sort of princes, as being out of God's favor for his disobedience against God in sparing (in a wrong pity) the King Agag, whom almighty God commanded to be slain, according to the justice of God against his sworn enemy.[6] And although Saul of a devotion meant to sacrifice such things as he spared of the Amalekites to the honor and service of God, yet Saul was reproved for his wrong mercy and devotion, and was told that obedience would have more pleased Him than such lenity, which sinful humanity (saith holy Chrysostom) is more cruel before God than any murder or shedding of blood when it is commanded of God. But yet, how evil soever Saul

5. treatise.
6. The story of King Saul, the Amalekites, and King Agag appears in 1 Samuel 15; the story of Saul and David follows, chapters 16–31, and 2 Samuel 1.

the King was and out of God's favor, yet was he obeyed of his subject David, the very best of all subjects and most valiant in the service of his prince and country in the wars, the most obedient and
loving in peace, and always most true and faithful to his sovereign
and lord, and furthest off from all manner rebellion. For the which
his most painful, true, and faithful service, King Saul yet rewarded
him not only with great unkindness, but also sought his destruction
and death by all means possible, so that David was fain[7] to save his
life, not by rebellion, nor any resistance, but by flight and hiding
himself from the King's sight. Which, notwithstanding, when King
Saul upon a time came alone into the cave where David was, so
that David might easily have slain him, yet would he neither hurt
him himself, neither suffer any of his men to lay hands upon him.
Another time also David, entering by night with one Abisai, a valiant and a fierce man, into the tent where King Saul did lie asleep,
where also he might yet more easily have slain him, yet would he
neither hurt him himself nor suffer Abisai, who was willing and
ready to slay King Saul, once to touch him. Thus did David deal
with Saul, his prince, notwithstanding that King Saul continually
sought his death and destruction. It shall not be amiss unto these
deeds of David to add his words, and to show you what he spake
unto such as encouraged him to take his opportunity and advantage to slay King Saul as his mortal enemy when he might: "The
Lord keep me," saith David, "from doing that thing and from laying
hands upon my lord, God's anointed. For who can lay his hand
upon the Lord's anointed and be guiltless? As truly as the Lord
liveth, except that the Lord do smite him, or his days shall come to
die, or that he go down to war and be slain in battle, the Lord be
merciful unto me that I lay not my hand upon the Lord's anointed"
(1 Sam. 24:6, 26:9–11).

These be David's words spoken at sundry times to divers his
servants, provoking him to slay King Saul when opportunity served
him thereunto. Neither is it to be omitted and left out how, when
an Amalekite had slain King Saul even at Saul's own bidding and
commandment (for he would live no longer now for that he had
lost the field against his enemies, the Philistines), the said Amalekite, making great haste to bring first word and news thereof unto
David as unto him for the death of his mortal enemy, bringing withal the crown that was upon King Saul's head and the
bracelet that was upon his arm, both as a proof of the truth of his
news and also as fit and pleasant presents unto David, being by
God appointed to be King Saul his successor in the kingdom. Yet
was that faithful and godly David so far from rejoicing at these

7. obliged.

news that he rent his clothes, wept, and mourned, and fasted; and so far off from thanksgiving to the messenger, either for his deed in killing the King, though his deadly enemy, or for his message and news, or for his presents that he brought, that he said unto him, "How happened it that thou was not afraid to lay thy hands upon the Lord's anointed to slay him?" Whereupon immediately he commanded one of his servants to kill the messenger, and said, "Thy blood be upon thine own head, for thine own mouth hath witnessed against thyself in confessing that thou hast slain the Lord's anointed" (2 Sam 1:13–16).

This example, dearly beloved, is notable, and the circumstances thereof are well to be considered, for the better instruction of all subjects in their bounden duty of obedience, and perpetual fearing[8] of them from attempting of any rebellion or hurt against their prince. On the one part, David was not only a good and true subject, but also such a subject as both in peace and war had served and saved his prince's honor and life and delivered his country and countrymen from great dangers of infidels, foreign and most cruel enemies, horribly invading the king and his country; for the which David was in singular favor with all the people, so that he might have had great numbers of them at his commandment if he would have attempted anything. Besides this, David was no common or absolute[9] subject, but heir apparent to the crown and kingdom, by God appointed to reign after Saul, which, as it increased the favor of the people that knew it towards David, so did it make David's cause and case much differing from the case of common and absolute subjects. And, which is most of all, David was highly and singularly in the favor of God. On the contrary part, King Saul was out of God's favor for that cause which is before rehearsed, and he, as it were, God's enemy, and therefore like in war and peace to be hurtful and pernicious unto the commonwealth; and that was known to many of his subjects, for that he was openly rebuked of Samuel for his disobedience unto God, which might make the people the less to esteem him. King Saul was also unto David a mortal and deadly enemy, though without David's deserving, who by his faithful, painful, profitable, yea, most necessary service had well deserved as of his country, so of his prince. But King Saul far otherwise: the more was his unkindness, hatred, and cruelty towards such a good subject both odious and detestable. Yet would David neither himself slay nor hurt such an enemy for that he was his prince and lord, nor would suffer any other to kill, hurt, or lay

8. frightening.
9. pure and simple.

hand upon him when he might have been slain without any stir, tumult, or danger of any man's life.

*   *   *

In foreign wars our countrymen in obtaining the victory win the praise of valiantness. Yea, and though they were overcome and slain, yet win they an honest commendation in this world and die in a good conscience for serving God, their prince, and their country, and be children of eternal salvation. But in rebellion, how desperate and strong soever they be, yet win they shame here in fighting against God, their prince, and country, and, therefore, justly do fall headlong into hell if they die, and live in shame and fearful conscience, though they escape. But commonly they be rewarded with shameful deaths, their heads and carcasses set upon poles, or hanged in chains, eaten with kites and crows, judged unworthy the honor of burial, and so their souls, if they repent not (as commonly they do not), the devil harrieth[1] them into hell in the midst of their mischief. For which dreadful execution Saint Paul (Rom. 13) showeth the cause of obedience, not only for fear of death but also in conscience to Godward[2] for fear of eternal damnation in the world to come.

Wherefore, good people, let us as the children of obedience fear the dreadful execution of God and live in quiet obedience to be the children of everlasting salvation. For as heaven is the place of good, obedient subjects, and hell the prison and dungeon of rebels against God and their prince, so is that realm happy where most obedience of subjects doth appear, being the very figure of heaven; and contrariwise, where most rebellions and rebels be, there is the express similitude of hell, and the rebels themselves are the very figures of fiends and devils, and their captain the ungracious pattern of Lucifer and Satan, the prince of darkness, of whose rebellion as they be followers, so shall they of his damnation in hell undoubtedly be partakers; and as undoubtedly children of peace the inheritors of heaven with God the Father, God the Son, and God the Holy Ghost, to whom be all honor and glory forever and ever, Amen.

1. carries off.
2. toward God.

JUAN DE MARIANA

[A Defense of Disobedience and Tyrannicide] (1599)†

Whether It Is Right to Destroy a Tyrant.

These are the defenses of each side, and after they have been carefully considered, it will not be difficult to set forth what must be decided about the proposed question. For certainly I see that the philosophers and theologians agree in this matter, that the prince who has taken possession of a republic by force and arms and, moreover, with no right and no public consent of the citizens can be killed by anyone and be deprived of his life and dominion.[1] Because he is a public enemy and oppresses his country with all evils, and because he truly and properly puts on the name and nature of a tyrant, he may be removed by any method and he may put off his power as violently as he took possession of it. (With this merit, then, Ehud, having insinuated himself into the graces of Eglon, King of the Moabites, slew him with a dagger plunged into the stomach; he snatched his people from the hard servitude which had oppressed them for eighteen years.)[2]

For if the prince holds power by the consent of the people or by hereditary right, his vices and lusts must be borne until he neglects those laws of honor and virtue by which he is bound. For princes must not be changed easily lest the republic fall into greater evils and serious disturbances arise, as was set down in the beginning of this disputation. But if, in truth, he destroys the republic, considers public and private fortunes as his own booty, holds public laws and sacred religion in contempt, and if he makes a virtue out of pride, brazenness, and impiety against heaven—this cannot be dissembled. One must consider carefully, however, what method of rejecting his prince should be taken, lest evil be piled upon evil and crime be avenged with crime.

---

† From Juan de Mariana, *De Rege et Regis Institutione* (Toledo, 1599), 74–82. Translation and footnotes by the editor of this Norton Critical Edition. Juan de Mariana (1536–1624), a Spanish Jesuit, argues that kings who act as tyrants forfeit their right to rule and that anyone may depose or kill them if there is no other remedy and if the will of the people so mandates. Mariana's work was widely condemned for instigating the assassination of Henri IV of France in 1610, about the time of *Macbeth*.
1. Mariana describes the tyrant in entrance (*ex defectu tituli*, "from defect of title"), the ruler who unlawfully seizes power; below, he will describe the tyrant in practice (*ex parte exercitii*, "from the part of practice"), the ruler who abuses his power.
2. For the Old Testament story of Ehud, Eglon, and the freeing of the Israelites, see Judges 3:12–4:1.

And the readiest and safest way is to debate what must be decided by common consent, if the opportunity for a public meeting may be given, and to ratify and validate what has been decided by the common opinion. In which matter one may proceed by these steps: first, the prince will have to be warned and summoned back to sanity; if he regulates his conduct, makes satisfaction to the republic, and corrects the faults of his past life, the process must be halted, I think, and no harsher remedies attempted. If he spits out the medicine, however, and no hope of sanity is left, it will be permissible for the republic by a declared sentence first to reject his sovereignty. And since war necessarily will be provoked, it will then be permissible to make plans for driving him out, to bring forth arms, to raise money from the people for the costs of war, and if the matter requires and if the republic cannot be protected otherwise, by its same right of defense and in truth by its better and proper authority, to declare the prince a public enemy and to slay him with a sword. Let there be the same opportunity to any private citizen whatsoever who, with all hope of impunity tossed aside and his own safety ignored, wishes to step forward in the attempt to help the republic.

You may ask what must be done if the opportunity to hold a public meeting will have been taken away, as often can happen. The same, certainly, in my opinion, will be the judgment when the republic is oppressed by the tyranny of a prince, when the capacity for public meeting has been taken away from the citizens, when the will is not lacking to destroy the tyranny, to avenge manifest and intolerable crimes of the prince, and to crush his destructive efforts, so that if the sacred fatherland should fall into ruins and attract public enemies into the province, I shall think that the man who, heeding the people's prayers, tries to kill the tyrant, has in no way acted as an enemy. And this is sufficiently confirmed by those arguments which are placed against the tyrant later in this disputation.

So the question of fact in this controversy is, "Who is properly considered to be a tyrant?" The question of law is clear, that it will be right to kill a tyrant. There is no danger that many by this example will rage against the life of princes as though they were tyrants; for we place the matter in the private will neither of any one citizen, nor of many, unless the public voice of the people is present and serious and learned men are brought together in council. Things would turn out very well in human affairs if many men of strong heart were found for the liberty of their country to be contemptuous of life and health; but the contrary desire for safety often holds back many in great endeavors. So, from such a great number of tyrants as have existed in ancient times, it is possible to reckon that only a few perished by the sword of their own people. In Spain scarcely one or two, although one should attribute this to the loyalty of the subjects and the clemency of princes, who received sovereignty with the best right and exercised it modestly and humanely.[3] Nevertheless, it is a salutary reflection that it may be impressed upon princes, if they oppress the republic and are intolerable because of their vices and foulness, that they live in such a condition that they may be killed, not only by right but also with praise and glory. Perhaps this fear will hinder someone, lest he allow himself to be deeply corrupted by vices and praises; it will put reins on madness. This is the main point, that it be impressed upon the prince that the authority of the whole republic is greater than that of one man; and that he not believe the worst men affirming something different in their desire to please him, which is a great wickedness.

There was not sufficient cause for David to kill King Saul,[4] it used to be objected, since David was able to reach safety by flight. If he, using this logic to save himself, were to slay a king especially established by God, it would have been impiety, not love of the republic. For Saul was not so depraved in morals that he was oppressing his subjects in tyranny, that he was overturning divine and human laws, that he was treating the citizens as spoil. The rights of rule certainly were transferred to David so that he might succeed the dead king, not, however, so that he might seize the life and power from the living one. Moreover, Augustine (*Contra Adimantus*, ch. 17) says this, namely that David did not wish to kill Saul, but that it would have been permissible.[5] It is not necessary to go on about the Roman emperors: by the blood and suffering of the pious the foundations of the church's greatness were laid out precisely to the very ends of the earth. And it was the greater miracle that the oppressed church was growing and, diminished in number, was gaining greater increments day by day. And in truth, the church was not free according to its doctrines in that time, nor even in this time, to do all the things which had been granted to it by right and laws. Thus, the famous historian Sozomen (Book 6, chapter 2) says that if a soldier happened to have killed the Emperor Julian,[6] since at that time they were actually accusing him specifically, he would have done so by right and with honor.

Finally, we think that upheavals in the republic must be avoided. Care must be taken lest joy from the expulsion of tyrants run wild in

---

3. Mariana wrote a popular history of Spain, *Historiae de rebus Hispaniae* (1592), which he revised several times and translated into Spanish (1601).
4. The story of King Saul and David appears in 1 Samuel 16–2 Samuel 1; for a different interpretation, see the *Homily*, pp. 210–12 in this Norton Critical Edition.
5. not merely for self-preservation, that is, but under certain circumstances.
6. Julian the Apostate was a Roman emperor from 361–63 and an enemy of Christianity; Christian lawyer in Constantinople, Sozomen (400–450) compiled a church history for the period 324–439.

a brief moment and turn out to be empty; and all remedies for restoring a prince to health must be tried before it comes to this last and most serious measure. But if it is the case that every hope has been taken away and the public safety and the holiness of religions are called into danger, who will be so poor in counsel as not to avow that it is allowable to strike at the tyrant by right, by law, and by arms? One, perhaps, would move to this extreme position of denial because the following proposal was rejected by the Fathers at the Council of Constance[7] in the 15th session, "A tyrant can and ought to be killed by any subject, not only by open force but also through plotting and deceit." But, in truth, I do not find that conciliar decree approved by the Roman Pope Martin V, nor by Pope Eugene or his successors, by whose consent the holiness of ecclesiastical councils stands.

✳   ✳   ✳

It is pleasing to conclude this disputation with the words of the Tribune Flavius, who, convicted of conspiracy against Domitius Nero,[8] in the midst of the questions about why he had acted oblivious to his oath of allegiance: "I hated you," he said, "but no soldier was more faithful to you while you deserved to be loved; I began to hate you after you became the murderer of your own mother and wife, a charioteer and actor, and an arsonist." A spirit soldierly and brave, according to Tacitus, Book 15.

Whether it is licit to kill a tyrant with poison.[9]

A wicked mind has unfathomable internal torments and the conscience of a tyrant is his own executioner. So even if no external adversary approaches, depravity of life and morals makes every joy and liberty of life bitter. For what condition of life, and how miserable, is it to singe off the beard and hair with burning coals for fear of the barber, as Dionysius the Tyrant[1] used to do? What pleasure was there to him who hid himself in the citadel like a snake in the time of quiet and sleep, as Clearchus, the Pontic tyrant,[2] was accustomed to do? What fruit of rule enjoyed Argive Aristodemus,[3] who used to conceal himself in a garret by means of a hanging door with a ladder added and removed? Or could there be greater

7. The sixteenth ecumenical council of the Church (1414–18), the Council of Constance settled rival claims to the papacy, combated heresy, and initiated some reforms.
8. fifth Roman emperor (54–68), infamous for debauchery and the persecution of Christians.
9. Mariana will answer the title question in the negative, arguing, remarkably, that such a method of assassination puts the victim's soul at risk by forcing him to commit a kind of suicide.
1. ruthless tyrant of Syracuse, ruling from 405–367 B.C.E.
2. severe Spartan governor of Byzantium, 411–401 B.C.E.
3. tyrant of Cumae, early sixth century C.E.

unhappiness than to trust no one, not even friends and family? To quake at any noise and shadow as if rebellion had broken out and the spirits of all were enraged against him? He clearly lives a miserable life whose life is such that the one who slays him will have great gratitude and praise.

It is a glorious thing to exterminate all of this pestilent and deadly species from the human community. For in truth certain limbs are cut off if they are rotten lest they infect the rest of the body; so the monstrosity of a beast in this likeness of a man ought to be removed from the republic as from a body and cut out with a blade. Certainly the tyrant who spreads terror ought to fear; but the terror he arouses is not greater than the fear he endures. There is not so much protection in military strength, arms, and troops as there is danger in the people's hatred, whence destruction threatens. All orders busy themselves to remove a monster conspicuous for his abominations of villainy and his sordid deeds of cowardice. After hatreds have grown daily, either insurrection breaks out and there is a rush to open force when the people have taken up arms (which admirable spirit of nature we ought to restore to our country, by which means not a few tyrants have perished by open force!), or else with greater caution, by fraud and plotting, tyrants perish by one or a few individuals gathering secretly and working to regain safety for the republic at their own peril. But if they succeed, they are regarded in every station of life as great heroes; if it should fall out otherwise, they fall as sacrifices pleasing to heaven and pleasing to men, famous to all posterity for their noble attempt.

Debate on Equivocation

HENRY GARNET

A Treatise of Equivocation (before 1606)[†]

And we may say with the logicians that there be four kinds of propositions. The first is a mental position, only conceived in the mind, and not uttered by any exterior signification; as when I think with

---

[†] From Henry Garnet, *A Treatise of Equivocation*, ed. David Jardine (London, 1851), 8–11. Spelling and punctuation have been modernized by the editor of this Norton Critical Edition. Henry Garnet, SJ (1553/4–1606) was Jesuit Superior in England from 1587 until his execution for complicity in the Gunpowder Plot, allegedly a scheme by Catholics to blow up Parliament. Garnet propounded a theory of equivocation, which enabled Catholics to tell partial truths or to deceive interrogators and thereby survive persecution. Condemning equivocation, the Porter in *Macbeth* (2.3.1–10) alludes to Garnet, who sometimes adopted the alias of "Farmer." See Cain's *Equivocation* below, 365–76.

myself these words, "God is not unjust." The second is a vocal proposition, as when I utter those words with my mouth. The third is a written proposition, as if I should set the same down in writing. The last of all is a mixed proposition, when we mingle some of these positions (or parts of them) together, as in our purpose, when being demanded whether John at Style be in such a place, I, knowing that he is there indeed, do say nevertheless "I know not"—reserving or understanding within myself these other words "to th'end for to tell you."[1] Here is a mixed proposition containing all this, "I know not to th'end for to tell you." And yet part of it is expressed, part reserved in the mind.

Now unto all these propositions it is common that then they are true when they are conformable to the thing itself; that is, when they so affirm or deny as the matter itself in very deed doth stand. Whereof we infer that this last sort of proposition, which partly consisteth in voice and partly is reserved in the mind, is then to be adjudged true, not when that part only which is expressed or the other only which is reserved is true, but when both together do contain a truth. For as it were a perverse thing in that vocal proposition, "God is not unjust," to say that position is false because if we leave out the last word the other three contain a manifest heresy (as if we affirmed God were not at all), the truth of every vocal proposition being to be measured not according to some parts but according to all together; even so that other proposition of which we spake, being a mixed proposition, is not to be examined according to the variety of the part expressed alone, but according to the part reserved also, they both together compounding one entire proposition.

Herein, therefore, consisteth the difficulty and this will we endeavor to prove: that whosoever frameth a true position in his mind and uttereth some part thereof in words, which of themselves being taken several from the other part reserved, were false, does not say false or lie before God, howsoever he may be thought to lie before men or otherwise commit therein some other sin. For yet we will not clear this party of sin herein, whereof we will speak hereafter, but only at this present we defend him not to have lied.

1. for the purpose of telling you. [Jardine's note]

SIR EDWARD COKE

Arraignment of Henry Garnet, S.J. (1606)[†]

He [Garnet] hath many gifts and endowments of nature, by art learned, a good linguist, and by profession a Jesuit and a Superior, as indeed he is superior to all his predecessors in devilish treason, a doctor of Jesuits, that is, a doctor of five D's as dissimulation, deposing of princes, disposing of kingdoms, daunting and deterring of subjects, and destruction. Their dissimulation appeareth out of their doctrine of equivocation. Concerning which, it was thought fit to touch something of that which was more copiously delivered in the former arraignment, in respect of the presence of Garnet there, who was the Superior of the Jesuits in England, concerning the treatise of Equivocation seen and allowed by Garnet and by Blackwell the Archpriest.[1] Wherein under the pretext of the lawfulness of a mixed proposition to express one part of a man's mind and retain another,[2] people are indeed taught not only simple lying but fearful and damnable blasphemy. And whereas the Jesuits ask why we convict and condemn them not for heresy, as it is for that they will equivocate and so cannot that way be tried or judged according to their words.

Now for the antiquity of equivocation, it is indeed very old, within little more than 300 years after Christ, used by Arius the heretic,[3] who having in a General Council been condemned and then by the commandment of Constantine the Emperor sent into exile, was by the said Emperor upon instant intercession with him and promise of his future conformity to the Nicene faith, recalled again.[4] Who, returning home and having before craftily set down in writing his heretical belief and put it into his bosom, when he came into the presence of the Emperor and had the Nicene faith propounded unto him, and was thereupon asked whether he then did indeed and so constantly would hold that faith, he, clapping his

---

[†] Anon., *A true and perfect relation of the whole proceedings against the late most barbarous traitors, Garnet a Iesuit, and his confederates* (London, 1606), sigs. T2–T3. Attorney General Edward Coke, later Chief Justice, prosecuted the Jesuit Henry Garnet for conspiracy in the Gunpowder Plot. Here he condemns Garnet's doctrine of equivocation, mentioned by the Porter in *Macbeth* (2.3.1–10). Coke equates equivocation to simple lying and blasphemy, traces its practice to the heretic Arius, and considers it a kind of unchastity.

1. George Blackwell, archpriest of England from 1597 to 1608.
2. A "mixed proposition" refers to a discourse wherein one's speaking, thinking and/or writing about a subject differed.
3. Arius (d. 336) denied the full divinity of Christ.
4. The First Council of Nicaea (325), convened to combat the Arian heresy, promulgated the Nicene Creed to affirm the full divinity of Christ, "God from God, light from light, true God from true God, begotten, not made, consubstantial with the Father."

hand upon his bosom where his paper lay, answered and vowed that he did, and so would constantly profess and hold that faith, laying his hand on his bosom where the paper of his heresy lay, meaning fraudulently by way of equivocation that faith of his own, which he had written and carried in his bosom.

For these Jesuits, they indeed make no vow of speaking truth, and yet even this equivocating and lying is a kind of unchastity, against which they vow and promise. For it hath been said of old, *Cor linguae faederat naturae sanctio, veluti in quodam certo connubio: ergo, cum disponent cor & eloquentio sermo concipitur in adulterio*, that is, "The law and sanction of nature hath, as it were, married the heart and tongue, by joining and knitting of them together in a certain kind of marriage; and, therefore, when there is discord between them two, the speech that proceeds from them is said to be conceived in adultery." And he that breeds such bastard children offends against chastity.

CRITICISM

SIMON FORMAN

[Eyewitness Account of *Macbeth*] (1611)[†]

In *Macbeth* at the Globe, 1610,[1] the 20 of April, Saturday, there was to be observed first how Macbeth and Banquo, two noblemen of Scotland, riding through a wood,[2] there stood before them three women fairies or nymphs,[3] and saluted Macbeth, saying three times unto him, "Hail Macbeth, King of Codon,[4] for thou shalt be a king, but shall beget no kings, etc" [1.3.51ff.]. Then said Banquo, "What, all to Macbeth and nothing to me?" "Yes," said the nymphs, "Hail to thee, Banquo, thou shalt beget kings, yet be no king" [1.3.68]. And so they departed and came to the court of Scotland, to Duncan, King of Scots, and it was in the days of Edward the Confessor. And Duncan bade them both kindly welcome, and made Macbeth forthwith Prince of Northumberland, and sent him home to his own castle,[5] and appointed Macbeth to provide for him,[6] for he would sup with him the next day at night, and did so. And Macbeth contrived to kill Duncan, and through the persuasion of his wife did that night murder the King in his own castle, being his guest. And there were many prodigies seen that night and the day before. And when Macbeth had murdered the King, the blood on his hands could not be washed off by any means, nor from his wife's hands, which handled the bloody daggers in hiding them, by which means they became both much amazed and affronted.[7] The murder being known, Duncan's two sons fled, the one to England, the [other to]

---

† From Forman's *Booke of Plaies*, which is at Oxford University (MS Ashmole 208). I have modernized and glossed F. J. Furnivall's transcription, reprinted in the revised New Variorum edition of *Macbeth*, ed. Horace Howard Furness, Jr. (Philadelphia: J. B. Lippincott Co., 1915), 356–57. The earliest eyewitness account of the play belongs to Simon Forman, a doctor and astrologer who made notes on four Shakespeare plays he saw at the Globe in the spring of 1611. Forman's reminiscence, demonstrably faulty in parts, nevertheless raises intriguing questions about the original performance, particularly its staging.

1. an error for 1611 (April 20 was a Saturday in 1611, not 1610).
2. Did Banquo and Macbeth ride horses onto a stage imagined as a wood rather than a heath? Probably not; Forman may be remembering an illustration in Holinshed's 1577 edition of the *Chronicles*, which shows Macbeth and Banquo on horseback meeting the witches in front of a tree.
3. The description possibly conflicts with the "black and midnight hags" (4.1.47) of Shakespeare's play.
4. Cawdor (another error).
5. Forman misrecalls the naming of Malcolm Prince of Cumberland (1.4.37–39). Malcolm does not return to his own castle in the play but accompanies the King to Macbeth's castle at Inverness.
6. Duncan.
7. ashamed. Forman recalls unwashable blood on the hands, a striking stage effect in apparent contradiction to the surviving text.

Ian McKellen and Judi Dench in Trevor Nunn's film (1979). Photo by Rex Features/courtesy of the Everett Collection.

Wales, to save themselves. They being fled, they were supposed guilty of the murder of their father, which was nothing so. Then was Macbeth crowned king, and then he for fear of Banquo, his old companion, that he should beget kings but be no king himself, he contrived the death of Banquo, and caused him to be murdered on the way as he rode. The next night, being at supper with his noblemen whom he had bid to a feast to the which also Banquo should have come, he began to speak of noble Banquo and to wish that he were there. And as he thus did, standing up to drink a carouse to him, the ghost of Banquo came and sat down in his chair behind him.[8] And he, turning about to sit down again, saw the ghost of Banquo, which fronted[9] him so, that he fell into a great passion of fear and fury, uttering many words about his murder, by which, when they heard that Banquo was murdered, they suspected Macbeth.

Then Macduff fled to England to the King's son, and so they raised an army and came into Scotland and at Dunsinane overthrew Macbeth. In the meantime, while Macduff was in England, Macbeth slew Macduff's wife and children, and after in the battle Macduff slew Macbeth.

Observe also how Macbeth's queen did rise in the night in her sleep, and walk, and talked and confessed all, and the doctor noted her words.

SAMUEL JOHNSON

Miscellaneous Observations on the Tragedy of *Macbeth* (1745)[†]

Act 1, Scene 1: *Enter three Witches.*

In order to make a true estimate of the abilities and merit of a writer it is always necessary to examine the genius of his age and the opinions of his contemporaries. A poet who should now make the whole action of his tragedy depend upon enchantment and produce the chief events by the assistance of supernatural agents would be censured as transgressing the bounds of probability. He would be banished from the theatre to the nursery and condemned to write fairy tales instead of tragedies. But a survey of the notions that prevailed

---

8. a possible indication of the original staging and its powerful dramatic effect.
9. confronted.

† From Samuel Johnson, *Miscellaneous Observations on the Tragedy of Macbeth* (London, 1745), 1–2, 4–6, 22–23, 44–47, 58–59. Footnotes are by the editor of this Norton Critical Edition. Spelling and punctuation have also been modernized by the editor. References to act, scene, and line numbers in this Norton Critical Edition have been added in brackets.

at the time when this play was written will prove that Shakespeare was in no danger of such censures, since he only turned the system that was then universally admitted to his advantage, and was far from overburdening the credulity of his audience.

The reality of witchcraft or enchantment—which, though not strictly the same, are confounded in this play—has in all ages and countries been credited by the common people, and in most by the learned themselves. These phantoms have indeed appeared more frequently in proportion as the darkness of ignorance has been more gross; but it cannot be shown that the brightest gleams of knowledge have at any time been sufficient to drive them out of the world. The time in which this kind of credulity was at its height seems to have been that of the Holy War,[1] in which the Christians imputed all their defeats to enchantments or diabolical opposition, as they ascribed their success to the assistance of their military saints.

*   *   *

The Reformation did not immediately arrive at its meridian,[2] and though day was gradually increasing upon us, the goblins of witch-craft still continued to hover in the twilight. In the time of Queen Elizabeth was the remarkable trial of the witches of Warbois, whose conviction is still commemorated in an annual sermon at Hunting-don.[3] But in the reign of King James, in which this tragedy was writ-ten, many circumstances concurred to propagate and confirm this opinion. The King, who was much celebrated for his knowledge, had before his arrival in England not only examined in person a woman accused of witchcraft, but had given a very formal account of the practices and illusions of evil spirits, the compacts of witches, the ceremonies used by them, the manner of detecting them, and the justice of punishing them, in his dialogues of *Dae-monologie*, written in the Scottish dialect and published at Edin-burgh.[4] This book was soon after his accession reprinted at London, and as the ready way to gain K. James's favor was to flatter his speculations, the system of *Daemonologie* was immediately adopted by all who desired either to gain preferment or not to lose it. Thus the doctrine of witchcraft was very powerfully inculcated, and as

1. The Crusades (1095–1281), a series of expeditions from Western Christendom to reclaim Eastern holy lands from Islamic rule.
2. midday position, highest point.
3. Hysterical girls in the Throgmorton family of Warbois in the county of Huntingdon accused an old woman, evidently ugly and half-witted, of bewitching them. On April 7, 1593, the woman, Alice Samuels, her husband, and their daughter were executed.
4. *Daemonologie* first appeared in 1597 (see the excerpt on pp. 205–08 in this edition); two publishers in London brought out editions of the book in 1603.

the greatest part of mankind have no other reason for their opinions
than that they are in fashion, it cannot be doubted but this persuasion made a rapid progress, since vanity and credulity cooperated in
its favor and it had a tendency to free cowardice from reproach. The
infection soon reached the Parliament, who in the first year of King
James made a law by which it was enacted (Ch. XII): That (1) "if any
person shall use any invocation or conjuration of any evil or wicked
spirit; (2) or shall consult, covenant with, entertain, employ, feed or
reward any evil or cursed spirit to or for any intent or purpose; (3) or
take up any dead man, woman or child out of the grave, or the skin,
bone, or any part of the dead person, to be employed or used in any
manner of witchcraft, sorcery, charm, or enchantment; (4) or shall
use, practice or exercise any sort of witchcraft, sorcery, charm, or
enchantment; (5) whereby any person shall be destroyed, killed,
wasted, consumed, pined, or lamed in any part of the body; (6) that
every such person being convicted shall suffer death."[5]

Thus, in the time of Shakespeare was the doctrine of witchcraft at
once established by law and by the fashion, and it became not only
unpolite but criminal to doubt it; and as prodigies are always seen in
proportion as they are expected, witches were every day discovered,
and multiplied so fast in some places that Bishop Hall mentions a
village in Lancashire where their number was greater than that of
the houses. The Jesuits and sectaries took advantage of this universal
error and endeavoured to promote the interest of their parties by
pretended cures of persons afflicted by evil spirits, but they were
detected and exposed by the clergy of the established Church.[6]

Upon this general infatuation Shakespeare might be easily allowed
to found a play, especially since he has followed with great exactness
such histories as were then thought true; nor can it be doubted that
the scenes of enchantment, however they may now be ridiculed, were
both by himself and his audience thought awful and affecting.

[Act 1, Scene 7]

The arguments by which Lady Macbeth persuades her husband to
commit the murder afford a proof of Shakespeare's knowledge of
human nature. She urges the excellence and dignity of courage,
a glittering idea which has dazzled mankind from age to age, and
animated sometimes the housebreaker and sometimes the conqueror;

---

5. Johnson cites "An Act against Conjuration, Witchcraft, and Dealing with Evil and
Wicked Spirits," 1604.
6. Johnson here articulates the standard anti-Catholic position, also evident in James I's
Daemonologie.

but this sophism Macbeth has forever destroyed by distinguishing true from false fortitude in a line and a half, of which it may almost be said that they ought to bestow immortality on the author, though all his other productions had been lost:

> I dare do all that may become a man,
> Who dares do more is none. [1.7.46–47]

This topic, which has been always employed with too much success, is used in this scene with peculiar propriety, to a soldier by a woman. Courage is the distinguishing virtue of a soldier, and the reproach of cowardice cannot be borne by any man from a woman without great impatience.

She then urges the oaths by which he had bound himself to murder Duncan, another art of sophistry by which men have sometimes deluded their consciences and persuaded themselves that what would be criminal in others is virtuous in them. This argument Shakespeare, whose plan obliged him to make Macbeth yield, has not confuted, though he might easily have shown that a former obligation could not be vacated by a latter.

Act 4, Scene 1

As this is the chief scene of enchantment in the play, it is proper in this place to observe with how much judgment Shakespeare has selected all the circumstances of his infernal ceremonies, and how exactly he has conformed to common opinions and traditions.

> Thrice the brinded cat hath mew'd. [4.1.1]

The usual form in which familiar spirits are reported to converse with witches is that of a cat. A witch who was tried about half a century before the time of Shakespeare had a cat named Rutterkin, as the spirit of one of those witches was Grimalkin; and when any mischief was to be done she used to bid Rutterkin, "go and fly!" But once, when she would have sent Rutterkin to torment a daughter of the Countess of Rutland, instead of going or flying he only cried "Mew," from which she discovered that the lady was out of his power—the power of witches being not universal but limited, as Shakespeare has taken care to inculcate.

> Though his bark cannot be lost,
> Yet it shall be tempest tost. [1.3.25–26]

The common afflictions which the malice of witches produced was melancholy, fits, and loss of flesh, which are threatened by one of Shakespeare's witches.

> Weary sev'nnights nine times nine
> Shall he dwindle, peak, and pine. [1.3.23–24]

It was likewise their practice to destroy the cattle of their neighbors, and the farmers have to this day many ceremonies to secure their cows and other cattle from witchcraft; but they seem to have been most suspected of malice against swine. Shakespeare has accordingly made one of his witches declare that she has been "killing swine," and Dr Harsnett[7] observes that about that time a sow could not be ill of the measles, nor a girl of the sullens,[8] but some old woman was charged with witchcraft.

> Toad, that under the cold stone
> Days and nights has forty-one
> Swelter'd venom sleeping got,
> Boil thou first i'th'charmed pot. [4.1.6–9]

Toads have likewise long lain under the reproach of being by some means accessory to witchcraft, for which reason Shakespeare in the first scene of this play calls one of the spirits "Paddock" or toad, and now takes care to put a toad first into the pot. When Vaninus[9] was seized at Toulouse there was found at his lodgings *ingens bufo vitro inclusus,* "a great toad shut in a vial," upon which those that prosecuted him, *Veneficium exprobrabant* ["they were exuding venom"], charged him, I suppose, with witchcraft

> Fillet of a fenny snake
> In the cauldron boil and bake;
> Eye of newt and toe of frog
> . . . .
> For a charm, etc. [4.1.12ff.]

The propriety of these ingredients may be known by consulting the books *De Viribus Animalium* and *De Mirabilibus Mundi,* ascribed to Albertus Magnus,[1] in which the reader who has time and credulity may discover very wonderful secrets.

> Finger of birth-strangled babe,
> Ditch-deliver'd by a drab. [4.1.30–31]

It has been already mentioned in the law against witches that they are supposed to take up dead bodies to use in enchantments,

---

7. Archbishop Samuel Harsnett (1561–1631) wrote several works exposing fraudulent possessions and exorcisms, including *A Declaration of Egregious Popish Impostures* (1603), which Shakespeare drew upon for *King Lear.*
8. fits of melancholy.
9. A pantheist, Giulio Cesare (or Lucilio Vanini), was convicted as an atheist and burned at the stake in 1619 in Toulouse, in southern France.
1. Albert the Great (1206–1280), scientist, philosopher, theologian, and Dominican priest.

which was confessed by the woman whom King James examined, and who had of a dead body that was divided in one of their assemblies two fingers for her share. It is observable that Shakespeare, on this great occasion which involves the fate of a king, multiplies all the circumstances of horror. The babe whose finger is used must be strangled in its birth; the grease must not only be human, but must have dropped from a gibbet,[2] the gibbet of a murderer; and even the sow whose blood is used must have offended nature by devouring her own farrow.[3] These are touches of judgment and genius.

[Act 5, Scene 5]

She should have died hereafter,
There would have been a time for such a word. [5.5.17–18]

This passage has very justly been suspected of being corrupt. It is not apparent for what "word" there would have been a "time," and that there would or would not be a "time" for any "word" seems not a consideration of importance sufficient to transport Macbeth into the following exclamation. I read, therefore:

She should have died hereafter.
There would have been a time for—such a world!—
Tomorrow, etc.

It is a broken speech in which only part of the thought is expressed and may be paraphrased thus: "The Queen is dead." Macbeth: "Her death should have been deferred to some more peaceful hour; had she lived longer, there would at length have been a time for the honours due to her as a queen, and that respect which I owe her for her fidelity and love. Such is the world—such is the condition of human life, that we always think tomorrow will be happier than today, but tomorrow and tomorrow steals over us unenjoyed and unregarded, and we still linger in the same expectation to the moment appointed for our end. All these days which have thus passed away have sent multitudes of fools to the grave, who were engrossed by the same dream of future felicity, and, when life was departing from them, they were like me reckoning on tomorrow."

2. gallows, structure for hanging.
3. offspring.

SAMUEL TAYLOR COLERIDGE

[On *Macbeth*] (1808–19)†

Macbeth stands in contrast throughout with *Hamlet*, in the manner of opening more especially. In the latter there is a gradual ascent from the simplest forms of conversation to the language of impassioned intellect—yet the intellect still remaining the seat of passion. In the former the invocation is at once made to the imagination and the emotions connected therewith. Hence the movement throughout is the most rapid of all Shakespeare's plays; and hence also, with the exception of the disgusting passage of the Porter (2.3), which I dare pledge myself to demonstrate to be an interpolation of the actors, there is not, to the best of my remembrance, a single pun or play on words in the whole drama. I have previously given an answer to the thousand times repeated charge against Shakespeare upon the subject of his punning, and I here merely mention the fact of the absence of any puns in *Macbeth* as justifying a candid doubt, at least, whether even in these figures of speech and fanciful modifications of language, Shakespeare may not have followed rules and principles that merit and would stand the test of philosophic examination. And hence, also, there is an entire absence of comedy, nay, even of irony and philosophic contemplation in *Macbeth*—the play being wholly and purely tragic.

For the same cause, there are no reasonings of equivocal morality, which would have required a more leisurely state and a consequently greater activity of mind; no sophistry of self-delusion except only that previously to the dreadful act, Macbeth mistranslates the recoilings and ominous whispers of conscience into prudential and selfish reasonings, and, after the deed done, the terrors of remorse into fear from external dangers, like delirious men who run away from the phantoms of their own brains, or, raised by terror to rage, stab the real object that is within their reach—whilst Lady Macbeth merely endeavours to reconcile his and her own sinkings of heart by anticipations of the worst and an affected bravado in confronting them. In all the rest Macbeth's language is the grave utterance of the very heart, conscience-sick, even to the last faintings of moral death. It is the same in all the other characters. The variety arises from rage, caused ever and anon by disruption of anxious thought and the quick transition of fear into it.

---

† From *The Literary Remains of Samuel Taylor Coleridge*, ed. Henry Nelson Coleridge, vol. 2 (London: William Pickering, 1836), 235–50. Spelling and punctuation have been modernized by the Norton editor. References to act, scene, and line numbers in this Norton Critical Edition have been added in brackets.

In *Hamlet* and *Macbeth* the scene opens with superstition, but in each it is not merely different but opposite. In the first it is connected with the best and holiest feelings; in the second, with the shadowy, turbulent, and unsanctified cravings of the individual will. Nor is the purpose the same: in the one the object is to excite, whilst in the other it is to mark a mind already excited. Superstition of one sort or another is natural to victorious generals; the instances are too notorious to need mentioning. There is so much of chance in warfare, and such vast events are connected with the acts of a single individual—the representative, in truth, of the efforts of myriads, and yet to the public, and doubtless to his own feelings, the aggregate of all—that the proper temperament for generating or receiving superstitious impressions is naturally produced. Hope, the master element of a commanding genius, meeting with an active and combining intellect, and an imagination of just that degree of vividness which disquiets and impels the soul to try to realize its images, greatly increases the creative power of the mind, and hence the images become a satisfying world of themselves, as is the case of every poet and original philosopher. But hope fully gratified, and yet the elementary basis of the passion remaining, becomes fear; and, indeed, the general, who must often feel, even though he may hide it from his own consciousness, how large a share chance had in his successes, may very naturally be irresolute in a new scene, where he knows that all will depend on his own act and election.

The Weird Sisters are as true a creation of Shakespeare's as his Ariel and Caliban, fates, furies, and materializing witches being the elements. They are wholly different from any representation of witches in the contemporary writers and yet presented a sufficient external resemblance to the creatures of vulgar prejudice to act immediately on the audience. Their characters consist in the imaginative disconnected from the good; they are the shadowy, obscure and, fearfully anomalous of physical nature, the lawless of human nature, elemental avengers without sex or kin.

* * *

The true reason for the first appearance of the witches is to strike the key-note of the character of the whole drama, as is proved by their reappearance in the third scene, after such an order as the King's as establishes their supernatural power of information.

* * *

[1.5]. Macbeth is described by Lady Macbeth so as at the same time to reveal her own character. Could he have everything he wanted, he would rather have it innocently—ignorant, as, alas, how many of us are, that he who wishes a temporal end for itself does in truth will the means, and hence the danger of indulging fancies. Lady Macbeth, like all in Shakespeare, is a class individualized; of high rank, left much alone, and feeding herself with day-dreams of ambition, she mistakes the courage of fantasy for the power of bearing the consequences of the realities of guilt. Hers is the mock fortitude of a mind deluded by ambition; she shames her husband with a superhuman audacity of fancy which she cannot support, but sinks in the season of remorse, and dies in suicidal agony. Her speech, "Come, all you spirits / That tend on mortal thoughts, unsex me here" [1.5.38ff.], etc., is that of one who had habitually familiarized her imagination to dreadful conceptions, and was trying to do so still more. Her invocations and requisitions are all the false efforts of a mind accustomed only hitherto to the shadows of the imagination, vivid enough to throw the everyday substances of life into shadow, but never as yet brought into direct contact with their own correspondent realities. She evinces no womanly life, no wifely joy, at the return of her husband, no pleased terror at the thought of his past dangers. Whilst Macbeth bursts forth naturally, "My dearest love" [1.5.56], and shrinks from the boldness with which she presents his own thoughts to him. With consummate art she at first uses as incentives the very circumstances, Duncan's coming to their house, etc., which Macbeth's conscience would most probably have adduced to her as motives of abhorrence or repulsion. Yet Macbeth is not prepared: "We will speak further" [1.5.69].

[1.6] The lyrical movement with which this scene opens, and the free and unengaged mind of Banquo, loving nature and rewarded in the love itself, form a highly dramatic contrast with the laboured rhythm and hypocritical over-much of Lady Macbeth's welcome, in which you cannot detect a ray of personal feeling, but all is thrown upon the "dignities," the general duty.

THOMAS DE QUINCEY

On the Knocking at the Gate in *Macbeth* (1823)[†]

From my boyish days I had always felt a great perplexity on one point in *Macbeth*. It was this: the knocking at the gate which succeeds to the murder of Duncan produced to my feelings an effect

---

† From Thomas De Quincey, *Confessions of an English Opium-Eater* (London: Walter Scott, 1886), 142–48. Footnotes are by the editor of this Norton Critical Edition. Spelling and punctuation have been modernized by the editor. References to act, scene, and line numbers in this Norton Critical Edition have been added in brackets.

for which I never could account. The effect was that it reflected back upon the murder[1] a peculiar awfulness and a depth of solemnity; yet, however obstinately I endeavoured with my understanding to comprehend this, for many years I never could see *why* it should produce such an effect.

* * *

My solution is this: Murder, in ordinary cases, where the sympathy is wholly directed to the case of the murdered person, is an incident of coarse and vulgar horror; and for this reason—that it flings the interest exclusively upon the natural but ignoble instinct by which we cleave to life, an instinct which, as being indispensable to the primal law of self-preservation, is the same in kind (though different in degree) amongst all living creatures. This instinct, therefore, because it annihilates all distinctions, and degrades the greatest of men to the level of "the poor beetle that we tread on," exhibits human nature in its most abject and humiliating attitude. Such an attitude would little suit the purposes of the poet. What then must he do? He must throw the interest on the murderer; our sympathy must be with *him* (of course, I mean a sympathy of comprehension, a sympathy by which we enter into his feelings and are made to understand them— not a sympathy[2] of pity or approbation). In the murdered person, all strife of thought, all flux and reflux of passion and of purpose, are crushed by one overwhelming panic; the fear of instant death smites him "with its petrific mace." But in the murderer, such a murderer as a poet will condescend to, there must be raging some great storm of passion—jealousy, ambition, vengeance, hatred—which will create a hell within him, and into this hell we are to look.

In *Macbeth*, for the sake of gratifying his own enormous and teeming faculty of creation, Shakespeare has introduced two murderers; and, as usual in his hands, they are remarkably discriminated. But—though in Macbeth the strife of mind is greater than in his wife, the tiger spirit not so awake, and his feelings caught chiefly by contagion from her—yet, as both were finally involved in the guilt of murder, the murderous mind of necessity is finally to be presumed in both. This was to be expressed; and on its own account, as well as to make it a more proportionable antagonist to the unoffending nature of their victim, "the gracious Duncan" [3.1.66], and adequately to expound "the deep damnation of his taking off"

---

1. De Quincey originally published this article in *London Magazine* (1823). *London Magazine* reads "murder" here; some later collections read "murderer."
2. In a note De Quincey argues against "the unscholar-like use of the word *sympathy*, at present so general, by which, instead of taking it in its proper sense as the act of reproducing in our minds the feelings of another, whether for hatred, indignation, love, pity, or approbation, it is made a mere synonym of the word *pity*."

[1.7.20], this was to be expressed with peculiar energy. We were to be made to feel that the human nature—i.e., the divine nature of love and mercy, spread through the hearts of all creatures and seldom utterly withdrawn from man—was gone, vanished, extinct, and that the fiendish nature had taken its place. And as this effect is marvellously accomplished in the dialogues and soliloquies themselves, so it is finally consummated by the expedient under consideration; and it is to this that I now solicit the reader's attention.

If the reader has ever witnessed a wife, daughter, or sister in a fainting fit, he may chance to have observed that the most affecting moment in such a spectacle is *that* in which a sigh and a stirring announce the recommencement of suspended life. Or if the reader has ever been present in a vast metropolis on the day when some great national idol was carried in funeral pomp to his grave, and, chancing to walk near the course through which it passed, has felt powerfully, in the silence and desertion of the streets, and in the stagnation of ordinary business, the deep interest which at that moment was possessing the heart of man—if all at once he should hear the death-like stillness broken up by the sound of wheels rattling away from the scene, and making known that the transitory vision was dissolved, he will be aware that at no moment was his sense of the complete suspension and pause in ordinary human concerns so full and affecting as at that moment when the suspension ceases and the goings-on of human life are suddenly resumed. All action in any direction is best expounded, measured, and made apprehensible by reaction. Now, apply this to the case in *Macbeth*. Here, as I have said, the retiring of the human heart and the entrance of the fiendish heart was to be expressed and made sensible. Another world has stepped in; and the murderers are taken out of the region of human things, human purposes, human desires. They are transfigured: Lady Macbeth is "unsexed"; Macbeth has forgot that he was born of woman; both are conformed to the image of devils; and the world of devils is suddenly revealed. But how shall this be conveyed and made palpable? In order that a new world may step in, this world must for a time disappear. The murderers and the murder must be insulated—cut off by an immeasurable gulf from the ordinary tide and succession of human affairs—locked up and sequestered in some deep recess; we must be made sensible that the world of ordinary life is suddenly arrested, laid asleep, tranced, racked into a dread armistice; time must be annihilated, relation to things without abolished, and all must pass self-withdrawn into a deep syncope[3] and suspension of earthly passion. Hence it is that, when the deed is

3. fainting spell.

done, when the work of darkness is perfect, then the world of darkness passes away like a pageantry in the clouds: the knocking at the gate is heard, and it makes known audibly that the reaction has commenced; the human has made its reflux upon the fiendish; the pulses of life are beginning to beat again; and the reestablishment of the goings-on of the world in which we live first makes us profoundly sensible of the awful parenthesis that had suspended them.

O mighty poet! Thy works are not as those of other men, simply and merely great works of art, but are also like the phenomena of nature, like the sun and the sea, the stars and the flowers, like frost and snow, rain and dew, hailstorm and thunder, which are to be studied with entire submission of our own faculties, and in the perfect faith that in them there can be no too much or too little, nothing useless or inert, but that, the farther we press in our discoveries, the more we shall see proofs of design and self-supporting arrangement where the careless eye had seen nothing but accident![4]

And what of the producer? It would be quite fatal for him to get his actors to underline the key images—to make them, as it were, italicize them with a knowing wink at the professors in the stalls or the students in the gallery. All we should ask of the producer in this matter is that he should give us what Shakespeare wrote, and all that Shakespeare wrote, and that he should not try to improve on the script provided by the dramatist.

HARRY LEVIN

Two Scenes from *Macbeth* (1982)[†]

Hamlet without the Prince would still be more of a spectacle than *Macbeth* without the Thane of Glamis. Though the latter is not introspective by nature, his soliloquizing is central to the play, as he considers intentions, casts suspicions, registers hallucinations, coerces his conscience, balances hope against fear, and gives thought to the unspeakable—all this while sustaining the most energetic role in the most intense of Shakespeare's plays. *Macbeth* is the fastest of them, as Coleridge pointed out, while *Hamlet*, at almost twice its length, is the slowest. Thus the uncut *Hamlet* has plenty of room for other well-defined characters and for highly

---

4. The last paragraph provides an example of the Shakespeare-worship that usually disables, rather than enables, critical judgment.

† From *Shakespeare's Craft: Eight Lectures*, ed. Philip H. Highfill, Jr. (Carbondale: Southern Illinois University Press: 1982), 48–68. Copyright © 1982 by The George Washington University. Reprinted by permission of Southern Illinois University Press.

elaborated subplots. Whereas *Macbeth*, which has come down to us in a version stripped for action, concentrates more heavily upon the protagonist. He speaks over thirty per cent of the lines; an overwhelming proportion of the rest bear reference to him; and Lady Macbeth has about eleven per cent, all of them referring to him directly or indirectly. Most of the other parts get flattened in this process, so that his may stand out in bold relief. Otherwise, as Dr. Johnson commented, there is "no nice discrimination of character." As Macbeth successively murders Duncan, Banquo, and Lady Macduff with her children, a single line of antagonism builds up through Malcolm and Fleance to the effectual revenger, Macduff. There is evidence, in the original text and in the subsequent stage-history, to show that the grim spareness of the plot was eked out by additional grotesqueries on the part of the Witches.

I make this preliminary obeisance to the centrality of the hero-villain because it is not to him that I shall be calling your attention, though it should be evident already that he will be reflected upon by my sidelights. In skipping over the poetry of his speeches or the moral and psychological dimensions of character, I feel somewhat like the visitor to a Gothic edifice whose exclusive focus is devoted to a gargoyle here and there. I should not be doing so if the monument as a whole were less memorably familiar than it is, or if the artistic coherence of a masterpiece did not so frequently reveal itself through the scrutiny of an incidental detail. My two short texts are quite unevenly matched, though not disconnected in the long run. One of them, the Porter's Scene, has been regarded more often than not as a mere excrescence or intrusion. The other, the Sleepwalking Scene, has become one of the high spots in the repertory as a set piece for distinguished actresses. The lowest common denominator between them is that both have been written in prose. Apart from more functional purposes, such as documents and announcements, Shakespeare makes use of prose to convey an effect of what Brian Vickers terms "otherness," a different mode of diction from the norm. To cite the clearest instance, Hamlet's normal personality is expressed in blank verse; he falls into prose when he puts on his "antic disposition." This combines, as do the fools' roles, the two major uses of Shakespeare's non-metrical speech: on the one hand, comedy, low life, oftentimes both; on the other, the language of psychic disturbance.

Our two scenes are enacted in these two modes respectively. But, before we turn to them, let us take a very brief glance at the outdoor stage of the Shakespearean playhouse. On that subject there has been an infinite deal of specific conjecture over a poor halfpenny-worth of reliable documentation, and many of those

conjectures have disagreed with one another. Over its most general
features, however, there is rough agreement, and that is all we need
here. We know that its large jutting platform had a roof supported
by two pillars downstage; one of which might conveniently have
served as the tree where Orlando hangs his verses in *As You Like It*.
We are also aware of an acting space "aloft" at stage rear, whence
Juliet or Prospero could have looked down. As for the curtained
space beneath, that remains an area of veiled uncertainty. Yet the
back wall of the tiringhouse had to include an outside doorway big
enough to accommodate the inflow and outflow of sizable properties, and possibly to present a more or less literal gate upon due
occasion. Hence it is not difficult to conceive of the stage as the
courtyard of a castle, into which outsiders would arrive, and off of
which branched chambers for the guests, who might hurriedly rush
out from them if aroused by some emergency. Moreover, the surrounding auditorium, open to the skies and rising in three tiers of
galleries, might itself have presented a kind of courtyard. Not that
this arrangement was representational. It was the stylization of the
theatrical arena that made possible its scope and adaptability.

Much depended, of course, upon the convention of verbal scenery. When the aged, gracious, and serene King Duncan appears at
the gate of Glamis Castle, his introductory words sketch the setting
and suggest the atmosphere:

> This castle hath a pleasant seat, the air
> Nimbly and sweetly recommends itself
> Unto our gentle senses. (1.6.1–3)

The description is amplified by Banquo with his mention of "the
temple-haunting marlet" (4), the bird whose presence almost
seems to consecrate a church, one of the succession of birds
benign and malign whose auspices are continually invoked. The
description of the marlet's "procreant cradle" (8)—and procre-
ation is one of the points at issue throughout—assures us that
"the heaven's breath / Smells wooingly here" (5, 6). And Banquo
completes the stage-design:

> Where they most breed and haunt, I have observ'd
> The air is delicate. (9, 10)

Knowing what we have been informed with regard to Duncan's
reception, and what he is so poignantly unaware of, we may well
find it a delicate situation. Stressing its contrast to the episodes
that precede and follow it, Sir Joshua Reynolds called it "a striking
instance of what in painting is termed *repose*." Repose—or rather,

the absence of it—is fated to become a major theme of the tragedy. It will mean not rest but restlessness for Macbeth, when Duncan all too soon is accorded his last repose. Are we not much nearer, at this point, to the fumes of hell than to the heaven's breath? Macbeth, as he will recognize in a soliloquy, "should gainst his murtherer shut the door," rather than hypocritically welcoming Duncan in order to murder him (1.7.15). Duncan has been a ruler who exemplified royalty, a guest who deserved hospitality, and a man of many virtues who has commanded respect, as Macbeth himself acknowledges. The scene is set for the crimes and their consequences by this two-faced welcome into the courtyard of Macbeth's castle.

By the end of the incident-crowded First Act, in spite of his hesitant asides and soliloquies, everything has fallen into place for the consummation of the Witches' cackling prophecies. The Second Act begins ominously with Banquo's muted misgivings; he supplicates the "merciful powers"—who seem less responsive than those darker spirits addressed by Lady Macbeth—to restrain in him "the cursed thoughts that nature / Gives way to in repose," and retires after Macbeth has wished him "Good repose" (2.1.7–9, 29). This exchange would seem to occur in the courtyard, which becomes the base of operations for the murder. The first scene culminates in the vision of the dagger, hypnotically drawing Macbeth to the door of Duncan's quarters. Leaving them after the deed, as he recounts to his wife in the second scene, he has experienced another hallucination: the voice that cried "Sleep no more!" (2.2.32). Meanwhile Lady Macbeth has soliloquized, fortified with drink, and he has cried out offstage at the fatal instant. One residual touch of humanity, the memory of her own father, has inhibited her from killing the king herself; but she is Amazonian enough, taking the bloody daggers from her badly shaken husband with a crude and cruel joke (the pun on "gild" and "guilt"), to reenter the death chamber and plant them upon the sleeping grooms (2.2.53–54). It is then that the tensely whispered colloquies between the guilty couple are suddenly interrupted by that most portentous of sound effects: the knocking at the gate.

This is the point of departure for a well-known essay by Thomas De Quincey, who argues, rather overingeniously, that the interruption helps to restore normality, calming the excited sensibilities of the spectator. "The reaction has commenced; the human has made its reflux upon the fiendish; the pulses of life are beginning to beat again," De Quincey concludes, "the reestablishment of the goings-on of the world in which we live makes us profoundly sensible of the awful parenthesis that had suspended them." Here De Quincey, who elsewhere styled himself "a connoisseur of murder," seems to have got his proportions wrong. Surely it is the Porter's Scene that forms a parenthesis in an increasingly awful train of events. "Every noise appalls me," Macbeth has said (2.2.55). For him—and for us as well—the knock reverberates with the menace of retribution, like the opening notes of Beethoven's Fifth Symphony. It heralds no resumption of diurnal business as usual. Let us bear in mind that the knocker is to be the avenger, the victim who will have suffered most from the tyrant's cruelty. Macduff's quarrel with Macbeth, according to Holinshed's chronicle, first arose because the Thane of Fife did not fully participate when commanded by the King of Scotland to help him build the new castle at Dunsinane. It is surprising that Shakespeare did not utilize that hint of motivation; possibly he did, and the scene was among those lost through the rigors of cutting. It would have added another turn of the screw to Macbeth's seizure of Macduff's castle at Fife and the domestic massacre therein.

As for Dunsinane Castle, it is ironic that Macbeth should count upon its strength and that it should be so easily surrendered, "gently rend'red," after a few alarums and excursions (5.7.24). It comes as a final reversal of the natural order that he, besieged and bound in, should be assaulted and overcome by what appears to be a walking forest. So, in the earlier scenes, the manifest presumption is that the pleasantly situated Glamis Castle would be a haven and a sanctuary, associated with temples by Macbeth as well as Banquo. Rapidly it proves to be the opposite for its guests, whereas those menacing thumps at the gateway announce the arrival not of a dangerous enemy but of their predestined ally. Despite his sacrifice and suffering, his quasi-miraculous birth, and his intervention on the side of the angels, I shall refrain from presenting Macduff as a Christ-figure. There are altogether too many of these in current literary criticism—many more, I fear, than exist in real life. Yet it is enlightening to consider the suggested analogy between this episode and that pageant in the mystery cycles which dramatizes the Harrowing of Hell. Some of those old guildplays were still being acted during Shakespeare's boyhood; nearby Coventry was a center for them; and we meet with occasional allusions to them in Shakespeare's plays, notably to Herod whose furious ranting had made him a popular byword. Without the Slaughter of the Innocents, over which he presided, the horrendous slaughter at Macduff's castle would have been unthinkable. Many later audiences, which might have flinched, have been spared it.

When Jesus stands before the gates of hell, in the Wakefield cycle, his way is barred by a gatekeeper suggestively named Rybald, who tells his fellow devil Beelzebub to tie up those souls which are about to be delivered: "how, belsabub! bynde thise boys, / sich

harow was never hard in hell." The command of Jesus that the gates
be opened takes the form of a Latin cadence from the liturgy, *Attol-
lite portas* . . . This, in turn, is based upon the vulgate phrasing
of the Twenty-fourth Psalm: "Lift up your heads, O ye gates; even
lift them up, ye everlasting doors; and the King of glory shall come
in." The liturgical Latin echoes the rite of Palm Sunday celebrating
Christ's entrance into Jerusalem. It was also chanted before the
portals of a church during the ceremonies of consecration. In the
mystery, Jesus enters hell to debate with Satan and ends by rescu-
ing therefrom various worthies out of the Old Testament. That is
the typological situation which prefigured Shakespeare's comic
gag. We must now turn back to his dilatory Porter, after having
kept the visitor waiting outside longer than the Porter will. Obviously the action is continuous between Scenes Two and Three,
with the repeated knocking to mark the continuity. "Wake Duncan
with thy knocking! I would thou couldst!" is the exit line (2.2.71).
Macbeth, unnerved, is guided to their chamber by his wife, as he
will be again in the Banquet Scene, and as she will imagine in the
Sleepwalking Scene. There should be a minute when the stage is
bare, and the only drama is the knocking.

But it will take a longer interval for the couple to wash off the
blood and change into night attire. This is the theatrical necessity
that provides the Porter with his cue and one of the troupe's come-
dians with a small part. Shakespeare's clowns tend to be more stylized than his other characters, most specifically the fools created
by Robert Armin, and probably to reflect the personal style of certain actors. Will Kemp, who preceded Armin as principal come-
dian, seems to have specialized in voluble servants. It may well have
been Kemp who created the rather similar roles of Launce in *The
Two Gentlemen of Verona* and Launcelot Gobbo in *The Merchant of
Venice*. Each of these has his characteristic routine: a monologue
which becomes a dialogue as the speaker addresses himself to
imagined interlocutors. Gobbo's is especially apropos, since it pits
his conscience against the fiend. Shakespeare did not abandon that
vein after Kemp left the company; indeed he brought it to its highest pitch of development in Falstaff's catechism on honor. The
Porter's little act is pitched at a much lower level, yet it can be better understood in the light of such parallels. The sleepy Porter
stumbles in, bearing the standard attributes of his office, a lantern
and some keys. He is not drunk now; but, like others in the castle,
he has been carousing late; and his fantasy may be inspired by the
penitential mood of the morning after. "If a man were Porter of
Hell Gate"—that is the hypothesis on which he is ready to act—"he
should have old turning the key"—he should have to admit innumerable sinners (2.3.1–3).

An audience acquainted with Marlowe's *Doctor Faustus* would not have to be reminded that the hellmouth had figured in the mysteries. And the dramatist who had conceived the Brothel Scene in *Othello* had envisioned a character, namely Emilia, who could be accused of keeping—as the opposite number of Saint Peter—"the gate of hell" (4.2.92). The Porter assumes that stance by choice, asking himself: "Who's there, i' th' name of Belzebub?" (3–4). He answers himself by admitting three social offenders. It has been his plan, he then confides, to have passed in review "all professions," doubtless with an appropriately satirical comment on each (18). But, despite the histrionic pretence that hellfire is roaring away, the Porter's teeth are chattering in the chill of early morning: "this place is too cold for hell" (16–17). Neither the time-serving farmer nor the hose-stealing tailor seems as pertinent a wrongdoer as the equivocator, "who could not equivocate to heaven" (10–11). Here the editors digress to inform us about the trial and execution of Henry Garnet, Superior of the Jesuit Order, in 1606. The topical allusion is helpful, insofar as it indicates how the word came to be in the air; and Garnet's casuistry had to do with treason and attempted regicide, the notorious Gunpowder Plot. But *Macbeth* is not exactly a satire on the Jesuits. Maeterlinck, in his translation, renders "equivocator" by "*jésuite*" because there is no cognate French equivalent. The thematic significance of the Porter's speech lies in its anticipation of the oracles ("these juggling fiends"), which turn out to be true in an unanticipated sense: "th' equivocation of the fiend" (5.8.19; 5.5.42).

The Porter, who has been parrying the knocks by echoing them, finally shuffles to the gate, lets in Macduff and Lenox, and stands by for his tip: "I pray you remember the porter" (20–21). Drink, which has inebriated the grooms and emboldened Lady Macbeth, is his poor excuse for tardiness. The after-effects of drinking are the subject of his vulgar and not very funny riddle: "nose-painting, sleep, and urine" (28). Then, licensed perhaps by the precedent of the devil-porter Rybald, he moves on to the equivocal subject of lechery. If drink provokes the desire but takes away the performance, it is a paradigm for Macbeth's ambition. For, as Lady Macbeth will realize: "Nought's had, all's spent, / Where our desire is got without content" (3.2.4–5). When liquor is declared to be "an equivocator with lechery," that equivocation is demonstrated by the give-and-take of the Porter's rhythms: "it makes him, and it mars him; it sets him on, and it takes him off; it persuades him, and disheartens him; makes him stand to, and not stand to; in conclusion, equivocates him in a sleep, and giving him the lie, leaves him" (2.3.32–36). Each of these paired clauses, here again, links a false promise with a defeated expectation, expiring into drunken slumber after a moment of disappointed potency. The seesaw of the cadencing is as much of a prophecy as the Witches' couplets, and it has the advantage of pointing unequivocally toward the dénouement. The repartee trails off, after a lame pun about lying, with the reentrance of Macbeth, for which the Porter has been gaining time by going through his turn.

That turn has regularly been an object of expurgation, both in the theater and in print. I am not digressive if I recall that, when I wrote the introduction to a school-edition several years ago, the publishers wanted to leave out the Porter's ribaldry. I insisted upon an unbowdlerized text; but their apprehensions were commercially warranted; the textbook, though it is in a well-known series, has hardly circulated at all. Thousands of adolescents have been saved from the hazards of contemplating alcoholism, sex, and micturition. On a higher critical plane—some would say the highest—Coleridge was so nauseated by the whole scene that he ruled it out of the canon, declaring that it had been "written for the mob by another hand." The sentence about "the primrose way to th' everlasting bonfire," Coleridge conceded, had a Shakespearean ring (2.3.19). Without pausing to wonder whether it might have been echoed from *Hamlet*, he characteristically assumed that Shakespeare himself had interpolated it within the interpolation of his unknown collaborator. This enabled him to beg the question with Coleridgean logic and to comment further on "the entire absence of comedy, nay, even of irony . . . in *Macbeth*." Wholly apart from the comedy or the authenticity of the Porter Scene, it must strike us as singularly obtuse to overlook the fundamental ironies of the play: its ambiguous predictions, its self-destructive misdeeds. It could be urged, in Coleridge's defense, that the concept of dramatic irony had not yet been formulated. Kierkegaard's thesis on it was published in 1840, having been anticipated by Connop Thirlwall just a few years before.

Coleridge's rejection is sustained by another high literary authority. In Schiller's German adaptation, the Porter is high-minded and cold sober. He has stayed awake to keep guard over the King, and therefore over all Scotland, as he tells Macbeth in an ambitious jest. Instead of masquerading as an infernal gatekeeper, he has sung a pious hymn to the sunrise and has ignored the knocking in order to finish his *Morgenlied*. Yet, for a century now, the current of opinion has run the other way; commentators have held, with J. W. Hales, that Shakespeare's Porter was authentic and by no means inappropriate. Robert Browning heartily agreed, and Bishop Wordsworth even allowed that the scene could be read with edification.

So it should be, given its eschatological overtones. We have long discarded the neo-classical inhibitions regarding the intermixture of tragic and comic elements. We have learned, above all from Lear's Fool, that the comic can intensify the tragic, rather than simply offer itself as relief. Those "secret, black, and midnight hags," the Witches, who for Holinshed were goddesses of destiny, come as close as anything in Shakespeare to the chorus of Greek tragedy (4.1.48). But their outlandish imminence seems elusive and amoral because of their mysterious connection with the machinery of fate. The Porter's role is grotesquely choric in another sense. Like the Gardener in *Richard II*, he stands there to point the moral, to act out the object-lesson. This castle, far from reaching up toward heaven, is located at the brink of hell. Even now its lord has damned himself eternally.

Damnation is portended by the curse of sleeplessness, which has been foreshadowed among the spells that the First Witch proposed to cast upon the sea-captain: "Sleep shall neither night nor day / Hang upon his penthouse lid" (1.3.19–20). No sooner has the King been murdered than Macbeth hears the voice crying "Sleep no more!" and begins to extoll the blessing he has forfeited. The word itself is sounded thirty-two times, more than in any other play of Shakespeare's. Repeatedly sleep is compared with death. Almost enviously, after complaining of the "terrible dreams" that afflict him nightly, Macbeth evokes the buried Duncan: "After life's fitful fever he sleeps well" (3.2.18, 23). When he breaks down at the Banquet Scene before the apparition of Banquo's ghost, it is Lady Macbeth who assumes command, discharges the guests, and leads her husband off to bed with the soothing words: "You lack the season of all natures, sleep" (3.4.140). It should be noted that she does not see the ghost or hear the voice, and that she skeptically dismisses the air-drawn dagger as a subjective phenomenon: "the very painting of your fear" (3.4.60). Unlike Macbeth, she has no intercourse with the supernatural forces. To be sure, she has called upon the spirits to unsex her, fearing lest she be deterred from murder by the milk— the feminine attribute—of human kindness. And from the outset it is he, not she, who feels and expresses that remorse she has steeled herself against, those "compunctious visitings of nature" (1.5.45). When they ultimately overtake her, his insomnia will have its counterpart in her somnambulism.

In keeping with her aloofness from supernaturalism, Shakespeare's treatment of her affliction seems so naturalistic, that it is now and then cited among the clinical cases in abnormal psychology. According to the seventeenth-century frame of reference, she may show the symptoms of melancholia or—to invoke theological concepts that still can grip the audiences of films—demonic possession. Psychoanalysis tends to diagnose her malady as a manifestation of hysteria, which compels her to dramatize her anxiety instead of dreaming about it, to reenact the pattern of behavior that she has tried so desperately to repress. Freud regarded this sleepwalker and her sleepless mate as "two disunited parts of a single psychical individuality," together subsuming the possibilities of reaction to the crime, and underlined the transference from his response to hers, from his hallucinations to her mental disorder. In more social terms, the closeness of their complementary relationship seems strongly reinforced by the sexual bond between them. Three of the exit-lines emphasize their going to bed together. Caroline Spurgeon and other interpreters of Shakespeare's imagery have noticed that the most recurrent metaphor in the play has to do with dressing and undressing, transposed sometimes into arming and disarming or crowning and uncrowning. The sense of intimacy is enhanced by the recollection that the nightgowns mentioned are dressing-gowns, that under the bedclothes no clothing of any sort was worn in that day; and nakedness exposed is one of the other themes (a recent film has welcomed the opportunity for presenting a heroine in the nude).[1] Lady Macbeth, as M. C. Bradbrook has observed, must have been a siren as well as a fury.

Inquiries into her motives have dwelt upon her childlessness, after having borne a child who evidently died, and that frustration seems to have kindled Macbeth's hostility toward the families of Banquo and Macduff. Deprived of happy motherhood, she takes a somewhat maternal attitude toward her spouse, and she seeks a vicarious fulfillment in her ruthless ambitions for his career. Holinshed had stressed her single-minded goading-on of her husband, "burning in unquenchable desire to bear the name of a queen." She may be a "fiend-like queen" to Malcolm and other enemies, but the characterization is highly nuanced when we contrast it with the termagant queens of Shakespeare's earliest histories (5.9.35). Criticism ranges all the way from Hazlitt ("a great bad woman whom we hate, but whom we fear more than we hate") to Coleridge ("a woman of a visionary and daydreaming turn of mind"). Coleridge had recreated Hamlet in his own image, after all, and his Lady Macbeth might pose as a model for Madame Bovary. The variance in interpretations extends from Lamartine's "perverted and passionate woman" to Tieck's emphasis on her conjugal tenderness, which provoked the mockery of Heine, who envisages her billing and cooing like a turtle dove. She may not be "such a dear" as Bernard

---

1. Roman Polanski's *Macbeth* (1971) [Editor's note].

Shaw discerned in Ellen Terry's portrayal; but she encompasses most of these images, inasmuch as Shakespeare clearly understood the ambivalence of aggression and sympathy in human beings. Her emotions and Macbeth's are timed to a different rhythm. As he hardens into a fighting posture, and his innate virility reasserts itself, she softens into fragile femininity, and her insecurities come to the surface of her breakdown.

Distraction of the mind is rendered by Shakespeare in a pithy, terse, staccato idiom which might not inappropriately be termed distracted prose. Madness, along with all the other moods of English tragedy, had originally been conveyed through blank verse, as when Titus Andronicus "runs lunatic." So it was in Kyd's operatic *Spanish Tragedy*, though the later and more sophisticated ragings of its hero would be added by another hand in prose. The innovation was Marlowe's:[2] in the First Part of *Tamburlaine* the captive queen Zabina goes mad over the death of her consort Bajazet, and before her suicide gives utterance to a short prose sequence of broken thoughts. Her farewell line, "Make ready my coach . . ." must have given Shakespeare a suggestion for Ophelia. He seized upon this technique and developed it to the point where it became, in the phrase of Laertes, "A document in madness, / Thoughts and remembrance fitted." Ophelia distributing flowers, like King Lear distributing weeds, obsessively renews the source of grief. Edgar in the guise of Tom o'Bedlam deliberately imitates such language as does Hamlet when he simulates insanity. Lear's Fool is exceptional, since he is both a jester and a natural; yet, in that dual role, he may be looked upon as a mediator between the comic and the distracted prose. And in *King Lear* as a whole, in the interrelationship between the Lear-Cordelia plot and the Gloucester-Edgar underplot, we have our most highly wrought example of the two plots running parallel. As a matter of dramaturgic tradition, that parallel tended in the direction of parody.

Thus, in the Second Shepherds' Play at Wakefield, the serious plot about the nativity is parodied by the sheepstealing underplot, since the lamb is an emblem of Jesus. In the oldest English secular comedy, *Fulgens and Lucres,* while two suitors court the mistress, their respective servants court the maid—probably the most traditional of all comic situations, harking back as far as Aristophanes' *Frogs.* In *Doctor Faustus* the clowns burlesque the hero's conjurations by purloining his magical book and conjuring up a demon. This has its analogue in *The Tempest*, where the conspiracy against Prospero is burlesqued by the clownish complot. Having defended the essential seriousness of the Porter's Scene, I am not moving

---

2. Christopher Marlowe (1564–1593), a London playwright [Editor's note].

toward an argument that there is anything comic per se in the Sleepwalking Scene; but there is something distinctly parodic about the virtual repetition of a previous scene in such foreshortened and denatured form. Murder will out, as the old adage cautions; the modern detective story operates on the assumption that the murderer returns to the locality of the crime. Lady Macbeth, always brave and bold when her husband was present, must sleep alone when he departs for the battlefield. It is then that her suppressed compunction, her latent sense of guilt, wells up from the depths of her subconscious anguish. Under the cover of darkness and semi-consciousness, she must now reenact her part, going through the motions of that scene in the courtyard on the night of Duncan's assassination, and recapitulating the crucial stages of the entire experience.

When the late Tyrone Guthrie staged his production at the Old Vic, he directed his leading lady, Flora Robson, to reproduce the exact gesticulation of the murder scene. Such an effect could not have been achieved within the Piranesi-like setting designed by Gordon Craig, where the sleepwalking was supposed to take place on the steps of a sweeping spiral staircase. One of the most theatrical features of this episode, however it be played, lies in the choreographic opportunity that it offers to the actress and the director. At the Globe Playhouse the principal problem in staging would have been the glaring fact that plays were performed there in broad daylight. That was simply met by a convention, which has been uncovered through the researches of W. J. Laurence. A special point was made of bringing out lanterns, tapers, or other lights, paradoxically enough, to indicate the darkness. But the lighting of the Sleepwalking Scene is not merely conventional. Lady Macbeth, we learn, can no longer abide the dark. "She has light by her continually," her Waiting Gentlewoman confides to the Doctor (5.1.22–23). It is the candle she carries when she enters, no mere stage property either, throwing its beams like a good deed in a naughty world. Banquo, on a starless night, has referred metaphorically to the overclouded stars as extinguished candles. Macbeth, when the news of his wife's suicide is subsequently brought to him, will inveigh against the autumnal prospect of meaninglessness ahead, and the yesterdays behind that have "lighted fools / The way to dusty death" (5.5.22–23). Life itself is the brief candle he would now blow out.

Lady Macbeth presumably carried her candle throughout the scene until the London appearance of Sarah Siddons in 1785. She was severely criticized for setting it down on a table, so that she could pantomime the gesture of rubbing her hands. Sheridan, then manager of the Drury Lane, told her: "It would be thought a presumptuous innovation." Man of the theater that he was, he congratulated her upon it afterwards. But many in the audience were put off by it, and even more by her costume. She was wearing white satin, traditionally reserved for mad scenes, and later on would shift to a shroud-like garment. Mrs. Siddons as Lady Macbeth became, by wide consent, the greatest English actress in her greatest role. Hence we have a fair amount of testimony about her performance. A statuesque figure whose rich voice ranged from melancholy to peevishness, subsiding at times into eager whispers, she was "tragedy personified" for Hazlitt, who reports that "all her gestures were involuntary and mechanical." More physically active than her candle-burdened predecessors, who seem to have mainly glided, she excelled particularly at stage-business. The hand-rubbing was accompanied by a gesture of ladling water out of an imaginary ewer. When she held up one hand, she made a face at the smell—a bit of business which Leigh Hunt considered "unrefined." Yet, after she had made her exit stalking backwards, one witness testified: "I swear that I smelt blood!" She herself has attested that, when as a girl of twenty she began to study the part, she was overcome by a paroxysm of terror.

Turning more directly to "this slumb'ry agitation," we are prepared for it by the expository conversation between the Gentlewoman and the Doctor (5.1.11). Lady Macbeth's twenty lines will be punctuated by their whispering comments. It is clear that there have been earlier visitations, and that Lady Macbeth has engaged in writing during one of them; but what she spoke the Gentlewoman firmly refuses to disclose. The Doctor, who has been watching with her during the last two nights, has so far witnessed nothing. But, from the account, he knows what to expect: "A great perturbation in nature, to receive at once the benefit of sleep and do the effects of watching!" (9–11). Sleep seems scarcely a benefit under the circumstances, much as it may be longed for by the watchful, the ever-wakeful Macbeth; and, though Lady Macbeth is actually sleeping, she is not only reliving the guilty past but incriminating herself. When she appears, the antiphonal comment ("You see her eyes are open." / "Ay, but their sense is shut.") raises that same question of moral blindness which Shakespeare explored in *King Lear* (24–25). If she could feel that her hands were cleansed when she washed them, her compulsive gesture would be a ritual of purification. Yet Pilate, washing his hands before the multitude, has become an archetype of complicity. Her opening observation and exclamation ("Yet here's a spot" . . . "Out, damn'd spot!") is a confession that prolonged and repeated ablutions have failed to purge her sins (31, 35). She continues by imagining that she hears the clock strike two: it is time for the assassination. Her revulsion

from it compresses into three words all the onus of the Porter's gar-
rulous commentary: "Hell is murky" (36).

That sudden glimpse of the bottomless pit does not keep her
from the sanguinary course she has been pursuing. But the grandiose iambic pentameter of her courtyard speeches, inspiriting and
rebuking her reluctant partner, has been contracted into a spas-
modic series of curt, stark interjections, most of them monosyl-
labic. "Yet who would have thought the old man to have had so
much blood in him?" (39–40). She had thought at least of her
father, and had momentarily recoiled. Macbeth had feared that the
deed might not "trammel up the consequence," might open the way
for retributive counteraction, and indeed Duncan's blood has clamored for a terrible augmentation of bloodshed, has set off the chain-
reaction of blood-feuds involving Banquo's progeny and Macduff's.
Hitherto we had not been aware of Lady Macbeth's awareness of
the latter, much less of how she might respond to his catastrophe.
Her allusion to Lady Macduff seems reduced to the miniature scale
of a nursery rhyme ("The Thane of Fife / had a wife"), but it culminates in the universal lamentation of *ubi est*: "Where is she now?"
Then, more hand-washing, more conjugal reproach. Her listeners
are realizing, more and more painfully, that they should not be listening; what she says should not be heard, should not have been
spoken, should never have happened. "Here's the smell of the blood
still" (50). The olfactory metaphor has a scriptural sanction, as
Leigh Hunt should have remembered: evil was a stench in righteous nostrils, and the offence of Claudius smelled to heaven. The
heartcry comes with the recognition that the smell of blood will be
there forever: "All the perfumes of Arabia will not sweeten this little hand" (50–51).

She had been clear-headed, tough-minded, and matter-of-fact in
tidying up after the murder: "A little water clears us of this deed." It
was Macbeth, exhausted and conscience-stricken after his monstrous exertion, who had envisioned its ethical consequences in a
hyperbolic comparison:

> Will all great Neptune's ocean wash this blood
> Clean from my hand? No; this my hand will rather
> The multitudinous seas incarnadine,
> Making the green one red. (2.2.57–60)

Her hand is smaller than his, and so—relatively speaking—is her
hyperbole. All the perfumes of Arabia, all the oilwells of Arabia,
could not begin to fill the amplitude of the ocean, and the contrast
is completed by the oceanic swell of his Latinate polysyllables. She
has come to perceive, unwillingly and belatedly, that the stigmata
are irremovable. He had perceived this at once and, moreover,

reversed his magniloquent trope. Never can the bloodstain be cleansed away; on the contrary, it will pollute the world. No one can, as she advised in another context, "lave our honors" (3.2.33). The sound that voices this perception on her part ("O, O, O!") was more than a sign when Mrs. Siddons voiced it, we are told (5.1.52). It was "a convulsive shudder—very horrible." The one-sided marital dialogue goes on, reverting to the tone of matter-of-factness. "Wash your hands, put on your nightgown, look not so pale" (62–63). If Duncan is in his grave, as Macbeth has mused, is not Banquo in a similar condition? Where is he now? Reminiscence here reverberates from the Banquet Scene: "I tell you yet again, Banquo's buried; he cannot come out on's grave" (63–64). These internalized anxieties that will not be so coolly exorcized are far more harrowing than the externalized ghosts that beset Richard III on the eve of battle. Having resumed his soldierly occupation and been reassured by the Witches' auguries, Macbeth has put fear behind him, whatever the other cares that are crowding upon him. It is therefore through Lady Macbeth that we apprehend the approach of nemesis.

And then her terminal speech: "To bed, to bed; there's knocking at the gate" (66–67). It is imaginary knocking; what we hear again is silence, a silence powerful enough to resurrect the encounter between those harbingers of revenge and damnation, Macduff and the Porter. Her fantasy concludes by repeating what we have already watched in both the Murder Scene and the Banquet Scene, when she led her faltering husband offstage. "Come, come, come, come, give me your hand" (67). Her next and penultimate remark harks back to the concatenation of earlier events. The First Witch, in her premonitory resentment against the sailor's wife, had promised him a swarm of nameless mischiefs (future tense): "I'll do, I'll do, and I'll do" (1.3.10). Macbeth's own ruminations at the edge of action had started from the premise (present tense, conditional and indicative): "If it were done, when 'tis done, then 'twere well / It were done quickly" (1.7.1–2). It was done quickly, whereupon Lady Macbeth sought to arrest his mounting disquietude with the flat affirmation (past, transitive): "What's done, is done" (3.2.12). Similar as it sounds, it was a far cry from her concluding negation, her fatalistic valediction to life: "What's done cannot be undone" (5.1.68). This implies the wish that it had not been done, reinforces Macbeth's initial feeling that it need not be done, and equilibrates the play's dialectical movement between free will and inevitability. The appeal, "To bed," is uttered five times. She moves off to the bedchamber they will never share again, as if she still were guiding her absent husband's steps and his bloodstained hand were still in hers.

The doctor, who has been taking notes, confesses himself to be baffled. The case is beyond his practise, it requires a divine rather than a physician. In the following scene he discusses it with Macbeth on a more or less psychiatric basis. Lady Macbeth is "Not so sick . . . / As she is troubled with thick-coming fancies, / That keep her from her rest" (5.3.37–39). The Doctor is not a psychiatrist; he cannot minister to a mind diseas'd" (40). Nor has he a cure for Scotland's disease, when Macbeth rhetorically questions him. Here we catch the connection with the one scene that passes in England, where the dramatic values center on Macduff's reaction to his domestic tragedy. His interview with Malcolm is a test of loyalty, and the invented accusations that Malcolm levels against himself— that he would, for instance, "Pour the sweet milk of concord into hell"—are more applicable to Macbeth, whose milky nature has gone just that way (4.3.98). We are at the court of Edward the Confessor, the saintly English king whose virtues make him a foil for the Scottish hellhound. A passage which might seem to be a digression expatiates on how the royal touch can cure his ailing subjects of the scrofula, known accordingly as the King's Evil. Shakespeare is complimenting the new Stuart monarch, James I, descendant of the legendary Banquo, who had revived the ancient superstition. But the pertinence goes further; for the spokesman of the English king is another doctor; and the antithesis is brought home when we compare the sickness of the one country with that of the other. The King's Evil? Given the omens, the tidings, the disaffections, is it not Scotland which suffers from that disease?

A. C. Bradley asserted that Lady Macbeth is "the only one of Shakespeare's great tragic characters who on a last appearance is denied the dignity of verse." That comment discloses a curious insensitivity not only to the ways of the theater, which never interested Bradley very much, but to the insights of psychology, for which he claimed an especial concern. It could be maintained that distracted prose constitutes an intensive vein of poetry. Somnambulism, though fairly rare as a habit among adults (much rarer than sleep talking), is such a striking one that we might expect it to have had more impact upon the imagination. Yet there seems to be little or no folklore about it, if we may judge from its omission in Stith Thompson's comprehensive *Index*. It has suggested the rather silly libretto of Bellini's opera, *La Sonnambula* (based upon a vaudeville-ballet by Scribe), where the sleepwalking heroine compromises herself by walking into a man's room at an inn, and then redeems her reputation by singing a coloratura aria while perambulating asleep on a rooftop. Dissimilarly, Verdi's *Macbetto* avoids such pyrotechnical possibilities. The prima donna, in her sleepwalking *scena*, sticks fairly close to Shakespeare's disjointed interjections, though her voice mounts to a Verdian lilt at the high point:

> Arabia intera
> rimandar sí piccol mano
> co' suoi balsami non puó,
> no, no, non puó . . . [3]

The only serious dramatization that I can recall, apart from Shakespeare's, is Kleist's *Prinz Friedrich von Hamburg*. In contradistinction to Lady Macbeth, Prince Friedrich has already made his promenade when the play opens; he is discovered at morning seated in a garden; and the garland he is unconsciously weaving adumbrates his dreams of future military glory. The title of Hermann Broch's fictional trilogy, *Die Schlafwandler*, is purely figurative. A melodrama made famous by Henry Irving, *The Bells*, culminates in the mesmerized reenactment of a crime. It is worth noting that the first *Macbeth* acted in German (1773), freely adapted by Gottlob Stefanie der Jüngere, replaced the sleepwalking scene by a mad scene in which Macbeth was stabbed to death by his lady. Shakespeare would seem to have been as unique in his choice of subject as in his handling of it.

There is nothing to prevent a mad scene from taking place in the daytime. But Lady Macbeth must be a noctambulist as well as a somnambulist, for her climactic episode brings out the nocturnal shading of the tragedy. *Macbeth,* from first to last, is deeply and darkly involved with the night-side of things. Both Macbeth and Lady Macbeth apostrophize the darkness, calling upon it to cover their malefactions. The timing of crucial scenes is conveyed, not merely by the convention of lighting candles, but by the recurring imagery of nightfall, overcast and dreamlike as in the dagger speech:

> Now o'er the one half world
> Nature seems dead, and wicked dreams abuse
> The curtain'd sleep. (2.1, 49–51)

Characters, habitually undressing or dressing, seem to be either going to bed or getting up, like the Porter when he is so loudly wakened. "Light thickens," and the mood can be summed up by the protagonist in a single couplet:

> Good things of day begin to droop and drowse,
> Whiles night's black agents to their preys do rouse.
> (3.2.52–53)

---

3. Italian: 'All the perfumes of Arabia will not sweeten this little hand. No, no, they cannot . . .' [Editor's note].

Critical decisions are reached and fell designs are carried out at hours when night is "Almost at odds with morning, which is which," when the atmosphere—like hell—is murky, and it is hard to distinguish fair from foul or foul from fair (3.4.126). The penalty for wilfulness is watchfulness, in the sense of staying awake against one's will, of fitfully tossing and turning between bad dreams. Existence has become a watching, a waking, a walking dream. Yet "night's predominance," as one of the Thanes describes it, cannot last forever (2.4.8). Malcolm offers consolation by saying: "The night is long that never finds the day" (4.3.240). Macduff is fated to bring in the head of Macbeth on a pike, like the Thane of Cawdor's at the beginning, and to announce the good word: "the time is free" (5.9.21). The human makes its reflux over the fiendish at long last. After so painful and protracted an agony, after a spell so oneiric and so insomniac by turns, we welcome the daylight as if we were awakening from a nightmare.

STEPHEN ORGEL

Macbeth and the Antic Round (1999)[†]

I begin my consideration of *Macbeth* some years before the Folio, for what seem to me good historical reasons: while it is certainly true, as historians of the book from Stanley Morison to Donald McKenzie and Randall McLeod have insisted, that works of literature do not exist independent of their material embodiment in texts, the printing of Shakespeare's plays is, nevertheless, really incidental. In their inception, in their conception, they are not books but scripts, designed to be realized in performance; and in this form they are not at all fixed by their material embodiment, whether Quarto or Folio (to say nothing of Riverside, Oxford or Norton), but fluid and open-ended. To realize them requires an infinite number of collaborative, often non-authorial, decisions, both textual and interpretive, which in turn eventuate in continual, increasingly non-authorial, revisions, excisions, additions. In this respect, Shakespeare plays have always been the free-floating signifiers of postmodern theory, standing for an infinitely variable range of signifieds. The play, that is, even in print, is always a process.

In the case of *Macbeth*, we are well into the process from the outset, since the earliest surviving version of the play, that included in the Folio, is demonstrably a revision. It includes songs for the witches, given in the text only as incipits ('Come away, come away,

† From *Shakespeare Survey* 52 (Cambridge: Cambridge University Press, 1999), 143–53.

etc.'; 'Black spirits, etc.'). These are songs from Middleton's play
The Witch. In performance they would have been accompanied by
dances, which means that in the theatre these scenes took a good
deal longer than they do on the page. The manuscript of Davenant's
version of the play,[1] prepared around 1664, includes the whole text
of the witches' songs from Middleton—these are really musical
dialogues, short scenes. The fact that Davenant did not supply his
own witches' material at these points, as he did elsewhere, suggests
that the Middleton material was already a standard feature of the
play (Stanley Wells and Gary Taylor, in the Oxford Shakespeare,
assume that the inclusion of all the Middleton material dates from
the revision printed in the Folio, and include the complete text of
the songs in their edition).

The elaboration of the witches' roles could have taken place anywhere up to about fifteen years after the play was first performed,
but the presence of the Middleton songs suggests that Shakespeare
was no longer around to do the revising, which presumes a date
after 1614. Why, only a decade after the play was written, would
augmenting the witches' roles have seemed a good idea? To begin
with, by 1610 or so witchcraft, magic and the diabolical were good
theatre business—Barnabe Barnes' *The Devil's Charter* was at the
Globe in the same season as *Macbeth*, and Marston's *The Wonder
of Women*, with its sorcery scenes, was at the Blackfriars. Jonson's
Masque of Queens, performed at court in 1609, inaugurated a
decade of sorcery plays and masques, including *The Tempest*, *The
Alchemist*, *The Witch*, *The Witch of Edmonton*, *The Devil is an Ass*,
and the revived and rewritten *Doctor Faustus*.

The ubiquitousness of theatrical magic is perhaps sufficient reason for the elaboration of the witches in *Macbeth*, but for me, it
does not account for everything. When Macbeth, after the murder
of Banquo, goes to consult the witches, and they show him a terrifying vision of Banquo's heirs, Hecate proposes a little entertainment to cheer him up:

> I'll charm the air to give a sound
> While you perform your antic round,
> That this great king may kindly say
> Our duties did his welcome pay. (4, I.145–8)

The tone of the scene here changes significantly: the witches are
not professional and peremptory any more, they are lighthearted,
gracious and deferential. We may choose to treat this as a moment
of heavy irony, though Macbeth does not seem to respond to it as
such; but if it is not ironic, the change of tone suggests that the

---

1. See excerpts below, pp. 309–20 [Editor's note].

'great king' addressed in this passage is not the king on stage, but instead a real king in the audience, Banquo's descendant and the king of both Scotland and England.

The editors of both the recent Oxford and Cambridge editions have resisted the suggestion that this moment in *Macbeth* reflects the local conditions of a court performance, observing that nothing in the scene positively requires such an assumption. This is true enough, but I also see nothing implausible about it, and though there is no record of a court performance, King James surely must have wanted to see a play that included both witches and his ancestors. What are the implications if we assume that the text we have is a revision to take into account the presence of the king, and that his interest in witchcraft also accounts for the augmentation of the witches' scenes, so that the 'filthy,' 'black and midnight hags' become graciously entertaining after they have finished being ominously informative? Such a play would be significantly less author-centred than our familiar text: first because it is reviser-centered—and the presence of the Middleton scenes implies that Shakespeare was not the reviser—and second, because it is patron-centred, taking a particular audience into account. To this extent Shakespeare's *Macbeth* is already, in the Folio version, a significantly collaborative enterprise. But if this is correct, it also means that this version of *Macbeth* is a special case, devised for a single occasion, a performance at court, not the play in repertory, the play for the public.

This leads us to another question: how did this text become the 'standard' version—why was it the right version to include in the Folio? It needs to be emphasized that this is a question whether we assume that a performance before the king is involved or not: there is no denying that this is a revised text with non-Shakespearian material. Most attempts to deal with this issue beg the question, assuming that what we have is indeed the wrong text, and that Shakespeare's first editors would never have included it if they had had any alternative. The right text, the text we want (the prompt-book, or even better, Shakespeare's holograph) must have been unavailable, lost—burned, perhaps, in the destruction of the Globe in 1613, as if only a conflagration could explain the refusal of Hemminge and Condell (who promise, after all, 'the true original copies') to give us what we want. But perhaps it was included precisely because it was the right text—whether because by 1620 this, quite simply, was the play, or, more interestingly, because the best version of the play was the one that included the king.

This would make it an anomaly in the Folio, a version of the play prepared for a single, special occasion, rather than the standard public theatre version. In fact, the play as it stands in the Folio is anomalous in a number of respects. It is a very unusual play textually: it is very short, the shortest of the tragedies (half the length of *Hamlet*, a third shorter than the average), shorter, too than all the comedies except *The Comedy of Errors*. It looks, moreover, as if the version we have has not only been augmented with witches' business, but has also been cut and rearranged, producing some real muddles in the narrative: for example, the scene between Lenox and the Lord, 3.6, reporting action that has not happened yet, or the notorious syntactic puzzles of the account of the battle in the opening scenes, or the confusion of the final battle, in which Macbeth is slain onstage, and twenty lines later Macduff re-enters with his head. Revision and cutting were, of course, standard and necessary procedures in a theatre where the normal playing time was two hours; but if theatrical cuts are to explain the peculiarities of this text, why was it cut so peculiarly, not to say ineptly? Arguments that make the muddles not the result of cutting but an experiment in surreal and expressionistic dramaturgy only produce more questions, rendering the play a total anomaly, both in Shakespeare's work and in the drama of the period.

The very presence of the witches is unusual. Shakespeare makes use of the supernatural from time to time—ghosts in *Richard III*, *Julius Caesar*, and most notably in *Hamlet*, fairies and their magic in *A Midsummer Night's Dream*, Prospero's sorcery in *The Tempest*, Joan of Arc's and Marjory Jordan's in the *Henry VI* plays, and Rosalind's claim to be a magician at the end of *As You Like It*—but there is no other play in which witches and witchcraft are such an integral element of the plot. Indeed, whether or not King James was in the audience, the fact that it is the witches who provide the royal entertainment can hardly be accidental. The king was intensely interested in witchcraft; his dialogue on the subject, *Dæmonology*, first published in Edinburgh in 1597, was reissued (three times) upon his accession to the English throne in 1603. This and the *Basilicon Doron*, his philosophy of kingship, were the two works that he chose to introduce himself to his English subjects, and as I have argued elsewhere, witchcraft and kingship have an intimate relationship in the Jacobean royal ideology.[2] This is a culture in which the supernatural and witchcraft, even for sceptics, are as much part of reality as religious truth is. Like the ghost in *Hamlet*, the reality of the witches in *Macbeth* is not in question; the question, as in *Hamlet*, is why they are present and how far to believe them.

Like the ghost, too, the witches are quintessential theatrical devices: they dance and sing, perform wonders, appear and

2. 'Jonson and the Amazons', in Elizabeth D. Harvey and Katharine Eisaman Maus, eds., *Soliciting Interpretation* (Chicago, 1990), pp. 119–39.

disappear, fly, produce visions—do, in short, all the things that, historically, we have gone to the theatre to see. They open the play and set the tone for it. On Shakespeare's stage they would simply have materialized through a trap door, but Shakespeare's audience believed in magic already. Our rationalistic theatre requires something more theatrically elaborate—not necessarily machinery, but some serious mystification. For Shakespeare's audience, the mystification is built into their physical appearance, which defies the categories: they look like men and are women. The indeterminacy of their gender is the first thing Banquo calls attention to. This is a defining element of their nature, a paradox that identifies them as witches: a specifically female propensity to evil—being a witch—is defined by its apparent masculinity. This also is, of course, one of the central charges levelled at Shakespeare's theatre itself, the ambiguity of its gender roles—the fact that on Shakespeare's stage the women are really male. But the gender ambiguity relates as well to roles within the play—Lady Macbeth unsexes herself, and accuses her husband of being afraid to act like a man. What constitutes acting like a man in this play: what other than killing? Lady Macbeth unsexing herself, after all, renders herself, unexpectedly, not a man, but a child, and thus incapable of murder: 'Had he not resembled / My father as he slept, I had done't' (2.2.12–13). Indeed, the definitive relation between murder and manhood applies to heroes as well as villains. When Macduff is told of the murder of his wife and children and is urged to 'Dispute it like a man,' he replies that he must first 'feel it as a man' (4.3.221–23). Whatever this says about his sensitivity and family feeling, it also says that murder is what makes you feel like a man.

The unsettling quality of the witches goes beyond gender. Their language is paradoxical: fair is foul and foul is fair; when the battle's lost and won. One way of looking at this is to say that it constitutes no paradox at all: any battle that is lost has also been won, but by somebody else. The person who describes a battle as lost and won is either on both sides or on neither; what is fair for one side is bound to be foul for the other. In a brilliantly subversive essay about twenty years ago, Harry Berger, Jr, suggested that the witches are in fact right, and are telling the truth about the world of the play— that there really are no ethical standards in it, no right and wrong sides.[3] Duncan certainly starts out sounding like a good king; the rhetoric of his monarchy is full of claims about its sacredness, about the deference that is due to it, how it is part of a natural hierarchy descending from God, how the king is divinely anointed, and

3. 'The Early Scenes of *Macbeth*: Preface to a New Interpretation' [1980, rpt.] in his collection *Making Trifles of Terrors* (Stanford, 1997), pp. 70–97.

so forth. But in fact none of this is borne out by the play: Duncan's rule is utterly chaotic, and maintaining it depends on constant warfare—the battle that opens the play, after all, is not an invasion, but a rebellion. Duncan's rule has never commanded the deference it claims for itself—deference is not natural to it. In upsetting that sense of the deference Macbeth feels he owes to Duncan, maybe the witches are releasing into the play something the play both overtly denies and implicitly articulates: that there is no basis whatever for the values asserted on Duncan's behalf; that the primary characteristic of his rule, perhaps of any rule in the world of the play, is not order but rebellion.

Whether or not this is correct, it must be to the point that women are the ones who prompt this dangerous realization in Macbeth. The witches live outside the social order, but they embody its contradictions: beneath the woman's exterior is also a man; beneath the man's exterior is also a woman; nature is anarchic, full of competing claims, not ordered and hierarchical; and to acknowledge that is to acknowledge the reality and force and validity of the individual will—to acknowledge that all of us have claims that conflict with the claims about deference and hierarchy. This is the same recognition that Edmund brings into *King Lear* when he invokes Nature as his goddess. It is a Nature that is not the image of divine order, but one in which the strongest and craftiest survive—and when they survive, they then go on to devise claims about Nature that justify their success, claims about hierarchies, natural law and order, the divine right of kings. Edmund is a villain, but if he were ultimately successful he would be indistinguishable from the Duncans and Malcolms (and James I's) of Shakespeare's world.

Here is a little history: the real Macbeth was, like Richard III, the victim of a gigantic and very effective publicity campaign. Historically, Duncan was the usurper—that is what the rebellion at the beginning of the play is about, though there is no way of knowing it from Shakespeare. Macbeth had a claim to the throne (Shakespeare does know this: Duncan at one point in the play refers to him as 'cousin' (1.4.14)—they were first cousins, both grandsons of King Malcolm II). Macbeth's murder of Duncan was a political assassination, and Macbeth was a popular hero because of it. The legitimate heir to the throne, whose rights have been displaced by the usurping Duncan, was Lady Macbeth. When Macbeth ascended the throne, he was ruling as Protector or Regent until Lady Macbeth's son came of age (she did have children—it is Shakespeare who deprives her and Macbeth those heirs). Macbeth's defeat at the end of the play, by Malcolm and Macduff, constituted essentially an English invasion—the long-term fight was between native Scottish Celts and Anglo-Norman invaders, with continental allies (such as the Norwegian king) on both sides. One way of looking at the action is to say that it is about the enforced anglicization of Scotland, which Macbeth is resisting.

Shakespeare knows some of this. In Holinshed, Macbeth not only has a claim to the throne, he also has a legitimate grievance against Duncan. Moreover, in Shakespeare's source, Banquo is fully Macbeth's accomplice, and the murder of Duncan has a good deal of political justification. All this would be very touchy for Shakespeare, because Banquo is King James's ancestor, and if Duncan is a saint, then Banquo is a real problem, the ancestor one wants to forget. Shakespeare's way of handling Banquo fudges a lot of issues. Should he not, as a loyal thane, be pressing the claim of Malcolm, the designated heir, after the murder? Should he remain loyal to Macbeth as long as he does? In fact, this is precisely the sort of question that shows how close the play is to *Hamlet:* in both plays, the issue of legitimacy remains crucially ambiguous. Nobody in *Macbeth* presses the claim of Malcolm until Malcolm reappears with an army to support him, any more than anyone in *Hamlet* presses the claim of Hamlet. In both plays, there is deep uncertainty about the relation between power and legitimacy—about whether legitimacy constitutes anything more than the rhetoric of power backed by the size of its army. Duncan tries to legitimize his son's succession by creating Malcolm Prince of Cumberland on the analogy of the Prince of Wales, thus declaring him heir to the throne. But this is not the way the succession works in Scotland— Cumberland is an English county, which was briefly ceded to the Scottish crown, and Malcolm's new title is the thin edge of the English invasion. James I himself became king of England not because he was the legitimate heir (he was one of a number of people with a distant claim to the throne), but because he was *designated* the successor by Queen Elizabeth; or at least several attendants at her death claimed that he was, and the people in control supported him. This is much closer to the situation in *Hamlet* and *Macbeth* than it is to any system of hereditary succession. And Macbeth is, even in the play, a fully legitimate king, as legitimate as Duncan: like Hamlet's Denmark, this is not a hereditary monarchy; Macbeth is *elected* king by the thanes, and duly anointed. The fact that he turns out to be a bad king does not make him any less the king, any more than the rebellion that opens the play casts doubt on Duncan's right to the throne.

Let us return to the witches' royal entertainment, with its songs and dances from Middleton. *The Witch* was written between 1610 and 1615; so by that time there was felt to be a need for more variety in the play, of a specifically theatrical kind, singing and dancing. I have suggested that witchcraft was good theatrical capital, but this does not really account for the revisions. Witchcraft was good theatre no matter what the witches did—spells, incantations, visions, appearances and disappearances, diabolical music were their stock in trade. It would not have been at all necessary to transform them into the vaudevillians they become for Macbeth's entertainment. If variety was required, Duncan's hosts could have entertained him at dinner as the King of Navarre entertains the Princess of France, with dances and a disguising; or Banquo's ghost, like Puck or Hamlet, could have interrupted a play within the play; or like Prospero, Duncan could have presented a royal masque to celebrate his son's investiture as Prince of Cumberland. Why bring the witches into it? But, to judge from the play's stage history, the vaudevillian witches constituted a stroke of theatrical genius.

Or did they? Consider the play's stage history. How successful, in fact, was *Macbeth* in its own time? Though it seems inconceivable that King James would not have been interested in the play, there is, as I have said, no record of a court performance—nor is there, in fact, *any* record of any pre-Restoration performance other than the one Simon Forman saw at the Globe in 1611, and reported in his diary. The Shakespeare Allusion Book records only seven other references to the play before 1649; of these, only three, all before 1677, seem to me allusions to performances. A fourth, from 1642, is quoting it as a classic text. The remaining examples merely refer to the historical figure of Macbeth.[4] This, it must be emphasized, is a very small number of allusions: for comparison, there are fifty-eight to *Hamlet*, thirty-six to *Romeo and Juliet*, twenty-nine to the *Henry IV* plays, twenty-three to *Richard III*, nineteen to *Othello*.

This is all we know of the stage history of the play up to the Restoration. So perhaps reinventing the witches was not a stroke of theatrical genius after all; perhaps all it did was undertake, with uncertain success, to liven up an unpopular play. When Davenant revised *Macbeth* for the new stage, he inserted the whole of the singing and dancing scenes from Middleton—this is, as I have indicated, at least arguably how the play had been performed on the public stage for two decades or more before the closing of the theatres in 1642, and it would thus have been this version of the play that Davenant saw throughout his youth. (Davenant was born in 1606, so he was going to the theatre in the 1620s and thirties).

4. The book tabulates seven allusions, but in fact includes eight. *The Knight of the Burning Pestle* and a play called *The Puritan* refer pretty clearly to Banquo's ghost, and *The Two Maids of Mortlake*, a parodic play by Robert Armin, the principal clown in Shakespeare's company, recalls Macbeth's 'Will all great Neptune's ocean wash this blood / Clean from my hands'. Since Armin's play was published in 1609, this must be a recollection of *Macbeth*, on the stage. Sir Thomas Browne in 1642 saying that he begins 'to be weary of the sun' is more likely a recollection of the printed text.

Indeed, since *The Witch* remained unpublished until 1778, it is likely that Davenant took his text not from Middleton at all, but directly from the King's Men's performing text of *Macbeth*. Pepys provides a good testimony to the success of these and Davenant's other additions. Between 1664 and 1669 he went to the play nine times. The first time he found it only 'a pretty good play, but admirably acted'—the admirable Macbeth was Betterton at the outset of his career. What Pepys saw on this occasion was certainly the folio text, with its Middleton additions. Thereafter he saw the play as Davenant refurbished it, and his response changed dramatically. It was, at various times, 'a most excellent play for variety'; 'a most excellent play in all respects, but especially in divertisement, though it be a deep tragedy; which is a strange perfection in a tragedy, it being most proper here and suitable'; and finally, 'one of the best plays for a stage, and a variety of dancing and music, that I ever saw.'[5]

The interesting point here is the relation between 'deep tragedy' and 'divertisement,' which clearly for Pepys is a critical one. It is what he likes best about the play—indeed, it is what makes him revise his opinion of the play from 'pretty good' to 'most excellent.' And what Davenant added to the play—songs, dances, spectacle—is not simply something to appeal to Restoration taste. He expanded and elaborated elements that were already being added even before the folio text was published in 1623. So that is something to pause over: the really striking theatricality of the tragedy, its emphasis not just on visions and hallucinations, but on spectacle of all kinds, and even overtly in scenes like the witches' dances—on entertainment, and its move toward the court masque. We see *Macbeth* as the most intensely inward of Shakespeare's plays, in which much of the action seems to take place within Macbeth's head, or as a projection of his fears and fantasies. But if we look again at the text we have, and fill in the blanks, we see that, as far back as our evidence goes, a great deal of the play's character was always determined by what Pepys called 'variety' and 'divertisement.' Perhaps for early audiences, then, these elements were not antithetical to psychological depth after all. In this respect *Macbeth* resembles *The Tempest* more than it does the other tragedies.

The play's 'divertisement' is a quality that is largely lost to us, partly because it is only hinted at in the folio text, which merely indicates that the songs are to be sung, but does not print them, and partly because it is so difficult to imagine doing the full-scale grotesque ballet they imply in a modern production. Pepys thought divertisement should have seemed radically indecorous too; but, to

---

5. For a fuller discussion of Pepys's response to the play, see my essay 'Shakespeare and the Kinds of Drama', *Critical Inquiry* 6: 1 (Autumn, 1979), 107–23.

his surprise, he did not find it so. What is the relation between tragedy and the antic quality of the witches? Why does that antic quality keep increasing in size and importance in the stage history of
the play from the seventeenth through the nineteenth century?
Addison, for example, recalls his attention being distracted at a
Betterton performance by a woman loudly asking 'When will the
dear witches enter?'[6] Garrick, despite his claim to have returned to
the text as originally written by Shakespeare, kept all Davenant's
witch scenes; and in 1793, when Mrs Siddons was the Lady Macbeth, Hecate and her spirits descended and ascended on clouds,
and the cauldron scene constituted a long interpolated pantomime.[7]
Clearly Mrs Siddons did not think she was being upstaged. Can we
imagine similar elements playing a similarly crucial role in the
stage history of *Lear* or *Hamlet*?

In fact, we can: in *Lear*, if it is the antic quality we are concerned
with, there are Lear's mad scenes and the fool's zany speeches,
which we find so hard to understand and pare down to a minimum,
but which must have been popular in Shakespeare's time because
new ones were added between the 1608 quarto and the 1623 folio.
As for *Hamlet*, perhaps the witches externalize that anarchic quality
that makes the prince so dangerous an adversary to the guilty king.

Suppose we try to imagine a *Hamlet* written from Claudius' point
of view, in the way that *Macbeth* is written from Macbeth's. Look at
it this way: the murder Claudius commits is the perfect crime; but
the hero-villain quickly finds that his actions have unimagined
implications, and that the world of politics is not all he has to contend with. Even as it stands, *Hamlet* is a very political play, and
does not really need the ghost at all: Hamlet has his suspicions
already; Claudius tries to buy him off by promising him the succession, but this is not good enough. It turns out that the problem is
not really conscience or revenge, it is Hamlet's own ambitions—he
wanted to succeed his father on the throne; Claudius, Hamlet says,
'Lept in between the election and my hopes' [*Hamlet*, 5.2.66]. The
ghost is really, literally, a deus ex machina. But in a *Hamlet* that did
not centre on Hamlet, Claudius' guilty conscience, which is not
much in evidence in the play, would have a great deal more work to
do. So would the ghost—who should, after all, logically be haunting Claudius, not Hamlet. This play would be not about politics but
about how the dead do not disappear, they return to embody our
crimes, so that we have to keep repeating them—just like *Macbeth*.
In this version of *Hamlet*, Hamlet is hardly necessary, any more
than in *Macbeth*, Malcolm and Macduff are necessary—the drama

6. *Spectator* 45 (1711).
7. *The Dramatic Mirror*, quoted in Gāmini Salgādo, *Eye-witnesses of Shakespeare* (Sussex,
1975), p. 299.

of *Macbeth* is really a matter between Macbeth and his ambition, Macbeth and the witches and his wife and his hallucinations and his own tortured soul, the drama of prophecies and riddles, and how he understands them, and what he decides to do about them, and how they, in themselves, constitute retribution.

What, then, about the riddles, those verbal incarnations of the imperfect speakers the witches? Macbeth is told that he will never be conquered till Birnam Wood comes to Dunsinane; and that no man of woman born will harm him. Are these paradoxical impossibilities realized? Not at all, really: the Birnam Wood prophecy does not come true, it just appears to Macbeth that it does—the wood is not moving, it merely looks as if it is. Or alternatively, we could say that 'Birnam Wood' is a quibble: Macbeth assumes it means the forest, but it could mean merely wood from the forest, the branches the soldiers are using for camouflage—it comes true merely as a stage device. As for 'no man of woman born,' maybe the problem is that Macbeth is not a close enough reader: he takes the operative word to be 'woman,'—'No man of *woman* born shall harm Macbeth'—but the key word turns out to be 'born'—'No man of woman *born* shall harm Macbeth.' If this is right, we must go on to consider the implications of the assumption that a Caesarian section does not constitute birth. This is really, historically, quite significant: a vaginal birth would have been handled by women, the midwife, maids, attendants, with no men present. But surgery was a male prerogative—the surgeon was always a man; midwives were not allowed to use surgical instruments—and the surgical birth thus means, in Renaissance terms, that Macduff was brought to life by men, not women: carried by a woman, but made viable only through masculine intervention. Such a birth, all but invariably, involved the mother's death.

Macbeth himself sees it this way, when he defies Macduff and says,

> . . . though Birnam Wood be come to Dunsinane,
> And thou opposed being of no woman born, (5.10.30–1)

where logically it should be 'being not of woman born': the key concept is not 'no woman' but 'not born.' But Shakespeare seems to be conceiving of a masculine equivalent to the immaculate conception, a birth uncontaminated by women, as the Virgin's was uncontaminated by man.

So this riddle bears on the whole issue of the place of women in the play's world, how very disruptive they seem to be, even when, like Lady Macduff, they are loving and nurturing. Why is it so important, for example, at the end of the play, that Malcolm is a virgin? Malcolm insists to Macduff that he is utterly pure, 'as yet / Unknown to woman' (4.3.126–7), uncontaminated by heterosexuality—this is offered as the first of his qualifications for displacing and succeeding Macbeth. Perhaps this bears too on the really big unanswered question about Macduff: why he left his family unprotected when he went to seek Malcolm in England—this is what makes Malcolm mistrust him so deeply. Why would you leave your wife and children unprotected, to face the tyrant's rage, unless you knew they were really in no danger?

But somehow the question goes unanswered, does not need to be answered, perhaps because Lady Macduff in some way is the problem, just as, more obviously, Lady Macbeth and the witches are. Those claims on Macduff that tie him to his wife and children, that would keep him at home, that purport to be higher than the claims of masculine solidarity, are in fact rejected quite decisively by the play. In Holinshed, Macduff flees only *after* his wife and children have been murdered, and therefore for the best of reasons. Macduff's desertion of his family is Shakespeare's addition to the story. Maybe, the play keeps saying, if it weren't for all those women . . . ? It really is an astonishingly male-oriented and misogynistic play, especially at the end, when there are simply no women left, not even the witches, and the restored commonwealth is a world of heroic soldiers. Is the answer to Malcolm's question about why Macduff left his family, 'Because it's *you* I really love'?

So, to return to the increasingly elaborate witches' scenes, the first thing they do for this claustrophobic play is to open up a space for women; and it is a subversive and paradoxical space. This is a play in which paradoxes abound, and for Shakespeare's audience, Lady Macbeth would have embodied those paradoxes as powerfully as the witches do: in her proclaimed ability to 'unsex' herself, in her willingness to dash her own infant's brains out, but most of all, in the kind of control she exercises over her husband. The marriage at the centre of the play is one of the scariest things about it, but it is worth observing that, as Shakespearian marriages go, this is a good one: intense, intimate, loving. The notion that your wife is your friend and your comfort is not a Shakespearian one. The relaxed, easygoing, happy time men and women have together in Shakespeare all takes place before marriage, as part of the wooing process—this is the subject of comedy. What happens after marriage is the subject of tragedy—Goneril and Regan are only extreme versions of perfectly normative Shakespearian wives. The only Shakespearian marriage of any duration that is represented as specifically sexually happy is the marriage of Claudius and Gertrude, a murderer and an adulteress; and it is probably to the point that even they stop sleeping together after only four months—not, to be sure, by choice.

In this context, Macbeth and Lady Macbeth are really quite well matched. They care for each other and understand each other deeply, exhibiting a genuine intimacy and trust of a sort one does not find, for example, in the marriage of the Capulets, or in Iago and Emilia (to say nothing of Othello and Desdemona), or in Coriolanus and Virgilia, or in Cymbeline and his villainous queen (who is not even provided with a name), or in Leontes and Hermione. The prospects for life after marriage in Shakespeare really are pretty grim. And in this respect, probably the most frightening thing in the play is the genuine power of Lady Macbeth's mind—not just her powers of analysis and persuasion, but her intimate apprehension of her husband's deepest desires, her perfect understanding of what combination of arguments will prove irresistible to the masculine ego: 'Be a man,' and 'If you really loved me you'd do it.'

But can the play's action really be accounted for simply by the addition of yet another witch? Macbeth's marriage is a version of the Adam and Eve story, the woman persuading the man to commit the primal sin against the father. But the case is loaded; surely Lady Macbeth is not the culprit, any more than Eve is—or than the witches are. What she does is give voice to Macbeth's inner life, release in him the same forbidden desire that the witches have called forth. To act on this desire is what it means in the play to be a man. But having evoked her husband's murderous ambition, having dared him to stop being a child, she suddenly finds that when he *is* a man she is powerless. Her own power was only her power over the child, the child she was willing to destroy to gain the power of a man.

Davenant, redoing the play, does some really interesting thinking about such issues. His version has had a bad press from critics since the nineteenth century, but like all his adaptations, it starts from a shrewd sense not merely of theatrical realities, but of genuine critical problems with the play—problems of the sort that editors and commentators lavish minute attention on, but directors and performers simply gloss over or cut. Many of his changes have to do with elucidation, clarifying obscurities in Shakespeare's text, especially in the opening scenes. There is also a move toward theatrical efficiency in casting. In the opening, for example, Macduff becomes Lenox, Seyton becomes the Captain—it is difficult to see why these are not improvements. Davenant also worries a lot, to our minds unnecessarily, about the location of scenes and the topography of the action, matters Shakespeare is resolutely vague about. Thus when Lady Macduff fears that she is lost, her servant is able to reassure her that 'this is the entrance o' the heath' (2.5.3)[8]—do heaths even have entrances? Such moments are the price of adapting the

---

8. Davenant's *Macbeth* is quoted from Christopher Spencer's edition, *Davenant's* Macbeth *from the Yale Manuscript* (New Haven, 1961).

play to a stage where topography is realized, location materialized in scenery.

The most interesting aspects of the revision involve the women. It has often been observed that since the Restoration theatre employed actresses, it made sense to increase the women's parts; but this is hardly adequate to account for Davenant's additions: for one thing, the witches continued to be played by men. It is the moral dimension of the woman's role that Davenant rethinks. Thus in a domestic scene that has no parallel in the folio, Lady Macduff sharply questions Macduff's motives, accusing him of ambition: 'I am affraid you have some other end / Than meerely Scotland's freedom to defend' (3.2.18–19)—doesn't he really want the throne himself? Lady Macduff here articulates the same critique of her husband that Hecate does of Macbeth, that he is out for himself alone. Her fear articulates that perennial problem in the play, Malcolm's question about Macduff that never gets answered—where are your real loyalties; why is coming to England to join my army more important than the lives of your wife and children? The problem remains in Davenant, but is mitigated by the fact that Lady Macduff encourages Macduff to flee after the murder of Banquo. If it was a mistake, it was her mistake as well as his. Davenant's Lady Macduff also expresses a conservative royalist line, insisting that the only thing that can justify Macduff's rebellion will be for him to place the true heir, Malcolm, on the throne, rather than claiming it himself—the women, for Davenant, consistently articulate the moral position. Even Lady Macbeth, in a scene of love and recrimination inserted before the sleepwalking scene, accuses Macbeth of being like Adam, following her when he should have led her. But as Davenant's women are more important, they are also less dangerous: the Restoration Malcolm does not claim to be a virgin.

Revisers and performers have never been happy with the way Lady Macbeth simply fades out, and Macbeth is perfunctorily killed. The play does not even provide its hero with a final speech, let alone a eulogy for Shakespeare's most complex and brilliant studies in villainy. Malcolm dismisses the pair succinctly as 'this dead butcher and his fiend-like queen.' Davenant added a rather awkward dying line for Macbeth ('Farewell vain world, and what's most vain in it, ambition,' 5.7.83), and tastefully resolved the problem of Macbeth's double death by leaving the body on stage and having Macduff re-enter with Macbeth's sword, instead of his head. By the mid-eighteenth century, Garrick—who was claiming to be performing the play 'as written by Shakespeare'—had inserted an extended death speech for the hero:

'Tis done! The scene of life will quickly close.
Ambition's vain, delusive dreams are fled,
And now I wake to darkness, guilt and horror;
I cannot bear it! Let me shake it off—
'Twill not be; my soul is clogged with blood—
I cannot rise! I dare not ask for mercy—
It is too late, hell drags me down; I sink,
I sink—Oh!—my soul is lost forever!
Oh!

This Faustian peroration went on being used until well into the nineteenth century.

The editors of Bell's Shakespeare in 1774 declared themselves pleased with the play's ending, observing, with characteristic condescension, that Shakespeare, 'contrary to his common practice . . . has wound up the plot, punished the guilty, and established the innocent, in such a regular progression of important events, that nothing was wanting but very slight alterations . . . [9] But there is a puzzling element in Shakespeare's conclusion, which is less symmetrical and more open-ended than this suggests. Why, in a play so clearly organized around ideas of good and evil, is it not Malcolm who defeats Macbeth—the incarnation of virtue, the man who has never told a lie or slept with a woman, overcoming the monster of vice? In fact, historically, this is what happened: Macbeth was killed in battle by Malcolm, not Macduff: Shakespeare is following Holinshed here, but why, especially in a play that revises so much else in its source material? Davenant recognizes this as a problem, and, followed by Garrick, gives Macduff a few lines of justification as he kills Macbeth: 'This for thy Royall Master Duncan / This for my Dearest friend my wife, / This for those pledges of our Loves; my Children . . . Ile as a Trophy bear away his sword / To wittness my revenge' (5.7.76–82). The addition is significant, and revealing: in Shakespeare, Macduff, fulfilling the prophecy, is simply acting as Malcolm's agent, the man not born of woman acting for the king uncontaminated by women. But why does virtue need an agent, while vice can act for itself? And what about the agent: does the unanswered question about Macduff abandoning his family not linger in the back of our minds? Does his willingness to condone the vices Malcolm invents for himself not say something disturbing about the quality of Macduff as a hero? Is he not, in fact, the pragmatic soldier who does what needs to be done so that the saintly king can stay clear of the complexities and paradoxes of politics and war? Davenant does not quite succeed in

---

9. *Bell's Edition of Shakespeare's Plays* (London, 1774), vol. 1, p. 71.

disarming the ambiguities of the ending. What happens next, with a saintly king of Scotland, and an ambitious soldier as his right hand man, and those threatening offspring the heirs of Banquo still waiting in the wings?

PETER HOLLAND

"Stands Scotland Where It Did?": The Location of *Macbeth* on Film (2004)[†]

In 1997 Michael Bogdanov, the energetic and irreverent English theater director and co-founder of the English Shakespeare Company, directed a production of *Macbeth* for the British independent television company Channel 4. Made originally for their schools programming and aimed at the United Kingdom equivalent of high school students, this *Macbeth* was first screened in a number of bite-sized segments before the film was broadcast as a complete work, the programming was Shakespeare made palatable for schools' consumption, but the production itself was anything but, offering instead a finely crafted vision of a thuggish world. Bogdanov, whose visual resources for theater or television productions are nothing if not eclectic, placed his weird sisters in the detritus of an urban world, the garbage of inner-city chaos, complete with smashed televisions, heaps of black trash bags, and a number of shopwindow mannequins, but this vision of the decay of late-twentieth-century civilization was displaced into a rural landscape, across which Macbeth and Banquo rode on motorbikes for their encounter with the women.

Placing Macbeth's court meeting in a wonderfully decaying cathedral, full of grand arches and peeling walls, and the final battle in a derelict factory complex, firmly planted Bogdanov's version in a contemporary world. Bogdanov's version was not created as a patronizing gesture of contemporary relevance to make schoolkids feel comfortable with the horrors of having to study Shakespeare but instead as a part of Bogdanov's serious and thoughtful commitment to help them understand Shakespeare as our contemporary and the play as a political commentary on the methods of the modern state.

But Bogdanov's playful bricolage of postmodern fragments also allowed for a lurking presence of the signs of Scotland, those iconic cultural devices that key in the ostensible location of the play's

† In an essay written for this collection, Peter Holland examines varying depictions of Scotland and England in five film versions of *Macbeth*.

fiction. Some of the military figures in the opening scenes wore plaid scarves over their uniforms as if their regimental allegiance was best encoded by their clan membership. Lady Macbeth announced that "Nought's had, all's spent / Where our desire is got without consent" (3.2.6–7) while wearing an immensely stylish, close-fitting jacket of tartan material, the kind of outfit one finds at an expensive shop catering to the businesswoman's wardrobe. In the English scene (4.3), set in the grand formal gardens of a nineteenth-century English country house (though Scottish country houses have formal gardens too), Macduff was wearing a kilt, that belated invention of Queen Victoria's Highland culture, as if Macduff needed to foreground his otherness in the polite English gentility of tea on the lawn. The Scottish doctor in Act 5 had an appropriately Scottish accent, though, since the English doctor was, as so often, cut, the contrast was not needed. Most wittily, while Fife Macduff's children were eating bowls of porridge, that quintessentially Scottish staple, the eldest child, angry at the murderer's comments, flicked a spoonful of his porridge straight into the murderer's face, to the guffaws of his partner.

Scotland leaves its traces on the film, as if it is only as trace could that country exist. As a nation-state Scotland had little meaning in the mid-1990s, even though the film was made, unknowingly, on the verge of the reestablishment of a Scottish parliament in the devolved structures of the nation Britain shortly afterwards. Had he made the film a year or two later or for a less educational context, perhaps Bogdanov would not have allowed the Scottish presence to be quite so jokingly allusive and quite so politically vestigial.

But at least Bogdanov's film sees Scotland as a commercial entity of food and clothing, a former nation now commodified into tartan couture and Scott's Porridge Oats, a set of visual relics of a national past. Jeremy Freeston's film of 1996 for Cromwell Productions, never, as far as I know, given a theater release but sent straight to video (and quite probably made for the TV/video market), is a low-budget attempt to film Shakespeare, in part financed by Grampian Television (a Scottish independent channel). Scotland, that is, exists as a source of funding for a company committed to making films about Scottish history, as in *The Bruce* (1996). Though the video's blurb announces that the film is "[a]uthentically set in eleventh-century Scotland"—without ever quite saying to what it is being authentic, since Shakespeare's play is hardly marked by anything much constituting historical authenticity—the visual style of the film is much more heavily dependent on the twin conventions of film costume-drama and nineteenth-century theater spectacle. For all the freshness of Jason Connery's Macbeth, son of a father who so brilliantly turned a Scots voice into a superbly manipulated film tool, the visual language of this film is locked into a set of conventions that it never questions or extends, but only absorbs.

The two films both watched by consumers, define a kind of overly neat polarity in the representation of place. The blandness of Freeston's acceptance of the accumulated modes of filmic history can be set against the pleasurable provocations and the analytic invitations of Bogdanov's method. Bogdanov's film, that is, demands response to its method—where Freeston's only emphasizes the watcher's passivity, as if visual context can be left unquestioned, resting in a clichéd aesthetic of landscape and the material texture of supposedly historicized—but non-national—clothing.

Since Scotland does not continue to stand "where it did"— indeed, since Shakespeare's Scotland is so self-evidently a construction of a convergence of twin histories, the constructed past of Holinshed and others and a present, as it were, under King James's construction—how various *Macbeth* films have created their worlds, the visual and aural definitions of their fictive placings, becomes a location of the films' locations, a definition of their senses of the play's landscapings. Precisely because film invites the presentation of a contextual real, an emphasized background contextualisation of the immanence of place, the choices of place made by Shakespeare films create meanings against which the action is played out. The meaning of Branagh's *Hamlet* (1996), for example, appears to be consequent on its setting against the exterior of Blenheim Palace, as grand a building as any post-early-modern castle could be. Film locations become dominant signals for the readings of the play they construct.

In the five films with which I shall be principally concerned, the range of meanings accorded to place sculpts the play's worlds into widely varying forms, enabling the particularities of Shakespeare's politics of nation to stand even clearer. Whether involving a space that includes Chicago gangsters or Japanese samurai, whether the territories are fought over by Italian-American mafiosi or between rival forms of religious practice, the Scotland of *Macbeth* films is always aware of the limits of its power as well as of its geography. The geography is dependant on precisely that sense of adjacency that leads Shakespeare to move the action here, (just as in the tantalizing incompleteness of the hero's comparable journey in *Hamlet*), from the place beyond (Scotland, Denmark) towards England, to that land imaged in *Macbeth* as a quasi-heavenly realm of calm and support.

What is at stake in the quest for the throne, be it by Macbeth or Malcolm, becomes present on film as things seen, whereas in theater the quest can rarely be more visibly defined than in the symbolic aspiration for "The sweet fruition of an earthly crown," as Marlowe's Tamburlaine calls it,[1] or potently heard in the play's dozen uses of the word Scotland. Significantly, after an initial reference to Duncan ("Mark, King of Scotland," 1.2.28), the word disappears until the English scene, where it chimes eight times to indicate that other place from which Malcolm and Macduff are temporarily exiled. Then it is heard in its final occurrences in the shout and echo that mark the new king ("Hail, King of Scotland! / Hail, King of Scotland!" 5.8.59) and in the new, more English world of earls, "the first that ever Scotland / In such an honor named" (5.8.63–64), rather than the more particular Scottishness of thanes. However we conceive of the territory over which Macbeth is king, the play never allows him to be named King of Scotland. What we see him achieve is dominion but not connection, authority but not a title, power displaced from its geographic and conceptual boundaries, those borders of the physical space and the imaginative existence of nation that will prove to be permeable, penetrable and vulnerable—like so much else in the play, from the opening battle against invaders and rebels to the last moments of turning Scotland into something more akin to England. Where Scotland precisely stands and what it looks like, its relation to England and the nature of its physical landscape, charts the films' senses of the play's political analysis. Location enables the film audience to read the play.

Scotland, IL

In 2001 Billy Morrissette wrote and directed his first feature film, *Scotland, Pa.*, a parodic displacement of *Macbeth* into a bleakly and blackly comic tale of ambition in a 1970s roadside fast-food restaurant in small-town Pennsylvania, where Joe "Mac" McBeth and his wife Pat take over Norm Duncan's eatery by murdering the owner, spurred on by the prophecies of the three hippies Joe encountered at a fair. Morrissette probably found the name of his comic hero in the title of a film that had moved Scotland to a location in the United States many years earlier: *Joe Macbeth*.

Joe Macbeth was made in England in 1955 for Columbia Studios, the third in their Shakespeare adaptations from this period (*House of Strangers* [1949]), directed by Joseph Mankiewicz and derived from *King Lear*, and *Lear's* transformation into a Western as *Broken Lance* [1954], directed by Edward Dmytryk). All three were ostensibly scripted or derived from work by Philip Yordan, though, as Tony Howard points out, Yordan "was often a 'front' for blacklisted

---

1. Christopher Marlowe, *"Doctor Faustus" and Other Plays*, ed. David Bevington and Eric Rasmussen (Oxford: Oxford University Press, 1995), *Tamburlaine, Part 1*, 2.6.29.

writers, and the precise nature of his role was not always clear."[2] At a time in which Hollywood was extremely wary of anything that might be seen as straight Shakespeare (especially after the comparative failure of Orson Welles's 1948 *Macbeth* and in spite of the comparative success of Joseph Mankiewicz's 1953 star-studded *Julius Caesar*), Columbia saw that Shakespeare as script-resource was well worth pursuing.

Directed by Ken Hughes, who had established his modest reputation in a series of Scotland Yard detective thrillers hosted by Edgar Lustgarten, *Joe Macbeth* cast a number of British actors opposite some Americans with reputations even more modest than the director's. Low budget in the extreme, the film uses the conventions of *film noir* as far as possible to disguise its necessary economies. Early reviews, wedded to the traditional high-culture notion of the transcendental status of both Shakespeare and his characters, often mocked the film as, for instance, "a comic-book version of an immortal piece of literature"[3] while "the sordid gangsters, realistically treated, are no parallels for Shakespeare's exalted personages, whose characters are illuminated by great poetry."[4] But Columbia's primary aim was to capitalize on the moviegoers' appetite for gangster movies rather than to make a statement about the banality of evil in Shakespeare's play. This is *Macbeth* set in a Chicago whose skyline is outlined behind the credits and whose grand Lakeshore Drive becomes the Lakeview Drive that Joe Macbeth rules.

Yet *Joe Macbeth*, from its title on, does nothing to disguise its relationship to Shakespeare. The opening action is played after a title quoting from Shakespeare ("Never in the Legions of Horrid Hell / Can come a Devil more damn'd / In evils to top Macbeth"[5] carefully ascribed to "*ACT 4, SCENE 3, MACBETH, WILLIAM SHAKESPEARE*"). The final sounds of sirens and gunfire suggest the continuation of the action now in tension with the otherwise invisible forces of law and order accompany a title quoting "It will have blood they say. / Blood will have blood."[6] Shakespeare's play is being invoked to suggest both the scale of the gangsters' actions and the universalism of Shakespeare's action in terms that ought to have endeared the film to the reviewers. With Banky as his partner, Mr. "The Duke" del Duca as the Duncan he will murder, and the three stages of

2. Tony Howard, "Shakespeare's Cinematic Offshoots," in Russell Jackson, ed., *The Cambridge Companion to Shakespeare on Film* (Cambridge: Cambridge University Press, 2000), 312.

3. Review in *America*, 3 December 1955, quoted by Robert F. Willson, Jr., *Shakespeare in Hollywood, 1929–56* (Madison, NJ: Fairleigh Dickinson University Press, 2002), 101.

4. Review in *National Parent Teacher*, March 1956, quoted in Willson, 101.

5. I preserve here the film's odd choices for capitalization.

6. Willson reads the ending sounds as "imply[ing] that the last of the gangsters has been destroyed" (96), but there seem in the film to be precious little grounds for seeing such a moralistic ending.

Macbeth's ascent defined as "Baron of the West Side," "Lord of Lakeview Drive," and "King of the City," a game of allusion is played out that sees modern forms of power and their consequential quests for control as only being explicable in terms of a gang's territory.

But Shakespeare's play is more than a discreet presence offering a grand allusive parallel for the action; *Macbeth* is also present as a precise echo of performance. Rosie, the ageing flower-seller who interrupts Joe's quiet wedding celebration *à deux* with his new wife Lily (a wedding delayed because Joe had to wait for Tommy, Duca's former right-hand hitman, to die—and, as Joe tells the dying Tommy over the phone in the film's remarkably brutal opening, "that Tommy sure hates to die") tells Joe's fortune using tarot cards that "came off the body of a hanged murderer." But Rosie greets Joe first with a theatrical salutation of "Ah, noble Macbeth," not because the screenwriter wanted some vestigial echo of Shakespeare but because Rosie had been an actress: as Joe says, "I would sure like to seen you when you played opposite Barrymore." This weird sister is an out-of-work actress, her theatricality some sign of the inappropriateness of theater as career but also of the irrelevance of *Macbeth* as play in a world even more violent and driven by ambition than Shakespeare's.

Rosie, later seen selling chestnuts in the street because the flower business is not going well, begins her second encounter with Joe by asking "Well, since we last met, how heavy hangs the crown?"—not a quote from *Macbeth* or elsewhere in Shakespeare but resoundingly Shakespearean—before warning him that "Banky casts a shadow over you . . . Nothing to fear from Banky, only his shadow," again a Shakespearean portent, especially since the film shows no concern with Malcolm. Retribution comes from Banky's son, Lenny, a Fleance who is able to exact revenge that only subsequent generations of Banquo's descendants will wreak on Shakespeare's Macbeth. The landscape of Joe *Macbeth* is, then, one in which Shakespeare is present as cultural artifact, the source of the voicing of the control over the narrative that prophecy provides. Other echoes of the play occur in the wheeling birds, for example, that are seen from time to time, a recurrent motif in the natural world of *Macbeth* films, and which Rosie sees in her crystal ball as a good omen.[7] Or the potent

7. "I saw birds—they were flying away. . . . Someone will die in this house. But the birds were all flying in one direction. That's a good omen. . . . With every death in this house, Macbeth shall rise." This scene, where Rosie reads her crystal ball for Lily, associates her tightly with the film's Lady Macbeth, much to Joe's annoyance: "I don't want that hag round here." Compare also Duca's comments on birds, the film's wryly witty transmutation of the "temple-haunting martlet" (1.6.4):

LENNY Did you ever see so many birds flying around outside. I guess they like it here.
DUCA Birds don't know from nothing. They're like people: they eat out of your hand one minute, bite it off the next.
BANKY You know, boss, you should a been a preacher.
DUCA I never got the call.

effect of the bell on the lake that stops Joe from sleeping ("Does it go on all night? Can a guy ever get any sleep?"). Both these motifs are naturalized into the fabric of the film, not calling attention to their status as echoes or allusions unless we wish them to be. Rosie and the consciously Shakespearean diction she uses summon up *Macbeth* as presence behind Joe's actions, the gaps between Macbeth and Joe being part of the film's reading of its own action.

Joe Macbeth is as striking for its careful and thoughtful adjustments to the hierarchies of Scotland as for its general vague faithfulness. The opening murder of Tommy, the film's Thane of Cawdor, raises Joe's status in a sequence that Lily has no difficulty presenting as a continuous cycle of eliminated potential rivals (like Tommy's unseen predecessor, Little Mike), something without Shakespearean parallel. If Joe clings to values of loyalty and modest ambition ("I'm as far as I want to go right now"), such traditional morality is seen as cowardice in a world in which the "air-drawn dagger" (3.4.63) becomes a knife that Lily hands Joe: "The knife knows where to go, Joe. Just follow it." There is nothing fully supernatural in *Joe Macbeth's* world, but there is an eeriness, embodied by Angus, the unnerving butler who comes with the Lakeview mansion. His offer of the housekeys to Lenny, Joe's apparent successor, is firmly rejected in the film's last lines of dialogue: "I suppose this means that you'll be the new master of the house, sir." "No, Angus. This is the end of the line. Better lock up and get yourself a new job."

The violent world of gangsterism is, though, seen as oddly beyond Joe. The murder of Lenny's wife and child (as it were, Lady Macduff and her son) is not planned by Joe but is a hostage-taking that went wrong when she refused to come meekly along and for which Joe is furious with the thugs who killed them. But such actions seem only too easy for Lenny, who moves in the film from being the nervy son who does not belong "in the racket," shooting his mouth off about his father's rights of succession (and earning a punch from his father in the process), into the dedicated avenger stalking his prey. If, as the doctor advises, it makes sense to treat Lily's ravings the modern way ("If you'll take my advice, you'll send for a psychiatrist"), then Lenny's neurotic, near-hysterical aggression deserves the same treatment.

If Lenny is the play's future, a continuation in a new guise of the film's view of the mobs, then the territory that is being fought over is defined as the nightclub, the mansion, and the continuing threat from neighbouring mob leaders, here the richly comic portrait of Dutch whose people muscle in on the Duke's land, burn out his club, and are only stopped when Dutch's crepes suzette are poisoned—and his greed stops Dutch from letting his personal

taster try them first. Dutch, who calculates for Joe how many oysters he has eaten in his lifetime (given that he consumes five dozen
a night), suggests the fragility of the borders of the Duke's land, how
little he is able effectively to be "kingpin" or "King of the City." With
borders unmarked on any map, the limits of this state—the Chicago
Scotland,—appear, in the joke of Dutch's name, to neighbour Holland as well as Capone's.

But the state also exists within another, as if Illinois has another
state of Duca or Macbeth or Dutch within it. In a film that manages so completely and so effectively to suppress the rest of the
community within which and alongside which the gangster world is
formed and run, the sense of states within states, countries and territories within others, is a disturbing effect. *Joe Macbeth* is not a
great film: for all the cleverness of some of its thinking it is often
poorly acted and weakly shot.[8] But the transpositions of place (not
least from Macbeth's castle to the bleak rich style of the Lakeview
mansion) redefine how modern territories are formed.

Scotland, NY

In the wake of the success of Coppola's *Godfather* trilogy, and especially Coppola's use of *King Lear* as an informing presence in the
third part (1990), the combination of Shakespeare and the mafia
must have seemed ripe for reconsideration. William Reilly, in his
first and only film as writer/director, rethought the virtues of *Joe
Macbeth* as *Men of Respect* (1991), set in New York. It is superbly
acted, especially by John Turturro as Michael Battaglia (whose very
name makes him the man of battles) and Katherine Borowitz as his
wife Ruthie, and Reilly achieves a remarkably neurotic transposi-
tion, as if the edginess of *Joe Macbeth*'s had penetrated the leading
roles. Turturro's wide-eyed stare is terrifying both in its danger to
others and its revelation of the permanent edge of fear with which
Mikey lives. Openly credited as "adapted" from *Macbeth, Men of
Respect* uses the possibilities of allusion, with continuous potency.
The film begins with the precredit sounds of news reports. Half-
heard among the stories of the KGB plotting to kill the Pope (a
KGB defector is quoted as saying "No secret lasts forever") or of
heroin in an "unusually pure and smokeable form" on the streets
("local police forces are powerless to stem the tide") is a report that
"unusual weather patterns continue to plague the metropolitan
area." Throughout, lines are transposed, their idiom changed but

8. Though it has nothing to do with the topic of this article, it is worth mentioning that
this is the only version of *Macbeth* known to me in which Macbeth kills his wife: when
Joe is preparing for the final shoot-out he forgets the gun by his bedside; Lily, the
devoted wife, brings it to him and, reacting to an unexpected noise, Joe shoots, only to
discover he has killed her—a neat and bleak ironic twist.

retaining a curious power: it is not so long a journey from "then, as his host, / Who should against the murderer shut the door, / Not bear the knife myself" (1.7.14–16) to "I should be watching his back, not sticking in the knife myself." Or from "If it were done when 'tis done, then 'twere well / It were done quickly" (1.7.1–2) to "If it's gonna get done, it better get done quick." Reilly wrote, as it were, with an open copy of *Macbeth* on his desk, and the film asks to be watched with a sustained awareness of Shakespeare's play.

Macbeth's opening war has here become an attack on the territory of "Charles 'the little Padrino' d'Amico" (Rod Steiger) by a rival mafioso, Cordero. The tide is turned by Battaglia's murder of a number of people at a restaurant table. When the news comes to d'Amico, suspicious of who might be a loyal and who a traitor, he sends out men to find Battaglia: "When you find him, you treat him as a Man of Respect, is that clear? . . . Cordero's loss, that's Battaglia's gain." Battaglia and his partner, Banky Como, encounter the witches (a campy young man, a dapper middle-aged man, and the woman who utters the prophecies in a semi-trance) in a shuttered room on some wasteland. Battaglia, who is told he will become "capo regime" and that "the time comes when you will be called Padrino, Padrino Battaglia," wonders "What do I have to do for this to happen?" "You only have to be yourself, to do what you're thinking." The awareness of the will is all-important; the self creates its own futures. By contrast, Banky's reaction to the news that "your son will be Padrino" is a brusque rejection: "My son Philly in this business. Over my dead body."

What in *Joe Macbeth* had been barely glimpsed becomes in *Men of Respect* a fully fledged exploration of the state within the state. Battaglia is admitted as a Man of Respect in a solemn ceremony: "We are a fraternity of great honour and we welcome only men of strength, courage and loyalty, men of respect. Our way comes before anything else in life, before God, before country, before family." Mikey has, Charlie tells him, "earned yourself a very special place in our thing." The creation of the ritual, especially after the scene with the "weird sisters" has been so full of Catholic religious images (crosses, icons, small statues, candles, offerings), suggests the interconnection of religious practice and a murderous subculture. Whereas Rosie's reading tarot cards could be ignored, here the full-blown potency of the supernatural solicitings is embedded in the culture it affects.

Men of Respect deserves full-scale examination and praise for its often brilliant re-imaginings: the mad Ruthie doggedly scrubbing at the bathtub to remove the long-gone bloodstains from Charlie's murder or the transformation of Birnam Wood into the prophecy that "not till the stars fall from the heavens will Battaglia's blood be shed," which comes true when there is a massive fireworks display. But if Scotland is only present as a joke (Battaglia at his "coronation" party as Padrino is given a tip for a horse called "Great Scot"), the exploration of "England" and of the future movement of this version of the nation-state is thoughtful and provocative. When d'Amico's power seems ebbing he becomes suspicious of Duffy, "a mean fucking Irishman." This criminal world is not wholly Italian-American—there is room for another nationality's involvement: we are encouraged to see Duffy as a representative of another Catholic nation since his name comes from Father Duffy who ran the orphanage on 149th Street in the Bronx outside which his dying mother was found in labour ("The intern ripped the little fucker from her belly."). D'Amico's *consigliere*, Carmelo Rossi, the film's Cawdor, urges d'Amico to retire to Florida. After defeating his enemies, d'Amico sends Rossi there. Not executed, this Cawdor will reappear later in "England."

Where *Joe Macbeth* eliminated Malcolm completely, *Men of Respect* leaves him in place as Mal (Stanley Tucci). Mal and his brother have fled not to England and Ireland but to Toronto (Canada as the American Ireland?) and Miami. Now, in the other space that constitutes this film's vision of that land outside Scotland, Mal consults with Cordero and Rossi, who agree to become Mal's *consigliere*: "I do not rest until we all spit on the grave of your father's murderer." In a switch from this increasingly murky world of deals in comfortable lounges, the conspirators meet Duffy in a bright garden, accompanied by troops of loyal men. Battaglia had been warned about Duffy by the "weird sister": "A large man with a red face . . . the complexion. An Irishman?" "Duffy." "This man is very dangerous to you. He doesn't respect you." Battaglia's response had been to blow up Duffy's car, killing his wife and child whom Duffy was taking for an outing at the zoo. Now Duffy promises to provide the muscle for the hit on Battaglia. Whatever else the film achieves, Reilly's revisioning of England into a conspiracy of rivals rather than as a repository for some ordered, blessed other concept of the state marks a considerable and effective act of imagination.

But it is less Mal d'Amico than Philip Como who shows the film's sense of a changing political order, a future that will relocate the nature of this Scotland, this world of violent power. If gangsters and hitmen are modern equivalents of the soldiers who can mean "to bathe in reeking wounds, / Or memorise another Golgotha" (1.2.39–40), then the new Scotland of Malcolm's intention becomes in *Men of Respect* the new way not of Mal but Philip. House-sharing with his father ("He cooks, I clean," says Banky proudly), Philip is not in the business as a hit man (as *Joe Macbeth*'s Banky had wanted to keep Lenny out of his world) but is, as his father even more proudly announces, "MBA Baruch." Banky urges Michael to talk with Philip, who can show new routes to legal profit, offering an echo of Coppola's Michael (Al Pacino), who desperately wants the Corleone family to be completely legitimate. If Duncan's world is unquestionably legitimate it is still founded on a culture and cycle of violence against which Malcolm's new regime may stand. Charlie and Mal come from and remain within a world of violence against which Philip offers an alternative. But when Philip is seen lurking behind the door while Mal plots with Rossi, spoken of as a useful man with a head for numbers, and when he is, in the film's final sequence, inducted as a Man of Respect, his final chilling smile indicates the new direction he will eventually take the thing when he becomes Padrino. Corporate America, rather than Jacobean England, is the destiny towards which this line of *padrini* will stretch.

Scotland, Japan

Both *Men of Respect* and *Joe Macbeth* are underrated achievements. Akira Kurosawa's version of *Macbeth*, known in English-speaking countries as *Throne of Blood*, though its Japanese title means *Cobweb Castle*,[9] has been accorded the proper respect due to its immense brilliance. The third of the cultural displacements I am considering, *Throne of Blood* (dis/re)places *Macbeth* into the Sengoku period of civil wars in Japan (1467–1568). Far from *Macbeth*'s suggestion of a previous period of relative stability and a subsequent history leading towards James, Kurosawa's film deliberately chooses a period of disruption in samurai culture and of continuous instability. As many critics have commented, Kurosawa's choice transforms the regicide from a profoundly transgressive act into one of almost routine occurrence. And as James Goodwin notes, the period was one "when there were frequent incidents of *gekokujo*, the overthrow of a superior by his own retainers."[1] Just as

---

9. The subtitles and the published screenplay both use this form but it sounds to me too much like a novel by the eighteenth-century novelist Thomas Love Peacock. "Spider's-Web Castle" might be better, if less alliterative. See Akira Kurosawa, *"Seven Samurai" and Other Screenplays* (London: Faber and Faber, 1992). There is a large and ever-growing critical literature on Kurosawa's film. I note, as particularly helpful with my thinking about its accomplishments, Anthony Davies, *Filming Shakespeare's Plays* (Cambridge: Cambridge University Press, 1988), 152–66; John S. Collick, *Shakespeare, Cinema and Society* (Manchester, Eng.: Manchester University Press, 1989); Peter S. Donaldson, *Shakespearean Films/Shakespeare Directors* (Boston: Unwin Hyman, 1990) 69–92; James Goodwin, *Akira Kurosawa and Intertextual Cinema* (Baltimore: Johns Hopkins University Press, 1994); Robert Hapgood, "Kurosawa's Shakespeare Films: *Throne of Blood, The Bad Sleep Well,* and *Ran*," in Anthony Davies and Stanley Wells, eds., *Shakespeare and the Moving Image* (Cambridge: Cambridge University Press, 1994), 234–49; and Donald Richie, *The Films of Akira Kurosawa* (3rd ed., expanded with a new epilogue; Berkeley: University of California Press, 1998).
1. Goodwin, 176.

Lily warns Joe Macbeth that Duca will have him killed if he doesn't eliminate him, so Asaji (Lady Macbeth) warns Washizu (Macbeth) that "Only two choices exist . . . sitting and waiting to be killed by our lord . . . or killing our lord to become Lord of Kumonosu Castle yourself."[2]

Asaji's argument depends on the risk of Miki's (Banquo) revealing the prophecy of the single witch the two have met in the enigmatic, labyrinthine space of Cobweb Forest:

> If . . . General Yoshiaki Miki should reveal the prophecy . . . then, we won't be left as we are. Our lord, taking you for a usurper threatening his throne . . . he will surely besiege the North Castle with his men without delay.[3]

It is not, of course, that killing one's superior becomes permissible: as Washizu responds, "It is high treason to kill our lord!" But in the system that Kurosawa is exploring through Asaji's voice, the process can be cyclical: "he himself ascended the throne by killing his previous lord, as you well know."[4]

The historical-political context, then, deliberately weakens the disruptive effect of the murder of the ruler. Only success matters, and the consequences have nothing to do with divine retribution and everything to do with holding one's nerve. But the conflicts are not only internal. Neither Duncan nor his successors seem to want to take further action against Sweno, the King of Norway who, helped by Cawdor, had besieged Fife. The defeat is so complete that Sweno "craves composition" and pays "Ten thousand dollars to our general use" before even being allowed to bury his dead (1.2.60–63). But Inui (Sweno), who had been helped by Fujimaki (Cawdor), poses a threat that is not resolved by the comparable victory. Clearly contiguous as landmass, Inui's territory is one from which he can invade easily—at the opening of the film he has crossed with four hundred men to besiege the First Fort, taking the opportunity created by seeing the success of Fujimaki's campaign against the Fifth and Fourth Forts. With Washizu's victory, Kuniharu's (Duncan) response is to order the border defences to be strengthened against future incursions.

Asaji's encouragement to murder Kuniharu is immediately met by the arrival at the North Castle (Inverness) of Kuniharu and a large army, ostensibly on a hunting expedition. There is no notion here that the opportunity for the regicide happens because Duncan

---

2. Kurosawa, *"Seven Samurai" and Other Screenplays*, 237 (ellipses original). The screenplay and the subtitles are rarely the same; unless otherwise noted I quote from the screenplay, even though it represents the script at an earlier stage of development from the shooting script.
3. Kurosawa, 237.
4. Kurosawa, 238.

wishes to accord Macbeth honor by visiting him. Instead the arrival of the troops, totally and unnervingly unexpected by Washizu, is part of a secret plan to crush Inui because, as Kuniharu says, "I can endure Inui's behaviour no longer." The political aftermath of the murder is that Kuniharu's son (Malcolm) will take refuge with Inui, that Washizu will claim Miki was murdered by a spy sent by Inui, that Miki's son (Fleance) will also turn to Inui, and that the invading army at the end, under the direct command of Noriyasu, Kuniharu's senior general (a figure who has no exact equivalent in *Macbeth*), will also be Inui's. At the end of *Ran*, Kurosawa's 1985 rethinking of *King Lear*, it is clear that the chaos (the meaning of the title) brought about in Hidetora's (Lear's) state will result in the invasion by neighboring lords whose troops are seen watching the final battles, ready to move in. By in effect, conflating Sweno and Edward the Confessor in *Throne of Blood*, Kurosawa makes Inui's land a physically adjacent geographic space as well as edged by a fluid border across which invasion can move in either direction. Just as in *Hamlet* Denmark is finally absorbed into the Norwegian empire, so in *Throne of Blood* it is the film's unseen equivalent of Norway that seems most likely to triumph.

But the political geography of the landscape in Kurosawa's film seems less significant than the physical geography. A film that makes castles appear and disappear in mists as it moves from the opening image of the site of the castle to its reality, proves profoundly to be exploring the natural landscape as a feature of human action in ways that we could call—for lack of a better word—Shakespearean. As Peter Donaldson has shown, Kurosawa's research on castles from the period taught him that some castles had mazes of forests deliberately grown in front of them.[5] The space in which Washizu and Miki encourage the spirit, one whose paths they ought to know, is a man-made defense mechanism, midway, as it were, between the human and the natural. The castle of the spider's web is protected by a forest whose intricately branching paths are the source of the castle's name.

For *Macbeth*s set in the twentieth-century city, like *Joe Macbeth* and *Men of Respect*, the nonurban is merely vestigial: the overgrown wasteland in which Battaglia will find the witches; the courtyard garden behind his restaurant, complete with stone birdbath for Ruthie's hand-washing in the sleepwalking scene, a space in which Mikey throws parties; the lake behind the Lakeview mansion in which Duca takes an early morning swim and where Joe murders him. If the play's emphasis on birds always seems to produce a corresponding avian excess in films, the nonhuman is only

5. Donaldson, 72.

an echo of a landscape imagined beyond the city. But in *Throne of Blood* the human world plants itself squarely, though vulnerably, in a rolling landscape, the bare space across which woods can move.

If filmed *Macbeths* have a natural yearning to produce swirling mists, Kurosawa's vision makes mist a sign of nature's wiping out of the human, the device that takes the film from the present, where Cobweb Castle is nothing more than a single pillar describing it as the castle's vestigial site, to the historic past of the film's main action. The unseen chorus intones a moral lesson that "The devil's path will always lead to doom," but it also defines the link of castle to human: "A proud castle stood in this desolate place / Its destiny wedded to a mortal's lust for power."[6] The castle and control over it is the path of human desire, given that Washizu's rise is charted as a move from fort to fort, much to the delight of his household (as Kurosawa makes clear in a series of short exchanges between the serving men, a workers' commentary that Shakespeare might well have admired). But the mist becomes also the defining feature of the fogginess of the maze. As they ride towards the castle, Washizu and Miki are lost in the rain-soaked forest, a labyrinth that even they, the great defenders of the castle's ruler, cannot penetrate by keeping to its confusing paths: its forest-spirit holds them, bringing them to the meeting with the witch. Whatever its origins, the forest is now not within human control but is, instead, the location of the supernatural. Following the prophecies, the spirit's hut, (the hut is a bamboo form that mediates the natural into the ambiguous, with its open walls) vanishes, while Washizu and Miki find the heaps of skulls and armour that seems the true end of their inquiry. But Kurosawa then makes their journey toward the castle defined by mist, not a wooded landscape. In the film's most famous and virtuosic sequence, the two horsemen ride to and fro, towards the camera and away from it, at diagonals to it and across its plane of depth, each time coming out of and back into mists as mazey as any forest trail. If the labyrinth of the spider's web forest is human in origin, this mistiness is most emphatically not, a murky feature of the film's supernatural. Mist and forest are the same thing: the space that confuses and disorients the riders—and the viewers.

It is hardly surprising then that the moving wood at the end should be accompanied by dawn mists, but Kurosawa also displaces the equivalent of Malcolm's instruction "Let every soldier hew him down a bough" (5.4.4) until after Washizu's death, when Noriyasu gives the order "Conceal yourselves among the branches"[7] What Washizu sees, the unnerving sight of "a moving grove" (5.5.38), is

6. Subtitles. The published screenplay's text is radically different here.
7. Kurosawa, 266.

Toshirō Mifune as Washizu (Macbeth) in Kurosawa's *Throne of Blood*
(1957). Courtesy of Rue des Archives/The Granger Collection, New York.

as inexplicable to the spectators as to Washizu and his men. The
natural really does seem to be moving, like some version of Tolk-
ien's Ents, and it will lead directly towards the hail of arrows that
will turn Washizu into a human pincushion. The film's buildings
are all wooden, extensions and transmutations of the forest, and

the arrows are as well. The final arrow that so memorably transfixes Washizu through the neck comes, as Donaldson accurately notes,

> from a place to which we have seen no archers ascend: off-screen right . . . The shot is not merely unexpected, then, but hints at a supernatural retribution. . . . [8]

Washizu, clattering down the ladders to the ground level of the mass of his troops, falls before them in a cloud of dust, as if the mists are enveloping him again and finally. It is only a short step from these mists to the ones that will take us back through time to the present, as if the natural and supernatural have swallowed up almost all traces the human world can leave on this landscape, leaving only those markers of former glory.

The moving wood is part of the merging of the nonhuman and human, but this merger is also established by Noriyasu's wise response to the barrier that the forest poses. If the forest paths are a maze controlled by the spirit world far more than as a man-made defense, then the answer is to ignore them: "Don't take the roads where you will go astray. When you have once entered the forest, proceed through the trees straight ahead."[9] When the army, spread out line abreast, enters the forest, it poses no problem, absorbing the army and eventually, as mobile camouflage, simply blends seamlessly with the army; the restorers of moral order and the natural are now intermingled. This disturbance of the separation between human and natural will also send its own message to the castle when, during the night before the siege, the castle is invaded by "a flock of wild birds,"[1] an ominous occurrence that Washizu tries unconvincingly to read as benign. The vulnerable borders of the state's political geography and the permeable divisions between the human and non-human are then explored by Kurosawa as structural parallels, dense signs of the fragility of the human will.

Only in one place in the film's locations does the human make a quasi-permanent mark: in the room in the North Castle where Fujimaki killed himself, leaving a bloodstain that cannot be scraped off, a mark seen on the room's wall. It is from this room, displaced from their own room by the need for Kuniharu to sleep in the castle's best room, that Asaji and Washizu will move to the murder, as if Fujimaki's blood produces a dynamic towards further bloodletting. The indelible trace of Fujimaki is a combination of

---

8. Donaldson, 87.
9. Kurosawa, 259. The screenplay describes the advancing army here as a "formation of troops . . . shaped like the wings of a crane", something that I cannot see on the film but which may be recognizable to a Japanese viewer.
1. Kurosawa, 262.

the human and the supernatural, a sign that "blood will have blood" (3.4.124) here too.

But it is also only in one place in the film that the human makes what one might define as a normative mark on the landscape: when Kuniharu and his "hunting party" ride towards Washizu's castle, they move through rice fields, the film's only signs of agriculture, of the cultivation of the natural for other than warlike ends.

Scotland, Wales

Of the five films, by far the most conventional in its approach to both a traditional view of the play and the realist modes of film is Roman Polanski's 1971 *Macbeth*.[2] The film's location work was shot in Wales (and, to a lesser extent, in England), creating a mostly predictable and uninteresting context of the real as the countryside behind the action. Scotland is only strongly marked in the king's banners and in the use of music (the sword dance at Macbeth's castle and the Celtic inflections of the unremittingly dreadful film score by the Third Ear Band) or in the occasional Scottish inflection of a voice (for example, Frank Wylie's Menteith). Otherwise it is no more than the cliched vague place of historical costume-drama, barely more interesting than that of Jeremy Freeston's 1996 film.

The locations' only special emphasis is a dirtiness, typified by the mud that covers the hems of everyone's robes and which weighs down Macbeth's nightgown as he leads Macduff to the discovery of Duncan's body. As much symbolic as authentic, the dirt is part of the sordid society Polanski charts, a world in which the Macbeths' evils are generated by a social practice of murder—for example, in the first shot after the credits where a soldier, finding that a face-down figure on the battlefield is not quite dead, promptly and brutally dispatches him.

Polanski chose to film in Britain because "I needed the kind of brooding, gray, autumnal skies so typical of the British Isles," but the filming in Wales enveloped the cast and crew

> in an icy, almost incessant downpour . . . [in which] makeup ran, beards came unstuck, horses panicked. When the rain stopped, fog reduced visibility to a few yards. The locations we'd chosen for the witches' scenes became accessible only to

2. Most work on Polanski's film has been pruriently obsessed by the connections with the Manson family's murder of Polanski's wife, Sharon Tate: see, for example, Bryan Reynolds, "Untimely Ripped: Mediating Witchcraft in Polanski and Shakespeare," in Lisa L. Starks and Courtney Lehmann, eds., *The Reel Shakespeare* (Madison, NJ: Fairleigh Dickinson Press, 2002), 143–64. But see the fine account of the successive scripts of the film in Bernice W. Kliman, "Gleanings: The Residue of Difference in Scripts: The Case of Polanski's *Macbeth*," in Jay L. Halio and Hugh Richmond, eds., *Shakespearean Illuminations* (Newark: University of Delaware Press, 1998), 131–46.

four-wheel-drive vehicles capable of crossing the sea of rich, greasy mud in which we spent our days.[3]

Not all the film's pervasive dampness is then deliberate, though Polanski is prone to heavy-handed weather symbolism like the thunderclaps that accompany Lady Macbeth's welcoming Duncan to Inverness, an overly portentous device inadequately naturalized into the real by the subsequent sudden downpour. If the film's first shot offers a similarly over-elaborated natural image in the blood-red sun spreading its potent color across the landscape, the location itself—the foreshore of an endless beach in which the weird sisters bury a hangman's noose, a severed arm, and a dagger, marking the spot with blood at least until the tide will obliterate the site—functions as a marginal space, a liminal transition that is ambiguously sea and land and where foul and fair might well be indistinguishable. It is in this space that the slaughter of the battle has taken place, and the bleak landscape seems appropriate for such pervasive human brutality: Macbeth is almost inevitably first seen supervising, with Banquo, the mass hanging of rebel soldiers, before he rides off (bored? disgusted?), and Banquo has to wheel and follow him.

Polanski's witches—one elderly and blind from birth, one middle-aged, and one young and dumb[4]—are not in the least spirits but instead poor women who are self-evidently extra-social, exactly the kind who were burnt as witches throughout early modern Europe. Kenneth Tynan, the English theater critic who collaborated with Polanski on the script, thought that "they should be presented in such a way that any sensible person in the audience might also find them trustworthy . . . more like spiritualist mediums than demons—morally neutral creatures who may inspire us with a faint twinge of unease but certainly should not make us shudder with revulsion."[5] But the result is nothing like the "Hindu holy men in loincloths with matted hair" Tynan envisaged. Though apparently semi-domesticated, living in a hovel, these weird sisters live beyond community. They do, however, become part of a greater network of female culture: Macbeth's second encounter with them begins with a young witch leading him into the underground hovel, a hell that is filled with naked women who prepare the cauldron brew and give it to him to drink, as if its psychotropic powers are a belated example of 1960s drug counterculture. The scene is a

3. Roman Polanski, *Roman by Polanski* (London: Heinemann, 1984), 293–94. On the making of the film, see also Barbara Learning, *Polanski: His Life and Films* (London: Hamish Hamilton, 1982), 76–89.
4. Did Polanski therefore want to hint that the middle one is deaf? If so, there is no apparent trace in the film.
5. Kenneth Tynan, *Letters*, ed. by Kathleen Tynan (London: Weidenfeld and Nicholson, 1994), 478.

remarkable combination of a conservative revulsion of hippiedom mixed with visual cliches of female heterodox activity.

What little remains of the "English" scene in the screenplay is not played in England at all but instead among the tents where the English troops are preparing for the war. Polanski also adds a scene where the English army unites with a Scottish one. There is, in effect, no land beyond Scotland here. What matters instead is the film's rather relentless exploration of the margins between inside and out, the border not of country but of the edge of human construction. *Macbeth*, of course, makes use of that sense of looking across the landscape, most obviously in the reported sight of Birnam Wood ("As I did stand my watch upon the hill" [5.5.33]). Shakespeare films have often been interested in the view from windows, especially in Olivier's *Henry V* (1944) and his *Richard III* (1955). But Polanski's *Macbeth* makes it into an obsessive motif so that Macbeth can only anticipate Banquo's murder by opening the window and looking across the countryside towards the spot where the murder will take place. While the film also emphasizes its castles' gates—like the gates Ross silently instructs Lady Macduff's servant to leave open for the murderers to enter or the one Macbeth's deserting soldiers unbar as they leave with their loot—windows function determinedly as signs of the look beyond, the means of connecting the closed inner world to the outer. Hence, for instance, Polanski signals Lady Macbeth's madness by having her slumped asleep on a stool at right angles to a window, making no attempt to look through it, her withdrawal defined by this disconnection from the vantage point she usually occupied.

If the film became notorious for the banality of its final sequence, in which the cyclical character of evil is indicated by having Donalbain, limping like a proto-Richard III, going to consult the witches, its presentation of the final battle shows a more striking approach to the conflict between human activity and the unnatural or supernatural of this film's world. The arrival of the besieging army is remarkably bombastic. The moving wood fools no one, except perhaps Macbeth himself, because the script has transferred "Let every soldier hew him down a bough" (5.4.4) from Malcolm to a glum conversation between two of Macbeth's soldiers who take one look at the wood on the move and knowingly tell each other "Every soldier has hewn him down a bough." "It shadows the numbers of their host and makes discovery err in report of them."[6] The army arrives with catapults firing flaming missiles and camouflaged battering rams, but none of this military paraphernalia is necessary

---

6. I have printed this as prose since, obviously, it is no longer quite in the rhythms of Shakespeare's verse.

since the castle is now deserted except for Macbeth himself, seated on his throne, waiting for all these men born of women.

The invaders may have "tied me to a stake" (5.7.1), but Polanski turns Macbeth's self-description as "bear-like" (2) into a literal reference, with Macbeth standing by the metal ring in the pillar to which the bear was tied as bait for the coronation celebrations. Polanski had wanted the bear-baiting to be an extensive scene, but it proved technically impossible.[7] Instead the animal, which, rather than Banquo, is jokingly identified by Macbeth as "our chief guest" (3.1.11), is seen dragged along as a dead carcass, leaving smears of blood across the castle floor. The bloodthirstiness that enjoys bear-baiting reappears at the end in the soldiers' jeering at Macbeth's decapitated head, a sight that Polanski shockingly films from Macbeth's point of view, the last images the dying eyes see.

The world Polanski creates is almost always determinedly secular. Though there is, surprisingly, a trio of rough crosses outside the weird sisters' hovel and a cross is briefly glimpsed in the flames that consume Macduff's castle at Fife, Polanski kept to Tynan's view of the play's secularity: "No Christianity except Banquo in 'the great hand of God' line. There is evil but no organized good in this universe."[8] The coronation of Macbeth takes place in a stone circle and is resolutely non-Christian. This has strange consequences for the film's look: as Pearlman rather pedantically comments, "[i]n order to salvage a dark-age setting, Polanski even falls into the anachronism of juxtaposing late medieval fortifications and armaments to neolithic religion."[9] Its secularism seems to be the social landscape out of which the violence of the film so unrestrainedly emerges. More than any other film of *Macbeth*, Polanski's understands the brutality of Shakespeare's play world.

Some Shakespeare films simply do not wear well over time, and Polanski's *Macbeth* now looks oddly timid in its solutions, trapped by a view of period and space that is too bound by cinematic convention to find anything approximating the demands of the play. Only in the brilliant conflation of various roles to create a version of Ross as the arch traitor, the ever-smiling true villain of the play, and an ironic choice to hail Malcolm as the new king, does the film's reading of the play seem lastingly powerful.[1] The deliberate use of realist location is only one part of a dull film-method that brought Shakespeare too close to costume epic for comfort.

7. For an account of the comic failure to film the scene, see Leaming, 83–84.
8. Tynan, *Letters*, 475.
9. See E. Pearlman, "*Macbeth* on Film: Politics," in Wells and Davies, eds., *op. cit.*, 253; this quotation unfairly represents an otherwise interesting article.
1. Kliman is especially interesting on the late decision to create this character, so superbly acted by John Stride.

Scotland, UT

In 1947 the Utah Centennial Commission and the American National Theater Association invited Orson Welles to direct and star in a stage production of *Macbeth* in Salt Lake City. Welles was already in negotiation with the Republic Studio to film the play, to make what would be the first American film-studio production of Shakespeare since the Reinhardt/Dieterle *A Midsummer Night's Dream* for Warner Brothers in 1935. Republic, even while defining the film project as one of their premiere projects, still stuck to a budget of only $800,000. The Utah production provided Welles with a number of ways to cut costs. Utilizing primarily the same cast, Welles could obviously economize on rehearsal time—something Shakespeare needed but which film budgets could not tolerate—but he also took more extreme measures: the sound for the film was prerecorded in Utah so that filming was done by the actors lip-synching to the already existing tracks. He also used the Utah sets as the primary locations for the film, leaving very visible shots of their origins all over the film in the flat platforms out of which the rocky structures emerge.

In the end the sound became one of the film's more notorious features. Shot in a mere twenty-three days (by comparison, Olivier's 1948 *Hamlet*, with which Welles's film was always unfavourably compared and whose success at the Venice Film Festival resulted in *Macbeth* being withdrawn from competition, was shot over thirty-two weeks), Welles's *Macbeth*'s rough and ready look was bound to rile critics. Before the film was properly distributed in 1951, the studio took over the product and butchered it, cutting the running time of approximately 107 minutes[2] by about 20 minutes and demanding that the actors' voices be rerecorded to eliminate the remarkable and distinctive timbre Welles wanted. The 1980 UCLA/Folger Shakespeare Library restoration of Welles's original, the only version currently available on video or DVD, still left in the quirky music score by Jacques Ibert that the studio incorporated but cut the explanatory prologue that Welles was made to include for the release print.[3]

2. There is some evidence that the film as Welles first delivered it ran for as much as 135 minutes; see Luke McKernan and Olwen Terris, eds., *Walking Shadows* (London: BFI Publishing, 1994), 92.
3. The multiple versions of the film are often discussed in the fine criticism the film has produced. See, for example, Michael Anderegg, *Orson Welles, Shakespeare and Popular Cinema* (New York: Columbia University Press, 1999), 74–97; Bernice W. Kliman, "Welles's *Macbeth,* A Textual Parable," in Michael Skovmand, ed., *Screen Shakespeare* (Aarhus: Aarhus University Press, 1994), 25–37; Pamela Mason, "Orson Welles and Filmed Shakespeare," in Jackson, *op. cit.*, 184–89; Neil Forsyth, "Shakespeare the Illusionist: Filming the Supernatural," in Jackson, *op. cit.*, 274–94, especially 282–86. Anthony Davies's often brilliant analysis of the film (*op. cit.*, 82–99) seems to have been made without having seen the restored version, though published in 1988.

Welles chose to record the soundtrack with the actors' using Scottish accents. The results are, to say the least, variable, but Welles's purpose was not primarily driven by the play's location. As Richard Wilson, Welles's assistant, noted,

> We didn't put a Scotch dialect in the picture because Macbeth was laid in Scotland. A Scotch dialect was put in because we determined **after careful tests,** that the intelligibility was greater with the Scotch accent, because it had a tendency to slow the actors down just enough to make it more comprehensible to the ear. The secondary reason was that it absolutely made it impossible for the actor to sing his lines ala Shakespearian declamation.[4]

Whatever the aim—and the result is slower, nondeclamatory, and comprehensible in spite of most actors' inability to sustain the effect—the result is to underpin the film's gestures towards realist Scottishness, just as the Caribbean accent of the African-American actors in Welles's 1937 stage production of the play at the Lafayette Theater in Harlem both helped the cast and emphasized Welles's setting in Haiti. The film score uses the distant sound of the skirl of bagpipes to indicate the advancing Anglo-Scots armies (though there is no sign of bagpipes in the shots of the troops), and costume often includes plaids thrown over a shoulder, draped across Macbeth's head, or, for Malcolm, accompanied by a full-dress kilt. There is no doubt of the geography with such referentiality.

Yet Welles's visual language for the play is emphatically not that of realist location. Mostly shot on the sets for the Utah production (themselves visibly derived as stage-forms from the 1937 designs), with flat stage-floor and vast rocky outcrops that somehow foreground their papier-mâché origins, the film almost ostentatiously shows off its cheapness, its sheer staginess. As Michael Anderegg argues,

> That Macbeth, just before his second encounter with the witches, stands in front of what appears to be a blank scrim against which, as lightning flashes overhead, we see his shadow projected, would not be notable on a stage; in a film, of course, it becomes an almost scandalous instance of showing the apparatus, of "baring the device."[5]

Overhead shots reveal the bold, coarse painting of the stage floor; scenes in entirely different fictive spaces are plainly shot on exactly the same set albeit from a slightly different angle; Lady Macduff is apparently murdered at Macbeth's castle; and Macbeth's throne

---

4. Quoted Kliman, 33 (emphasis original).
5. Anderegg, 83.

seems to be placed on a staircase in the castle courtyard. None of these disjunctions would surprise in the theater, but all work aggressively against cinematic forms and expectations.

Perhaps the most remarkable sequence in such respects is Macbeth's receiving the report of Banquo's murder and then walking towards the banquet scene. He appears to be in a subterranean maze hewn from the rock, with water dripping off the ceiling (and onto the soundtrack) or cascading down the walls—the water is forceful enough for Macbeth to wash in it before he emerges for the banquet from between two inordinately large barrels. Jean Cocteau, in one of the most sympathetic readings the film received early in its life, saw the effect as a kind of temporal ambiguity supporting a dream vision:

> Coiffed with horns and crowns of cardboard, clad in animal skins like the first motorists, the heroes of the drama move in the corridors of a kind of dream underground, in devastated caves leaking water, in an abandoned coal-mine . . . at times we ask ourselves in what age this nightmare is taking place, and when we encounter Lady Macbeth for the first time before the camera moves back and places her, we almost see a lady in modern dress lying on a fur couch next to the telephone.[6]

In this form of reading, where the defects of budget become the strengths of the film's constructed meaning, even the voices can be heard as deliberately and effectively odd. Cocteau knew that the sound might be "unbearable to English ears" but thought that "this is what one can expect from these bizarre monsters who express in a monstrous language the words of Shakespeare, which remain their words."[7]

If we see the film's sets as a kind of realist definition of eleventh-century Scottish castles, then it becomes willfully disruptive. If the set is left as a form of expressionist cinema in which place is only meaning and never context, if, that is, space is allowed to be as metaphorical as anything in the play's densely imagistic spoken language, then Welles's landscape is supremely functional because it denies the realist functionality that landscape on film is supposed to have. For all its frequent banality and even cliché, Welles's use of space in *Macbeth* never fails to provoke. Thus the caverns of the castle are seen as the tunnels of the mind through which Macbeth wanders, a space of deliberate interiority accompanied by voice-over echoes of Banquo's parting lines, a journey of confrontation

6. Quoted in Joseph McBride, *Orson Welles* (London: Secker and Warburg, 1972), 112. Compare Claude Beylie's definition of the film as "redolent of both the Paleolithic and atomic eras" (quoted in Anderegg, 84) and Anderegg's own sense of the film's Scotland as "not so much prehistoric as outside history" (84).
7. McBride, 112–13.

with what has been done that necessarily conjures up the ghost of Banquo in the next sequence, at a banquet claustrophobically compressed by the canopy that overhangs the entire length of the table. Thought generates event here and, as Anthony Davies argues persuasively, space and the body are conjoined:

> The spatial substance, in some affinitive way, takes on the involuntary biochemistry of Macbeth. Its cavernous walls exude drops of moisture just as Macbeth's skin glistens with the torrid sweat of panic.[8]

The struggle with the forms of space is part of the film's more generalized struggle to create form. Macbeth and his wife, in particular, are repeatedly threatened by swirling mists that define the lure of formlessness, of an undefined universe in which action becomes freer or at least morally disengaged. André Bazin called Welles's universe prehistoric—a prehistoric "not that of our ancestors, the Gauls or the Celts, but a prehistory of the conscience at the birth of time and sin."[9] The opening shots that move between mists and the bubbling contents of the weird sisters' cauldron resolve into a mass of clay which the witches sculpt into an image of Macbeth (and which they will later crown and decapitate as the action moves forward), a new version of the voodoo doll of the 1937 stage production. Form emerging out of formlessness is thus the witches' landscaping of the play.

Welles's prologue for the release-print spoke of the film's time frame:

> Our story is laid in Scotland, ancient Scotland, savage, half lost in the mist which hangs between recorded history and the time of legends. The cross itself is newly arrived here. Plotting against Christian law and order are the agents of chaos, priests of hell and magic; sorcerers and witches.[1]

If there is little sense in the film of a political alternative (England becomes a stage set of a hillock dominated by a massive stone Celtic cross), the true opposition that underpins the film is between Christianity and the witches' paganism. For Welles, Macbeth was "a member of the Christian community" whom "the forces of evil" that "represent ancient religion, paganism" are "fighting to win . . . over. Even at the end, Macbeth remains a member of the Christian world and continues to fight to save his integrity."[2] Welles here may be retrospectively rewriting his film: borrowing a process that was a

---

8. Davies, 89.
9. Quoted Davies, 89.
1. Quoted Davies, 87; note Welles's use of mist here.
2. Interview with Richard Marienstras in 1974, reprinted in Mark W. Estrin, ed., *Orson Welles: Interviews* (Jackson, MS: University Press of Mississippi, 2002), 151–52.

fundamental part of his voodoo *Macbeth* of 1937, the witches are present at various unexpected junctures, and the film ends with them outside the castle chanting the displaced line, "Peace, the charm's wound up" (1.3.38). The sheer power of these figures, whose faces are barely seen, clutching their tall two-pronged staves, become explicitly an infernal trinity set against the film's pervasive presence of a Christian alternative. The Scottish soldiers, for example, carry three-pronged, Trinitarian spears; the English army is accompanied by a veritable forest of Celtic crosses; and Malcolm and Macduff have crosses on their helmets.

Most emphatically of all, where the sordid political world of Polanski's film would be defined by the aggregation of various characters into the smiling Ross, Welles's created character—whom he named the Holy Father, whose lines come from Ross, Angus, and the Old Man—seeps into every aspect of the film. As Duncan arrives to visit the Macbeths, the Holy Father leads the assembled troops in a baptismal catechism ("Dost thou renounce Satan and all his works?") while they stand holding lighted candles. By invoking the need for St. Michael to be "our safeguard against the wiles and wickedness of the devil," the Holy Father becomes the play's sign of a Christian good. At his first appearance, for instance, he sends the witches scurrying for cover; as Macbeth muses aloud whether "This supernatural soliciting / Cannot be ill," he looks at the Holy Father and firmly asserts "cannot be good" (1.3.134), as if otherwise subject to a religious reproof; and it is the Holy Father who warns Lady Macduff and later encourages Macduff to join the invaders. During the siege of Macbeth's castle at the end of the play, Macbeth throws his spear at the Holy Father, killing him and thereby provoking the invaders to burst through the gates, as if this act of "sacrilegious murder" (2.3.62) is an echo from Duncan, a sign of Macbeth's final capitulation to the dark forces of the pagan world. If the Holy Father's wig of long, dangling braids looks now irresistibly comic, his presence is the most profound definition of the moral landscape Welles seeks to create. In the politics of Welles's *Macbeth* the play becomes set in a location of religious conflict, its moral choices ultimately defined as the acceptance of a Christian state religion or its subversive opposite, the demonic powers whose presence in the film's last shots unnervingly suggests the incompleteness of Christianity's triumph. Welles's rejection of a realist landscape, in part forced on him by the exigencies of the tiny budget, result in the creation of an interior moral space, a landscape more congruent with Shakespeare's than that of any other filmmaker.

ROBERT S. MIOLA

A Note on the Authorship Controversy (2014)

Since 1778 scholars have detected the presence of another play-wright in *Macbeth*, one Thomas Middleton (1580–1627), who also seems responsible for parts of Shakespeare's contemporary *Timon of Athens* (c. 1605–8). Arguing that Thomas Middleton adapted the 1623 Folio *Macbeth* in about 1616, Gary Taylor included *Macbeth* in his *Thomas Middleton: The Collected Works* (Oxford, 2007). Brian Vickers, along with Marcus Dahl and Marina Tarlinskaya, denied Middleton's presence in *Macbeth* in "An Enquiry into Middleton's supposed "adaptation" of *Macbeth*" (2010), available online, http:// ies.sas.ac.uk/events/seminars/LFAS/index.htm (under "Projects"), and in "Disintegrated: Did Middleton Adapt *Macbeth*?" (*Times Literary Supplement*, May 28, 2010, pp. 13–14). Though Middleton's *The Witch* includes the two witches' songs that are simply cued in *Macbeth* (3.5, 4.1), Vickers argues, this coincidence does not indicate Middleton's revising hand. Furthermore, the evidence from stage directions, particularly the formulas for simultaneous entrance ("*Enter A, meeting B*" and "*Enter A and B meeting*"), is ambivalent, pointing to Shakespeare as well as to Middleton. In addition, Marcus Dahl's computer assisted study of "trigrams," collocations of three consecutive words that may be used to discover characteristic verbal patterns and identify individual authors, attests to Shakespeare's hand alone in the disputed scenes. Finally, the metrical analyses of Marlina Tarlinskaya show the proposed Middletonian revisions to conform to Shakespearean verse norms. The Folio text of *Macbeth* shows evidence of revision, Vickers concludes, but the reviser was Shakespeare himself, not Thomas Middleton.

Gary Taylor responds to these objections in the following article written for this Norton Critical Edition.

Thomas Middleton, playwright and possible reviser of *Macbeth* (engraving, 1887).

The debate between the principals will doubtless continue and there will be also contributions from other scholars; but the exchange here reveals the present controversy over *Macbeth* and the methods currently used to determine authorship.

GARY TAYLOR

Macbeth and Middleton (2014)[†]

Brian Vickers and I agree that the earliest extant text of *Macbeth* contains material from two different periods in the play's evolution: its original composition by Shakespeare alone (1606), and a later adaptation that incorporated two songs from *The Witch*. Vickers attributes that later adaptation to Shakespeare. I have argued for thirty years that Shakespeare revised his plays, but "new additions" by other playwrights were often written for theatrical revivals, and in this instance I join most other Shakespeare scholars in attributing the alterations to Middleton. How can we determine which hypothesis is correct?

Vickers is right that the presence of two Middleton songs does not in itself prove that Middleton wrote the material surrounding those songs, or anything else in *Macbeth*. Grace Ioppolo, whose 1991 book he quotes, is also correct in claiming that song cues *might* be written by a bookkeeper. But Ioppolo goes further. She conjectures that an author would "presumably" have rewritten the full text of the songs, and hence that "&c." is evidence *against* Middleton's involvement. That claim is not justified by the historical evidence. Tiffany Stern (2009) has demonstrated that theatre songs were intrinsically mobile, and the cue with "&c." establishes only that the song already existed and was familiar to the acting company. Moreover, added passages, with or without songs, were often pasted into an existing playbook (as happened in Middleton's *The Lady's Tragedy*). Such paste-ins demand economy of space, so it would make sense to abbreviate reference to a song-lyric that the company owned and had performed. Raphael Seligman (2012) shows that Middleton sometimes re-used his own songs in different plays. And one scene in his play *The Widow* contains abbreviated references to two songs: "Kuck before and kuck behind, etc." (3.1.6) and "Come, my dainty doxies" (18). The first is otherwise unknown, but the second comes from Middleton's *More Dissemblers Besides Women*. All this does not prove that Middleton personally added

---

† Written for this edition.

the two *Witch* songs to *Macbeth*, but it certainly makes his intervention possible.

Vickers claims that "modern scholarship" dates *The Witch* "to between 1609 and 1616". That range comes from the 1950 edition by W. W. Greg and F. P. Wilson. But all recent editors (Esche 1993, Schafer 1994, O'Connor 2007) date Middleton's play in late 1615 or 1616. Indeed, the most detailed discussions prefer "mid-1616" (O'Connor, 382) or "August of 1616" (Esche, 25)—both after Shakespeare's death in April 1616. Vickers does not acknowledge or refute their evidence. If Shakespeare revised *Macbeth* after Middleton wrote *The Witch*, he did so in the last months of his life, in a style strikingly unlike his writing in *Henry VIII* and *Two Noble Kinsmen*.

My attribution of the adaptation to Middleton (*Companion* 2007, pp. 383–98) is hardly iconoclastic or revolutionary. The "151 lines" I attribute to Middleton include the fifty-seven lines of the two songs (3.5.34–73, 4.1.44–60); Vickers does not dispute their authorship. Although my summary (p. 397) does not attempt to differentiate the exact authorial shares in the seventy-two lines of "mixed writing", the earlier full discussion of particular passages does so; for instance, I provide new evidence for Shakespeare's authorship of specific lines in the "mixed" passages in 1.2 and 4.1.

Vickers ignores most of my evidence, focusing instead on a few items that he labels misrepresentations. One of these, my account of the significance of the two directions in *Macbeth* that contain the present participle "*meeting*", summarizes thirty pages of analysis by R. V. Holdsworth (pp. 189–219 of his 1982 dissertation, which I have placed online at thomasmiddleton.org/macbeth). Holdsworth has recently published an essay (2012) based on this chapter of the dissertation, and he calls the claim by Vickers "a wholly misleading distortion of my argument" (email, October 1, 2012). I believe that anyone who reads Holdsworth's analysis will see that Vickers is guilty of a "false report" of the evidence and its importance.

Vickers elsewhere cites unusual stage directions as reliable evidence of authorship (*Co-Author,* 211). Holdsworth surveyed instances of *Enter . . . meeting* in the stage directions of 644 plays in 670 variant texts from 1580 to 1642. He found six examples in the Shakespeare canon (p. 189), including two in *Macbeth*: 1.2.0.1–3 (*Enter King Malcome, Donalbaine, Lenox, with attendants, meeting a bleeding Captaine*) and 3.5.0.1 (*Enter the three Witches, meeting Hecat*). The "four other instances of this form occurring in Shakespearean texts" include one from 4.1 of *Henry VIII*—a scene attributed, by Vickers and me among many others, to John Fletcher. Two others come from scenes of *Timon of Athens* (3.4, 3.5) that Vickers and I both attribute to Middleton. That leaves, as evidence of Shakespeare's own habits, only the single example Vickers cites from the quarto text of *King Lear* (*Enter Bast. and Curan meeting*).

But Holdsworth demonstrated that the *Lear* direction differed, crucially, from those in *Macbeth*. He carefully distinguished the grammatical formula "Enter A, meeting B" (which occurs in *Timon* 3.4 and *Macbeth* 1.2 and 3.5) from other formulas, including "Enter A and B, meeting" (which occurs in *King Lear*). That second formula is unambiguous, because it specifies the entrance of two characters. Notably, the first formula *is* ambiguous, because it does *not* specify whether "B" is already on stage: in early modern plays, sometimes B is, sometimes not. The ambiguous formula "Enter A, meeting B" (or "Enter A, B meeting" him or them) occurs in the Shakespeare canon only four times: these two stage directions in the 1623 text of *Macbeth*, and the two directions in scenes of *Timon of Athens* that Vickers himself attributes to Middleton (as do recent texts of that play in the Arden, Oxford, and RSC editions of Shakespeare). By contrast, the ambiguous *meeting* occurs twelve times in undisputed Middleton plays, and once in *The Revenger's Tragedy*, now almost universally attributed to Middleton; Vickers has elsewhere praised, deservedly, David Lake and MacDonald P. Jackson, who confirmed Middleton's authorship of *Revenger* and of these scenes of *Timon*. Thus, if we disregard the disputed examples in *Macbeth* itself, the ambiguous formula ("Enter A, meeting B" or "Enter A, B meeting him") never appears in Shakespeare's approximately 2500 stage directions. But Middleton's much smaller dramatic canon contains fifteen examples (if we accept, as Vickers does, his share of *Timon*). Two of those fifteen are in Middleton's own handwriting, in a manuscript of *A Game at Chess*. Final score: Middleton 15 Shakespeare 0.

According to Vickers, Holdsworth found *"meeting"* almost equally often in Middleton ("ten") and Heywood ("nine"). Does Vickers want to suggest the wildly implausible idea that Heywood revised *Macbeth*? I do not think so, although it would be accurate to say that Heywood is much likelier than Shakespeare to be responsible for those stage directions. The Middleton/Heywood comparison confuses the issue, and is inaccurate. The numbers "ten" and "nine" do occur in Holdsworth's 1982 discussion, but they are quickly superseded. Middleton has ten only if we disregard *Revenger, Timon*, and the equally ambiguous formula "Enter A, B meeting him". Moreover, Holdsworth established that "B" was never already onstage in the Middleton examples of *meeting*, whereas "B" was present in five of the nine Heywood examples. If we include Middleton's scenes of *Timon* and disregard the contested case of *Macbeth*, Middleton's thirty two dramatic texts contain fifteen examples (in ten plays) of the ambiguous meeting-requiring-simultaneous-entrance, but it appears only fourteen times (in fourteen plays) in 637 early modern dramatic texts by other writers.

Holdsworth did not calculate the statistical significance of this contrast, but a simple chi-square test (explained on thomasmiddleton .org/macbeth) demonstrates that the probability of such a distribution occurring randomly is just a sliver short of absolute zero. Only six plays from 1580–1624 contain more than one example; five are by Middleton, and the sixth is *Macbeth*. In the entire period up to 1642, only two scenes contain a stage direction that combines (a) the ambiguous simultaneous *meeting* and (b) the phrase "with attendants": *Timon* 3.4 (by Middleton) and *Macbeth* 1.2. Three different features of the stage directions in *Macbeth*—the presence of the ambiguous simultaneous *meeting*, the fact that it occurs twice, and the juxtaposition of "with attendants"—all point to Middleton uniquely or with near certainty. The two directions in *Macbeth* are not only likelier to be by Middleton than Shakespeare; Middleton is more likely to have written them than any other Renaissance playwright.

To summarize: Holdsworth demonstrated that a rare, Middletonian stage direction, using the grammatically ambiguous participle *meeting* to indicate simultaneous entrance, occurred in two scenes of *Macbeth* (1.2, 3.5)—two scenes where scholars had, for different and independent reasons, long suspected Middleton's intervention. One of those scenes (3.5) contains a song from *The Witch*. Holdsworth thus provided strong evidence, based on a comprehensive survey of early modern drama, that *Macbeth* contained rare features characteristic of Middleton but not Shakespeare. Holdsworth alone deserves credit for that discovery.

Vickers also accuses me of misrepresenting the work of John Dover Wilson, claiming that Wilson's position is the "complete opposite" of my own. I have provided, on the Middleton website, the full context of the discussions by Wilson and myself. Wilson believed, as I do, that 3.5 and 4.1 contain new material written by Middleton, and that 1.2 represents Middleton's abridgement of Shakespeare's original text, perhaps combining "two or more original scenes not too carefully stitched together" (p. xxiv). Wilson felt that "the verse, *except for a word or two here and there,* is certainly Shakespeare's" (p. xxv; italicizing the words omitted by Vickers), and I provide a paragraph of new evidence that "most of what remains in the scene is Shakespeare's" (p. 386). Wilson cited (p. 98) a parallel from *A Chaste Maid in Cheapside* ("rip my belly up to the throat then") for "unseamed him from the nave to the chops"

(1.2.22). I provide an additional Middleton parallel for the same
phrase—"rip thee down from neck to navel" (*Witch* 5.1.14)—and
note that Shakespeare never used the word *seam* at all, which
occurs five times in Middleton. In *Meeting of Gallants* (1604) the
verb "seamed" is applied to "a lieutenant" (201); shortly thereafter,
"seam-rent suits" are compared to "torn bodies" (271–72); in *The
Widow* (1615–16) "an open seam in his shirt" is immediately followed by "shall I run him through there" with "my sword" (1.2.195–
96); in *Masque of Heroes* (1619), "their faces seamed" (266.12)
combines the verbal past participle with the unusual idea of seam-
ing a body. These Middleton passages stretch from 1604 (before
the original composition of *Macbeth*) to 1615–19 (before and after
composition of *The Witch*). They illustrate what Vickers elsewhere
calls "the superior value of parallelisms existing in both thought
and language" (*Co-Author*, 166). Middleton associated the noun
seam and the rare verb *seamed* with torn human bodies, military
figures, violence, and swords; he imagined human bodies ripped
open between the *nave(l)* and neck. Such unShakespearian language suggests that Middleton wrote bridging material to compen-
sate for the cuts suspected by Wilson, myself, and other scholars.

As for Jonathan Hope's linguistic evidence, it cannot by itself provide statistical proof that Middleton rather than Shakespeare wrote
all of 3.5 or 4.1. Hope does not claim that, and neither do I. We
simply note that two scenes, which contain cues for songs by Middleton, also resemble Middleton in their usage of "do". In particular,
Hope notes (p. 105) that 3.5 and 4.1 "together have a regulation rate
of 88 percent", which "makes them look less 'Shakespearean' than
the play as a whole" (which has a "rate of 84 per cent"). Elsewhere,
he notes that his larger control samples from other, uncontested
Middleton and Shakespeare plays are also "only four per cent apart"
(p. 101). He gives figures (p. 105) showing that none of the four
scenes in *Macbeth* with a total of more than fifty examples has so
high a percentage rate as the combined 3.5 and 4.1 (with a total of
seventy-three). Hope acknowledges that this small sample cannot be
"conclusive", but that does not mean it is worthless. All such evidence establishes probabilities, and multiple independent tests
increase the likelihood of another author's presence. In *Shakespeare,
Co-Author* (2002), Vickers stressed "the importance in authorship
studies of co-ordinating several different approaches, each testing
the others" (198). I agree. I also agree that the five Shakespeare
plays he examined in that book were co-written with a collaborator.
(In fact, I had anticipated his conclusions in 1987.)

In support of Shakespeare's authorship of the passages usually
attributed to Middleton, Vickers provides his own stylistic analysis of
a few passages. It's true that, like Hecate, Oberon and Titania

command lesser fairies, and true too that the deities in *Pericles*, *Cymbeline*, and *The Tempest* speak "rhymed iambics." But none of Shakespeare's supernatural figures speak rhymed iambic *tetrameter*, as Hecate does in 3.5 and 4.1. By contrast, Middleton's Hymen does so in *Women Beware Women* (5.1.90–91, 100–101); his Succubus in *A Mad World, My Masters* mixes rhymed iambic tetrameter with rhymed trochaic tetrameter (4.1.43–62), as does Levity in *Honourable Entertainments* 7.4–25; Error in *Triumphs of Truth* mixes rhymed iambic and trochaic tetrameter with a concluding pentameter couplet (625–34); the resurrected Raynulph in *Hengist* speaks rhymed tetrameters throughout his five speeches, but with occasional rhymed pentameters (1.0.4, 1.2.14–16, Epi.9–10). Hecate's rhymed speeches in *Macbeth* similarly mix iambic tetrameter with random iambic pentameter (3.5.2–3, 12, 21). So does Hecate in *The Witch* (1.2.15–28), in a scene where she gives orders to her subordinates. Formally, Middleton provides better parallels than Shakespeare for Hecate's speeches in *Macbeth*. But Vickers, like most scholars and students, knows Shakespeare better than he knows Middleton.

However, his online collaborators provide two new kinds of evidence, apparently objective, for Shakespeare's authorship of the contested material. Marina Tarlinskaya, a specialist in metrical analysis, carefully and usefully distinguishes Shakespeare's blank verse from Middleton's. Unfortunately, her analysis of "105" iambic pentameter lines in *Macbeth* was based on the confusing typography in the Middleton *Collected Works* (which does not distinguish added lines from mixed or transposed ones). My attributions in the Middleton *Companion* are much clearer, and are now readily accessible on the website. Of the lines I explicitly attribute to Middleton, most are lyric verse or prose, and blank verse is both rare and scattered. ("Units", in this table, refers to a succession of complete iambic pentameter lines attributed to Middleton; for example, 1.3.44 is a single unit, and so is 4.1.163–7.)

Complete Iambic Pentameter Lines in the Folio Text of *Macbeth*, attributed by Gary Taylor to Thomas Middleton

1.1.8 (lineation disputed by Vickers)
1.2.21–23, 26–29
1.3.44
3.5.1–3, 12, 21, 35–36, 74 (surrounded by tetrameters and song lyric)
4.1. 79–80, 86, 92, 140–42 (in the first half of the scene, surrounded by tetrameters and song lyric), 153–55, 158–60, 163–67, 172–73
TOTAL: 37

UNDISPUTED TOTAL: 36
UNRHYMED UNDISPUTED TOTAL: 28
TOTAL NUMBER OF SEPARATE UNITS: 18
AVERAGE LENGTH OF UNIT: 2 LINES

Once I pointed out these figures to Tarlinskaya, she immediately withdrew her conclusions. As she wrote, "36 scattered lines are not nearly enough material for my kind of analysis to use for attribution" (January 5, 2012). The distribution of these lines across so many different passages prevents an author from establishing what she calls "rhythmical momentum". When a writer is entangled in small changes in someone else's verse, his own rhythmical tendencies are inhibited and redirected. And rhymed iambic pentameter often differs, rhythmically, from blank verse. Consequently, these few scattered lines cannot be confidently attributed, on metrical grounds, to anyone. Nothing neither way.

Marcus Dahl prepared the databases used to search for parallels, and then applied to them software that identifies sequences of three or more words. Again, the problems with this analysis are structural; the claims made by Vickers and Dahl about Thomas Kyd using these methods (never subjected to peer review) have been criticized in great detail in peer-reviewed publications by Hugh Craig (2009) and MacDonald P. Jackson (2008, 2010, 2012). There are additional problems specific to this example. Dahl's procedures identify as "rare" any sequence of three or more words that does not appear in his database. But the contents of the database are not publicly identified, and Dahl has privately acknowledged (email, December 14, 2011) that it fully represented Shakespeare's dramatic canon, but included only a fraction of the smaller Middleton canon. Moreover, all texts are old-spelling, so the search engine will not identify the same phrases if they are spelled differently. As a result, many of the allegedly unique Shakespearian phrases are not unique at all. Gabriel Egan (2012) independently checked twelve of their examples of "Shakespearian" wordstrings in disputed passages of *Macbeth*. In all twelve cases, he found Middleton parallels—sometimes more parallels in Middleton than Shakespeare. For instance, in the Captain's speech Egan found two Middleton parallels for "Shew'd like a" (1.2.15), four more for "him/till he" (21–2), four more for "him from the" (22), and five for "And fix'd" (23). (These last three occur in the same sentence as "unseamed him from the nave to the chops".) "At this point I stopped checking their claims systematically," Egan writes, "as it is clear that either most of the Middleton canon is not in whatever database Dahl, Tarlinskaja and Vickers use for their searches or else their search methodology is failing to find the matches."

None of the new evidence offered by Vickers or his collaborators rules out Middleton, makes a plausible case for Shakespeare, or matches the statistical weight of Holdsworth's survey of stage directions. But we can perhaps solve the problem by replacing Dahl's limited database with comprehensive, public databases that do not favor one writer over another. All Middleton's work can now be searched on Oxford Scholarly Editions Online; Literature Online and Early English Books Online provide comprehensive databases of Shakespeare and the rest of extant early modern drama. I cannot fit a full re-examination of *Macbeth* against these databases into this short response to Vickers. Nevertheless, using these search engines, I have looked at all possible words strings and juxtapositions of key words in the passage (4.1.39–43) between Hecate's entrance and the cue for Middleton's song "Black spirits". Which early modern playwright is most likely to have written these lines?

> *Enter Hecat, and the other three Witches.*
> *Hec.* O well done: I commend your paines,
>   And euery one shall share i'th' gaines:
>   And now about the Cauldron sing
>   Like Elues and Fairies in a Ring,
>   Inchanting all that you put in.
> *Musicke and a Song. Blacke Spirits, &c.*

Full details of the results are given on the Middleton website. Once again, Dahl and Vickers under-report the Middleton parallels. They cite "in a ring" from *Merry Wives,* but do not notice its appearance in Middleton's *No Wit* 6.26 or *Honourable Entertainments* 3.44. Vickers observes that Shakespeare uses the gerund "enchanting" four times, but does not report Middleton's "enchanting" in *Wisdom of Solomon* 18.174 and *Revenger* 1.3.113. In cases like this, the Shakespeare and Middleton parallels simply cancel each other out. But other evidence points compellingly in one direction. For "*Enter . . . the other three*", "O well done", and "well done" juxtaposed with "I commend your" there are parallels in Middleton but no other early modern playwright. Only one other playwright (John Ford) provides even a single unique three-word parallel. Shakespeare's larger canon does not contain any. Middleton, but not Shakespeare, also provides rare parallels for "I commend your" (eight), "the gains and" (one), "and now about" (one), "now about the" (two), and "you put in" (one). Against these eight Middleton parallels (three of them unique), the larger Shakespeare canon provides only two. To "elves and fairies" in *Macbeth,* Vickers compares "elf and fairy" in *Midsummer*—not an exact or unique parallel, and possibly suggested by Reginald Scot's *Discovery of Witchcraft*, the source of the following Middleton song. By contrast, the stage direction "*Music and a song*" is exactly paralleled in *Julius Caesar* (but also in four other early modern plays, and in *Macbeth* 3.5, where it precedes the cue for the other Middleton song). Both *Macbeth* and *Caesar* were published after Shakespeare's death, and "Music and a song" might, as Ioppolo conjectures, have been added by a King's Men bookkeeper. But even if we accept Shakespeare's authorship of the stage direction in *Caesar,* it is not unique. Notably, the two Shakespeare parallels come from the first half of his career (before 1600), rather than its end (where Vickers places the revision of *Macbeth*). If we limit ourselves to exact matches, Shakespeare provides only one (possibly due to a bookkeeper, in a single play written sixteen years earlier), against Middleton's eight (with eighteen occurrences in thirteen different works, written before and after the adaptation). A comprehensive survey of unusual collocations thus confirms the scholarly consensus assigning this iambic tetrameter speech to Middleton.

This passage, immediately preceding the cue for a Middleton song, was written by Middleton, not Shakespeare. Middleton was thus demonstrably involved in the adaptation of *Macbeth* printed in the 1623 Folio, which contains three rare Middletonian stage directions, cues for two Middleton songs, and at least one Middletonian iambic tetrameter speech. Only when every detail of *Macbeth* has been subjected to equally comprehensive, equally objective examination will we know what is Shakespeare's, what is Middleton's, and what difference it makes.

WORKS CITED

Craig, Hugh, and Arthur Kinney, eds. *Shakespeare, Computers, and the Mystery of Authorship.* Cambridge: Cambridge University Press, 2009.

Egan, Gabriel. "Shakespeare: Editions and Textual Matters." *The Year's Work in English Studies, Volume 91: Covering Work Published in 2010* (2012): 390–92.

Esche, Edward J., ed. *A Critical Edition of Thomas Middleton's "The Witch."* New York: Garland, 1993.

Greg, W. W., and F. P. Wilson, eds. *The Witch.* Malone Society, 1950.

Holdsworth, R. V. "Middleton and Shakespeare: The Case for Middleton's Hand in *Timon of Athens.*" Unpublished Ph.D. thesis. University of Manchester, 1982.

Holdsworth, Roger. "Stage Directions and Authorship: Shakespeare, Middleton, Heywood." *Memoria di Shakespeare,* 8, Special issue on Authorship. Ed. Rosy Colombo and Daniela Guardamagna. Rome: Bulzoni, 2012. 185–200.

Hope, Jonathan. *The Authorship of Shakespeare's Plays: A Sociolinguistic Study.* Cambridge: Cambridge University Press, 1994.

Ioppolo, Grace. *Revising Shakespeare*. Cambridge: Harvard University Press, 1991.

Jackson, MacDonald P. *Studies in Attribution: Middleton and Shakespeare*. Jacobean Drama Studies 79 (Salzburg, 1979).

———. "New Research on the Dramatic Canon of Thomas Kyd." *Research Opportunities in Medieval and Renaissance Drama* 47 (2008): 107–27.

———. "Parallels and Poetry: Shakespeare, Kyd, and *Arden of Faversham*." *Medieval and Renaissance Drama in England* 23 (2010): 17–33.

———. "Reviewing Authorship Studies of Shakespeare and His Contemporaries, and the Case of *Arden of Faversham*." *Memoria di Shakespeare*, 8, Special issue on Authorship. Ed. Rosy Colombo and Daniela Guardamagna. Rome: Bulzoni, 2012. 149–67.

Lake, David J. *The Canon of Thomas Middleton's Plays: Internal Evidence for the Major Problems of Authorship*. Cambridge: Cambridge University Press, 1975.

Middleton, Thomas. *The Collected Works*. Gen. eds. Gary Taylor and John Lavagnino. Oxford: Oxford University Press, 2007.

O'Connor, Marion, ed. *The Witch* (2007). In Middleton, *Collected Works*, 1124–64, and Taylor and Lavagnino, *Companion*, 382–83, 995–1009.

Schafer, Elizabeth, ed. *The Witch*. New Mermaids. New York: Norton, 1994.

Seligmann, Raphael. "Passionate Tunes for Amorous Poems: Middleton's Way with Music." In *The Oxford Handbook of Thomas Middleton*. Ed. Gary Taylor and Trish Thomas Henley. Oxford: Oxford University Press, 2012. 80–97.

Stern, Tiffany. *Documents of Performance in Early Modern England*. Cambridge: Cambridge University Press, 2009.

Taylor, Gary. "The Canon and Chronology of Shakespeare's Plays." In Stanley Wells et al., *William Shakespeare; A Textual Companion*. Oxford: Clarendon Press, 1987. 69–144.

Taylor, Gary, and John Lavagnino, gen. eds. *Thomas Middleton and Early Modern Textual Culture: A Companion to "The Collected Works."* Oxford: Oxford University Press, 2007.

Vickers, Brian. *Shakespeare, Co-Author: A Historical Study of Five Collaborative Plays*. Oxford: Oxford University Press, 2002.

Wilson, John Dover, ed. *Macbeth*. Cambridge: Cambridge University Press, 1947.

AFTERLIVES

WILLIAM DAVENANT

Macbeth (1674)†

[1.5]

Enter LADY MACBETH *and* LADY MACDUFF, *Lady Macbeth*
having a letter in her hand.

LADY MACBETH   Madam, I have observed since you came hither,
You have been still disconsolate. Pray tell me,
Are you in perfect health?

LADY MACDUFF   Alas, how can I?
My lord, when honor called him to the war,
Took with him half of my divided soul,
Which, lodging in his bosom, liked so well
The place that 'tis not yet returned.

LADY MACBETH   Methinks
That should not disorder you, for no doubt
The brave Macduff left half his soul behind him
To make up the defect¹ of yours.

LADY MACDUFF   Alas,
The part transplanted from his breast to mine,
As 'twere by sympathy, still bore a share
In all the hazards which the other half
Incurred, and filled my bosom up with fears.

LADY MACBETH   Those fears, methinks, should cease now he is safe.

LADY MACDUFF   Ah, madam, dangers which have long prevailed
Upon the fancy, even when they are dead,
Live in the memory awhile.

LADY MACBETH   Although his safety has not power enough to put
Your doubts to flight, yet the bright glories which
He gained in battle might dispel those clouds.

LADY MACDUFF   The world mistakes the glories gained in war,
Thinking their luster true. Alas, they are

---

† From William Davenant, *Macbeth, A Tragedy with All the Alterations, Amendments,*
Additions, and New Songs (London, 1674), sigs. B1v–B2, B3v–B4, D1–D2v, D4v–F1 [no
sig. E], F4–F4v, G1v–G2, G2v–G3, H2–H3v, K1. Footnotes are by the editor of this
Norton Critical Edition. Spelling and punctuation have also been modernized by the
editor. William Davenant (1606–1668), an accomplished poet, dramatist, and manager
of the Drury Lane Theatre, produced several adaptations of Shakespeare. His *Macbeth*
tinkered with phrasing, expanded spectacle, especially the witches' parts, developed
Lady Macduff into a foil for Lady Macbeth, omitted the Porter scene, and flattened the
tragedy into a tale of ambition.
1. deficiency. The conversation turns on the conception of marriage as a state in which
two souls become one.

But comets, vapors by some men exhaled
From others' blood,[2] and kindled in the region
Of popular applause, in which they live
Awhile then vanish; and the very breath
Which first inflamed them blows them out again.

LADY MACBETH [*Aside*] I willingly would read this letter but
Her presence hinders me; I must divert her.
—If you are ill, repose may do you good;
You'd best retire and try if you can sleep.

LADY MACDUFF My doubtful thoughts too long have kept me
waking,
Madam. I'll take your counsel.   *Exit* LADY MACDUFF.

[1.7]

Enter MACBETH.

MACBETH If it were well when done, then it were well
It were done quickly; if his death might be
Without the death of nature in myself,
And killing my own rest, it would suffice.
But deeds of this complexion[3] still return
To plague the doer and destroy his peace.
Yet, let me think: he's here in double trust.
First, as I am his kinsman and his subject,
Strong both against the deed; then, as his host,
Who should against his murderer shut the door,
Not bear the sword myself. Besides, this Duncan
Has born his faculties[4] so meek, and been
So clear in his great office that his virtues
Like angels plead against so black a deed.
Vaulting Ambition! Thou o'erleapst thyself
To fall upon another.

[2.5] *An heath.*

Enter LADY MACDUFF, MAID, *and* SERVANT.

LADY MACDUFF Art sure this is the place my lord appointed
Us to meet him?

SERVANT This is the entrance o'th'heath; and here

---

2. Glory is a brief flash like a comet or an insubstantial vapor drawn forth (**exhaled**) from bloodshed.
3. kind.
4. powers.

He ordered me to attend him with the chariot.
LADY MACDUFF   How fondly[5] did my lord conceive that we
  Should shun the place of danger by our flight
  From Inverness! The darkness of the day
  Makes the heath seem the gloomy walks of death.
  We are in danger still; they who dare here
  Trust Providence may trust it anywhere.
MAID   But this place, madam, is more free from terror.
  Last night methoughts I heard a dismal noise
  Of shrieks and groanings in the air.
LADY MACDUFF   'Tis true, this is a place of greater silence,
  Not so much troubled with the groans of those
  That die, nor with the outcries of the living.
MAID   Yes, I have heard stories how some men
  Have in such lonely places been affrighted
  With dreadful shapes and noises.   *Macduff* [*within*] *hollows.*[6]
LADY MACDUFF   But hark, my lord sure hollows!
  'Tis he; answer him quickly.
SERVANT [*Shouting*]   Illo, ho, ho, ho!

                  Enter MACDUFF.

LADY MACDUFF   Now I begin to see him. Are you afoot, My lord?
MACDUFF   Knowing the way to be both short and easy,
  And that the chariot did attend me here,
  I have adventured. Where are our children?
LADY MACDUFF   They are securely sleeping in the chariot.

         [*Enter* WITCHES.] *First Song by Witches.*

FIRST WITCH   Speak, sister, speak; is the deed done?
SECOND WITCH   Long ago, long ago—
  Above twelve glasses[7] since have run.
THIRD WITCH   Ill deeds are seldom slow
  Nor single. Following crimes on former wait.
  The worst of creatures fastest propagate.
  Many more murders must this one ensue,
  As if in death were propagation[8] too.
SECOND WITCH   He will—
FIRST WITCH   He shall—
THIRD WITCH   He must spill much more
  blood
  And become worse to make his title good.

5. foolishly.
6. cries out a greeting.
7. hourglasses.
8. birth and increase.

FIRST WITCH   Now let's dance.

SECOND WITCH   Agreed.

THIRD WITCH   Agreed.

FOURTH WITCH   Agreed.

CHORUS[9] [*Singing and dancing*]   We should rejoice when good
   kings bleed.
  When cattle die, about we go,
  What then, when monarchs perish, should we do?

MACDUFF   What can this be?

LADY MACDUFF   This is most strange, but why seem you afraid?
  Can you be capable of fears, who have
  So often caused it in your enemies?

MACDUFF   It was a hellish song. I cannot dread
  Aught that is mortal, but this is something more.

Second Song.

Let's have a dance upon the heath;
We gain more life by Duncan's death.
Sometimes like brinded[1] cats we show,
Having no music but our mew.
Sometimes we dance in some old mill,
Upon the hopper,[2] stones, and wheel,
To some old saw or bardish rhyme,
Where still the mill-clack[3] does keep time.
Sometimes about a hollow tree,
Around, around, around dance we.
Thither the chirping cricket comes,
And beetle, singing, drowsy hums.
Sometimes we dance o'er fens and furze,[4]
To howls of wolves and barks of curs.
And when with none of those we meet,
We dance to th'echoes of our feet.
At the night-raven's dismal voice,
Whilst others tremble, we rejoice;
And nimbly, nimbly dance we still
To th'echoes from an hollow hill.

MACDUFF   I am glad you are not afraid.

LADY MACDUFF   I would not willingly to fear submit;
  None can fear ill but those that merit it.

MACDUFF [*Aside*]   Am I made bold by her? How strong a guard

---

9. all the witches.
1. streaked or spotted.
2. container for feeding grain into the grinding machines.
3. instrument that strikes the hopper (a funnel-shaped receptacle) to pour out the grain.
4. marshes and spiny shrubs.

Is innocence!—If anyone would be
Reputed valiant, let him learn of you.
Virtue both courage is, and safety too.

A dance of witches. Enter two WITCHES.

MACDUFF   These seem foul spirits; I'll speak to 'em.
—If you can anything by more than nature know,
You may in those prodigious times foretell
Some ill we may avoid.
FIRST WITCH   Saving thy blood will cause it to be shed.
SECOND WITCH   He'll bleed by thee, by whom thou first hast bled.
THIRD WITCH   Thy wife shall, shunning danger, dangers find,
And fatal be to whom she most is kind.   *Exeunt Witches.*
LADY MACDUFF   Why are you altered, sir? Be not so thoughtful.
The messengers of darkness never spake
To men but to deceive them.
MACDUFF   Their words seem to foretell some dire predictions.
LADY MACDUFF   He that believes ill news from such as these,
Deserves to find it true. Their words are like
Their shape—nothing but fiction. Let's hasten to our journey.
MACDUFF   I'll take your counsel; for to permit
Such thoughts upon our memories to dwell,
Will make our minds the registers of hell.   *Exeunt all.*

[3.2]

Enter MACDUFF *and* LADY MACDUFF.

MACDUFF   It must be so. Great Duncan's bloody death
Can have no other author but Macbeth.
His dagger now is to a scepter grown;
From Duncan's grave he has derived his throne.
LADY MACDUFF   Ambition urged him to that bloody deed.
May you be never by ambition led.
Forbid it, heav'n, that in revenge you should
Follow a copy that is writ in blood.
MACDUFF   From Duncan's grave methinks I hear a groan
That calls aloud for justice.
LADY MACDUFF   If the throne
Was by Macbeth ill gained, heavens may
Without your sword sufficient vengeance pay.
Usurpers' lives have but a short extent;
Nothing lives long in a strange element.
MACDUFF   My country's dangers call for my defense
Against the bloody tyrant's violence.

LADY MACDUFF   I am afraid you have some other end,
    Than merely Scotland's freedom to defend.
    You'd raise yourself, whilst you would him dethrone,
    And shake his greatness to confirm your own.
    That purpose will appear, when rightly scanned,
    But usurpation at the second hand.
    Good sir, recall your thoughts.
MACDUFF   What if I should
    Assume the scepter for my country's good?
    Is that an usurpation? Can it be
    Ambition to procure the liberty
    Of this sad realm, which does by treason bleed?
    That which provokes will justify the deed.
LADY MACDUFF   If the design should prosper, the event
    May make us safe, but not you innocent;
    For whilst to set our fellow subjects free
    From present death or future slavery,
    You wear a crown not by your title due,
    Defense in them is an offense in you.
    That deed's unlawful though it cost no blood,
    In which you'll be at best unjustly good.
    You, by your pity which for us you plead,
    Weave but ambition of a finer thread.
MACDUFF   Ambition does the height of power affect,[5]
    My aim is not to govern but protect.
    And he is not ambitious that declares,
    He nothing seeks of scepters but their cares.
LADY MACDUFF   Can you so patiently yourself molest,
    And lose your own, to give your country rest?
    In plagues what sound physician would endure
    To be infected for another's cure?
MACDUFF   If by my troubles I could yours release,
    My love would turn those torments to my ease;
    I should at once be sick and healthy too,
    Though sickly in myself, yet well in you.
LADY MACDUFF   But, then, reflect upon the danger, sir,
    Which you by your aspiring would incur:
    From fortune's pinnacle you will too late
    Look down, when you are giddy with your height.
    Whilst you with fortune play to win a crown,
    The people's stakes are greater than your own.
MACDUFF   In hopes to have the common ills redressed,
    Who would not venture single interest?[6]

5. desire.
6. private gain or advantage.

[3.6]

Enter MACDUFF *and* LADY MACDUFF.

LADY MACDUFF   Are you resolved then to be gone?

MACDUFF   I am.
   I know my answer cannot but inflame
   The tyrant's fury to pronounce my death;
   My life will soon be blasted by his breath.

LADY MACDUFF   But why so far as England must you fly?

MACDUFF   The farthest part of Scotland is too nigh.

LADY MACDUFF   Can you leave me, your daughter, and young son,
   To perish by that tempest which you shun?
   When birds of stronger wing are fled away,
   The ravenous kite[7] does on the weaker prey.

MACDUFF   He will not injure you; he cannot be
   Possessed with such unmanly cruelty.
   You will your safety to your weakness owe,
   As grass escapes the scythe by being low.
   Together we shall be too slow to fly;
   Single, we may outride the enemy.
   I'll from the English King such succors[8] crave,
   As shall revenge the dead, and living save.
   My greatest misery is to remove,
   With all the wings of haste from what I love.

LADY MACDUFF   If to be gone seems misery to you,
   Good sir, let us be miserable too.

MACDUFF   Your sex, which here is your security,
   Will by the toils of flight your danger be.

Enter MESSENGER.

   What fatal news does bring thee out of breath?

MESSENGER   Sir, Banquo's killed.

MACDUFF   Then I am warned of death.
   Farewell. Our safety us awhile must sever.

LADY MACDUFF   Fly, fly, or we may bid farewell for ever.

MACDUFF   Flying from death, I am to life unkind,
   For leaving you, I leave my life behind.   *Exit.*

LADY MACDUFF   Oh, my dear lord, I find now thou art gone,
   I am more valiant when unsafe alone.
   My heart feels manhood; it does death despise,
   [*Weeps*] Yet I am still a woman in my eyes.
   And of my tears thy absence is the cause;
   So falls the dew when the bright sun withdraws.   *Exeunt.*

7. bird of prey.
8. supports.

[3.8]

[*Enter* HECATE *and three* WITCHES.] *Music and Song.*[9]

[SPIRITS *within*] Hecate, Hecate, Hecate, oh, come away!
[HECATE]   Hark, I am called. My little spirit, see,
    Sits in a foggy cloud and stays for me.
[SPIRITS *within*] Come away, Hecate, Hecate, oh, come away!

Machine descends [*carrying* SPIRITS.][1]

HECATE   I come, I come, with all the speed I may.
    With all the speed I may. Where's Stadling?
SECOND SPIRIT   Here.
HECATE   Where's Puckle?
THIRD SPIRIT   Here, and Hopper too, and Hellway too.
FIRST SPIRIT   We want[2] but you, we want but you!
    Come away, make up the count.
HECATE   I will but 'noint,[3] and then I mount;
    I will but 'noint, and then I mount.
FIRST SPIRIT   Here comes down one to fetch his due,
    A kiss, a coll,[4] a sip of blood;
    And why thou stayst so long I muse,[5]
    Since the air's so sweet and good.
[HECATE]   Oh, art thou come? What news?
SECOND SPIRIT   All goes fair for our delight.
    Either come, or else refuse.
[HECATE]   Now I'm furnished for the flight;
    Now I go, and now I fly,
    Malkin,[6] my sweet spirit, and I.
THIRD SPIRIT   Oh, what a dainty pleasure's this,
    To sail i'th'air while the moon shines fair,
    To sing, to toy, to dance, and kiss.
    Over woods, high rocks, and mountains,
    Over hills and misty fountains,

---

9. The song "Come away, come away" is sung off-stage in Shakespeare's play (3.5.35 S.D.), as is the song following, "Black spirits" (4.1.43 S.D.). Both songs occur in Thomas Middleton's play *The Witch* (1610–15, pub. 1778), and suggest that Middleton had a hand in revising *Macbeth*. William Davenant's versions of the songs may derive from the King's Men's performing text of *Macbeth*, to which he had acquired the rights, and so may present the verses as sung in Shakespeare's play.
1. A mechanical contrivance that is used to lower the spirits and other characters increases the spectacle of the scene. The ensuing lines identify Hecate's companions as spirits, who may or may not differ in production from the witches.
2. lack.
3. anoint (myself).
4. hug.
5. wonder.
6. a name for a familiar, i.e., attendant spirit, often in the shape of a cat.

Over steeples, towers, and turrets,
We fly by night 'mongst troops of spirits!
No ring of bells to our ears sounds,
No howls of wolves nor yelps of hounds,
No, nor the noise of water's breach,
Nor cannons' throats our height can reach.

                              [*Exeunt Hecate and the spirits.*]
FIRST WITCH   Come, let's make haste; she'll soon be back again.
SECOND WITCH   But whilst she moves through the foggy air,
Let's to the cave and our dire charms prepare.   [*Exeunt all.*]

[4.3]

Enter HECATE *and the other three* WITCHES [*to the three witches*].[7]

HECATE   Oh, well done; I commend your pains.
And everyone shall share the gains.
And now about the cauldron sing,
Like elves and fairies in a ring.

                              Music and song.

Black spirits and white,
Red spirits and gray,
Mingle, mingle, mingle,[8]
You that mingle may.
FIRST WITCH   Tiffin, Tiffin, keep it stiff in.
Firedrake[9] Pucky, make it lucky.
Liar Robin, you must bob in.
CHORUS   Around, around, about, about,
All ill come running in, all good keep out.
FIRST WITCH   Here's the blood of a bat!
HECATE   Oh, put in that, put in that!
SECOND WITCH   Here's lizard's brain!
HECATE   Put in a grain!
FIRST WITCH   Here's juice of toad, here's oil of adder,
That will make the charm grow madder.
SECOND WITCH   Put in all these; 'twill raise the stench.
HECATE   Nay, here's three ounces of a red-haired wench.
CHORUS   Around, around, about, about,
All ill come running in, all good keep out.

7. i.e., to those already onstage.
8. mix together (also, have sexual intercourse).
9. a mythological dragon.

SECOND WITCH   I, by the pricking of my thumbs,
   Know something wicked this way comes.
   Open locks, whoever knocks.

Enter MACBETH.

[4.4]

Enter MACBETH *and* SEYTON.

MACBETH   Seyton, go bid the army march.
SEYTON   The posture of affairs requires your presence.
MACBETH   But the indisposition of my wife
   Detains me here.
SEYTON   Th'enemy is upon our borders; Scotland's in danger.
MACBETH   So is my wife, and I am doubly so.
   I am sick in her and in my kingdom too.
   Seyton!
SEYTON   Sir?
MACBETH   The spur of my ambition prompts me to go
   And make my kingdom safe, but love, which softens
   Me to pity her in her distress, curbs my resolves.
SEYTON [*Aside*]   He's strangely disorder'd.
MACBETH   Yet why should love, since confined, desire
   To control ambition, for whose spreading hopes
   The world's too narrow. It shall not; great fires
   Put out the less. Seyton, go bid my grooms
   Make ready; I'll not delay my going.
SEYTON   I go.
MACBETH   Stay, Seyton, stay; compassion calls me back.
SEYTON [*Aside*]   He looks and moves disorderly.
MACBETH   I'll not go yet.
SEYTON   Well, sir.

Enter a SERVANT, *who whispers* [*to*] *Macbeth.*

MACBETH [*To the Servant*]   Is the Queen asleep?
SEYTON [*Aside*]   What makes 'em whisper and his countenance
      change?
   Perhaps some new design has had ill success.
MACBETH   Seyton, go see what posture our affairs are in.
SEYTON   I shall, and give you notice, sir.   *Exit Seyton.*

Enter LADY MACBETH.

MACBETH   How does my gentle love?
LADY MACBETH   Duncan is dead.

MACBETH   No words of that.
LADY MACBETH   And yet to me he lives.
  His fatal ghost is now my shadow, and pursues me
  Where e'er I go.
MACBETH   It cannot be, my dear;
  Your fears have misinformed your eyes.

                          [*Enter* DUNCAN'S GHOST.]

LADY MACBETH   See there! Believe your own!
  [*To the Ghost*] Why do you follow me? I did not do it.
MACBETH   Methinks there's nothing.
LADY MACBETH   If you have valor, force him hence!
                               [*Exit Ghost.*]

  Hold, hold, he's gone. Now you look strangely.
MACBETH   'Tis the strange error of your eyes.
LADY MACBETH   But the strange error of my eyes
  Proceeds from the strange action of your hands.
  Distraction does by fits possess my head
  Because a crown unjustly covers it.
  I stand so high that I am giddy grown.
  A mist does cover me, as clouds the tops
  Of hills. Let us get down apace.
MACBETH   If by your high ascent you giddy grow,
  'Tis when you cast your eyes on things below.
LADY MACBETH   You may in peace resign the ill-gained crown.
  Why should you labor still to be unjust?
  There has been too much blood already spilt.
  Make not the subjects victims to your guilt.
MACBETH   Can you think that a crime, which you did once
  Provoke me to commit? Had not your breath
  Blown my ambition up into a flame,
  Duncan had yet been living.
LADY MACBETH   You were a man.
  And by the charter of your sex you should
  Have governed me; there was more crime in you
  When you obeyed my counsels than I contracted
  By my giving it. Resign your kingdom now,
  And with your crown put off your guilt.
MACBETH   Resign the crown, and with it both our lives.
  I must have better counselors.
LADY MACBETH   What, your witches?
  Curse on your messengers of hell! Their breath
  Infected first my breast. See me no more.
  As king your crown sits heavy on your head,
  But heavier on my heart. I have had too much

Of kings already.

                                    [DUNCAN'S] GHOST *appears.*

                    See, the ghost again!
MACBETH   Now she relapses.
LADY MACBETH [*To Macbeth*]   Speak to him if thou canst.
  [*To the Ghost*] Thou lookst on me, and showst thy wounded
    breast.
  Show it the murderer!   [*Exit Ghost.*]
MACBETH [*Calling*]   Within there, ho!

                                        Enter WOMEN.

LADY MACBETH   Am I ta'en prisoner? Then the battle's lost.

                        Exit Lady Macbeth, led out by women.

MACBETH   She does from Duncan's death to sickness grieve,
  And shall from Malcolm's death her health receive.
  When by a viper bitten, nothing's good
  To cure the venom but a viper's blood.

                        [5.8]

MACBETH   I scorn to yield! I will in spite of enchantment
  Fight with thee, though Birnam Wood be come to Dunsinane,
  And thou art of no woman born; I'll try
  If by a man it be thy fate to die.

                They fight. Macbeth falls. They shout within.

MACDUFF   This for my royal master, Duncan,
  This for my dearest friend, my wife,
  This for those pledges of our loves, my children.
                                        (*Shout within.*)
  Hark, I hear a noise. Sure, there are more
  Reserves to conquer. I'll as a trophy bear
  Away his sword to witness my revenge.
                        Exit Macduff [*with Macbeth's sword.*]
MACBETH   Farewell vain world, and what's most vain in it,
  ambition. *Dies.*

MACBETH TRAVESTIES (1820–66)[†]

[1.1, By Francis Talfourd, 1850]

A blasted heath, rain, thunder, and lightning.

Enter MACBETH *and* BANQUO, *under an umbrella.* (*L.*)

The three WITCHES *discovered crouching, one smoking a short pipe.* (*R.*)

BANQUO   So foul and fair a day I never saw.
MACBETH   No! You don't say so—well, I never—Lor'.
BANQUO   I think so, really. Macbeth, my fine feller,
  Confess 'twas well I brought the umberella.
MACBETH   You'll just allow me to observe, my pippin,[1]
  You get its shelter, and give me the dripping.
  But who (*Seeing witches*) are these abominable hags?
  Why, Banquo, did you ever see such scrags?[2]
  What ugly brutes! How rough and wild in dress!
  —Who and what are ye? Answer.
WITCHES   Can't you guess?
MACBETH   You should be women, but I never heard
  Of women wearing whiskers, and a beard!
  Speak, if you can, and if you can't, why don't;
  Come, speak out plainly—won't you—oh, you won't?
                                    (*Menaces them.*)
FIRST WITCH   Hail! Thane of Glamis!
SECOND WITCH   Thane of Cawdor, hail!
THIRD WITCH   Macbeth, by perseverance, shall not fail
  To be the king of Scotland
ALL   Hail! Hail! Hail!
MACBETH   What mean these salutations, noble Thane?
BANQUO   These showers of "hail!" prognosticate your "reign"!
MACBETH (*To Witches*)   Young women, do you see aught in my eye,

---

† From Rush Moore, *Macbeth Travestie, in Three Acts* (Calcutta, 1820); W. K. Northall, *Macbeth Travestie* (New York, 1847); Francis Talfourd, *Macbeth Travestie: A Burlesque* (Oxford, 1850; 3rd ed.); and *Macbeth, A Burlesque* (Nottingham, 1866). Poking irreverent fun, the travesties ridicule perceived excesses, puncture pretensions, and, in Francis Talfourd's rewriting, cheerfully reverse the irreversible forces of evil and doom. The Norton editor has excerpted scenes from these four plays to provide a parodic version of *Macbeth*. Act and scene numbers in brackets refer to Shakespeare's play; the abbreviations *L.* and *R.* indicate stage left and right, respectively. Footnotes are by the editor of this Norton Critical Edition. Spelling and punctuation have also been modernized by the editor.
1. fine fellow (slang).
2. lean, wretched people.

That smacks at all of verdure, that you try
To gammon me?[3] I'm far too old a bird
Thus to be caught with chaff—it's too absurd.
In what the first fair creature says no harm is,
By Sinel's death I know I'm Thane of Glamis.
But this fact is in my digestion sticking:
The Thane of Cawdor is alive—and kicking—
A jolly sort of cove[4]—and to be a king!
Oh, gemini, who'd dream of such a thing?
No more than to be Cawdor (*Aside*)—yet, good gracious,
To be a king would really be splendacious!

BANQUO (*To Witches*)   Really, young ladies, you are rather going it,
For my lot I don't care much for the knowing it;
But since you are in a prophesying vein,
Just tell us what you think of me. Again,
I say, with nonsense don't attempt to cram one,
And, as you'd save your bacon, spare your gammon.[5]

WITCHES   Thou shalt get kings, though thou thyself be none!

BANQUO   Oh, stuff and nonsense!

MACBETH   I am diddled—done!
Don't go, young women, till you've said from whence
You owe this very strange intelligence:
D'ye think that we don't know the time o' day,
That on this blasted heath you stop our way?
Stay—none of that. If you don't quickly speak,
I'll send you on a visit to next week.   (*Witches vanish. R.*)
They've vanished!

BANQUO   I am sorry this you troubles;
The earth, sir, like the water, has its bubbles.

[1.7, By W. K. Northall, 1847]

Enter MACBETH, *thoughtfully R.*

MACBETH   If it were done when 'tis done, there's no doubt
'Twere quite as well 'twere quickly set about.
If the same knife which cuts poor Duncan's life supporters
Could only cut the throats of common news reporters,
And thus make dumb the press—it's pretty clear
This cut would be the be-all and the end-all here.

---

3. Do you see anything green (from inexperience) in my eye that you try to trick (**gam-mon**) me?
4. fellow.
5. And as you'd save yourselves, spare us your tricks.

But this even-handed justice is a sorry jade,[1]
And may commend to my own throat the self-same blade.
He's here in double trust, but then he's had long credit,
And yet I'm called upon to write more debit.
But still I am his kinsman, and his subject too;
In either case, the bloody work is hard to do.
I think I'll hire a man to do the deed:
I shouldn't murder when I ought to feed.
And who can bear to be the common scoff,
For "the deep damnation of his taking off"?
I have no spur to prick me on—full well I know it—
So, vaulting ambition, I say, prithee, go it!
Don't overleap yourself, and then come tumbling down
With dislocated neck or broken crown.

Enter LADY MACBETH, *R.*

How now, Mrs. M., did he eat those oysters that you stewed?
LADY MACBETH   He supped on nothing else—your leaving us was
    rude.
MACBETH   I will not do this deed; he has honoured me of late,
    And bought me golden pippins,[2] which I ate.   *(Walks L.)*
LADY MACBETH   Coward! You much desire to be a king,
    But tremble at the means which do the thing.
MACBETH   I dare do all that becomes a man, so do not vex me,
    If more you want, why, damn it, ma'am, unsex me.

[1.7 *continued,* By Francis Talfourd, 1850]

LADY MACBETH   The old boy's abed, and now's your time to do it.
MACBETH   I'm out of sorts—I feel a kind of dizziness,
    And won't proceed no farther in this business.
LADY MACBETH   Pooh! you're a spoon.[3]
MACBETH   To tell the truth, I'm loath
    To stop the old man's wizen.[4]
LADY MACBETH   But your oath!
    You're bold enough when there's no danger nigh—
    When once it comes then you're for "fighting shy."
MACBETH   I dare do all that may a man become.

1. horse.
2. apples.
3. fool.
4. throat.

LADY MACBETH   To an oath once made you should stick fast—by
   Gum!
  If 'tis not from cowardice you keep aloof,
  Strike off the prince, and let me have a proof.
MACBETH   Suppose the king disposed of—yet, my dear,
  It seems my next course isn't over clear—
  Malcolm, my cousin, nine times removed, or so!
  I'm in a fix—I fear it is no go.
LADY MACBETH   Nine times removed already! Then it's plain
  It can't hurt to remove him once again!
  Macbeth, pluck up a little courage, do, man!
MACBETH   Who would believe you were a female woman?
  We shall be sorry for it!
LADY MACBETH   For a warrior
  I may say that I never saw a sorrier!
  Say, who hast sought in battle undismayed
  The hot affray,[5] of what thou art afraid!
MACBETH   Egad—I'll do it!
LADY MACBETH   Why do you turn so pale?
MACBETH   An awkward thought's just struck me—should we fail!
LADY MACBETH   Fail! Stuff and nonsense—Fail! Your courage
  screw
  But to the sticking-place, and we shall do.
  Come, "if you['d] die a pantile, be a brick!"[6]
MACBETH   The sticking-place is exactly where I stick!
LADY MACBETH   Duncan's attendants are so full of beer,
  They'll be quite muddled, that is very clear;
  When they're asleep, bedaub their faces o'er—
MACBETH   With blood? I understand. O my! O Lor!
  Is this a clasp-knife,[7] such as plough-boys use
  For cutting bread-and-cheese? You'll me excuse,
  —Perhaps you are but a clasp-knife of the brain.

                           (*Snatches at it.*)

  Egad, I missed it—there it is again!
  And o[n]'ts blade gouts[8] of—No—the maker's name,
  Which was not there before—it's all a sham!   (*Bell rings.*)
LADY MACBETH   Of course it is! Now go, d'ye hear the bell?
MACBETH   Hear it not, Duncan, for it is a knell

---

5. fray.
6. If you want to amount to something, be strong now. A **pantile** is a roofing tile; **brick**
  refers literally to the construction element of clay and figuratively to strength.
7. a knife that folds its blade into the handle.
8. on its blade drops.

That tolls you into heaven, or to—never mind,
Which of the two it is, you'll too soon find.   (*Exit R.*)

> *Lady Macbeth sings. Air "Lucy Neal."*

Softly slip your shoes off,
Soft to the chamber steal;
When Duncan finds you by his side,
How happy he will feel.

Oh, poor King Duncan!
When he finds the steel
In his bread-basket,[9] I should guess,
Will wriggle a great deal!

But soft, he is about it,
I thought I heard a squeal;
When Duncan has it in his side,
How happy he will feel.

> *Re-enter* MACBETH, *with daggers.*

LADY MACBETH   Is't done, my husband? What's the matter now?
MACBETH   I've done the deed; didn't you hear the row?[1]
   I stumbled (where I hadn't seen them standing)
   Over the old boy's bluchers[2] on the landing;
   You heard it?
LADY MACBETH   No one else did.
MACBETH   That's all right,
   But just look here—this is a sorry sight.
                                 (*Looking at his hands*)
LADY MACBETH   Pshaw! Stuff!
MACBETH   One sung out in his sleep—how soon,
   I fear he'll sing to quite another tune!
   They were both beery—one declared outright
   He'd no intention to go home that night.
   The other in no high state of sobriety,
   Heedless of manners, sung out—*"Tulla-li-ety"*;
   I couldn't echo it—What was amiss?

9. stomach.
1. commotion.
2. boots.

LADY MACBETH   Oh! nonsense, now, you mustn't think of this.

MACBETH   How much more need of joyousness had I, yet he
Sung, and I couldn't echo *"Tulla-li-ety."*

LADY MACBETH   Why did you bring those daggers from their
places?
Go, take them back, and smear the sleepers' faces
With blood.

MACBETH (*Doggedly*)   No, come you know, I've done one murder;
That's quite enough, and I sha'nt go no furder.

LADY MACBETH   Don't leave the job unfinished, come now, don't;
Go!

MACBETH   If I do I'm—, never mind, I won't!

LADY MACBETH   Be mine the task, since you the courage lack;
Give me the daggers, I shall soon be back.   (*Exit R.*)

MACBETH (*Alone*)   Were all the waters of the Serpentine,
With those of the New River to combine—
Were e'en the potent Thames to lend its aid,
And Regent Park's canal, I am afraid,
Failing to wash from off my hands this gore,
They'd make red what mud-coloured was before.

                    Re-enter LADY MACBETH.

LADY MACBETH   My hands are like yours, p'raps a little redder.
                              (*Loud knocking*)
I thought I heard a knock; we'd best to bed.

MACBETH   Ah!
And not to lose the public's good opinion—

LADY MACBETH   We'll red our eyebrows with a Spanish onion!
                              (*Knocking repeated*)

            Air—*"Who's dat knocking at the door?"*

MACBETH   Who's that knocking at the door?   (*Knock*)

LADY MACBETH   Who's that knocking at the door?   (*Knock*)

MACBETH   I don't care a pin,
He sha'nt come in.

LADY MACBETH   Our hands are not clean,
So he can't come in!

BOTH   Whoever is a-knocking at the door, at the door?
Whoever is a-knocking at the door?   (*Loud knocking*)

[1.7 *continued,* From *Macbeth,*
A Burlesque, 1866][1]

Macbeth and Lady M. perform "Duncan Gray," Lady Macbeth singing and beating time.

DUNCAN, *dressed in night-gown and night-cap, puts his head in at the door.*

Music continues for some time after he has begun to speak.

DUNCAN   Oh, murder! Oh, stop there! Oh, stop, I say. I command you to stop that excruciating duet! 'Tis passing horrible. I can't sleep, upon my soul, I can't. Macbeth doth murder sleep. My noble hosts, you forget the supper and the repose needed after such a feast. I haven't had a wink, and the sun is already beginning to shine in the east. Your pie, fair hostess, I mean the blackbird pie, was so uncommonly good, that I thought I'd *like* to eat it, and I thought I *could* eat it, and I thought I *would.* So the whole four-and-twenty blackbirds disappeared one after the other down the red lane, not omitting the crust; and I feel just now, craving your pardon, as the American showman would say, "kinder like to bust." Besides, the worst remains to be told. When you your music begin, all the four-and-twenty birds flutter about and begin to sing; isn't that a pretty comfortable state of things for the home affairs of a constitutional king?[2] Here take this crown for your music (*flings to him a crownpiece*), and once more, good night.   (*Retires.*)

[4.1, By Rush Moore, 1820]

A dark cave. In the middle a cauldron boiling.

Enter HECATE *and three* WITCHES.

HECATE   By the itching of my noddle,[1]
Some great rogue does this way toddle.

Enter MACBETH.

The thumb of my left hand too itches.

---

1. In this burlesque Duncan eats a pie with twenty-four blackbirds baked in it, according to the nursery rhyme; they wake inside him and escape, causing his death.
2. "Isn't that a dainty dish to set before the king?" says the nursery rhyme.
1. head.

MACBETH   How now, ye sacred midnight bitches!
   What's the rig,[2] I'm going to task[3] you,
   And beg you'll answer what I ask you.
   Though you untie the winds and let,
   Eunuchs twins of maidens get,[4]
   Who shall upon the throne be set,
   Though St. Paul's steeple should be bent,
   Until it meet the monument,
   Or though a mare at Drury Lane,
   Should tread the boards as Crazy Jane?[5]
HECATE   Speak, we'll answer all your queries.
FIRST WITCH   With us there sure no cause for fear is.
HECATE   Will you from us instruction gather,
   Or from our masters had you rather?

*   *   *

Thunder. The APPARITION of an armed head rises.

Song: Tune: "Moll in the Wad."

APPARITION   Macbeth, Macbeth, be up to snuff.
   Beware of that thundering rogue, Macduff.
   For well I know the Thane of Fife,
   Has whetted for you a shear[6] steel knife.
MACBETH   The which I suppose he does intend,
   Unto my ribs to recommend:
   But he shall lose his aim for once,
   And find his friend Macbeth no dunce.   *Apparition vanishes.*

Thunder. An APPARITION of a bloody child rises.

APPARITION   Macbeth!
MACBETH   Go on, I'll hear thee through't.
APPARITION   Be bloody, bold, and resolute,
   Laugh the power of man to scorn,
   Fear none that are of woman born.
MACBETH   Tip us your daddle,[7] old two shoes,
   I thank ye kindly for your news.

---

2. swindle.
3. test.
4. eunuchs beget twins from maidens.
5. Macbeth imagines St. Paul's steeple bending over and then another impossible eventuality, a horse playing the role of Crazy Jane, a mad woman, at Drury Lane Theatre.
6. strengthened.
7. shake our hands.

I'd grind[8] my sword, my shield I'll brighten,
You've put me in a mood for fighting!   *Apparition descends.*

Thunder. An APPARITION *of a child crowned rises.*

APPARITION   None shall vanquish thee, bold Thane,
  Till Birnam Wood to Dunsinane,
  Shall its respects, obsequious pay,
  And 'fore its walls, its branches lay.
MACBETH   My thanks that you'll accept, I beg;
  I'm now all right as my left leg.
  Yet much I wish to know one thing.
  Shall Banquo's line produce a king?   *Apparition descends.*
  Deny me this and by Saint Paul,
  I'll kick you soundly one and all.
FIRST WITCH   Show.
SECOND WITCH   Show.
ALL   Show his eyes,
  Sights that would Old Nick[9] surprise.

Eight KINGS *pass over the stage,* BANQUO *following.*

MACBETH   Down, Banquo, to thy hell go down,
  What the deuce brought you to town?
  The sight of thee doth make me blind;
  I, therefore, hope you'll be so kind,
  As to be off, sans hesitation,
  And with you take this generation
  Of unsubstantial looking things,
  Who are rigged out[1] in the garb of kings,
  And which that horrid smile of thine,
  Doth seem to say shall reign ere mine.
HECATE   Now that your wishes are fulfilled,
  You seem as though you had been drilled,
  By something which has made a hole,
  Through your pure, majestic soul.
  But we must all now elsewhere fly.
  Farewell, Macbeth, Mac'mind your eye.
                        Hecate and witches vanish.
MACBETH   Where the devil are they gone?
  I wonder what they ride upon.
  This day of all my life the worst,
  Shall stand i'th' calendar accurst.

---

8. sharpen.
9. name for the devil.
1. dressed up.

[*He orders offstage.*] Without there, ho! Pray, walk within,
And with thee some kind cordial bring.

     Enter ROSS, *holding a glass of gin, which Macbeth drinks.*

MACBETH   Oh, the virtue that lays in
A simple glass of English gin!
It gives one's vitals such relief,
As really is beyond belief.
But, Ross, what I should first have asked you,
Is which way those damned witches passed you?

[5.5, By W. K. Northall, 1847]

MACBETH   Wherefore was that cry?
SEYTON   The Queen, my lord, is dead, and I—
MACBETH   She should have died hereafter, but she'll keep;
And perhaps tomorrow I shall have time to weep.
Tomorrow—and tomorrow—and tomorrow—
Ay, that's well thought of—I've a note to pay,
And the last recorded dollar to me lent,
Was yesterday in whiskey-punches[1] spent!
Out, out, short candle! For burn brightly as you may,
You cannot burn much longer anyway.
Life's but a walking shadow—or a poor player at most—
Who murders Hamlet once, and then is cast the ghost.

     Enter OFFICER, *with bill, R.*

MACBETH   How now, thy message? Let not thy tongue stand still.
OFFICER   As I stood looking at my watch upon the hill,
A cartman bade me give you this little bill,
For a load that he brought you of Birnam's wood.
MACBETH   Liar! Slave!
OFFICER [*Kneels.*]   I could not have misunderstood;
And if it be not so, why, take my head and thump it—
I'll swear I saw him at your door but just now dump it.
MACBETH   If that thou liest and deceivest me,
I'll have thee hung alive upon a tree,
A thing for rooks and daws[2] to pick at,
And men and women to turn sick at.   *Exit Officer. R.*

---

1. mixed drinks containing whiskey.
2. large and small crows.

[5.8, By Francis Talfourd, 1850]

MACDUFF   Then yield, beast, and to badger ye
 We'll have you in a traveling menagerie,
 Stirred up between the bars with heartless poles,
 Or poked at by the ladies' parasols!
 And o'er it thus inscribe, for want of betterer,
 "Here may you see the live"—you know—*et cetera,*
 Adding moreover, "He's put here because
 He led a life he *didn't ought to was!*"
MACBETH   Have you been draining cups of whiskey toddy,
 That thus you boast? No, no, before my body
 I throw my shield!
MACDUFF   Hallo! That's not a bad one!
MACBETH   I mean I should have thrown it, if I had one,
 At it like one o'clock.[1] Lay on, Macduff,
 Perhaps you'll sing out when you've had enough.

> *They fight in the extreme of melodrama; a pause.*

MACDUFF   Why, you're sewn up. (*To audience*) I'll into him now
 pitch.
MACBETH   No, not sewn up, I've only got one stitch.

> *They fight as before. Macbeth falls.*

MACBETH   Oh, lor! Will someone a physician run for?
 For I've a strange suspicion that I'm done for!   (*Dies.*)
MACDUFF   Ha! Ha! My boy, hurrah! His neck I'll wring,
 Cut off his head, then cut off to the king.

> *Enter* MALCOLM, LORDS, ARMY, ATTENDANTS, *etc.*

MALCOLM   There is no need for, see, the King is here!
 —Refresh our soldier with a pint of beer.

> *A pint of beer is brought to Macduff; he drinks and
> passes it on to the army, etc.*

MACDUFF   The tyrant's dead! You now the kingdom claim;
 Receive the crown.   (*Presenting it*)

> DUNCAN *enters, comes between them, nods and winks at
> them, takes the crown and places it on his own head.
> They fall back in astonishment.*

DUNCAN   Thank you! If it's all the same

1. vigorously.

To you, I'll wear it!   (*Puts it on.*)
MALCOLM   Well, this is a balker![2]
I thought you were spifflicated.[3]
DUNCAN   Walker![4]
I'm not the cove,[5] my boy, so soon to die.
MACDUFF   Well, well, I never!
MACBETH (*Rising to a sitting posture, and looking round.*)
                        No more did I!
If that old cock can jest and sport his squibs[6]
After those several one-ers in the ribs,
I don't see why I shouldn't live as well,
And so here goes. (*Rises.*)
MACDUFF   I say, hallo, my swell![7]
You're an ex-Monarch, but it don't appear;
If treble-ex you'd think yourself small beer![8]
MACBETH (*To Duncan*)   I tender, sir, of course, my resignation,
                              (*They appear satisfied.*)
Since all's in train[9] for me to leave my station.
So at your feet I lay my regal diadem
Without regret, nor wish again that I had 'em.

            Enter at back BANQUO *and* LADY MACBETH, *arm-in-arm,*
            the latter with an extravagant bonnet, parasol, and shawl.
                They make their way through the army to the front.

My wife and Banquo too! This is a treat.
BANQUO   You don't down there get half enough to eat;
I didn't like it; and so, with your wife,
Gave up the ghost.
MACBETH   Died?
LADY MACBETH   No, we came to life.
MACBETH   We live at present, but how long depends
Upon the kind indulgence of our friends;
Let me entreat them but their favour give,
And kind applause, and we shall truly live!

---

2. stopper, disappointment.
3. utterly destroyed.
4. no way!
5. chap.
6. show off his sarcasms and satires.
7. fine fellow.
8. Three x's, apparently, marked a current brand of beer; **small beer**: i.e., insignificant.
9. ready, with puns on **train** and **station**.

GIUSEPPI VERDI

Macbeth (1865)†

[Piave's Libretto][1]

Macbeth
Ma le spirtali donne
Banco padre di regi han
    profetato—
Dunque I suoi figli regneran?
    Duncano
Per costor sarà spento?
Lady Macbeth[2]
Egli, e suo figlio vivono, è ver—
Macbeth
Ma vita immortale non hanno—

Lady Macbeth
Ah, sì, non l'hanno!
Macbeth
Forz'è che scorra un altro
    sangue,
            o donna!
Lady Macbeth
Dove? Quando?
Macbeth
Al venir di questa notte.
Lady Macbeth
Immoto sarai tu nel tuo
    disdegno?

Macbeth
But the weird women
Greeted Banquo as father of
    kings—
Then will his sons reign?
    Duncan
For them has been killed?
Lady Macbeth
He and his son live, it is true—
Macbeth
But they do not have immortal
    life—

Lady Macbeth
Ah, yes, they do not have that!
Macbeth
Perhaps, there will flow more
    blood,
            o wife!
Lady Macbeth
Where? When?
Macbeth
This very night.
Lady Macbeth
Will you be constant in your
    purpose?

---

† Giuseppe Verdi (1813–1901) wrote a four-act opera of *Macbeth* (performed Florence, 1847, and revised, Paris, 1865), which, unlike previous Shakespearean operas, seriously attempted to translate the poetic drama into music. As Verdi wrote to Marianna Barbieri-Nini (his Lady Macbeth) on January 2, 1847: "The plot is taken from one of the greatest tragedies the theatre boasts, and I have tried to have all the dramatic situations drawn from it faithfully, to have it well versified, and to give it a new texture, and to compose music tied so far as possible to the text and to the situations. . . . I wish the performers to serve the poet better than they serve the composer," *Verdi's Macbeth: A Sourcebook*, ed. David Rosen and Andrew Porter (New York: Norton, 1984), 29. Verdi expanded the roles of the witches and Lady Macbeth, reduced Duncan to a mute part, and added a chorus of Scottish refugees, men, women, and children. The opera is readily available in CD versions.
1. Francesco Maria Piave wrote the libretto for *Macbeth*. I quote the Italian text from the revised Paris version 1865, rpt. (New York: Kalmus, n.d.), 108ff., 234ff. (Translation mine.)
2. In contradistinction to Shakespeare's play, Lady Macbeth here takes an active role in plotting the death of Banquo and his son.

Macbeth
Banco! L'eternità t'apre il suo
    regno!

(*Parte*)

Lady Macbeth
La luce langue, il faro spegnesi

Ch'eterno scorre per gl'ampi
    cieli!
Notte desiata provvida veli
La man colpevole che ferirà.

Nuovo delitto! È necessario!
Compiersi debbe l'opra fatale.

Ai trapassati regnar non
    cale;
A loro un requiem, l'eternità.
O voluttà del soglio!
O scettro, alfin sei mio!
Ogni mortal desio
Tace e s'acqueta in te.

Cadrà fra poco esamine
Chi fu predetto re.

* * *

Macbeth
Ancora le streghe interrogai.

Lady Macbeth[2]
E disser?
Macbeth
"Da Macduff ti guarda."
Lady Macbeth
Segui.
Macbeth
"Te non ucciderà nato di
    donna."
Lady Macbeth
Segui.
Macbeth
"Invitto sarai finchè la selva

Di Birna contro te non mova."

Macbeth
Banquo, eternity opens for you
    its reign!

(*Leaves*)

Lady Macbeth
Light dims, the eternal light
    goes out
That courses through the wide
    heavens!
Desired night providently hides
The guilty hand that strikes the
    blow.
A new crime. It is necessary!
The fatal work must be
    completed.
The dead do not care to reign;

For them a rest—eternity.
O joy of the throne!
O scepter, finally you are mine!
Every mortal desire
Becomes silent and rests in
    thee.
Soon he will fall lifeless,
Who was predicted to be the king.

* * *

Macbeth
I have questioned the witches
    again.
Lady Macbeth
And what did they say?
Macbeth
"Beware Macduff."
Lady Macbeth
Go on.
Macbeth
"None of woman born shall kill
    you."
Lady Macbeth
Go on.
Macbeth
"You will be invincible until
    Birnam
Wood moves against you."

Lady Macbeth
Segui.

Macbeth
Ma pur di Banco apparevemi
    la stripe—
E regernà!

Lady Macbeth
Menzogna!
Morte e sterminio sull'iniqua
    razza!

Macbeth
Si, morte! Di Macduffo arda la
    rocca!
Perano moglie e prole!

Lady Macbeth
Di Banco il figlio si rinvenga, e
    muoia!

Macbeth
Tutto il sangue si sperda a noi
    nemico!

Lady Macbeth
Or riconosco il tuo coraggio
    antico.

Macbeth and Lady Macbeth
Ora di morte e di vendetta,
Tuona, rimbomba per l'orbe
    intero,
Come assordante l'atro
    pensiero
Del cor le fibre tutte intronò.
Ora de morte, ormai t'affreta!

Incancellabile il fato ha scritto:

L'impresa compier deve il
    delitto
Poichè col sangue s'inaugurò.
                          [*Exeunt.*]
*Luogo deserto ai confini della
    Scozia e dell'Inghilterra.*
Coro (*profughi scozzesi*)[3]

Lady Macbeth
Go on.

Macbeth
And yet Banquo's issue
    appeared—
And will reign!

Lady Macbeth
A lie!
Death and extinction to that
    wicked race!

Macbeth
Yes, death! Macduff's castle
    will burn!
His wife and children will die!

Lady Macbeth
Banquo's son will be found and
    killed!

Macbeth
Let all blood hostile to us be
    spilled!

Lady Macbeth
Now I recognize your former
    courage.

Macbeth and Lady Macbeth
Hour of death and vengeance,
Thunder, resound through all
    the world,
Like the deafening dark
    thought
Thunders in the heart's core.
Hour of death, come swiftly
    now!

Fate has written an indelible
    script.

The enterprise must end in
    crime,
Because it began in blood.
                          [*Exeunt*]
*A deserted place on the borders
    of Scotland and England.*
Chorus (*Scottish refugees*)

---

3. The solemn Chorus comprises men, women, and children near Birnam Wood. On
December 10, 1846, Verdi wrote to Piave, "In this chorus I'd like (as Shakespeare did
in a dialogue between Ross and Macduff) a genre scene, a sublime, affecting picture of
Scotland's misery," *Verdi's Macbeth*, 21.

Patria oppressa! Il dolce nome

No, di madre aver non puoi,

Or che tutta a' figli tuoi
Sei conversa in un avel!
D'orfanelli e di piangenti

Chi lo sposo e chi la prole

Al venir del nuovo sole
S'alza un grido e fere il ciel.
A quell grido il ciel risponde
Quasi voglia impietosito
Propagar per l'infinito,
Patria oppressa, il tuo dolor!

Suona a morto ognor la squilla,

Ma nessuno audace è tanto
Che pur doni un vano pianto
A chi soffre ed a chi muor.

Macduff (*scena ed aria*)
O figlie, o figli miei! Da quel
    tiranno
Tutti uccisi voi foste, e insiem
    con voi
La madre sventurata! Ah, fra
    gli artigli
Di quel tigre io lasciai

La madre e i figli?
Ah, la paterna mano
Non vi fu scudo, o cari,
Dai perfii sicari
Che a morte vi ferir!
E me fuggiasco, occulto,
Voi chiamavate in vano,
Coll'ultimo singulto,
Coll'ultimo respir.
Trammi al tiranno in faccia,

Signore, e s'ei mi sfugge,
Possa a colui le braccia,

Oppressed country! The sweet
    name,
Of mother, no, you cannot
    have,
Now that for all your children
You have become a tomb.
From orphans and those
    grieving,
This one a spouse and that one
    a child,
At each new break of day,
Arises a cry that strikes heaven.
To that cry heaven responds,
As if, moved to pity, it would
Multiply infinitely,
Oppressed country, your
    sorrows.
The bell tolls at death
    evermore.
But no one is bold enough
To shed a vain tear
For the one who suffers and
    who dies.

Macduff (scene with aria)
Oh, my children, my children!
    By that
Tyrant you have all been killed,
    together
With your ill-fated mother. Ah,
    to the
Claws of that tiger did I
    abandon the
Mother and children?
Alas, a father's hand
Did not shield you, dear ones,
From the wicked killers
Who struck you to death!
And me, a fugitive, hiding,
You called to in vain,
With your last gasp,
With your last breath.
Bring me to the face of the
    tyrant,
Lord, and if he escape me then,
You can open for him your arms

Del tuo perdon aprir.	In pardon.
(*Al suono del tamburo entra Malcolm, conducendo molti soldati inglesi.*)	(*At the sound of a drum, Malcolm enters, leading many English soldiers.*)
Malcolm	**Malcolm**
Dove siam? Che bosco è quello?	Where are we? What wood is that?
Coro	**Chorus**
La foresta di Birnamo.	Birnam Wood.
Malcolm	**Malcolm**
Svelga ognuno, e porti un ramo,	Let every man cut off and carry a branch
Che lo asconda, innanzi a sè!	Before him to hide behind!
(*a Macduff*)	(*to Macduff*)
Ti conforti la vendetta.	Revenge will comfort you.
Macduff	**Macduff**
Non l'avrò—di figli è privo!	I shall not have it—he has no children.
Malcolm	**Malcolm**
Chi non odia il suol nativo	Whoever does not hate his native land,
Prenda l'armi e segua me.	Take up arms and follow me.
Tutti	**All**
La patria tradita	Our country betrayed,
Piangendo ne invita!	Weeping, invites us!
Fratelli! Gli oppressi	Brothers! The oppressed
Corriamo a salvar.	Let us run to save!
Già l'ira divina	Already divine wrath
Sull'empio ruina;	Falls on his sinful ruin;
Gli orribili eccessi	His horrible excesses
L'Eterno stancàr.	Weary the Everlasting.

Verdi's Letters (1847, 1865)[†]

To Felice Varesi, February 4, 1847[1]

Now here's the last piece for you. Have a copyist write it out in full so that you can study it, and then you'll have your entire part. I urge you to learn it well before arriving in Florence, so that you can go straight into stage rehearsals. This final scene I put into your hands.

[†] *Verdi's Macbeth*, 41, 66–67, 90–91, 99. Reprinted by permission of the American Institute for Verdi Studies.
1. Felice Varesi, the baritone who played Macbeth in 1847.

There's an *adagio* in D flat, every detail of which needs coloring, *cantabile* and *affettuoso*.[2] As for the lines in the intervening passage, "Life—What does it matter! / 'Tis a tale told by a poor idiot: / Wind and sound, signifying nothing," I want you to declaim them with all the irony and contempt possible. You'll be able to make much of the death scene, if together with your singing, your acting is well thought out. You can see very well that Macbeth mustn't die like Edgardo, Gennaro,[3] etc.; therefore it has to be treated in a new way. It should be affecting, yes; but more than affecting, it should be *terrible*. All of it sotto voce, except for the last two lines, which, in fact, you'll also accompany with acting, bursting out with full force on the words "Vile . . . crown . . . and only for you!" You're on the ground, of course, but for this last line you'll stand almost straight up and will make as great an impression as possible.

To Salvatore Cammarano, November 23, 1848[4]

Tadolini's qualities are far too good for that role [Lady Macbeth].[5] This may perhaps seem absurd to you. . . . Tadolini has a beautiful and attractive appearance; and I would like Lady Macbeth to be ugly and evil. Tadolini sings to perfection; and I would like the Lady not to sing. Tadolini has a stupendous voice, clear, limpid, powerful; and I would like the Lady to have a harsh, stifled, and hollow voice. Tadolini's voice has an angelic quality; I would like the Lady's voice to have a diabolical quality! Submit these remarks to the management, to Maestro Mercadante, who will approve these ideas of mine more than the others will, and to Tadolini herself. Then do in your wisdom what you think best.

Note that there are two principal numbers in the opera: the duet between the Lady and her husband and the sleepwalking scene.[6] If these numbers fail, then the opera is ruined. And these pieces absolutely must not be sung: "They must be acted out and declaimed with a very hollow and veiled voice; otherwise, they won't be able to make any effect. (The orchestra with *mutes*)."[7] The

---

2. "with tender and passionate expression"; *adagio*: a notation for slow tempo; *cantabile*: "song-like."
3. characters from Donizetti's *Lucia di Lammermoor* and *Lucrezia Borgia*.
4. Cammarano was librettist and stage director at the San Carlo Theater, Naples.
5. Eugenia Tadolini, an Italian soprano, despite these objections, did sing the role of Lady Macbeth.
6. Barbieri-Nini recalled that "the sleepwalking scene cost me three months' study: for three months, morning and evening, I tried to imitate those who talk in their sleep, uttering words (as Verdi would say to me) while hardly moving their lips, leaving the rest of the face immobile, including the eyes. It was enough to drive one crazy. As for the duet with the baritone that begins 'Fatal mia donna, un murmure' ['My deadly lady, a noise,' 2.2.14]—you may think I am exaggerating, but it was rehearsed more than a hundred and fifty times so that it might be closer to 'speech' than 'singing,' the Maestro would say," *Verdi's Macbeth*, 51.
7. Verdi, apparently, quotes here one of his earlier instructions.

stage is extremely dark. In the third act (I've seen it done in London)[8] [the apparition scene] must take place behind an opening in the scenery, with a fine, ashen veil in front of it. The kings should not be puppets, but eight men of flesh and blood. The floor over which they pass must resemble a mound, and they must be seen clearly to ascend and descend. The scene must be completely dark, especially when the cauldron disappears, and lighted only where the kings pass. The music beneath the stage must be reinforced (for the large San Carlo Theatre), but be sure there are neither trumpets nor trombones. The sound must seem distant and muted, and must therefore be composed of bass clarinets, bassoons, contrabassoons, and nothing else.[9]

To Léon Escudier, January 23, 1865[1]

The appearance of Hecate, goddess of night, is good because it interrupts all those devilish dances and gives way to a calm and severe *adagio*. I don't need to tell you that Hecate should never dance, but only assume poses. Nor do I need to advise you that the *adagio* must be played by the clarinet and bass clarinet (as indicated), which, in union with the cello and bassoon, will result in a hollow and severe sound, as the situation demands. Also, ask the conductor to supervise the ballet rehearsals from time to time so that he can indicate the tempos I have marked.[2] Dancers always alter all the tempos, and if that were done with this ballet, it would lose all its character and would not produce the effect that, it seems to me, it should have. . . .

Another observation, on Macbeth's banquet scene in Act II. I have seen this play performed several times in France, England, and Italy. Everywhere they have Banquo appear from a revolving wing; he gesticulates, inveighs against Macbeth, and then goes off calmly behind another wing. In my opinion, that creates no illusion or effect, and it is not clear whether he is a ghost or a man. When I staged *Macbeth* in Florence, I had Banquo appear (with a large wound on his forehead) through a trapdoor from underground, precisely in Macbeth's place. He did not move but only raised his head at the proper moment. It was terrifying. . . .

A final observation. In the duet between Macbeth and the Lady in Act I, there is the *primo tempo*,[3] which always makes a big effect,

---

8. perhaps a production at the Princess Theatre starring William Macready in 1847.
9. Rosen and Porter (67) note that the 1847 score featured neither bass clarinets nor contrabassoons but did include trumpets, contrary to Verdi's later conception here.
1. Escudier (1821–1881), French publisher, impresario, and agent, overseer of the Paris production of *Macbeth*, 1865.
2. Verdi added a ballet (usually not performed today) for the 1865 production.
3. the first movement or section of rhymed lines in a single meter.

and there is the passage on the words, "Follie follie che sperdono / I primi rai del di" ["Foolish thoughts, foolish thoughts, which the first rays of dawn will dispel"; cf. 2.2.36–7]. The French translator must retain the words "Follie follie," because the whole secret of the effect of this number may well lie in these words and in the Lady's infernal derision.

To Léon Escudier, February 8, 1865

Above all, bear in mind that there are three roles in this opera and three is all there can be: Lady Macbeth, Macbeth and the chorus of witches. The witches dominate the drama; everything derives from them—coarse and gossipy in the first act, sublime and prophetic in the third. They are truly a character and a character of the utmost importance. So far as Macduff's part is concerned, no matter what you do, you will never succeed in making it very important. On the contrary, the more prominence you give it, the more it will show its insignificance. He does not become a hero until the end of the opera. He has, however, enough music to distinguish himself, if he has a good voice; but there is no need to give him a single note more. To have him sing a part of the *brindisi*[4] in Act II [the Banquet scene, 3.4] would be a mistake and a dramatic contradiction. In this scene, Macduff is just a courtier like everyone else. The important character, the dominating demon of this scene, is Lady Macbeth; and however much Macbeth can distinguish himself as an actor, Lady Macbeth, I repeat, dominates and controls everything. She scolds Macbeth for being "not even a man" and tells the courtiers to pay no attention to her husband's delirium—"it is a nervous affliction"—and to better reassure them she repeats the *brindisi* with the utmost nonchalance. In this way it is beautiful, and coming from her lips it has great meaning; from Macduff it means nothing and is a contradiction. True or no?—admit that I am right.

EUGÈNE IONESCO

Macbett (1972)†

DUNCAN   Hear us, O Lord.
OFFICER *(kneeling)*   Hear us, O Lord.

---

4. a drinking song.
† Eugène Ionesco, *Macbett*, trans. Charles Marowitz (New York: Grove Press, 1973), 72–86.
  English translation copyright © 1973 by Grove Press, Inc. © 1972 by Editions Gallimard.
  Used by permission of Grove/Atlantic, Inc., Editions Gallimard, and Georges Borchardt,

MONK   Hear us, O Lord. May hatred and anger waft away like smoke in the wind. Grant that man may prevail against nature, where suffering and destruction reign. May love and peace be freed from their chains, may all destructive forces be chained up that joy may shine forth in heavenly light. May that light flood us that we may bathe ourselves in it. Amen.

DUNCAN *and* OFFICER   Amen.

MONK   Take your scepter with my blessing. With it you are to touch the sick.

> *Duncan and the Officer get up. The Monk kneels*
> *before Duncan who mounts the throne and sits.*
> *The Officer stands on Duncan's left.*
> *This scene should be played with solemnity.*

DUNCAN   Bring in the patients.

> *The Monk rises and goes and stands on Duncan's right. The First*
> *Sick Man comes in upstage left. He is bent double and walks with*
> *difficulty. He is wearing a cape with a hood. His face is a ravaged*
> *mask—like a leper's.*

Come here. A little nearer. Don't be afraid.

> *The Sick Man approaches and kneels on one of*
> *the bottom steps of the throne.*
> *He has his back to the audience.*

FIRST SICK MAN   Have pity on me, my lord. I've come a long way. On the other side of the ocean, there is a continent and beyond that continent, there are seven countries. And beyond those seven countries there's another sea, and beyond that sea there are mountains. I live on the other side of those mountains in a damp and sunless valley. The damp has eaten away my bones. I'm covered in scrofula, in tumors and pustules which break out everywhere. My body is a running sore. I stink. My wife and children can't bear me to come near them. Save me, lord. Cure me.

DUNCAN   I shall cure you. Believe in me and hope. (*He touches the Sick Man's head with his scepter.*) By the grace of our Lord Jesus Christ, by the gift of the power vested in me this day, I absolve you of the sin which has stained your soul and body. May your soul be as pure as clear water, as the sky on the first day of creation.

The First Sick Man stands up and turns toward the audience.
He draws himself up to his full height, drops his stick
and lifts his hands to heaven. His face is clear and smiling.
He shouts for joy and runs out left. The Second Sick
Man enters right and approaches the throne.

DUNCAN What is your trouble?

SECOND SICK MAN My lord, I'm unable to live and I can't die. I can't sit down, I can't lie down, I can't stand still, and I can't run. I burn and itch from the top of my head to the soles of my feet. I can't bear to be indoors or on the street. For me, the universe is a prison. It pains me to look at the world. I can't bear the light nor sit in the shade. Other people fill me with horror, yet I can't bear to be alone. My eyes wander restlessly over trees, sheep, dogs, grass, stars, stones. I have never had a single happy moment. I should like to be able to cry, my lord, and to know joy. (*During this speech, he has come up to the throne and climbed the steps.*)

DUNCAN Forget you exist. Remember that you are.

Pause. Seen from behind, one can read in
the twitching of the Sick Man's shoulders that it's
impossible for him to comply.

I order you. Obey.

The Second Sick Man who was twisted in agony, relaxes
his back and shoulders and appears to be calming down.
He gets up slowly, holds out his arms and turns around.
The audience can see the contorted face relax and light up.
He walks off left, jauntily, almost dancing.

OFFICER Next!

A Third Sick Man approaches Duncan, who cures him in the
same way. Then in quick succession a Fourth, Fifth, Sixth . . .
Tenth, Eleventh come on stage right and go out left
after having been touched by Duncan's scepter. Before each
entrance, the Officer shouts "Next!" Some of the Patients
are on crutches or in wheel-chairs. All this should be
properly controlled and toward the end should be
accompanied by music which gradually gets faster
and faster.
While this is going on, the Monk has slowly dropped away
till he is sitting rather than kneeling on the floor. He looks poised.
After the Eleventh Sick Man, the tempo becomes slower
and the music fades into the distance. Two last patients come in,
one from the left, the other from the right. They are wearing
long capes with hoods that come down over their faces.
The Officer who shouted "Next" fails to notice
the last patient, who creeps up behind him.

Suddenly the music cuts out. At the same moment, the MONK
*throws back his hood or takes off his mask, and we see that it's
Banco in disguise. He pulls out a long dagger.*

DUNCAN *(to Banco)* You?

*At the same moment, Lady Duncan throws off her
disguise and stabs the Officer in the back. He falls.*

DUNCAN *(to Lady Duncan)* You, madam?

The other beggar—Macbett—also pulls out a dagger.

DUNCAN Murderers!

BANCO *(to Duncan)* Murderer!

MACBETT *(to Duncan)* Murderer!

*Duncan dodges Banco and comes face to face with Macbett.
He tries to go out left but his escape is cut off by Lady Duncan,
who holds out her arms to stop him. She has a dagger in one hand.*

LADY DUNCAN *(to Duncan)* Murderer!

DUNCAN *(to Lady Duncan)* Murderess! *(He runs left, meets Macbett.)*

MACBETT Murderer!

DUNCAN Murderer! *(He runs right. Banco cuts him off.)*

BANCO *(to Duncan)* Murderer!

DUNCAN *(to Banco)* Murderer!

*Duncan backs toward the throne. The three others close in on him,
slowly drawing their circle tighter. As Duncan mounts the first step,
Lady Duncan snatches off his cloak. Duncan backs up the steps,
trying to cover his body with his arms. Without his cloak he feels
naked and exposed. He doesn't get very far, however, for the others
are after him. His scepter falls one way, his crown the other,
Macbett pulls at him and brings him down.*

DUNCAN Murderers!

He rolls on the ground. Banco strikes the first blow, shouting.

BANCO Murderer!

MACBETT *(stabbing him a second time)* Murderer!

LADY DUNCAN *(stabbing him a third time)* Murderer!

The three of them get up and stand over him.

DUNCAN Murderers! *(Quieter.)* Murderers! *(Feebly.)* Murderers!

*The three conspirators draw apart, Lady Duncan by the body,
looking down.*

LADY DUNCAN He was my husband, after all. Now that he's dead,
he looks just like my father. I couldn't stand my father.

Blackout.

*A Room in the palace. In the distance we can hear the crowd
shouting, "Long live Macbett! Long live his bride! Long live
Macbett! Long live his bride!" Two servants enter upstage, one from
one side, one from the other. They meet downstage center.
They can be played by two men, or a man and a woman,
possibly even two women.*

SERVANTS (*looking at each other*)   They're coming.

They go and hide upstage. Enter left Duncan's widow, the future Lady Macbett, followed by Macbett. They have not as yet acquired the regal attributes. The cheering and shouts of "Long live Macbett and his bride" are louder. They go to the exit stage left.

LADY DUNCAN   Thank you for bringing me to my apartments. I'm going to lie down. I'm quite tired after my exertions.

MACBETT   Yes, you could do with a rest. I'll come and pick you up at ten o'clock for the marriage ceremony. The coronation is at midday. In the afternoon, at five o'clock, there will be a banquet—our wedding feast.

LADY DUNCAN (*giving her hand to Macbett to be kissed*)   Till tomorrow then, Macbett.

She goes out. Macbett crosses to go out right. The sound of scattered cheering. The two Servants who had hidden reappear and come downstage.

FIRST SERVANT   Everything is ready for the wedding ceremony and the breakfast afterward.

SECOND SERVANT   Wines from Italy and Samoa.

FIRST SERVANT   Bottles of beer coming by the dozen.

SECOND SERVANT   And gin.

FIRST SERVANT   Oxen.

SECOND SERVANT   Herds of deer.

FIRST SERVANT   Roebuck to be barbecued.

SECOND SERVANT   They've come from France, from the Ardennes.

FIRST SERVANT   Fishermen have risked their lives to provide sharks. They'll eat the fins.

SECOND SERVANT   They killed a whale for oil to dress the salad.

FIRST SERVANT   There'll be Pernod from Marseille.

SECOND SERVANT   Vodka from the Urals.

FIRST SERVANT   A giant omelette containing a hundred and thirty thousand eggs.

SECOND SERVANT   Chinese pancakes.

FIRST SERVANT   Spanish melons from Africa.

SECOND SERVANT   There's never been anything like it.

FIRST SERVANT   Viennese pastries.

SECOND SERVANT   Wine will flow like water in the streets.

FIRST SERVANT   To the sound of a dozen gypsy orchestras.

SECOND SERVANT   Better than Christmas.

FIRST SERVANT   A thousand times better.

SECOND SERVANT   Everyone in the country will get two hundred and forty-seven black sausages.

FIRST SERVANT   And a ton of mustard.

SECOND SERVANT   Frankfurters.

FIRST SERVANT   And sauerkraut.

SECOND SERVANT   And more beer.

FIRST SERVANT   And more wine.

SECOND SERVANT   And more gin.

FIRST SERVANT   I'm drunk already, just thinking about it.

SECOND SERVANT   Just thinking about it I can feel my belly bursting.

FIRST SERVANT   My liver swelling. (*They throw their arms around each other's necks and stagger out drunkenly, shouting "Long live Macbett and his bride."*)

> *Banco enters right. He crosses to stage center and stops, facing the audience. He appears to reflect for a moment. Macbett appears upstage left.*

MACBETT   Ah, it's Banco. What's he doing here all by himself? I'll hide and overhear him. (*He pretends to pull invisible curtains.*)

BANCO   So Macbett is to be king; Baron Candor, Baron Glamiss, then king—as from tomorrow. One by one the witches' predictions have come true. One thing they didn't mention was the murder of Duncan, in which I had a hand. But how would Macbett have come to power unless Duncan had died or abdicated in his favor—which is constitutionally impossible? You have to take the throne by force. Another thing they didn't mention was that Lady Duncan would be Lady Macbett. So Macbett gets everything—while I get nothing. What an extraordinarily successful career—wealth, fame, power, a wife. He's got everything a man could possibly want, I struck down Duncan because I had a grudge against him. But what good has it done me? True, Macbett has given me his word. He said I could be chamberlain. But will he keep his promise? I doubt it. Didn't he promise to be faithful to Duncan—and then kill him? People will say I did the same. I can't say I didn't. I can't get it out of my mind. I'm sorry now—and I haven't any of Macbett's advantages, his success, his fame, to stifle my remorse. The witches told me I shouldn't be archduke or king, but they said I should father a whole line of kings, princes, presidents, and dictators. That's some consolation. They said it would happen, yes, they said it would happen. They've proved conclusively that they can see into the future. Before I met them I had no desire, no ambition beyond that of serving my king. Now I'm consumed with envy and jealousy. They've taken the lid off my ambition and here I am carried away by a force I can't control—grasping, avid, insatiable. I shall father dozens of kings. That's something. But yet I have no sons or daughters. And I'm not married. Whom shall I marry? The Lady in Waiting is rather sexy. I'll ask her to marry me. She's a bit spooky but so much the better. She'll be able to see danger coming and we can take steps to avoid it. Once I'm married, once I've started a family, once I'm chamberlain, I'll curtail Macbett's powers. I'll be his *éminence gris*. Who knows, perhaps the witches will reconsider their predictions. Perhaps I will reign in my own lifetime after all.   (*He goes out right.*)

MACBETT   I heard every word, the traitor! So that's all the thanks I get for promising to make him chamberlain. I didn't know my wife and her maid had told him that he'd be father to a line of kings. Funny she never mentioned it. It's disturbing to think she kept it from me. Who are they trying to fool, me or Banco? Why? Banco father to a line of kings. Have I killed Duncan to put Banco's issue on the throne? It's all a sinister plot. Well, we'll soon see about that. We'll soon see if my initiative can foil the snares of destiny the devil has set for me. Let's destroy his issue at the fountainhead—that is, Banco himself. (*He crosses right and calls.*) Banco! Banco!

BANCO'S VOICE   Coming, Macbett. Coming.

(*Banco comes on.*)

[BANCO]   What do you want?

MACBETT   Coward, so that is how you repay me for all the favors I was going to grant you. (*He stabs Banco in the heart.*)

BANCO (*falling*)   O my God! Have mercy.

MACBETT   Where are all those kings now? They're going to rot with you and in you, nipped in the bud.

(*He goes.*)
Blackout.

Lights up. Shouts of "Long live Macbett! Long live Lady Macbett! Long live our beloved king! Long live the bride!" Macbett and Lady Macbett come on right. They are in robes of state. They wear crowns and purple robes. Macbett is carrying his scepter. Sound of bells ringing and the enthusiastic cheering of the crowd, Macbett and Lady Macbett stop center stage with their backs to the audience and wave left and right to the crowd. Noise of the crowd: "Hurrah! Long live the Archduke! Long live the Archduchess!" Macbett and Lady Macbett turn and salute the audience, waving and blowing kisses.
They turn and face each other.

MACBETT   We'll discuss it later.

LADY MACBETT   I can explain everything, dear.

MACBETT   Well, I've canceled your prediction. I've nipped it in the bud. You've no longer got the upper hand. I discovered your little arrangements and took steps accordingly.

LADY MACBETT   I didn't mean to hide anything from you, love. As I said, I can explain everything. But not in public.

MACBETT   We'll discuss it later.

Macbett takes her hand and they go out right,
smiling at the crowd.
The cheering continues.
Pause. The stage is empty, Lady Macbett comes on with her Lady
in Waiting. She is in the same costume as in the previous scene.

LADY IN WAITING   It suits you, being a bride. The crowd cheering. The way you held yourself. Such grace. Such majesty. He cut a fine figure, too. He's looking much younger. You made a lovely couple.

LADY MACBETT   He's gone to sleep. He had a few too many after the ceremony. And there's still the wedding feast to come. Let's make the most of it. Hurry up.

LADY IN WAITING   Yes, ma'am. (*She collects a case from offstage right.*)

LADY MACBETT   Away with this sacred and anointed crown. (*She throws the crown away. She takes off the necklace with a cross on it which she had been wearing.*) This cross has been burning me. I've got a wound, here on my chest. But I've doused it with curses.

Meanwhile the Lady in Waiting has been opening
the case and taking out her witch's costume.
She proceeds to dress Lady Macbett in it.

The cross symbolizes the struggle of two forces, heaven and hell. Which will prove the stronger? Within this small compass a universal warfare is condensed. Help me. Undo my white dress. Quickly, take it off. It's burning me as well. And I spit out the Host which fortunately stuck in my throat. Give me the flask of spiced and magic vodka. Alcohol 90 proof is like mineral water to me. Twice I nearly fainted when they held up the icons for me to touch. But I carried it off. I even kissed one of them. Pouah, it was disgusting. *During all this, the Lady in Waiting is undressing her.*

Hurry up. I hear something.

LADY IN WAITING   Yes, ma'am. I'm doing my best.

LADY MACBETT   Hurry, hurry, hurry. Give me my rags, my smelly old dress. My apron covered in vomit. My muddy boots. Take this wig off. Where's my dirty gray hair? Give me my chin. Here, take these teeth. My pointed nose, and my stick tipped with poisoned steel.

The Lady in Waiting picks up one of the sticks left by
the pilgrims. As Lady Macbett issues her orders, "Unhook my
white dress!" etc., the Lady in Waiting carries them out.
As indicated in the text, she puts on her smelly old dress, her apron
covered in vomit, her dirty gray hair, takes out her teeth,
shows the plate to audience, puts on her pointed nose, etc.

FIRST WITCH   Hurry! Faster!

SECOND WITCH   I am hurrying, my dear.

FIRST WITCH   They are waiting for us.

The Second Witch produces a long shawl from the case and puts it around her shoulders, at the same time pulling on a dirty gray wig. The two witches are bent double and sniggering.

I feel much more at home, dressed like this.

SECOND WITCH   He, he, he, he!

She shuts the case. They both sit astride it.

FIRST WITCH   Well, that's that, then.

SECOND WITCH   A job well done.

FIRST WITCH   We've mixed it nicely.

SECOND WITCH   He, he, he, he. Macbett won't be able to get out of it now.

FIRST WITCH   The boss will be pleased.

SECOND WITCH   We'll tell him all about it.

FIRST WITCH   He'll be waiting to send us on another mission.

SECOND WITCH   Let's skedaddle. Suitcase, fly!

FIRST WITCH   Fly! Fly! Fly!

The First Witch, who is sitting in front of the case, mimes a steering wheel. It's a very noisy engine. The Second Witch spreads her arms, like wings. Blackout. Spotlight on the case which appears to be flying.

WELCOME MSOMI

uMabatha (1996)[†]

Characters

MABATHA, *later* Chief Mbathazeli (Macbeth), the King's cousin
KAMADONSELA (Lady Macbeth), his wife
DANGANE / MDANGAZELI (Duncan), King
DONEBANE (Donalbain), Prince
MAKHIWANE (Malcolm), Prince
ISANGOMA 1, 2 & 3 (3 Witches), witchdoctors[1]

[†] From Welcome Msomi, *uMabatha: An Adaptation of Shakespeare's "Macbeth"* (Praetoria: Johannesburg: Via Afrika/Skotaville Publishers, 1996). Reprinted by permission of Welcome Msomi. Copyright © by Welcome Msomi. (The "u" before Mabatha is an honorific Zulu prefix, roughly equivalent to "Mr.") Footnotes are by the editor of this Norton Critical Edition. Welcome Msomi adapts Shakespeare's *Macbeth* into *uMabatha*, a tale of Zulu ambition, murder, greed, and fear. *uMabatha* is based on the story of Shaka (1787–1828), a legendary, brutal Zulu warrior who built a formidable army and created an empire in South Africa before being murdered.

1. (I)Sangoma, usually female, are witchdoctors with powers of healing and divination.

BHANGANE (Banquo), the King's Induna[2]
FOLOSE (Fleance), Bhangane's son
MAFUDU (Macduff), King's cousin
KAMAKHAWULANA (Lady Macduff), Mafudu's wife
INDODANA (Boy), Mafudu's son
IMBONGI the King's praise singer
HOSHWENI (Captain)
LINOLO (Lennox), attendant
ANGANO (Angus), attendant
INYANGA (Doctor), herbal doctor
ISALUKAZI (Gentlewoman), nurse
MSIMBITHI (Messenger), a messenger
3 MURDERERS
SPIRITS
WARRIORS
SWAZI IMPI[3]
WOMEN

1.3

Thunder and strong winds. Enter SANGOMA I, II & III.

SANGOMA I   Where have you been, Mngoma?[4]
SANGOMA II   I have been spitting strange spells.
SANGOMA III   What spells have you been spitting, Mngoma?
SANGOMA II   I have been spitting my venom
  To the spirits of darkness and misfortune.
SANGOMA II   Spit them Mngoma, spit so that we can hear.
SANGOMA III   Yes, spit, Mngoma, spit so that we can hear.
SANGOMA I   Elele! Elele! Elele![5]
SANGOMA II & III   Spread your venom!
SANGOMA I   I spit to the moon.
SANGOMA II & III   Spit them!
SANGOMA I   I spit to the sun so that the world becomes dark.
SANGOMA II & III   Spit them!
SANGOMA I   I spit to the sun,
  So that the world becomes dark.
SANGOMA II & III   Spit! Spit! Spit your venom!
SANGOMA II   I! I will spit to the spirits of misfortune,
  And spread the shadow of my venom

2. chief counselor.
3. Impi(s) are warriors organized into a regiment; these come from Swaziland in South Africa.
4. diviner.
5. a cry of joy.

Between the sun and the new day.

SANGOMA III   I will spit to the wind;
   My venom will cloud the clear water with blood.

                                        (*Slow drumbeat*)

SANGOMA I   That is the sign
   Mabatha is near.

ALL THREE (*Sing and dance*)   We miss the wisdom of the stones
   When we shake and throw our bones.

                              Enter MABATHA *and* BHANGANE.

MABATHA   This day's battle
   Will beat in my veins
   Until my life runs out.

BHANGANE   The night is at our heels;
   If we linger
   Its shadow will reach Umfolosi before we do.
   Hawu![6] Spirit of my father! What are these!
   By the heavens above!—What are you doing here?
   Speak! What are you doing?
   You just stare at me, dumb as the stones,
   Hissing like angry mambas.[7]

MABATHA   Speak! Who are you?

SANGOMA I (*Throwing bones*)   Mabatha! Chief of Dlamasi!

SANGOMA II (*Throwing bones*)   Mabatha! Chief of Mkhawundeni![8]

SANGOMA III   Mabatha! The bones rattle for a mighty chief.

ALL THREE   Elele! Elele! Elele!

BHANGANE   Hawu, my friend! What is it? You shake
   Like an old tree, struck by lightning,
   Whose roots have lost their hold.
   Why do you let the breath of these Sangomas
   Blow through your branches
   Like truth?
   Listen to me, you serpents!
   You tell my friend all that will befall him hereafter,
   Hailing him as a chief,
   But to me you are dumb.
   Throw your bones for me, too, if you can.
   But I want you to know
   I do not beg for food like an old hungry dog.
   In my eyes you are the beggars,
   You are less than dirt.

6. an exclamation of surprise or shock.
7. venomous African snakes.
8. The Dlamasi are the people of uMabatha's (Macbeth's) village; the Mkhawundeni are
   the people of Khondo's (Cawdor's) village.

Do you hear what I say?

ALL THREE   Oh, Great One!

SANGOMA I (*Throwing bones*)   You who seem so very small,
Like an ant in Mabatha's shadow,
You have your own power.

SANGOMA II (*Throwing bones*)   Your life is like an empty pool,
But soon the water will overflow.

SANGOMA III (*Throwing bones*)   Your seeds will grow to be the
    tallest trees of the forest,
But your leaves will never see the light.

ALL THREE   Mabatha! Bhangane! Mabatha! Bhangane!

MABATHA   Stay, you serpents, I say, stay!
After my father's death
I know that I will be chief of Dlamasi,
But when you talk of Mkhawundeni
Your tongues are forked
Because I know Khondo is still alive.
No, these Sangomas prick our ears with thorns.
Tell me,
From which bad egg did you suck your wisdom?
Answer me!

ALL THREE   Elele! Elele! Elele!   *The Sangomas disappear.*

2.1 *Mvanencane, Mabatha's kraal.*[9]

Enter KAMADONSELA *with four* WOMEN *bearing pots on
their heads and singing. They busy themselves with
stamping corn and preparing tshwala.*[1] *Distant drumbeat.*

KAMADONSELA (*Listening*)   On the day of our victory
Came three Sangomas out of the earth
And spoke strange truths.
(*Drumbeat*) When we challenged them
With taunts, they became shadows of the night.
(*Drumbeat*) As we stood wrapped in wonder,
Mdangazeli's word was brought,
Hailing me as Chief of Mkhawundeni.
This title these Sangomas' bones foretold,
And further, greatest of all chiefs.
(*Drumbeat*) Let this drumbeat echo in your heart
Till I return.
—Chief of Dlamasi, when you went hence.

---

9. Mvanencane is the name of Macbeth's kraal, or enclosed village, comprised of huts.
1. traditional beer.

When you return, I welcome Khondo,
Chief of Mkhawundeni.
And more shall befall as they foretold.
But yet I fear
The gentle dove that nestles in your heart,
Where I would have the wind-swift hawk
That falls like lightning on his prey.
What can you grasp
Without the strong claws of the hawk,
And what advantage take
Without his sharp eye and his swift flight?
Yes, my Khondo,
The prey that lies in wait was meant for you.
And therefore I have called
On all the spirits of my ancestors
To breathe fire in your heart
And burn away your fears.

                                        Enter MSIMBITHI.

What has happened?
MSIMBITHI   Mother of the Great Kraal!
KAMADONSELA   What is it? Speak, what is your news?
MISIMBITHI   Oh, Great One, I bring word
    That King Mdangazeli will visit Mvanencane today.
KAMADONSELA   What! Do you speak the truth?
MISIMBITHI   I swear this is the truth.
    My Prince Mabatha
    Follows close behind me
    To tell the news again.
    Oh, pardon me, I gasp for breath.
    This news gave my feet wings
    For they hardly touched the ground.
KAMADONSELA [*To women*]   Drown his thirst with tshwala;
    He has brought good news this day.
                            Exeunt women singing, with Msimbithi.
This messenger rolls his eyes
And gasps the name of Dangane in our kraal;
Even so will Dangane gasp his life away;
The skies crash down on him.
I call again
On all the spirits of my ancestors:
Let my heart be like the devil's thorn,
My blood of mamba's poison,
That where I strike no life returns;
Dry up my woman's tears,

And let my breasts shrivel with serpent's milk.
I call on you
To shade my eyes
And fill my ears with earth,
So none can see or hear
Iklwa,
The assegai's clean path[2]

Enter MABATHA.

Khondo! Greatest of all warriors!
I heard your message carried on the wind.
Although the sky is red tonight,
Our tomorrow will be clear and bright.
MABATHA   Dangane, our Chief, comes here today.
KAMADONSELA   And when will he depart?
MABATHA   With the rising of the sun.
KAMADONSELA   Never will he rise again!
Khondo, I see your face
As in a still pool,
Starting from the waters.
Look and see yourself.
Walk bravely, laugh,
And welcome our great guest,
While in your hand a hissing mamba waits.
Dangane comes like a tame bull
To the slaughter-block.
Sharpen your spear,
Be ready for the sacrifice.
MABATHA   Let us think about this further.
KAMADONSELA   Yes, my Khondo,
The fruit is ripe and must be plucked,
Or else waste on the branch.   *Exeunt all.*

2.4

Enter KAMADONSELA.

KAMADONSELA   The guards robbed of their senses give me
     strength.   (*A dog howls.*)
Khondo is busy now. The guards
Are snoring deep in their last sleep.
                         (*A muffled shout from the hut*)

---

2. **Assegai** is a slender iron-tipped spear; **Iklwa** is a short spear.

KAMADONSELA   I am afraid they have awakened before his work is
   done.
   Then this attempt will mean our death.
   I left the assegai where he could not miss it.

Enter MABATHA [*with bloody hands and knife*].

MABATHA   It is done. Did you hear any sound?
KAMADONSELA   I heard the dog howl.
MABATHA   Did you cry out?
KAMADONSELA   When? Now?
MABATHA   As I left the hut.
KAMADONSELA   Who, me?
MABATHA   Wait! Who sleeps in the next hut?
KAMADONSELA   Donebane.
MABATHA   Donebane! These hands smell of death.
KAMADONSELA   It is foolish to nurse these thoughts.
MABATHA   I heard the sound of weeping in the dark,
   Then someone cried, "The earth is gaping!"
KAMADONSELA   The King's sons are both asleep.
MABATHA   They called upon the spirits of their ancestors for help;
   I thought they had seen my hands, stained with blood.
KAMADONSELA   Khondo, pluck this thorn out of your mind.
MABATHA   I, too, wanted to summon the spirits of my ancestors.
KAMADONSELA   When the rains come we cannot hold back the
   flood.
   If you let this dark stream rush into your mind,
   It will lead to madness.
MABATHA   My eyes were blind,
   The blood in my ears drummed out the watchman's cry:
   "Awake! Mabatha comes to steal your life away."
   A warrior's life should not end with this slow horror.
KAMADONSELA   What do you mean?
MABATHA   A voice was singing in my head,
   "All your days, Mabatha,
   Men will hunt you like the cowardly jackal."
KAMADONSELA   What voice did you hear?
   You make me wonder, Khondo; are you not a warrior,
   And does a warrior shake when a shadow crosses his path?
   Khondo! Khondo, why did you bring the assegai?
   It must lie with the drunken guards.
MABATHA   No! The darkness smothers me.
   I cannot go back to that foul place.
KAMADONSELA   Give me the assegai!
   The sleeping guards are harmless as their King.
   I will smear them with his blood.   *Kamadonsela exits.*

Calls from within: "Mabatha!"

MABATHA   What voice is that?
Why do I shake like a fevered child?
See how the sun's wound stains the sky;
Even so this blood will stain my hands forever.

Re-enter KAMADONSELA.

KAMADONSELA   Khondo, my hands are like yours
But my heart is firm.   *(Calls from within)*
There is someone calling at the gate!
Let us wash this blood from our hands.
Come, Khondo, let us return to our hut
And be found sleeping.   *Exit.*
MABATHA   There is no hole deep enough to hide my fear.
(Calls from within)
All your breath cannot wake Mdangazeli now.   *Exit.*

3.3 *Mvanencane, Mabatha's kraal.*

Sounds of feasting and rejoicing. Warriors and maidens
perform a dance, and sing the song of welcome:
"Mbathazeli has come!"
Enter MABATHA *(as the Chief Mbathazeli),* KAMADONSELA,
HOSHWENI, LINOLO *and* ATTENDANTS.

ALL   Mbathazeli!
MABATHA   Sit now. Let our chiefs and counselors be near me.
Let the tshwala flow;
Attend to all their needs, my wife.

MURDERER I *appears.*

Your face is streaked with blood!
MURDERER I   It is Bhangane's
MABATHA   You should not then come here
Where every eye can see your deed.
MURDERER I   Yes, my Chief, his breath is stopped.
MABATHA   That is well. You are, indeed, brave warriors.
And Folose lies with his father?
MURDERER I   No, Mbathazeli, Folose escaped.
MABATHA   Hawu! You have failed me. Folose still lives?
MURDERER I   It was not our aim, my Chief,
But the night's dark hand that was at fault.
MABATHA   Do you swear that Bhangane is no more?
MURDERER I   As I stand here, my Chief,
The vultures will enjoy his flesh.

MABATHA   I thank you for what you have done.
Go now, we will meet tomorrow.   *Exit Murderer I.*
KAMADONSELA   Khondo, the feast is cold
When the Chief does not drink with his guests.
MABATHA   I have not forgotten, my wife;
A pressing matter held me back.

> *The* SPIRIT OF BHANGANE *enters.*

LINOLO   Here is your place, Mbathazeli.
MABATHA   Where?
LINOLO   Here, my Chief. What is it? Why does Mbathazeli shake?
MABATHA   All! Who did this?
ALL   What, Mbathazeli?
MABATHA [*To the Spirit*]   Do not look at me! My hands are clean.
HOSHWENI   I think it would be wise to bid the guests farewell.
Mbathazeli is not well.
KAMADONSELA   Stay, friends. This sickness is like a cloud
That soon will pass and show the sun again.
He is often thus. If you depart
You will do him wrong. Sit and drink.

> [*Kamadonsela and Mabatha converse apart.*]

Khondo! What foolishness is this?
MABATHA   You do not know what witchcraft is practised here!
KAMADONSELA   You disappoint me, Khondo.
When all our plans have reached this height,
And all men hail you as their King,
You show your weakness and your fears to every eye.
What is it now? Why do you stare so wildly?
MABATHA   What do you say? Look! Look there!
This is witchcraft when those we know are dead
Appear once more.

> *The Spirit disappears.*

KAMADONSELA   What do you mean?
MABATHA   I saw him sitting there!
KAMADONSELA   Khondo, there is no such thing.
MABATHA   I have killed many men in battle.
When they fell by my assegai, the earth swallowed them,
Their bones were food for ants.
Now they rise and follow us.
KAMADONSELA   Khondo, you have alarmed our guests.
MABATHA   I do forget, my wife.
—Friends and warriors,
I ask you all

To pardon me. This is a sickness.
Which means nothing to those that know me.
Come, let us drink and enjoy the feast.
Give me some tshwala. There is only one small cloud
That darkens our feast, my brother
Bhangane's absence.
Drink, my friends.
ALL   Mbathazeli!

> *Re-enter the* SPIRIT OF BANGHANE.

MABATHA   Keep away! Keep away from me!
   Why do you follow me and glare
   With your dead eyes. Keep away, evil spirit!
KAMADONSELA   Khondo! Khondo, what is the matter?
   Why do you disrupt our feast
   With these wild words?
MABATHA   This is witchcraft!
   The spirits of the dead have risen,
   And you ask why I stare.
   This horror turns my blood to water.
HOSHWENI   What horror, Mbathazeli?
KAMADONSELA   I beg you not to question him,
   His sickness grows. I entreat you now
   To leave and return to your homes.
LINOLO   Stay in peace, Great Lady.
   We hope Mbathazeli soon shakes off this sickness
   And is himself again.
>   *Exeunt all except Mabatha and Kamadonsela.*
KAMADONSELA   Khondo, what poisonous beetles feed on your mind?
MABATHA   I swear by my ancestors I saw him standing there.
KAMADONSELA   It is almost day; come, Khondo,
   Sleep is your only medicine.
MABATHA   Tomorrow when the sun sets
   I will visit the three Sangomas.
   They will make all things known to me,
   Uncover all dark secrets with their bones.
   I cannot now turn back;
   The path behind is washed with blood
   And I must climb, whatever dangers lie ahead.
KAMADONSELA   Khondo, sleep and rest will cool the fever of your
      thoughts.
MABATHA   Leave me! Keep away!
   You cannot see or feel
   This horror that follows me.
>   *Exit Mabatha followed by Kamadonsela.*

4.1 *In the veld.*[3]

Enter SANGOMA I, II, & III [*with a pot*].

SANGOMA I   The jackal howls three times.
SANGOMA II   Three times the Tokoloshe[4] screams.
SANGOMA III   The evil bird cries three times.
SANGOMA I   Yes, Bangoma, that means it is time
To prepare our medicine in the pot.
ALL THREE (*Dancing and singing*)   It boils and boils here in the
    pot,
The fire burns, the juice is hot.
SANGOMA II   Into the pot I throw the skin of
An old horned snake, a horse, and beetles,
Strong medicine to call up the spirits of our ancestors.
ALL THREE   It boils and boils here in the pot,
The fire burns, the juice is hot.
SANGOMA III   A sheep's ear and the eye of an ox,
Cow-dung mixed with the hoof of a goat,
All boil together in the pot.
ALL THREE   It boils and boils here in the pot,
The fire burns, the juice is hot.
SANGOMA I   And now the blood of an old baboon,
Slaughtered when the moon was full.

The three Sangomas sneeze.[5] *Slow beating of a drum.*

I smell out a stranger approaching our circle.
ALL THREE (*Softly*)   It boils and boils here in the pot,
The fire burns, the juice is hot.

Enter MABATHA.

MABATHA   Yes, evil ones, what are you doing?
ALL THREE   Work we perform in the dark.
MABATHA   Where did you learn this wisdom?
Answer me! You may hiss with the serpent,
And listen to the whisper of the wind,
But listen now to me.
SANGOMA I   Speak!
SANGOMA II   Ask!
SANGOMA III   We will answer!
SANGOMA I   Do not forget, the voices that speak through us are
the spirits of the dead.

---

3. the open plain.
4. a mischievous, lascivious hairy dwarf in South African folklore.
5. a sign of divine inspiration.

MABATHA   Let me hear them speak for your tongues are forked.
SANGOMA I   We will call them, they will appear.
ALL THREE   Rise! Rise from the earth!
    Awake and rise, spirits of the dead.

> Drumbeats and cries. The Sangomas perform a frenzied
> dance and fall exhausted.
> The FIRST SPIRIT appears.

FIRST SPIRIT   Mabatha! Mabatha! Mabatha!
    Beware of someone. I warn you,
    Beware of someone
    Who is of unnatural birth.
    That is all.   Exit.
MABATHA   I thank you for this warning. Wait
    There is more—
SANGOMAS   He will not stay. Here is another
    Greater than the first.

> [SECOND SPIRIT] appearing.

SECOND SPIRIT   Mabatha! Mabatha!
    Be great as the lion who scorns
    The assegai of men.
    No ordinary warrior can match your strength.   Exit.
MABATHA   These are words that gladden my heart.

> Thunder and drumbeats. THIRD SPIRIT appears.

What is this that rises like a mighty chief?
SANGOMAS   Be still! Listen to his words!
THIRD SPIRIT   The lionhearted Mbathazeli will be the only chief
        to reign
    Until the leaves of the forest become impis and approach his
        kraal.   Exit.
MABATHA   Hah! These are wonders that only children dream of.
    How can the leaves of Mdansane[6] grow legs and become impis?
    You have poured cool water on the fire in my head.
    But the thorn that pricks me still is this:
    Will the sons of Bhangane
    Ever grow to be chiefs?
SANGOMAS   Do not question more!
MABATHA   If you disobey
    My warriors will tear out your hearts
    And leave your flesh for jackal meat.

---

6. a jungle region (equivalent to Birnam Wood).

Tell me what witchcraft this is!
Which spirits do you summon now?

> *The Sangomas sway and chant over the pot.*

SANGOMAS   Appear! Appear! Appear!
Show! Show! Show!
Shadows of the night, destroy his sight.

> A ROW OF SPIRITS *with identical masks appears.*
> *The last one is the* SPIRIT OF BANGHANE.

MABATHA   Who are these that appear
In number like the fingers of my hands,
One like the other,
And all like Bhangane?
Out of my sight! Be gone, evil spirits!
They all point and stare at me.
What does this mean?
And last of all is Bhangane,
Who laughs at me and mocks me.
Are these all the seeds of Bhangane
Grown to be mighty chiefs?
Answer me!

> *The Sangomas dance and then disappear.*

MABATHA   Where are they?
Their words still echo in my ears.
Who is there?

> *Enter* LINOLO.

LINOLO   How can I serve you, my King?
MABATHA   Did you see the three Sangomas?
LINOLO   No, Mbathazeli.
MABATHA   Did they not pass near you?
Let any man who sees them kill them.
Their breath is like the rotten smell
That rises from the still, green pool,
And brings a sickness with it.
Do you bring me any news?
LINOLO   Your messengers, my King, came to report.
Mafudu has fled to Swaziland.
MABATHA   Swaziland!
LINOLO   Yes, great King.
MABATHA   Fool, not to listen to the message of my blood!
My thoughts were children, tortoise-slow,
But now I will strike

Swifter than the crouching lion
Who smells the terror of his prey.
I will destroy Mafudu's kraal,
His wife, his children, all, and waste no time.
Lead me to these warriors.   *Exeunt.*

5.1 *At Mvanencane.*

Enter INYANGA *and* ISALUKAZI.

INYANGA   The moon's eye has closed
  Since first you summoned me.
  When did you last see this madness seize her?
ISALUKAZI   I have attended her since
  Mbathazeli climbed his high mountain,
  And thrice have I heard her sing so strangely,
  Seen her seize the hide around her loins
  And tear it with hands and teeth
  Like some wild animal.
INYANGA   No, old woman,
  My gums are too soft to chew this bone.
  We are like two old dogs
  Shivering as we guard the kraal,
  When we should be sleeping by the fireside.

Enter KAMADONSELA, *singing and playing the*
makhweyana.[7]

Hush! Here she comes!
Hawu, what grief can make her wail
And sway so wildly?
ISALUKAZI   She is sick. It seems
  There is a poison within her
  That she must vomit out.

Kamadonsela kneels and drops the makhweyana.

INYANGA   No, this woman is not sick.
  There is some animal caged within her
  That fights to be free.
ISALUKAZI   That is true, my son.
KAMADONSELA   Here is blood! Here is blood!
INYANGA   What is she doing now?
  Why does she rub her hands?
ISALUKAZI   She is often seen clasping her hands

7. a wooden musical bow with a single string that is struck by a grass stalk.

And rubbing them thus.
KAMADONSELA   Khondo! It is time.
  Be brave and fearless.
  Why do you shake with fear
  When no eyes can see your deed?
  Mafudu has fled to Swaziland,
  Where is his wife, where is she?
  Khondo! Your weakness is an open pit
  That will swallow us both.
INYANGA   Let us go! What she has spoken
  Should not be uttered or heard.
ISALUKAZI   She has opened the sore,
  And we have seen the poison.
INYANGA   Her guilt is a load too heavy to bear.
ISALUKAZI   It is a sorrowful sight.
INYANGA   I have not the skill to cure her sickness.
KAMADONSELA   The smell of the blood follows me.

                    She picks up the makhweyana and caresses it.

INYANGA   What is she doing now?
ISALUKAZI   I cannot tell. This madness is like a fever.
KAMADONSELA   Go, wash your hands;
  Be not afraid. Bhangane is with his ancestors;
  He cannot trouble us.   *She moves off, singing.*
INYANGA   Will she sleep now?
ISALUKAZI   Yes, the fit has left her weak.
KAMADONSELA   Someone is calling! Someone is calling!   *Exit.*
INYANGA   Strange things have happened,
  But my old eyes have never seen such nights before.
  Go now, old man, go and rest,
  And do not speak what you have seen this night.
ISALUKAZI   I am a dumb beast. Farewell.
INYANGA   No, my father, he must find another Inyanga.
  I cannot cure her sickness.
  I must seek some way to leave this evil place.

                         5·4

  Drums and chanting. The WARRIORS *at Bhanganoma near
  Mvanencane perform a war dance.
  Enter* MAKHIWANE, DONEBANE, MAFUDU, HOSHWENI, *and
  the* SWAZI IMPI. *The two Impis engage in battle, and
  MABATHA's warriors are driven off. Mabatha fights
  Donebane and slays him.
  MAFUDU enters and challenges Mabatha.*

MAFUDU   I have returned! Turn and face me, murdering dog!

MABATHA   Mafudu, there is no hatred in my heart
For you. Come not near
Lest I be forced to spill your blood.

MAFUDU   You talk of spilling blood!
What about the blood of my children?
The blood of my wife?
The blood of all those dear to me.
You are not a man, Mabatha,
But a stinking dog.

MABATHA   Mafudu, to see you die
For a cause that is not your own—

MAFUDU   What do you mean?

MABATHA   Even your children died because of your ill thinking,
Fighting a battle of Mdangazeli.
Donebane, the son of Mdangazeli,
Is now food for the vultures;
His death is justified.
Only the sons of Mdangazeli
Must fight this battle—not you!

MAFUDU   Mabatha, your hands are steeped in blood
Of thousands of our people of KwaZulu[8]
That you have sent to our ancestors.
Your calabash[9] of greed
Has left thousands without kraals,
Without food, without hope.

MABATHA   Stop hiding behind words;
Fight like a man.

MAFUDU   You, Mabatha, have destroyed
The spirit of tranquility;
The bones of the innocent speak to me.
They say that the vicious dog must die.
Your time has come, Mabatha!

MABATHA   You cannot tell me anything.
The Sangomas prophesied that Bhangane's sons
Shall be kings, but they are all dead.
Mafudu, you will bend like a reed
Before my blows.
The only warrior I fear in my life
Is the one who came into this world
Like a spirit from the dead.

MAFUDU   Then turn and fight.

---

8. name of the province in South Africa that (with Natal) is home to the Zulu nation.
9. gourd or pumpkin, the shells of which function as a vessel.

Mabatha! I am the one who came
Into this world in a way unnatural,
Like a spirit from the dead.
MABATHA   If that is so, I will not fight you, Mafudu.

> *Mabatha runs to stage right. Warriors push him down to
> stage right, and he tries to escape through other exits,
> finally being surrounded by more warriors.*

MAFUDU   You have nowhere to go, Mabatha.
MABATHA   I know now, the Sangomas' words have confirmed the
truth.
MAFUDU   This is your day to meet your ancestors.

> *Mabatha and Mafudu fight until Mabatha is slain.
> MAKHIWANE, who enters with a group of WARRIORS,
> rejoices at the death of Mabatha.
> Makhiwane congratulates Mafudu.*

MAKHIWANE   Warriors! Brave warriors!
What you have done this day
Will always make you honoured
In my father's land,
ALL   Mntwana!¹
MAKHIWANE   The dog who snarled and showed his teeth
Is dead. And the evil one, his wife,
Has taken her own life.
ALL   Mntwana!
MAKHIWANE   All those loyal warriors who fled
From the tyrant's cruel hand
Can return and live in peace.
The spear has broken.

> *He throws the spear into the ground. Makhiwane is
> crowned the new king.*

ALL   Mntwana!
Makhiwane, son of Mdangazeli,
Makhiwane, son of Mdangazeli,
Makhiwane, son of Mdangazeli,

> *Drums and chanting. Warriors exeunt, led by Makhiwane.*

1. Prince.

BILL CAIN

Equivocation (2009)[†]

Act 1, Scene 12

Cecil and Shag and a manuscript between them.
But the men and the script have changed. What was once
a negotiation is now a battle to the death.

CECIL ([*holding up*] *the text he brought in*)   Now this is a shoddy piece of work.

SHAG   That's not the script. Only company members have the new draft.

CECIL   This is it. (*Laser focus on Shag*) The most interesting aspect is the idea of the composite character. You took Digby's youth, Wintour's rage and Bates'[1] remorse and conflated them into one sympathetic, lovable traitor. This is not the script I commissioned.

Shag is stunned Cecil has the script.

SHAG   Where, where did you get that?

CECIL   Now, the problems. You say the King promised religious toleration. Not true and, in fact, treasonous.

SHAG   I will not discuss this until you tell me where—

CECIL   You say Catesby came to see me. He did, but the implications are unfair to me. Now, the priests—

SHAG   I will discuss nothing with you, until you tell me where you—

CECIL   I bought it.

SHAG   It was not for sale.

CECIL   Everything is for sale.

SHAG   I am not!

[†] *Equivocation*, by Bill Cain, a Jesuit playwright, premiered at the Oregon Shakespeare Festival, 2009, and has played in New York and Washington. The play presents a radically alternative reading of the Gunpowder Plot (1605), allegedly a Catholic attempt to blow up Parliament, and of *Macbeth*. In *Macbeth* the Porter's drunken welcome of an equivocator to hell has long been read as an allusion to Henry Garnet, the Jesuit executed for treason in the Gunpowder Plot, who had propounded a theory of equivocation, by which Catholics could licitly deceive interrogators and escape persecution. (See above, 218–19). Cain, however, portrays Garnet as a hero and Robert Cecil, secretary of state, as the equivocating villain who invents the threat of the plot to enable his persecution of Catholics. In Cain's work Cecil commissions Shakespeare (Shag) to write a play celebrating the victory over the conspirators, but Shakespeare instead writes *Macbeth* to portray Cecil as a bloodthirsty tyrant. Used with permission of Bill Cain and Abrams Artists Agency.

1. Three of the conspirators, Everard Digby, Thomas Wintour, and Thomas Bates.

CECIL I can go to any printer's stall and buy one-hundred and fifty of your most explicit love letters[2] for pocket change! Don't tell me you're not for sale. William, where's my play?

SHAG Answer me one question and I'll write it. (*A nod, then—*) A dozen ill-equipped young men dug a hole, dumping dirt, bringing in lumber, making noise enough to wake the dead? They dug a hole—under Parliament—a hole big enough to store thirty-eight barrels of gunpowder?

CECIL Your question?

SHAG How could a man like you, who, without leaving his office, knows the whereabouts of every grain of pepper in London (*with growing disbelief*)—how could such a well-informed man possibly not have not known that those men were digging that hole, when the hole that they were digging—digging every day from March until November—was being dug under the very building in which you have your office?

Silence. Then—

CECIL I don't understand theater. (*Then*) I have neutralized Europe, set France and Spain at one another's throats to keep them from our door. This is harder.

SHAG You'll never understand. Theater's a small world, but it's built on affection and trust.

CECIL And yet from your little world I have this.

Cecil holds up the script.

SHAG So, you have a spy among us.

CECIL Just the one, do you think? Now (*all business*) what do you require to write this play? Name it; it's yours.

SHAG Show me the tunnel!

CECIL I think we both know that would be impossible.

SHAG Very well. No tunnel. Was there a letter?

CECIL Of course there was a letter.

SHAG Forged?

CECIL If no one knows who wrote it, why would you have to forge it?

SHAG I want to see it.

CECIL Next you'll be asking me to see the gunpowder.

SHAG Very well, show me the—

CECIL It's been dispersed. It's far too dangerous to have weapons that could cause that much destruction in one place.

SHAG There was no gunpowder in the Gunpowder Plot?

---

2. Cecil refers to Shakespeare's 154 sonnets, first published in print in 1609, however, some years after the events here portrayed (1606).

CECIL   There was, but there didn't have to be.

SHAG (*dawning realization*)   There was no plot in the Powder Plot.
I am a fool.

CECIL   Don't blame yourself. People might want to know about the
dirt in theater. In life, they leave the dirt to me. (*Then, boldly*)
William, will you write this play—yes or—

SHAG (*triumphant*)   No!

CECIL (*pleased*)   Very well. (*Then, more pleased*) Guards!

> *Drums, powerful, sustained, threatening, under.*

SHAG   I won't write your lies.

CECIL   By the time you're done, they won't be lies. (*Handing files*)
Here are the specifications on the dirt. The water. The wood.
Anything else you need will be provided. There will have been a
plot when you have written the history of it as real as Richard's
hump and I will provide a punishment for deviation from the story
so appalling that no one will so much as raise his voice to question
it. William, we can heal this nation of a hundred years of division.

> *The guards (Richard and Armin)[3] arrive in armor,*
> *hands on sheathed swords.*

SHAG   You want to found the nation on a lie.

CECIL   You think Rome was founded by twins suckled by wolves?

SHAG   So, we are Rome now?

CECIL   Rome is over, and so is Wittenberg.

SHAG   And when both religions are gone, what will be left?

> *Cecil is amazed that Shag doesn't know.*

CECIL   Why (*with wonder and admiration*)—you. You will be left.
You will be the measure of all things. People will go to your plays
as they used to go to church. Reverently. And they will leave
exactly as they went in, unchanged but feeling somehow improved.
Have you ever looked at one of your audiences? You make them
happy, but not so happy as to make them reject their unhappiness.
You make them angry, but not so angry as to inspire action. You
reduce all of reality to spectacle, making action unnecessary,
even impossible—you are the perfect civic religion. (*Deep
admiration*) Your work will outlast the Bible—which it resembles,
but you've improved on it.

SHAG   How?

CECIL   You've kept the willing suspension of disbelief and gotten
rid of the moral demands.

---

3. *Equivocation* has a cast of six characters: Shag, Nate, Sharpe, Richard, Armin, and
Judith (Shakespeare's daughter). These six actors play all the other roles and the script
often indicates which actor plays which other role.

SHAG   You know what the precise problem is here—you're insane—and I will not write your play.

> *Shag starts out. Guards draw swords. Flank Shag.*
> *Block his exit.*

SENIOR [RICHARD]   Sir, you have a letter in your possession I require of you.
(*Shag is puzzled.*) A letter from a prisoner.

> *Shag realizes Tom Wintour's letter is in his pocket.*
> *Takes out letter.*

SHAG (*an appeal to Cecil*)   It's to his wife. Do you know what it is to love your wife?
JUNIOR [ARMIN]   You're asking the wrong man, sir. He worked the day of his wife's funeral.
CECIL (*shrugging it off*)   I worked the day she died.
SENIOR   The letter is from a traitor. It is treason to possess it.

> *The Guards take a step towards him. Shag fights his*
> *desire to hand it over.*

SHAG   No. I won't.
CECIL (*absolute command*)   Won't! Of course you will. You don't wake up one morning and decide to perform an act of moral courage. It takes practice. That's why Fawkes and Catesby, Wintour and the others will be remembered and you will be forgotten.
SHAG   I will be remembered. You just said my plays would live forever.
CECIL   Your plays, yes. But you? (*Total contempt*) You will be the only major writer whose very existence will be a matter of debate. (*Then, disgusted*) Why should anyone remember you? You have done nothing. You are nothing. Nothing!

*   *   *

Act 2, Scene 8

Garnet's cell in the Tower.
GARNET   Then all is lost.
COKE[4]   Mr. Garnet, your sentence has been pronounced. (*Public reading of the sentence*)
"Mr. Garnet shall be drawn to the common place of execution—

---

4. Sir Edward Coke, the Chief Justice who prosecuted the conspirators in the plot and condemned Garnet to death for treason. See above, pp. 220–21.

JUDITH   "and there to be hanged by the neck—
SHARPE   "cut down alive—
CECIL   "his privy-member cut off, to be burnt before his face—
COKE   "his head to be severed from his body—
COKE, JUDITH, SHARPE, CECIL   "and his body divided into four parts—
JAMES[5] (*signing the order*)   "to be disposed of as the King should think fit."

All but Shag and Garnet depart.

GARNET (*sadly amused at himself*)   Master Shagspeare, Will, for the first time, I am afraid.
SHAG   We are all afraid of death.
GARNET   Not death.
SHAG   What then?
GARNET (*taking stage*)   That I shall cease to be myself. I am afraid that, stepping out on a platform, in front of a crowd—unprotected, exposed—I will not be sufficient to the occasion.
SHAG   You're like my actors.
GARNET   They lose hope?
SHAG   No, actors always have hope. And after they get their first laugh, they think they are gods.
GARNET   I should like to laugh again before I die. Is there anything funny in your play?
SHAG   It's the least funny play ever written.
GARNET   Pity. Even a tragedy should have something—

Knock, Knock, Knock. Silence. Then—

SHAG   Well, there is one bit.
GARNET   What's it about?
SHAG (*strangely enough*)   Equivocation.
GARNET   Tell me.
SHAG   A king is killed. The killers have gone to wash blood off their hands when there's a knocking at the gate. (*Knock, knock, knock.*) A porter arrives.
PORTER [ARMIN]   (*intense Scottish accent*) Knock, knock, knock! Who's there, in the name of Beelzebub? (*To Garnet*) Faith, here's an equivocator, that could swear in both the scales against either scale; who committed treason enough for God's sake, yet could not equivocate to heaven. Oh, come in, equivocator. But this place is too cold for hell. I'll devil-porter it no further. I had thought to have let in some of all professions that go the primrose way to the everlasting bonfire.

5. King James VI of Scotland, who ruled as King James I of England from 1603 to 1625.

Act 2, Scene 9

Macbeth performed onstage [with a] backstage audience.[6]

> *James enters to watch the play.*
> *He sits center and anchors all activity around him. Shag*
> *throws lines to the Porter.*

SHAG   Was it so late, friend, ere you went to bed that you do lie so late?

PORTER   Faith, sir, we were carousing till the second cock. And drink, sir, is a great provoker of three things.

JAMES (*Scot to Scot*)   What three things does drink especially provoke?

PORTER   Marry, sir, nose-painting, sleep and urine. Lechery, sir, it provokes and unprovokes; it provokes the desire but it takes away the performance. Therefore, much drink may be said to be an equivocator with lechery. (*Playing to James and Garnet*) It makes him and it mars him. It sets him on and it takes him off. It persuades him and disheartens him. Makes him stand to and not stand to. In conclusion, equivocates him in a sleep and giving him the lie, leaves him. (*Then, soliciting applause*) Pray you, remember the porter.

> *James and Porter disappear as Garnet laughs*
> *into silence. Then—*

SHAG (*with compassion*)   Do not despair.

GARNET   What is there left for which to hope?

SHAG   Soon, very soon, you will see my son.[7] He is a sweet boy. He will make you at home. Give him a kiss for me.

GARNET   You will see him again yourself. Look to your daughter and you will see your son again. On my word. Give her a kiss for me!

SHAG   I shall. *Benedicite.*

GARNET (*a hand gently on Shag's head*)   *Benedicite.*

> *Garnet disappears.*
> *Shag is instantaneously surrounded by the first produc-*
> *tion of Macbeth.*
> *Actors rush on.*
> *[Backstage]*

[SHAG]   How's it going?

ARMIN (*over the moon*)   The King laughed at the Porter.

---

6. The action below consists of the onstage production of *Macbeth* before the onstage audience of James and Cecil and the backstage audience of Shag, Garnet, Judith, and the actors who step out of their *Macbeth* roles.

7. Hamnet Shakespeare, who died of the plague at age eleven in 1596.

SHAG Cecil?

ARMIN (*under the moon*) Not so much.

      Sharpe, pumped, arrives with Nate.

NATE Where were you! James almost shat himself with the witches. He's on the edge of his seat!

SHARPE (*serious actor preparation*) And in the next scene I intend to push him over the edge.

      Richard comes offstage.

RICHARD You're back.

SHAG How's it going?

RICHARD James loves it.

SHAG And Cecil?

      Cecil enters. Sits as audience.

RICHARD He never comes to see us. What's he doing here? When I did the speech about insomnia—

SHAG Macbeth hath murdered sleep; Macbeth shall sleep no more?

RICHARD ([*nods*] *yes*) Cecil stood up like I had called his name. I almost stopped the performance.

SHAG He's not used to theater. Here's a new speech. Play right to him.

SHARPE (*ready to enter*) Watch this. (*Then, on stage*) Oh, horror, horror, horror!

JAMES [SHARPE] Laddie, calm yourself.

MACDUFF [SHARPE] Confusion now hath made his masterpiece! Most sacrilegious murder hath broke ope the Lord's anointed temple, and stole thence the life o' the building.

JAMES [SHARPE] What is't you say—the life? Mean you his majesty? Beagle,[8] I think they killed the king.

MACDUFF [SHARPE] Approach the chamber, and destroy your sight with a new Gorgon! See, and then speak yourselves.

JAMES [SHARPE] (*applauding*) The lad's tremendous. He's brilliant! Bloody brilliant!

      Lady Macbeth [Armin] enters.

Well, hello lassie.

LADY MACBETH Those of his chamber as it seemed had done't.

      Richard walks on stage and plays directly to Cecil.

MACBETH O yet I do repent me of my fury that I did kill them.

---

8. James's nickname for Cecil.

Macbeth's hands are covered with blood. All look at him. Silence.
Then, a drop of blood falls onto Cecil's hands. He looks at the
blood. Does anyone see it but him? He wipes it off.

SHAG [*backstage*]   Good.
MACDUFF   And when we have our naked frailties hid, let us meet
and question this most bloody piece of work. In the great hand of
God I stand; and thence against the undivulged pretence I fight
of treasonous malice.
MACBETH   And so do I!
ALL   So all.

> *Backstage*

SHAG (*handing Richard the crown*)   Here, put this on during that
new speech. And throw in a little Richard the Third.
RICHARD (*amused*)   Right. Good business.

> *Macbeth [Richard] enters, limping. Cecil, provoked, rises.*[9]

JAMES   Sit, Beagle. Stay.
SHAG [*backstage*]   Good.
MACBETH (*to James*)   The weird sisters prophet-like hail'd Banquo
father to a line of kings while (*to Cecil*) upon my head they placed a
fruitless crown, no son of mine succeeding. If't be so, for Banquo's
issue have I murder'd and mine eternal soul given to the common
enemy of man, to make them kings, the seed of Banquo kings!

> *Richard crowns himself king, exactly as Cecil did.*[1]

MACBETH   To be thus is nothing.

> *Armin [as Lady Macbeth] enters, saving the moment.*

LADY MACBETH   How now, my lord! Why do you keep alone, of
sorriest fancies your companions making? What's done is done.
MACBETH   I will tomorrow to the weird sisters.
JAMES (*thrilled*)   The witches? The witches are coming?

> *All actors nod yes.*

MACBETH   More shall they speak, for I am bent to know by the
worst means, the worst, for mine own good. I am in blood stepped
in so far that, should I wade no more, returning were as tedious
as go o'er.

> *Richard III-like, [Macbeth] limps off. Cecil is not amused.*

---

9. Both Richard III and Cecil limped.
1. Cecil had crowned himself in an earlier scene.

RICHARD [*backstage*] Cecil is watching this play like a death sentence. What have you done? You haven't cunted[2] me on this, have you?

SHAG [*backstage*] You said we hold the mirror up.[3] Well, that's what we're doing. Shhhhhhhhh—

> *As Cecil cleans traces of the blood from his hand—*

LADY MACBETH Here's the smell of blood still. Out, damned spot. Out I say. What? Will these hands ne'er be clean?

> *Cecil, murderous, approaches Richard—*

RICHARD [*backstage*] That's it. I'm ending this.

> *By the time Cecil gets to Richard, Cecil has become Nate.*

NATE [*backstage*] (*to Richard*) You're on.

> *Thunder and lightning.*

ALL WITCHES Double, double, toil and trouble. Fire burn and cauldron bubble.

MACBETH How now, you secret black and midnight hags. What is't you do?

WITCH 1 [ARMIN] A deed without a name.

ALL WITCHES Macbeth! Macbeth! Macbeth!

WITCH 1 [ARMIN] Be bloody, bold and resolute and laugh to scorn the power of man for none of woman born shall harm Macbeth.

JAMES (*exactly*) Then what need he fear any man?

MACBETH Then what need I fear any man!

ALL WITCHES Macbeth, Macbeth, Macbeth!

WITCH 1 [ARMIN] Shall never vanquished be until great Birnam Wood to high Dunsinane Hill shall come against him.

JAMES Why, that shall never be!

MACBETH [*aside*] Right again! [*To Witches*] That will never be. Yet my heart throbs to know one thing. Tell me, shall Banquo's issue ever reign in this kingdom?

ALL WITCHES Seek to know no more!

MACBETH Show, show!

JAMES Tell him! Shall Banquo's issue ever reign in this kingdom!

> *Thunder and lightning!*

NATE [*backstage*] Here we go.

ALL WITCHES Show!

---

2. double-crossed.
3. You said that we hold the mirror up to nature, in other words, that we represent things as they truly are.

> *With James holding center, the actors approach*
> *him with mirrors, each mirror picking up the king's*
> *image and reflecting it to another mirror.*
> *An infinite progression of Jameses.*

MACBETH   A parade of kings! Thy crown does sear mine eyeballs.
What, will thy line stretch out to the crack of doom? And yet
another. Enough!

> *The illusion suddenly vanishes, James stands,*
> *applauds, cheers, whistles loudly. Until—*

SETON [ARMIN]   The queen, my lord, is dead.

MACBETH   She should have died hereafter. There would have been
a time for such a word. (*Cecil's least favorite word*) Tomorrow.

JAMES   Tomorrow, eh?

MACBETH   And tomorrow.

JAMES   And tomorrow?

MACBETH   And tomorrow.

JAMES   Tomorrow and tomorrow and tomorrow, eh? (*Then*) Aye,
Beagle, that's a good one! Comic relief!

> *[Backstage] Judith walks to her father.*

SHAG   It's a soliloquy. Sorry.

JUDITH   I like this one. It tells the truth. Life is a tale told by an
idiot. Full of sound and fury signifying nothing.

SHAG   I'm so sorry that you like it.

> *[Onstage] Build to the final battle.*

SETON [ARMIN]   My lord, as I did stand my watch upon the hill, I
look'd toward Birnam and anon methought the wood began to move!

MACBETH   Liar and slave!

MACDUFF (*entering, sword in hand*)   What is thy name?

MACBETH   Thou'lt be afraid to hear it.

MACDUFF   No, though thou call'st thyself a hotter name than any
is in hell.

MACBETH   My name's Macbeth.

MACDUFF   Turn, hell-hound, turn.

MACBETH   Swords I smile at. Weapons laugh to scorn. For none of
woman born shall harm Macbeth!

MACDUFF   Despair thy charm and let the angel whom thou still hast
served tell thee Macduff was from his mother's womb untimely
ripp'd.

JAMES [SHARPE] (*to Cecil*)   That's poetry for caesarean section.

MACBETH   Lay on, Macduff, and damned be him that first cries
hold, enough!

Sword fight, sword fight, sword fight.

ARMIN [*backstage*]   Looks like we're going to be alright.

Richard [Macbeth] and Sharpe [Macduff]
hack each other with swords.

Macduff cuts off Macbeth's head. Raises it high.

MACDUFF   Behold where stands the usurper's cursed head. The time is free. Hail, king of Scotland!

ALL (*to James*)   Hail, King of Scotland!

James leaps from his seat, bravoing and cheering and
whistling and repeating—

JAMES (*beside himself*)   Hail, King of Scotland! Hail, King of Scotland!

Act 2, Scene 10

Aftermath of Macbeth. Backstage.

James gushes over the cast.

JAMES   You were wonderful. You were wonderful. How do you do it? How do you remember all those lines? I loved it. Where's the lassie? Where's—?

He finds Armin in Lady Macbeth costume.

(*ogling Lady Macbeth*) You could almost believe . . .

ARMIN   Majesty, this ([*indicating*] *the dress, the breasts*) is an illusion.

JAMES ([*indicating*] *his robe, crown*)   Well, so's this. So is this. Do you know what I liked best, Writer?

SHAG   The mirrors, Majesty?

JAMES   The mirrors, the mirrors! The way one image caught another and it went on and on! But no. That wasn't my favorite.

RICHARD   Perhaps his Majesty enjoyed "Double, double, toil and trouble"?

JAMES   The witches were wonderful! And they tricked him, the poor man. They did. They equivocated him, didn't they, Beagle? (*Then, to Cecil*) And how did you like your play, Beagle?

CECIL   If it pleased your Majesty, I am content.

JAMES (*confidential*)   He hated it. I sat next to him. You could feel waves of hate rolling off him through the whole thing.

CECIL   I commissioned a play about the Powder Plot, Majesty.

JAMES   Yes and, wicked creatures (*delighted*), you gave him a play about a man of no conscience, with ambitions above his station, a killer of royalty, careless of his wife, with a spy in every house, who dies utterly unpitied. They did a play (*then, to Cecil*) about you!

> *James casually tosses Cecil Macbeth's severed head.*
> *Cecil stands exposed. Blood on his hands.*

Resources

The annual bibliographies of *Shakespeare Quarterly* and *PMLA* (*Publications of the Modern Language Association*) provide comprehensive listings of publications.

• indicates works excerpted or included in this Norton Critical Edition.

ONLINE

DEEP: Database of Early English Playbooks A user-friendly database that enables research in the publishing, printing, and marketing of every playbook produced in England, Scotland, and Ireland up to 1660. http://deep.sas.upenn.edu/

Early English Books Online An indispensable and searchable digital library of over 100,000 English books from 1475 to 1700. http://eebo.chadwyck.com/home/

English Short Title Catalog A listing of over 460,000 items published between 1473 and 1800, mainly but not exclusively in English. http://estc.bl.uk/

Folger Shakespeare Library Links to many scholarly and popular Shakespeare sites and an impressive Digital Image Collection. www.folger.edu/

Geneva Bible (1560/1599) Transcriptions of the Bible translation Shakespeare is likely to have used. www.genevabible.org/

Google Book Search A digital archive of many scholarly monographs and reference books (see also The Online Books Page, Project Gutenberg, and The Universal Digital Library). http://books.google.com

Internet Shakespeare Editions A database of plays and poems, facsimiles of early editions, Shakespeare's life and times, and play performances. http://internetshakespeare.uvic.ca/

JSTOR An archive of scholarly articles and reviews (see also Project Muse). www.jstor.org/

Literature Online A database of many works of English and American Literature as well as many literature journals. http://lion.chadwyck.com/

Modern Language Association Bibliography Citations of scholarly books and articles from 1926 to the present. www.mla.org/bibliography/

OpenSourceShakespeare Site that enables text, word, and character searches in Shakespeare's works (see also The Works of the Bard). www.opensourceshakespeare.com/concordance/

Oxford Dictionary of National Biography Authoritative, illustrated biographies of people important in British history. www.oxforddnb.com/

Oxford English Dictionary Authoritative historical dictionary. www.oed.com/

Oxford Scholarly Editions Online Searchable database of modern editions of early modern texts. www.oup.com/online/us/oseo/

PBS Video: Great Performances: Patrick Stewart's *Macbeth* An online version of the chilling Rupert Goold production, starring Patrick Stewart and Kate Fleetwood. http://video.pbs.org/video/1604122998/

Royal Shakespeare Company A resource on theatrical productions (click on the Education link for a complete Internet guide to Shakespeare). www.rsc .org.uk/

Shakespeare in Europe A collection of resources including many adaptations. http://pages.unibas.ch/shine/linkstragmacbethwf.html

Shakespeare: An International Database of Shakespeare on Film, Television, and Radio An international database from 1899 to the present. www .bufvc.ac.uk/shakespeare/

World Shakespeare Bibliography Annotated citations for books, articles, reviews, and productions related to Shakespeare from 1960 to the present. www.worldshakesbib.org/

PRINT

Adelman, Janet. *Suffocating Mothers: Fantasies of Maternal Origin in Shakespeare's Plays from* Hamlet *to* The Tempest. London: Routledge, 1992.

Bartholomeusz, Dennis. Macbeth *and the Players.* Cambridge: Cambridge University Press, 1969.

Bate, Jonathan, and Eric Rasmussen, eds. *Macbeth.* New York: Modern Library, 2009.

• Bell, G. J. "Notes," ed. H. C. Fleeming Jenkin, "Sarah Siddons as Lady Macbeth and Queen Katherine, with an introduction by Brander Matthews." *Publications of the Dramatic Museum of Columbia University,* 2nd Series, Papers on Acting 3. New York: Corlies, Macy, 1915.

Berger, Harry, Jr. "The Early Scenes of *Macbeth*: Preface to a New Interpretation." *English Literary History* 47 (1980): 1–31.

Blayney, Peter M. W. *The First Folio of Shakespeare.* Washington: Folger Library Publications, 1991.

• Boaden, James, ed. *The Private Correspondence of David Garrick.* 2 vols. London: H. Colburn and R. Bentley, 1831–32.

Bradley, A. C. *Shakespearean Tragedy: Lectures on* Hamlet, Othello, King Lear, Macbeth. London: Macmillan, 1904.

Braunmuller, A. R., ed. *Macbeth.* Cambridge: Cambridge University Press, 1997, updated, 2008.

Brown, John Russell Brown, ed. *Focus on* Macbeth. London: Routledge & Kegan Paul, 1982.

• Campbell, Thomas. *Life of Mrs. Siddons.* 2 vols. London: Effingham Wilson, 1834.

Carroll, William C., ed. Macbeth: : *Texts and Contexts.* Boston: Bedford/St. Martin's, 1999.

Cliff, Nigel. *The Shakespeare Riots: Revenge, Drama, and Death in Nineteenth-Century America.* New York: Random House, 2007.

• Coleridge, Samuel Taylor. *The Literary Remains of Samuel Taylor Coleridge.* Ed. Henry Nelson Coleridge. 4 vols. London: William Pickering, 1836–39.

• Davenant, William. Macbeth: *A Tragedy with all the Alterations, Amendments, Additions, and New Songs.* London, 1674.

• Davies, Thomas. *Dramatic Micellanies: Consisting of Critical Observations on Several Plays of Shakespeare.* 3 vols. London, 1783–84.

Dent, R. W. *Shakespeare's Proverbial Language: An Index*. Berkeley: University of California Press, 1981.

• De Quincey, Thomas. *Confessions of an English Opium-Eater*. London: Walter Scott, 1886. Ed. John E. Jordan. *DeQuincey as Critic*. Boston: Routledge & Kegan Paul, 1973.

• Erasmus, Desiderius. *Collected Works of Erasmus*, volume 76: *Controversies*. Ed. Charles Trinkaus et al. Toronto: University of Toronto Press, 1999.

• Fleetwood, Kate. *Macbeth*. Illuminations Media, DVD (2011), Extras.

• Forman, Simon. F. J. Furnivall's transcription, reprinted in the Horace Howard Furness, Jr.'s revised New Variorum edition of *Macbeth*. Philadelphia: J. B. Lippincott, 1915. 356–57.

Gardner, Helen. "Milton's 'Satan' and the Theme of Damnation in Elizabethan Tragedy." *English Association Essays and Studies* 1 (1948): 46–66.

• Garnet, Henry. *A Treatise of Equivocation*. Ed. David Jardine. London, 1851.

Greenblatt, Stephen. "Shakespeare Bewitched." *New Historical Literary Study*. Ed. Jeffrey N. Cox and Larry Reynolds. Princeton: Princeton University Press, 1993. 108–35.

Hazlitt, William. *Characters of Shakespear's Plays*. London, 1817.

Hinman, Charlton, ed. *The Norton Facsimile: The First Folio of Shakespeare*. New York, 1968.

• Holinshed, Raphael. *The First and Second Volumes of Chronicles*. London, 1587.

Holland, Peter, ed. *Garrick, Kemble, Siddons, Kean: Great Shakespeareans Volume II*. London: Continuum, 2010.

• *An Homilie agaynst disobedience and wylful rebellion*. London, 1570.

• Ionesco, Eugène. *Macbett*, trans. Charles Marowitz. New York: Grove Press, 1973.

• James I. *Daemonologie*. Edinburgh, 1597.

• ———. *Newes from Scotland*. London, 1592.

• Johnson, Samuel, *Miscellaneous Observations on the Tragedy of Macbeth*. London, 1745.

Jacobi, Derek. "Macbeth," *Players of Shakespeare* 4. Ed. Robert Smallwood. Cambridge: Cambridge University Press, 1998. 193–210.

Kliman, Bernice, W. *Macbeth: Shakespeare in Performance*, 2nd edn. Manchester: Manchester University Press, 2004.

Knight, G. Wilson. *The Imperial Theme*. London: Oxford University Press, 1931.

Knights, L. C. "How Many Children Had Lady Macbeth?" *Explorations*. 1933; rpt. New York, 1964.

• Levin, Harry. "Two Scenes from *Macbeth*." *Shakespeare's Craft: Eight Lectures*. Ed. Philip H. Highfill, Jr. Carbondale: Southern Illinois University Press, 1982. 48–68.

• Macready, William. *Macready's Reminiscences and Selections from his Diaries and Letters*. Ed. Sir Frederick Pollock. New York: Macmillan, 1875.

• Mariana, Juan de. *De Rege et Regis Institutione*. Toledo, 1599.

McDonald, Russ. *Look to the Lady: Sarah Siddons, Ellen Terry, and Judi Dench on the Shakespearean Stage*. Athens: University of Georgia Press, 2005.

• McKellen, Ian. "Interview with Julian Curry." *Shakespeare on Stage: Thirteen Leading Actors on Thirteen Key Roles*. London: Nick Hern Books, 2010. 143–69.

• Mikijirô, Hira. "Interview." *Performing Shakespeare in Japan*, eds. Minami Ryuta, Ian Carruthers, and John Gillies. Cambridge: Cambridge University Press, 2001.

Miola, Robert S. "Two Jesuit Shadows in Shakespeare: William Weston and Henry Garnet." *Shakespeare and Religion: Early Modern and Postmodern Perspectives*. Ed. Ken Jackson and Arthur F. Marotti. Notre Dame: University of Notre Dame Press, 2011. 25–45.

• Moore, Rush. *Macbeth Travestie, in Three Acts.* Calcutta, 1820.
• Msomi, Welcome. *uMabatha: An Adaptation of Shakespeare's* Macbeth. Praetoria: Via Afrika/Skotaville Publishers, 1996.
Muir, Kenneth. "Image and Symbol in *Macbeth.*" *Shakespeare Survey* 19 (1966): 45–54.
———. *The Sources of Shakespeare's Plays.* London: Methuen, 1977.
Mulryne, Ronnie. "From text to foreign stage: Yukio Ninagawa's Cultural Translation of *Macbeth*," *Shakespeare from Text to Stage.* Ed. Patricia Kennan and Mariangela Tempera. Bologna: Clueb, 1992. 131–43.
• N-Town Cycle. *Ludus Coventriae: or The Plaie called Corpus Christi, Cotton MS Vespasian D. VIII.* Ed. K. S. Block. London: Oxford University Press, 1922. 169–77.
Newstok, Scott L., and Ayanna Thompson, eds. *Weward* Macbeth: *Intersections of Race and Performance.* New York: Palgrave Macmillan, 2010.
Norbrook, David. "*Macbeth* and the Politics of Historiography." *Politics of Discourse: The Literature and History of Seventeenth-Century England.* Ed. Kevin Sharpe and Steven N. Zwicker. Berkeley: University of California Press, 1987. 78–116.
• Northall, W. K. *Macbeth Travestie.* New York, 1847.
• Orgel, Stephen. "Macbeth and the Antic Round." *Shakespeare Survey* 52 (1999): 143–53.
Rank, Sven. *Twentieth-Century Adaptations of Macbeth. Writing between Influence, Intervention, and Cultural Transfer.* Frankurt: Peter Lang, 2010.
• Ristori, Adelaide. *Memoirs and Artistic Studies,* trans. G. Mantellini. New York: Doubleday, 1907. 161–74.
Rosenberg, Marvin. *The Masks of Macbeth.* Berkeley: University of California Press, 1978.
Schoenbaum, S., ed. *Macbeth: Critical Essays.* New York: Garland, 1991.
• Scot, Reginald. *The Discouerie of Witchcraft.* London, 1584.
• Seneca. *Seneca his Tenne Tragedies.* Ed. Thomas Newton. London, 1591.
Shaheen, Naseeb. *Biblical References in Shakespeare's Plays.* London: Associated University Presses, 1999.
• Shakespeare, William. *The Historical Tragedy of Macbeth.* Dublin, 1761 [with Garrick's additions].
• Sher, Antony. *Macbeth.* Illuminations Media, DVD (2001), Extras.
———. "Leontes in *The Winter's Tale* and Macbeth," *Players of Shakespeare* 5. Ed. Robert Smallwood. Cambridge: Cambridge University Press, 2003. 91–112.
• Stewart, Patrick. "*Macbeth*: A Conversation with Sir Patrick Stewart," Public Broadcasting Service, October 6, 2010 [with Paula Zahn].
Stoppard, Tom. *Dogg's Hamlet and Cahoot's Macbeth.* London: Faber and Faber, 1980.
• Talfourd, Francis. *Macbeth Travestie.* 3rd edn. Oxford, 1850.
Taylor, Gary, et al., eds. *Thomas Middleton: The Collected Works.* Oxford, Oxford University Press, 2007. (Also his *Thomas Middleton and Early Modern Textual Culture: A Companion to the Collected Works.* Oxford: Oxford University Press, 2007.)
• Yukio, Ninagawa. "Interview." *Performing Shakespeare in Japan,* ed. Minami Ryuta, Ian Carruthers, and John Gillies. Cambridge: Cambridge University Press, 2001.
Vickers, Brian, ed. *Shakespeare: The Critical Heritage.* 6 vols. London: Routledge & Kegan Paul, 1974–81.
———. "Disintegrated. Did Middleton adapt *Macbeth*?" *Times Literary Supplement,* May 28, 2010, pp. 13–14.
———. Marcus Dahl and Marina Tarlinskaya. "An Enquiry into Middleton's supposed "adaptation" of *Macbeth*" (2010). http://ies.sas.ac.uk/events/seminars/LFAS/index.htm.
• *Verdi's Macbeth: A Sourcebook.* Ed. David Rosen and Andrew Porter. New York: Norton, 1984.

• Walter, Harriet. *Macbeth*. Illuminations Media, DVD (2001), Extras.
• Welles, Orson. "Orson Welles: Shakespeare, Welles, and Moles," *Orson Welles: Interviews* [with Richard Marienstras]. Ed. Mark W. Estrin. Jackson: University Press of Mississippi, 2002. 146–72. [Interview conducted in 1976, published in French 1998, translated by Alisa Hartz.]

Wills, Garry. *Witches and Jesuits: Shakespeare's* Macbeth. New York: Oxford University Press, 1995.

Wheeler, Thomas. Macbeth: *An Annotated Bibliography*. New York: Garland, 1990.